"Abraham Lincoln had less schooling than all but a couple of other presidents, and more wisdom than every one of them. In this original, insightful book, Michael Gerhardt . . . explains how this came to be. He focuses on five men he calls Lincoln's mentors, but the book is really an account of how Lincoln educated himself. Crucially, it does not stop at the inauguration; more than any other president, Lincoln grew in office. Until the very end of his life, his self-education never ceased. . . . Gerhardt's emphasis on Lincoln's education casts his presidency in a distinctive light. This is no small accomplishment given all that has been written about Lincoln. Mr. Gerhardt stresses that Lincoln was 'educable,' a quality never more necessary in an occupant of the White House than during the Civil War."

—H. W. Brands, *Wall Street Journal*

"*Lincoln's Mentors* . . . has a vital lesson for anyone who's trying to succeed, or trying to help others succeed. The book's big idea is that Lincoln, for all his gifts, was *intentional* about seeking out mentors who could help him master oratory, speechwriting, party politics, campaigning, conventions, executive power, managing a cabinet."

—Mike Allen, Axios

"Michael J. Gerhardt has devised an ingenious solution for demystifying America's most enigmatic president: examining the key people who influenced Lincoln as he developed his own unique skills and leadership style. These pages trace how a poor, backwoods farm boy rose to become among the most eloquent defenders of America's highest ideals as well as a steely and tenacious source of unity when the nation needed it most. Gerhardt shows that Lincoln's genius was in borrowing selectively from the examples of his mentors—both the famous and the obscure—to become an unsurpassed original."

—Russell L. Riley, co-chair of the Presidential Oral History Program at the University of Virginia's Miller Center

"Understanding the ideas that shaped Lincoln's mind helps us understand the ideas that shaped the American mind. In this illuminating book, Michael Gerhardt brings Lincoln's intellectual and political mentors to life, offering vivid and unexpected insights about Lincoln and the teachers who inspired him."

—Jeffrey Rosen, president and CEO of the
National Constitution Center

"A worthy addition to the Lincoln bibliotheca. . . . Professor Gerhardt is a splendid writer of nonfiction. His storyline is clear and resonant. The author is fluent in Lincoln history and political philosophy, but he stays close to his aspiration for the book—not to cover every event, but to demonstrate how an untutored, Western, small-town lawyer could make himself into the most eloquent and influential president the country has ever had."

—New York Journal of Books

"Gerhardt's Lincoln's Mentors is a remarkably probing examination of what Lincoln read, how he learned, and how he was constantly reaching out for friends, mentors, and role models. His is an especially valuable analysis of how both Henry Clay and Andrew Jackson influenced the Lincoln presidency. This superb treatment of Lincoln as a political thinker and operative ranks right up there with the prize-winning biographies of David Donald and James McPherson."

—Thomas E. Cronin, president emeritus of Whitman College
and co-author of The Paradoxes of the American
Presidency and Leadership Matters

"Gerhardt makes solid cases for his choices as major influences. A satisfying general biography that concentrates on Lincoln's political career."

—Kirkus Reviews

LINCOLN'S MENTORS

LINCOLN'S MENTORS

THE EDUCATION OF A LEADER

MICHAEL J. GERHARDT

MARINER BOOKS

Boston   New York

HarperCollins books may be purchased for educational, business, or sales promotional use. For information, please e-mail the Special Markets Department at SPsales@harpercollins.com.

A hardcover edition of this book was published in 2021 by Custom House, an imprint of William Morrow.

FIRST MARINER BOOKS PAPERBACK EDITION PUBLISHED 2022.

Designed by Leah Carlson-Stanisic
Photograph by Everett Collection/Shutterstock, Inc.

Library of Congress Cataloging-in-Publication Data

Names: Gerhardt, Michael J., 1956– author.
Title: Lincoln's mentors : the education of a leader / Michael J. Gerhardt.
Description: First edition. | New York, NY : Custom House, [2021] | Includes bibliographical references and index.
Identifiers: LCCN 2020038379 (print) | LCCN 2020038380 (ebook) | ISBN 9780062877192 (hardcover) | ISBN 9780062877185 (trade paperback) | ISBN 9780062877208 (ebook)
Subjects: LCSH: Lincoln, Abraham, 1809-1865—Friends and associates. | Lincoln, Abraham, 1809–1865—Political career before 1861. | United States—Politics and government— 19th century.
Classification: LCC E457.2 .G44 2021 (print) | LCC E457.2 (ebook) | DDC 973.7092—dc23
LC record available at https://lccn.loc.gov/2020038379
LC ebook record available at https://lccn.loc.gov/2020038380

ISBN 978-0-06-287718-5

22 23 24 2 26 LSC 10 9 8 7 6 5 4 3 2 1

IN MEMORY OF MY MOTHER, SHIVIA LEE GERHARDT (1929–2020). HER SELFLESS DEVOTION, LOVE, PATIENCE, COURAGE, AND SUPPORT ARE ENDURING BLESSINGS AND MODELS TO US ALL.

Upon the subject of education, not presuming to dictate any plan or system respecting it, I can only say that I view it as the most important subject we as a people can be engaged in.

—ABRAHAM LINCOLN, *First Campaign Speech, March 9, 1832*

CONTENTS

INTRODUCTION **THE SEARCH FOR LINCOLN'S TEACHERS** 1

CHAPTER ONE **FINDING HIS MENTORS (1809–1834)** 9

CHAPTER TWO **FINDING THE PATH TO CONGRESS (1834–1844)** 47

CHAPTER THREE **CLAY MAN IN THE HOUSE (1844–1850)** 93

CHAPTER FOUR **LEARNING FROM FAILURE (1849–1856)** 147

CHAPTER FIVE **BECOMING PRESIDENT (1856–1860)** 201

CHAPTER SIX **"HE WAS ENTIRELY IGNORANT NOT ONLY OF
THE DUTIES, BUT OF THE MANNER OF DOING BUSINESS" (1860–1861)** 261

CHAPTER SEVEN **COMMANDER IN CHIEF (1861–1864)** 305

CHAPTER EIGHT **FINAL ACT (1864–1865)** 359

EPILOGUE 409

ACKNOWLEDGMENTS 427

NOTES 431

INDEX... 467

LINCOLN'S MENTORS

THE SEARCH FOR LINCOLN'S TEACHERS

In times of crisis, Americans look to Abraham Lincoln. That impulse has been especially strong in the year 2020, as the nation has simultaneously grappled with a pandemic costing more than a quarter of a million American lives, a recession causing unemployment exceeding Depression-level numbers, mass protests against racism and police brutality, waves of violence across the land, and an impending presidential election bound to inflame divisions among America's public. For such a fraught time, Lincoln's eloquence, steady hand, and determination in leading an embattled nation to overcome secession, brutal civil war, and a severely weakened economy have become touchstones for Americans yearning for unifying, calming leadership.

Yet, at the heart of Abraham Lincoln's successes and story is a mystery that has intrigued historians and admirers. How did a man with no executive experience and only a single term in Congress become America's greatest president? That is the question nearly everyone asks about Lincoln. This book suggests an answer. The most common view of Lincoln as a political genius does not give Lincoln his due. To be certain, his political acumen and soaring rhetoric are matched by few others in American history. But Lincoln had a handful of men to whom he turned for guidance and inspiration throughout his life. Even as a young man, Lincoln knew enough to know he needed mentors. He could not learn in isolation all the skills he needed to become a great leader.

Consider, for example, the popular depiction of Abraham Lincoln in the years 1849–1856 as lost, alone, and in desperate need

of inspiration. True, when Lincoln returned home to Springfield, Illinois, after his seemingly lackluster two years in the U.S.
House of Representatives, his prospects were bleak. After years of
struggling to make a mark in national politics, he worried that he
had failed and that his political career was over. The Whig Party
opposed nominating him for a second term, in spite of his loyal
service to the party for more than a decade. He did not want to
leave office, but the strong stance he had taken in opposition to the
Mexican War had eroded his local support, given that Illinois had
been among the states with the largest numbers of volunteers for
the conflict. Many of the people back home, including his fellow
Whigs, mocked him as "Spotty Lincoln," a nickname they coined
after he failed to persuade the House to approve a resolution criticizing President James Polk for lying to Congress about the exact spot where Mexicans had fired the first shots that started the
Mexican War. Lincoln had campaigned for Zachary Taylor in 1848,
but, once in office, Taylor denied his application to become the
commissioner of the Land Office. Worse still, Taylor died in 1850,
elevating to the presidency his vice president, Millard Fillmore, a
Whig who did not take Lincoln seriously.

By the time Fillmore left office in 1853, Lincoln had to confront
the fact that the Whig Party was dying. Its demise left him without a party apparatus to sustain his political future. Dispirited,
he turned his attention to reviving his law practice with William
Herndon, building it into a highly respected but ultimately not
very lucrative firm. His dreams of becoming a great lawyer were
crushed when the nationally renowned Edwin Stanton of Pennsylvania dismissed him from the biggest case of his career in 1855.

As Lincoln's fortunes dimmed in the 1850s, his longtime Democratic rival, Stephen Douglas, had become a senator for Lincoln's
home state of Illinois and a rapidly rising star in national politics.
In 1854, Douglas took center stage nationally in drafting and securing passage of the controversial Kansas-Nebraska Act, a law that
allowed voters in the territories of Kansas and Nebraska to decide
for themselves whether or not to permit slavery within their borders. As violence erupted in Kansas and President Franklin Pierce

ordered the federal government to support proslavery forces there, Lincoln did little. Home was no respite. His sagging prospects exacerbated tensions with his wife, Mary Todd, who had great ambitions for him. Seemingly adrift, he read Euclid to sharpen his mind. He worried that he would never make a lasting mark on the world. His friends worried about his sanity.

Yet Lincoln's vexation was of a deliberative sort, a pause—albeit forced by circumstance—and not a surrender. His aspirations had not eroded, nor had much of his support for high office. In fact, his development as a serious presidential contender had begun many years earlier, and in 1849–1856, Lincoln was not so much reinventing himself as adapting the lessons he had learned over more than two decades in politics and law. In every critical phase of his life, including those seven years, Lincoln followed the same strategy, and it was not to turn completely inward. Besides reading voraciously to learn more about political philosophy, issues, and history of concern to him, he looked to others for guidance on the skills, vision, and strategies he needed in order to achieve his ambitions.

Certainly, the books, newspapers, plays, and poetry he read offered him a foundation that went beyond the accumulation of facts and phrases; they filled the vacuum left by the traumatizing absence of his father and the death of his mother when he was nine. An older, wiser Lincoln, who had benefited from years of self-education, noted that "a capacity, and taste, for reading, gives access to what has already been discovered by others. It is the key, or one of the keys, to the already solved problems. And not only so. It gives a relish, and a facility, for successfully pursuing the unsolved ones."[1] Books, unlike people, would never let him down. Yet he also realized that the words he read on the page could tell him only so much. To ascend in the tumultuous world of politics required a different sort of study.

Many people who knew Lincoln in his middle to late years spoke of how he read purely for utilitarian purposes, forgoing the pleasures of fiction. Even his study of poetry and drama was in pursuit of mastering the cadence of public speaking and better understanding human nature. Both as a boy and later in his life, Lincoln was intrigued with the founding of the republic, particularly with stories of the great men who were responsible for it, giants who still tread the earth in his lifetime. The books and speeches he read and reread sparked a lifelong fascination with politics, rhetoric, and the Constitution, and the debates in Illinois and throughout the nation were extensions of those the Founders had had in framing and ratifying the Constitution. Those men were hardly a distant memory for Lincoln and his generation. The nation had elected its first president only twenty years before Lincoln was born.

Lincoln's ambition to make an enduring mark on the world led him to five men, whose experiences, political insights, vision of the Constitution, example, and guidance helped him navigate the path to the presidency. From these five, Lincoln learned valuable lessons on how to master party politics, to campaign for office, to understand and use executive power, to negotiate, to manage a Cabinet, to craft a speech, and to develop policies and a constitutional vision that fit the times and became his most enduring legacy. In the nineteenth century, it was common, particularly for enterprising young men, to find flesh-and-blood mentors, men who would serve not only as father figures but also as teachers of the skills they needed to succeed. Lincoln's mentors were something different. For him, mentors were not just the men he actually interacted with but also sources of inspiration and instruction— men to be emulated, men whose mistakes he was determined to avoid, and men with whom he could argue or take issue without fear of alienation or retaliation. There is no reliable evidence that he ever met two of the men who so profoundly helped him steer his course to the White House. Yet Lincoln referred to these two men as mentors, seeing them as far more than inspirational figures. I have followed Lincoln's lead.

It is common for those who adore Lincoln to dismiss Andrew Jackson as a mentor because Lincoln campaigned so vigorously against Jackson and his political heirs, Martin Van Buren, James Polk, and Franklin Pierce, and for Jackson's most notable foe,

Henry Clay. Yet Jackson bracketed Lincoln's life: he was the president during Lincoln's formative years, and he was the first president to appoint Lincoln to federal office. Jackson was the president who initiated the Black Hawk War, in which Lincoln became captain of a company of volunteers, and Jackson was the only other president who formulated a coherent and compelling case against secession and the only one whose portrait hung in Lincoln's office throughout his presidency. Furthermore, Lincoln agreed with Jackson's declaration of the unique position of the president as the only federal official elected by and therefore representative of all the people of the Union. He adapted Jackson's understanding of democracy to the circumstances the nation confronted in a civil war, and he emulated Jackson's suspension of habeas corpus and Supreme Court–defying strategy.

Throughout his life, Lincoln was surrounded by Democrats who revered Jackson and by Whigs who cheered Jackson's great rival Henry Clay. Navigating this world sharpened Lincoln's ability to maintain lasting friendships with men who opposed him politically.

In 1832, Lincoln cast his first vote in a presidential election for Clay, not Jackson. For the rest of his life, he proudly proclaimed himself a Clay Whig and praised Clay as his "teacher," "mentor," and "beau ideal of a statesman." Lincoln followed both Clay and Jackson into the law, as a means for earning a living and making political and social connections. He considered himself to be a "self-made man" like Clay.

Clay was someone Lincoln cited often, not only in his debates with Douglas, but also later as president. Clay's oratory was more than a model that Lincoln studied and emulated. Lincoln also followed Clay's lead and that of Thomas Jefferson, whom Clay followed, in developing his vision, as a Senate candidate and later as president, of a connection between the promise of the Declaration of Independence that "all men are created equal" and the Constitution as the implementation of that pledge.

Lincoln's third mentor was Zachary Taylor. Lincoln followed Taylor closely when he led his army to important victories in the

Mexican War, and Lincoln was among the first national politicians to back Taylor for the presidency in 1848. Lincoln admired Taylor as another "self-made man" and lauded Taylor's devotion, like that of Clay and Jackson, to standing firmly against secession and against rebels threatening the Union.

Taylor bookends the years 1849 to 1861 for Lincoln, who eulogized him in 1850 and then, as he traveled to his own inauguration as president, singled Taylor out to a friendly audience in Pittsburgh as the man responsible for "my political education." The phrase *political education* meant something special to Lincoln and his generation; it referred to what people learned from real political experiences rather than books. Lincoln was not so idealistic that he perpetually ignored the chilly pragmatism of several of his mentors, especially Clay and Jackson. Recognizing the political advantages of such hardheaded expediency, he not only changed his mind about issues but also changed allegiances—even when it meant undermining those who had guided his ascent. He'd backed Taylor for president at the expense of Clay's candidacy, despite the fact that there may have been no politician who shaped Lincoln's beliefs more than Clay. Lincoln cited many of Taylor's actions as precedent for his own, including making record numbers of recess appointments and treating Southern forces as rebels and traitors. Lincoln followed Taylor in believing (as Jackson did) that a president must sometimes lead Congress, not the other way around, in fashioning national policy—in some ways a rejection of his earlier Whig conviction that legislative bodies should be paramount. On the other hand, Lincoln was not blinded by his mentors' virtues. The strategy he used to form his Cabinet was a barbed rejection of Taylor's choice not to use appointments to unify his party and administration.

A fourth mentor was Mary Todd's cousin John Todd Stuart. Lincoln met Stuart when Lincoln was assisting Sangamon County surveyor John Calhoun, a staunch Jacksonian (and no relation to the famous South Carolina senator of the same name). Stuart and Lincoln had crossed paths earlier during the Black Hawk War. Jackson had appointed among his officers as colonel Zachary Taylor, a personal friend who had served with him in the Second Seminole War begun in 1835. Stuart introduced Lincoln to law and politics in Illinois. He was a model for Lincoln in debating political opponents (they both faced off against Stephen Douglas, but Stuart did so much earlier) and in courtroom appearances, particularly in jury trials. Stuart made it possible for Lincoln to meet many of the people who would help him rise in Illinois politics. Lincoln sought Stuart's counsel and respected him even after Stuart joined the Democratic Party in 1856.

Orville Browning is the least likely of any of these men to have been a mentor to Lincoln. Whereas Browning, like Stuart, was a friend of Lincoln's, Browning, unlike Stuart, was a sometime rival. Yet Lincoln repeatedly turned to him for advice throughout his life. Their alliance helped move Whig policies through their respective chambers of the Illinois state legislature. Sometimes Browning (and Stuart, too) counseled Lincoln about his personal life. Browning and his wife tried to advise Lincoln through several amorous relationships, including the one they (as well as Stuart) thought the most troublesome, Lincoln's marriage to Mary Todd. Browning helped to found the national Republican Party as well as the Republican Party in Illinois. He constructed the Illinois Republican Party platform in 1856, on which Lincoln ran against Douglas. And Browning's advice after Lincoln's election to the presidency foreshadowed the strategy that Lincoln followed to keep the two promises he made in his First Inaugural Address—not to initiate hostilities with the South and to protect the Union.

The impact of these mentors on Lincoln's life is evident in his rise to power and his years as president. Only in the last few months of his presidency, with his reelection secured and the war won, did he begin to forgo consulting them. By then, his confidence in his political acumen, vision, and rhetoric was at its peak.

The giant figure of Lincoln seated in the iconic monument honoring him in the nation's capital captures the myth of Lincoln sitting alone, nearly godlike, contemplating the great issues of his day, head and shoulders above the fray. That is not how Lincoln learned to lead. This book is the story of how he did.

CHAPTER ONE

FINDING HIS MENTORS
(1809-1834)

In 1832, the United States was at a crossroads. It was hurtling toward its twelfth presidential election. The young nation, slightly more than four decades old, was sharply divided—politically, economically, regionally, and racially. No conflict generated more controversy and division than the legitimacy and maintenance of the institution of slavery. In 1832, there were twenty-four states, nearly equally divided over the future of slavery. The newest state, Missouri, was a slave state. Neighboring Illinois, admitted into the Union in 1818, was relatively small and had a peculiarly mixed record on slavery—with a state constitution adopted in 1819 forbidding it but a harsh Black Code adopted by the state legislature that restricted the presence and activities of African Americans.

The deep political divisions in the nation were reflected in the two fierce rivals vying for the nation's highest office. The contest pitted the stubborn, combative incumbent and champion of ordinary citizens and states' rights to regulate commercial interests and slavery without federal oversight, Andrew Jackson, against his most hated rival, Henry Clay, America's best-known orator and legislator, who championed a strong national government devoted to economic development and compromise, even on the question of the future of slavery in America.

As flatboats and other vessels navigated the Mississippi and between these two westernmost states, their crews and passengers could not help but see their stark differences. Among those pilots was a young man who reputedly expressed his revulsion when he saw African Americans in chains auctioned along his route. Abraham Lincoln was not alone in such sentiments, but in his case his thoughts may well have gone beyond mere observation. Perhaps he might be the one to change things, to eradicate such demonic commerce. Enamored with the exploits of great men, he yearned to become one of them, though he did not come from a prosperous or powerful family and regularly had no money in his pocket. He had to start somewhere, and he chose to settle in the small town of New Salem, Illinois, home to no more than a few hundred people. Many of its residents came from Kentucky, where he had been born, but although the frontier could be merciless, young Abraham Lincoln believed there were no immutable limits on what a determined man might become. The only things he needed were the opportunities to educate himself and to find the right men who could help him earn his place in America's story.

I

He was born with a thirst for learning but had no teacher.

Lincoln never met his paternal grandfather, Abraham. Twenty-eight years before he was born, his namesake, then only forty-one, was killed by a Native American, while his three sons, including the younger Abraham's father, Thomas, watched in horror.[1] Abe's uncle Mordecai, aged fifteen, shot the native, giving rise to a story the family embellished over the years. Lincoln himself told and retold the story throughout his life, never missing the chance to imbue it with the character of a legend that underscored the harshness of the frontier, where he was born in a one-room cabin on February 12, 1809.

The realities of childhood are difficult to reconstruct, even more so when the man was a child in the early 1800s and later grows up to become president. In Lincoln's case, contemporaneous records of his childhood are hard to come by; most people who interacted with him were illiterate, and most who wrote about his youth did so later with the knowledge of what he became almost certainly shaping their memories. Even so, we can separate some clues of the boy who became Lincoln from the legends of his origins.

Neighbors recalled young Abe's mother, Nancy, as "superior"[2] to her husband because she knew how to read. To young Abe's delight, she regularly read aloud to him from the King James Bible. At seven, he was sent, with his sister, Sarah, to a one-room school a mile away from their home in Kentucky, where he learned the fundamentals of reading and ciphering. When Abe was nine, Nancy died after consuming tainted milk, writhing in excruciating agony in front of him and the rest of her family.

Dennis Hanks, who was ten years older than Abe, was an illegitimate cousin who had lived with Nancy's family and later with the Lincolns after she died. Dennis claimed to have given young Abe "his first lesson in spelling—reading and writing,"[3] explaining that he had "taught Abe to write with a buzzards [sic] quill, which I killed with a rifle and having made a pen—put Abes [sic] hand in mine and moving his fingers by my hand to give him the idea of how to write."[4] It is possible there is some truth to his recollections, for he was reputed to be "the best-educated" member of the Hanks family, though what passed for best might not have been all that good. It is equally if not more possible that his recollections were hyperbole, given that they were recorded later, after Lincoln's death, and Dennis may have surrendered to the temptation to overstate his importance, as many later did, in the education of a man who became president.

A more likely story, historian David Herbert Donald suggested, was that "Dilworth's Spelling-Book," which Abe and Sarah had begun to use in school in Kentucky, provided Abe's first serious introduction to the basics of grammar and spelling. He more likely credited his stepmother rather than his biological mother with the other essential help he received in learning how to read and write, declaring in the 1850s, "All that I am, or hope to be, I owe to my angel mother."

Beginning with the alphabet and Arabic and Roman numerals, Dilworth's

> proceeded to words of two letters, then three letters, and finally four letters. From these, students learned to construct sentences, like the one Abe constructed in school, "No man may put off the law of God." Dilworth's then went on to more advanced subjects, and the final section included the prose and verse selections, which were accompanied by crude woodcuts, which may have been the first pictures [Abe] had ever seen.[5]

Other texts used in school, "like *The Columbian Class Book* and *The Kentucky Preceptor,* expanded and reinforced what [Abe] learned from Dilworth's."[6] Most contemporaries, particularly after Lincoln died, remembered him as a prodigy, while John Hanks, another cousin who lived with the Lincolns for a short while, remembered young Abe as "somewhat dull, not a brilliant boy—but worked his way by toil: to learn was hard for him, but he worked slowly, but surely."[7]

When Abe was ten, his father, Thomas, abandoned both him and his sister, Sarah, for several months. He left the children with Dennis Hanks while he searched for a new wife. Thomas found her in Kentucky, where they married in late 1819. He returned with his new wife, Sarah, along with her two children, to Indiana. She found Abe, Sarah, and Dennis not just emaciated and "wild," but Abe, she thought, was "the ugliest chap that ever obstructed her view."[8] No matter her initial apprehension, she came to love and be beloved by Lincoln, partly due to her unrelenting efforts to nurture the boy and support his dreams. Though not literate herself, she had brought with her a few books. One was *Robinson Crusoe,* the stirring story of a castaway who survived because of his courage and self-reliance. Another was *The Arabian Tales,* a collection of folk tales mostly told in prose but some in riddles and verse, which Lincoln read, reread, and used to entertain his friends.[9] (Dennis Hanks told a story, which may be more legend than fact, of Thomas berating Abe for the book, which he thought was nothing but "a pack of lies." "Mighty fine lies," Abe answered, "mighty fine lies.") Yet another book was *Webster's Speller,* one of many such guides Abe had on hand in school and at home. It is unclear how much they helped him. He made spelling mistakes all his life, such as writing "appologies," "opertunity," "immancipation," "Anapolis," "apparant," "inaugeral" . . . the list goes on. Some scholars believe these mistakes show that Lincoln was dyslexic, others, that he sometimes wrote in haste, but, at least as important, they showed that Lincoln cared less about how to write them correctly than about how the words sounded when spoken aloud.

Though these books might not have helped Lincoln to fully master written English, they pulled him out of the depression caused by his mother's death. They "reignited Abraham's love of learning,"[10] his stepmother said. Books were scarce on the frontier, so he read carefully rather than extensively. He memorized a good deal of what he read: "When he came across a passage that Struck him," his stepmother recalled, "he would write it down on boards if he had no paper & keep it there till he did get paper— then he would re-write it—look at it [and] repeat it" to himself until "it was fixed in his mind to suit him he . . . never lost that fact or his understanding of it."[11] Sarah stressed, too, that Abe was not just interested in reading but in writing, and in his writing, clarity of expression was all important. She said that Abe "seemed pestered to give Expression to his ideas and got mad almost at [any] one who couldn't Explain plainly what he wanted to convey." Lincoln had the same recollection that as a boy he was never satisfied "until I had put it in language plain enough, as I thought, for any boy I knew to comprehend." (His interest in writing and speaking plainly intensified with age.)

"Abe was getting hungry for book[s], reading everything he got his hands on," Dennis Hanks recalled, as did other friends and schoolmates of Lincoln.[12] "I never seen Abe after he was twelve 'at he didn't have a book some'ers 'round," he explained. Abe's stepmother agreed: "He read all day the books he could lay his hands on. He read diligently—studied in the day time—went to bed early—got up Early and then read."[13] "He'd put a book inside his shirt an' fill his pants pockets with corn dodgers," Dennis Hanks remembered,

> an' go off to plow or hoe. When noon come he'd set down under a tree, an' read an' eat. In the house at night, he'd tilt a cheer by the chimbly, an' set on his backbone an' read. I've seen a feller come in an' look at him, Abe not knowin' anybody was round, an' sneak out again like a cat, an' say, "Well, I'll be darned." It didn't seem natural, nohow, to see a feller read like that.[14]

Abe read so much that he allegedly once told a friend that "he had read through every book he had ever heard of in that county, for a circuit of 50 miles."[15]

First cousin John Hanks remembered that when Lincoln returned home after work, he "would go to the cup-board, snatch a piece of corn bread, take down a book, sit down in a chair, cock his legs up as high as his head, and read."[16] Abe's contemporaries, David Herbert Donald wrote, "attributed prodigies of reading to him." Lincoln supposedly told his cousin Dennis Hanks, "The things I want to know are in books," adding, according to biographer Carl Sandburg, "My best friend is the man who'll git me a book I ain't read."[17] Books were, for him, "the main thing" in life.

Looking back in 1859, as he was mounting his presidential campaign, Lincoln wrote a letter to Jesse Fell, a close friend of David Davis, who was in charge of his campaign and a fellow lawyer. Fell had written Lincoln to inquire about whether the two might be related, and Lincoln wrote back that, while he doubted they were, "when I came of age I did not know much. Still somehow I could read, write, and cipher to the Rule of Three."[18] In a campaign biography, which he ghostwrote in 1860, Lincoln declared, "All told, the aggregate of his schooling did not amount to one year."[19] If Lincoln was underselling his formal education, it was not by much.

Abe's stepmother, Sarah, was careful not to blame Lincoln's father, Thomas, for ending Abe's formal education, recalling, "As a usual thing, Mr. Lincoln never made Abe quit reading to do anything if he could avoid it. He would do it himself first."[20] That was not how Dennis Hanks remembered it. He said Thomas thought his son wasted too much time on books, "having sometimes to slash him for neglecting his work by reading."[21] That is how Lincoln remembered it, too.

When neighbors complained to Thomas about Abe's propensity to tell jokes and stories rather than to do the fieldwork they were paying him for, additional beatings might follow. Though Thomas was over average height, he was burly, and Dennis Hanks remembered that Lincoln's "father would sometimes knock him a rod."[22] It was unsurprising that when asked what he wanted to be when he grew up, Lincoln said, "NOT a carpenter or a farmer like my father." It was little surprise that he yearned for "emancipation" from his father.

II

Several of the books in Lincoln's home were not unusual for a frontier working family of the 1820s. Indeed, because of the lessons, examples, virtues, and religious fidelity that they instilled, they were among the most popular of the time, especially among young families.

The first, of course, was the King James Bible, which Abe's mother, Nancy, had introduced him to. It was said that by the age of ten, Lincoln recited Bible verses and sermons for his friends and family. His stepsister, Matilda Johnson, said, "When father & mother woud go to church, . . . Abe would take down the Bible, read a verse—give out a hymn—and we would sing. . . . he would preach & we would do the Crying—sometimes he would join in the Chorus of Tears."[23] She further recalled, "One day my bro John Johnston caught a land terrapin—brought it to the place where Abe was preaching—threw it against the tree—crushed the shell and it Suffered much—quivered all over—Abe preached against

Cruelty to animals, Contending that an ant's life was to it, as sweet as ours to us. . . ."[24]

While his siblings and friends were impressed when he quoted or satirized biblical passages or verses, it is unclear how much of the Bible Lincoln actually read. He may have simply been well versed in the sections he liked best. Dennis Hanks said that Abe "didn't read the Bible half as much as [is] said." Hanks thought the Bible "puzzled" Lincoln, "especially the miracles. He often asked me in the timber or sittin' around the fireplace nights, to explain scripture."[25] Lincoln's stepmother agreed: "Abe read the bible some, though not as much as [is] said: he sought more congenial books—suitable for his age."[26] He certainly didn't seem to engage with the scriptures in total solemnity. Once she asked him to entertain guests by reading aloud from the Bible. Unhappy to do this, the boy began reading through passages as quickly as he could; the more she admonished him, the faster he read. Finally, as Michael Burlingame notes, "In exasperation, she grabbed a broom and chased him out of the cabin, much to his relief. Another time, he read aloud from the Book of Isaiah, playfully interpolating passages from Shakespeare."[27]

Such incidents are early signs of the skepticism Lincoln had about the Bible as fact, yet he never doubted the powers of its language and stories. "In regard to this Great Book," he reputedly wrote in response to several former slaves who had given him a copy of the Bible in 1864, "I have but to say, it is the best gift God has given to man. All the good the Savior gave to the world was communicated through this book. But for it we could not know right from wrong. All things most desirable for man's welfare, here and hereafter, are to be found portrayed in it."[28] Though he often questioned the scriptures as fact and ridiculed organized religion, he recognized its words and lessons as profound and enduring, not just for him but also for the townspeople and country folk who became his public.

While the Bible was apparently the first book Abe had tried to read, the second, *Aesop's Fables,* was equally if not more influential. The collection of 725 morality tales was written in Greek by a former slave in the sixth century BCE. As one of Abe's friends recalled, "He kept the Bible and *Aesop's* always within reach, and read them over and over again."[29] Abe read the book so often, he memorized much of it. (Decades later, he would make powerful use of Aesop's fable about the Lion and the Four Bulls: "A kingdom divided against itself cannot stand.")

A childhood friend, James Ewing, recalled,

I doubt if he ever told a story just because it was a story. If he told an anecdote it was to illustrate or make clear some point he wanted to impress. He had a marvelous aptitude for that—to illustrate the idea he wanted to convey. He was a wonderful observer, and he had the rare ability to remember what he had seen and heard and read, so as to apply such information to the point of anything that struck him as ludicrous. . . . He applied this wonderful gift of observation and appreciation of humor to a situation or to something which somebody had said.[30]

Judge Owen Reeves, a friend from Lincoln's law-practicing days, agreed: "I heard Lincoln tell hundreds of anecdotes and stories, but never one that was not told to illustrate or give point to some subject or question that had been the theme of conversation, or that was not suggested by an anecdote or story told by someone else."[31]

In addition to the Bible and Aesop, Lincoln loved reading about the lives of the American Founders and their struggles to break free from British tyranny and to establish the United States. He had little taste for novels. He reputedly tried to read *Ivanhoe* but never finished. There are records of James Fenimore Cooper's novels in Lincoln's possession when he was a boy, but even as an adult he owned books by none of the great novelists of his time, such as Charles Dickens and Nathaniel Hawthorne. Instead, it was the history of politics that captured his imagination at an early age. He discovered "during my earliest days of being able to read Parson Weems' popular biography of George Washington, *A History of the Life and Death, Virtues and Exploits of General George Washington.*"

Weems's biography, first published in 1800, was more sermon

than actual history. It aimed to popularize the view of Washington as leading the colonists to victory in the Revolution because his military tactics were distinctly "American" in their ingenuity, courage, and independence, and his fight was for "American" ideals. By 1809, the year of Lincoln's birth, the book was in its fortieth edition, and Weems had added more anecdotes and myths to further promote the impression that Washington was wiser and, in a way that could only be American, more virtuous. (For instance, Weems created the purely fictional tale of young George chopping down a cherry tree and then declining to lie about what he had done.) The book effectively deified Washington as "the hero," the "Demigod," and "the 'Jupiter Conservator,' the friend and benefactor of men."[32] Weems went so far as to not only depict Washington as smarter, braver, and more ingenious than anyone else at the time, but also as more successful with the ladies.

The book perpetrated myths about the martial potency of superior American rectitude. For example, Weems declared that Washington at the 1753 Battle of Monongahela was immune to "[s]howers of bullets" from Native Americans and had "that TRUE HEROIC VALOUR which combats malignant passions—conquers unreasonable self—rejects the hell of hatred, and invites the love into our own bosoms, and into those of our brethren with whom we may have had a falling out."[33] It is unlikely that Lincoln, at fifteen, would have realized the book was filled with "effectual truths" (Niccolo Machiavelli's terms for myths serving political purposes) that Weems hoped would define American values. At fourteen or fifteen, Abe discovered that a neighbor had another, well-regarded biography of Washington written by David Ramsay, a physician and one of America's first self-proclaimed historians. Yet Abe never tired of recalling how he had walked two miles to a neighbor's house to first borrow Weems's book and spent months working off the cost of the book after it had been damaged in the rain.

Weems had been a friend of Thomas Jefferson, and his story of Washington constructed an inspiring vision of a new nation founded on the values of charity, modesty, and bravery. In contrast, Ramsay was one of the first Americans who aspired to do genuine historiography, researching primary documents, correspondence, diaries, and other authentic texts from the founding era. However, Ramsay was not without his own political agenda. He had fought in the Revolutionary War, and he hoped to validate republicanism's elevation of public service as a means to inculcate appropriate virtues, such as duty, mercy, loyalty, justice, and selflessness, in the governed as well as in the governors—as well as to reinforce national unity. Ramsay believed that Washington's story, more than any other, could inspire the values indispensable for a good life and a good society. Whereas Weems depicted Washington as a near-deity, Ramsay emphasized that he was a man, albeit a remarkable one with extraordinary qualities, including humility and courage. In addition, Ramsay depicted the new nation as bent on reform and determination to improve on English governance.

It was Weems's book that stuck with Lincoln. When he traveled to Washington for his first inaugural, Lincoln told the New Jersey Senate he could not forget Weems's account of Washington's struggles at Trenton—"the crossing of the river; the contest with the Hessians; the great hardships . . . I recollect thinking then, boy even though I was, that there must have been something more than common that those men struggled for."[34] Lincoln knew by then, if not well before, that Weems's book was as much fiction as real history, but it never bothered him. Decades before his political ascent, Lincoln understood that the myth could count even more than the facts because what people believed, what drove them to action, was what mattered most.

As late in his life as 1865, he told his friend and law partner William Herndon that the biographies of great men "are all alike. You might as well print up these biographies with blank titles and fill in the name of any subject that you please."[35] They "are written as false and misleading," he told Herndon, "never once hinting at [the subject's] failures and blunders." Those "failures and blunders" were as important to Lincoln as their successes, because he learned from them both. But instead, the biographies then available "can fill up eloquently and grandly at pleasure, thus commemorating a lie, an injury to the dying and to the name of the dead." Lincoln suggested that booksellers should have "blank biographies on their shelves always already for sale—so that, when a man dies, and his heirs—children and friends wish to perpetuate the memory of the dead, they can purchase one already written, but with blanks, which they can fill up eloquently and grandly at pleasure, thus commemorating [the] names of the dead."[36] Lincoln lived in an age without professional biographies and thus could shape his "tale" as he liked. If left unattended, his story would be up for grabs. Properly tended and with stretches of truth but not outright lies, it could be enduring.

Another book that Lincoln likely read was Lindley Murray's *Reader*, which was popular in homes and schools throughout Lincoln's youth. A strong supporter of the war for independence, Murray became a grammarian and editor of many books that were in large demand as manuals for instructing young children on reading, grammar, and writing. Issued at the end of the eighteenth century, Murray's *Reader* was full of classical moral axioms from the ancient Greeks and Romans as well as from British magazines like *The Spectator* and other Enlightenment moral sources. Such readings enriched the appreciation of young Lincoln for writing to convey moral instruction and for constructing allegories, fables, and stories.[37]

The Bible, Aesop, Murray, chronicles of the lives of public figures—Lincoln considered them dynamic, elastic tools to influence opinions, not accounts of facts and not to be interpreted as such. Another influential book that shaped Lincoln's understanding of the founding of the republic was William Grimshaw's *History of the United States*, first published in 1821. Grimshaw considered himself an objective historian and wrote many history textbooks that were widely used in Lincoln's day. This book, Grimshaw's most popular, was intended to inspire young people to adopt the values (as Grimshaw understood them to be) of the men who wrote the Constitution and won independence. It began with the discovery of the United States and ended with Florida's acquisition in 1819. It finished with an account of Northern states establishing laws for emancipation and prohibiting slavery. Grimshaw exhorted his readers, "Let us not only declare by words, but demonstrate by our actions, 'That all men are created equal, that they are endowed, by their Creator, with the same unalienable rights; that, amongst these, are life, liberty, and the pursuit of happiness.'"[38]

These stirring words were, of course, the self-evident truths set forth in the second paragraph of the Declaration of Independence. Lincoln memorized the entire document, and of all that he read in his life, its words might well have been the most influential. Indeed, he devoted his adult life to reminding the American people that these words were the promises that the American Constitution was established to ensure. In an 1856 speech, he described it as the "sheet anchor of our principles."[39] Two years earlier in Peoria, he had instructed his audience, "Let us readopt the Declaration of Independence, and with it the practices and policy which harmonizes with it."[40]

But not everything Lincoln read was as civic-minded. Humor delighted him; he mimicked the styles of the different speakers he heard and the writers he loved, and he adored telling funny stories and jokes. There was good reason to believe his gift of storytelling came naturally or at least ran in the family. Dennis Hanks recalled that Lincoln's father, Thomas, "could beat his son telling a story—cracking a joke."[41] Watching his father bring laughter to a room was a powerful example of how even someone whose reputation did not much include amusement and diversion could win the crowd in the right circumstance with skilled deployment of narrative.

Lincoln's cheekiness is evident in two poems he wrote when he was in his teens if not younger, penned in his arithmetic book. The first announced, "Abraham Lincoln / His hand and pen / He will be good / But God knows when," and the other, "Abraham Lincoln is my name / And with my pen I wrote the same / I wrote in both hast and speed / And left it here for fools to read."[42] While these rhymes may not suggest a sophisticated fascination with poetry, in fact Lincoln was genuinely entranced by the art. As a boy, he read Thomas Gray's "Elegy in a Country Churchyard," a poem he quoted often. As president, he once told campaign biographer John Locke Scripps, "It is a great piece of folly to attempt to make anything out of my early life. It can all be condensed into a single sentence, and that sentence you will find in Gray's Elegy: 'The short and simple annals of the poor.'"[43]

Besides the poems he encountered in the readers he had at school, Lincoln would have come across poetry in William Scott's *Lessons in Elocution*, another of the books that his stepmother had brought into their home. Around 1825, Lincoln began to read the Scott collection closely, which included Shakespeare, a writer who, along with Robert Burns, Lincoln quoted frequently throughout his life. (Later, as president, he wrote, "I think nothing equals *Macbeth*. It is wonderful.")

Lincoln's facility with rhyme and wit was not always used virtuously. Around the age of nineteen, he wrote "Chronicles of Reuben," based on incidents dating back to 1826, when Lincoln's sister married Aaron Grigsby, whose family were neighbors of the Lincolns. When Sarah died in childbirth, Lincoln blamed Aaron and the Grigsbys for waiting too long to call a doctor to save her. His bitterness increased when he was not invited to the joint wedding celebration of Aaron's brothers Reuben and Charles, who were married on the same day. Lincoln purportedly arranged, through a friend, for Reuben and Charles to be brought to the wrong bedrooms, where each other's wife awaited after the wedding party. Lincoln wrote a description of the incident in "Chronicles of Reuben" as payback. Patterned after biblical scripture, a prose narrative was followed by a poem about Billy Grigsby, another of Aaron's brothers, who, it says, "married Natty," who was another man. Lincoln's neighbor Joseph Richardson claimed that "Chronicles of Reuben" was "remembered here in Indiana in scraps better than the Bible."[44] The episode was among Lincoln's earliest exploitations of the power of public ridicule and the sway it conferred on those who wield it. What he called "the power to hurt," a phrase he borrowed from a Shakespeare sonnet, would remain useful, though not the "chief weapon in his rhetorical arsenal."

A final book that fed Lincoln's love of language and allegory was John Bunyan's *The Pilgrim's Progress*, first published in 1678 and quickly translated into over a hundred languages. By the time Lincoln's father gave him a copy of the book (borrowed from a neighbor), it was second only to the Bible in its popularity in the United States. The youngster may have first discovered it when Benjamin Franklin referred to it in his autobiography, another book Lincoln loved. When Abe first discovered Bunyan's tale, his "eyes sparkled, and all that day he could not eat, and that night he could not sleep."[45] Sometimes called (erroneously) the first lengthy prose narrative in English, *The Pilgrim's Progress* tells the story of an everyman known as Christian who flees the City of Destruction (this world) and is instructed to follow the narrow path to the Celestial City, "That Which Is to Become" as the full title puts it. The quest is filled with set pieces that became some of Lincoln's favorite fables, and the tale as a whole was inspiring to a young man who dreamed of beating the odds to become a hero.

III

The histories and biographies Abe read sparked an interest in politics, as did the nearly daily conversations in his house and in the neighborhood. Thomas was a proud Democrat, as were most of the people in Abe's family and the neighboring homes. They all felt betrayed by the federal government, which was tightening their credit and backing the big businesses gouging them. As is the wont of many children, Lincoln adopted his father's party affiliation.

Nineteenth-century America was not ripe with the sort of "nonprofit" organizations that now constellate our daily lives. A political career held the greatest promise for a young man who saw public service, not family or acquiring money, as his principal calling. To feed his interest in what he saw as this much more virtuous pursuit, Lincoln discussed politics every chance he had with friends and neighbors. In 1828, he went to work for Colonel

William Jones, a local postmaster only six years older than Lincoln. Jones hired Lincoln as a farmhand and as a land clerk in his
tiny general store, where Lincoln sometimes slept, even though his
family's cabin was only about a mile and a half away. Jones was a
graduate of the first public university in Indiana, Vincennes University, and his store became a popular gathering place for young
men to debate political issues. Henry Clay Whitney, an Illinois
friend of Lincoln's, recalled Abe telling him, "The sessions were
held in Jones' store, where the auditors and disputants sat on the
counter, on inverted nail kegs, or lolled upon barrels or bags, while
the wordy contest raged."[46] He further said Lincoln explained that
"the questions selected for discussion were not concrete. At one
time there would be a debate upon the relative forces of wind
and water; at another, upon the comparative wrongs of the Indians and the negro; the relative merits of the ant and the bee; also
of water and fire."[47] Dennis Hanks, who sometimes joined in the
sessions, recalled that "Lincoln would frequently make political
speeches to the boys; he was always calm, logical, and clear. His
jokes and stories were so odd, original, and witty all the people
in town would gather around him. He would keep them all till
midnight. Abe was a good talker, a good reasoner, and a kind of
newsboy."[48]

Similarly, Nathaniel Grigsby, who had made his peace with Lincoln by this time and had become, like Lincoln, a regular partici-
pant in the Jones's store debate, recollected that "we attended [the
debates]—heard questions discussed—talked everything over and
over and in fact wore it out."[49] Grigsby acknowledged, "We learned
much in this way," and, as for Lincoln, Grigsby added (perhaps in
a rose-colored recollection), "His mind and the ambition of the
man soared above us. He naturally assumed the leadership of the
boys. He read and thoroughly read his books whilst we played."[50]
Grigsby found that "Lincoln was figurative in his speeches, talks,
and conversations. He argued much from analogy and explained
things hard for us to understand by stories, maxims, tales, and figures. He would almost always point [out] his lesson or idea by some
story that was plain and near, as that we might instantly see the

force and bearing of what he said."[51] Grigsby agreed that Jones was "Lincoln's guide and teacher in politics."[52]

In the 1828 presidential election, the Democrats' champion was John Quincy Adams's foe, Andrew Jackson, who had lost to Adams four years before. Lincoln and Dennis Hanks "went to political and other speeches" and heard "all sides and opinions." Hanks remembered that "Lincoln was originally a Democrat after the order of Jackson—so was his father—so we all were."[53] David Turnham and Elizabeth Crawford, who both knew Lincoln in Indiana, recalled Lincoln and his father as "Jackson men" when they left for Illinois in 1830.[54] Abe had even been heard singing, "Let auld acquaintance be forgot / And never brought to mind. / May Jackson be our president /And Adams left behind."[55] This was the song of a Jackson man.

However, something happened that changed the political scene in the 1820s and 1830: Henry Clay took the lead in assembling a new political party. He called it the Whig Party, a name he borrowed from the British political party that favored legislative rather than executive dominance, emphasizing the importance of Parliament over the king as the best and most effective representatives of the people. Dennis Hanks remembered that "Colonel Jones made [Abraham] a Whig."[56] Jones backed John Quincy Adams in 1828, and though Clay was not a candidate in that election, several contemporaries in Indiana remembered Lincoln's memorizing Clay's speeches, reciting them for his friends, and praising Clay, as the newspapers did, as "Harry of the West." Jones had a library, and he subscribed to several newspapers as well as having at least temporary access to all the others that came through his office as postmaster. In those days, newspapers were the lifeblood of American democracy. They were the principal sources of news and notable speeches, particularly on the national stage. They also generally adhered to their owners' politics. Jones introduced Lincoln to the *New York Telescope,* the *Washington Intelligencer,* the *Western Register,* and the *Louisville Gazette,* all of which were Whig papers. Thus informed and influenced, as Lincoln prepared to leave his father's home for good, his choice on which of the two men to follow was already taking shape.

IV

For most of Abraham Lincoln's life, Andrew Jackson and Henry Clay were the two titans fighting over the future of America. They both were born before the American Revolution ended, and both men were tall. Jackson was six one, thin and sinewy. Clay was six three, and those who came to hear his oratory often remarked how he slowly unfurled to his full height as he rose to make his point. Lincoln grew to be the tallest of the three. His stature—in both the literal and figurative sense—would one day come to dwarf both men.

Jackson was ten years older than Clay and had fought in the War of Independence. It was a well-known fact in Lincoln's era that Jackson and his brother Robert had been captured by the British in 1781, and while in captivity, both had famously refused to shine the boots of a British officer, who slashed Jackson's face, giving him a scar that he wore proudly for the rest of his life.

Clay and Jackson both came from modest backgrounds, though Jackson's family was poorer. Jackson's father had died before he was born, and Clay's father had died when he was four. Jackson's mother moved in with her sister's family, while Clay's mother remarried, so Clay grew up in a crowded home with siblings and stepsiblings. Jackson attended a one-room schoolhouse for a year before entering a local academy for a year or two, while Clay was put on a fast track to become educated in Richmond. Both men took great pains to emphasize—indeed, exaggerate—their humble origins,[57] which did not slow either of them down. They both studied law. Jackson did it almost entirely on his own: he briefly apprenticed for a lawyer in Salisbury, North Carolina, and then, with the help of several other local attorneys, was admitted to the

North Carolina bar in 1787. Clay secured a coveted clerkship with the Virginia Court of Chancery, and his neat handwriting caught the eye of one judge, the esteemed George Wythe, America's first law teacher, who had mentored both Thomas Jefferson and the great chief justice John Marshall. Because Wythe had a crippled hand, he could not write for himself, so he hired Clay, then sixteen, as his secretary for the next four years. Wythe's influence on Clay was profound. "To no man," Clay said in 1851, "was I more indebted by his instructions, his advice, and his example."[58] Clay said that he learned his lifelong opposition to slavery from Wythe.

For a short while, Jackson practiced law but quickly moved on to become a prosecutor, land speculator, and most important, protégé of one of Tennessee's most colorful and controversial leaders, William Blount. Blount had been one of North Carolina's delegates to the Constitutional Convention and a signatory to the Constitution. With Blount's support, Jackson became Tennessee's first attorney general and a delegate to Tennessee's constitutional convention in 1796. When Tennessee became a state the next year, Jackson was elected as its first and only representative in the U.S. House of Representatives. A year later, Jackson was elected to the Senate, arriving there shortly after the House had impeached his mentor, Blount, and the Senate then expelled him for having conspired with the British to take control of Spanish Florida in exchange for money that would have helped him to pay off the enormous debts he had incurred as a land speculator.[59] Jackson left the Senate less than a year later to return to Tennessee, where he was elected to the Tennessee Supreme Court, on which he served until 1804.

Clay was experiencing his own meteoric rise to power. Already established as a lawyer (who sometimes corresponded with Andrew Jackson on legal matters), he was elected to the Kentucky General Assembly at the age of twenty-six. In 1804, Aaron Burr, Jefferson's vice president, killed Alexander Hamilton in a duel and then headed west to make a fortune. He was in Kentucky when he was charged with treason. (Burr had apparently been in discussions with William Blount over some "land scheme.") Burr turned to Clay and, with co-counsel John Allen, convinced him that the real plot was a Republican vendetta against him. Clay got the charges dismissed when a key witness failed to appear at trial. As Clay, already renowned for his eloquence, later explained,

> *Such was our conviction of the innocence of the accused, that, when he sent a considerable fee, we resolved to decline accepting it, and accordingly returned it. We said to each other, Col. Burr has been an eminent member of the profession, has been attorney general of the State of New York, is prosecuted without cause, in a distant State, and we ought not to regard him in the light of an ordinary culprit.*[60]

When he was defending Burr, Clay was elected in 1806 to complete the U.S. Senate term of the incumbent, who had resigned in anger after losing reelection. Clay, then twenty-nine, was already the speaker of the state house of representatives but was four months shy of the minimum age of thirty required in the Constitution for service in the Senate. Nonetheless, the Senate seated him with no objection. As Clay was preparing to go to Washington, Burr contacted him to let him know he was about to be indicted a second time for treason.[61] Clay was concerned that he might have a conflict of interest due to his new Senate duties, but Burr assured him in writing that he was innocent of the charges that he had promoted the dissolution of the United States in any way.[62] When Clay appeared in court on Burr's behalf, the prosecution again conceded that an important witness had failed to appear. Clay angrily denounced the prosecution's shenanigans, and two days later the jury acquitted Burr.[63]

Eager to get to Washington to begin his life as a senator, Clay left almost immediately after procuring Burr's acquittal, but before he arrived in the nation's capital, President Jefferson got word to him that he was in possession of a coded message from Burr in which his treacherous schemes were evident. Jefferson issued a proclamation warning the nation of a military conspiracy and urging the capture of the traitors, including Burr. Once Clay arrived in Washington, he tried to reassure everyone that he had believed Burr was innocent, but at the White House, President Jefferson showed Clay some of the decoded documents demonstrating Burr's guilt. "It seems," Clay wrote his father-in-law, "that we have been much mistaken about Burr."[64] Clay refused to appear on Burr's behalf at his treason trial conducted later before the chief justice of the United States, John Marshall. Clay told people that Burr had "deceived" him and that he would not give Burr "an opportunity for deceiving him [another] time."[65] Clay's association with Burr would follow him for the rest of his life, a warning to other lawyers, including Lincoln, on the risks of both representing and becoming too closely associated with unpopular clients.

The legal careers of Jackson and Clay each consistently took a backseat to their political ambitions. In 1812, Clay supported the United States' declaration of war against Britain after it attempted to stop American traders from supplying Russian and American hemp to France for salt-resistant cordage for Napoleon's navy. The British forced captured American sailors into servitude and encouraged Native American attacks on American settlers on the frontier. Jackson enthusiastically joined the cause and became a hero as the prevailing general when his ragtag army of roughly hundreds of American men defeated the larger, better financed and armed forces of the British in the Battle of New Orleans in 1815. In that case, he'd marched his band of volunteers from Tennessee to Mississippi, but, once he arrived, he was ordered to disband his men. He refused. Instead, he funded their march back hundreds of miles to Tennessee and then to New Orleans. Thinking he was as tough as the hardest wood they knew, they dubbed him Old Hickory. The name stuck.

Jackson had a hair-trigger temper. He fought two duels; in one of them, the man he killed had struck him first near the heart. The bullet was so close to his heart that surgeons decided they could not remove it without killing Jackson. He caned various enemies and made numerous challenges that were not accepted. He had two shootouts with the governor of Tennessee and another with his then aide-de-camp Thomas Hart Benton, whose bullet struck him in his left arm. Nevertheless, Benton later became a friend and political ally, and Jackson later would sometimes make a show of being angry to intimidate people he wished to be rid of.

In 1817, President James Monroe directed Jackson to lead military forces to rebuff Native American attacks in Spanish Florida. Jackson succeeded, but not before ordering the brutal killing of Native Americans in his charge as well as two British citizens who had traded with them. When it became clear that Spain could not defend or control the Florida territory, President Monroe, through his secretary of state, John Quincy Adams, negotiated the transfer of sovereignty over it from Spain to the United States. Monroe then placed Jackson in control of the territory as military governor.[66]

With the 1824 presidential election fast approaching, Jackson and Clay both tried to position themselves to succeed President Monroe, who was finishing his second term. Jackson got off the mark faster. A young man named John Eaton, a friend of Jackson's family in Tennessee, published a biography of Jackson in 1817, the first campaign biography in American politics. Young Abraham Lincoln would likely have read it. Eaton's book and Jackson's campaign portrayed the candidate as a war hero, defender not only of his country but the common man, unbeholden to the banks and businesses, and a champion of states' rights.[67]

For his part, Clay had become the youngest speaker of the U.S. House of Representatives in its history, having been elected to the position when he first entered the House in 1811. Up until 1820, Clay had been an agitator rather than a peacemaker in Congress. His introduction of the Missouri Compromise in 1820 changed all that. A slave owner, he had founded the American Colonization Society in 1817 to provide a solution for the slavery problem by buying slaves their freedom and then funding their travel back to Africa. Clay was an early president, Andrew Jackson an inactive vice president. Alarmed that sectional differences over slavery were threatening to rip the country apart, Clay saw an opportunity he could not resist: his chance to exercise leadership on the question of slavery. On March 3, 1820, the House approved Clay's proposed compromise—allowing Maine to be admitted into the Union as a free state and Missouri as a slave state. The proposal further barred the expansion of slavery north of the 36°30' parallel, excluding Missouri. As the first successful attempt to broker a compromise between the proslavery and antislavery members of Congress, Clay's effort, including detailed accounts of his four-hour oration, delivered over two days, was widely reported by newspapers throughout the country.

Clay split each part of the compromise into separate bills, which were supported by different coalitions in the House. Clay earned the nickname the Great Compromiser for his kind of tactic, and he would use the same technique thirty years later in his crowning achievement as a legislator—the Compromise of 1850, yet another attempt to find a solution to the slavery problem that, in the end, merely postponed a final reckoning.

Over the course of two legislative days (and over 40 pages in the *Annals of Congress*), Clay delivered a speech that foreshadowed the eloquence to come. He set forth his belief in tariffs to protect fledgling American industry, in federal funds for internal improvements, and in a national bank that would give credit to help people improve the quality of their lives. "The object of the bill under consideration," he declared, "is to create the home market, and to lay the foundations of a genuine American policy."[68] In characteristic fashion, he proceeded to systematically address ten arguments made against the tariff, and concluded, "But there is a remedy, and that remedy consists in modifying our foreign policy, and in adopting a genuine AMERICAN SYSTEM. We must naturalize the arts in our country, and we must naturalize them by the only means which the wisdom of nations has yet discovered to be effectual—by adequate protection against the otherwise overwhelming influence of foreigners."[69] As described by Lincoln's biographer David Herbert Donald, "Clay's American System sought to link the manufacturing of the Northeast with the grain production of the West and the cotton and tobacco crops of the South, so that the nation's economy would become one vast interdependent web. When economic interests worked together, so would political interests, and sectional rivalries would be forgotten in a powerful American nationalism."[70]

From an early age, Clay and Jackson had each regarded himself as the true heir to the political vision of Thomas Jefferson; at the turn of the nineteenth century, they each shared Jefferson's skepticism of a strong federal government and commitment to expanding access to voting for ordinary American citizens. In time, Clay, unlike Jackson, became increasingly concerned that relying too much on the uninformed opinions of the vast electorate was in conflict with the interests of American businesses whose success was crucial for ensuring the nation's prosperity. Clay thus developed confidence in a potent national government that backed ambitious public works, such as a vast transportation infrastructure that would have included canals, roads, harbors, and navigation improvements, as well as funds for schools. Clay's vision, which became known as the American System, was in sharp conflict with Jackson's certitude that the hard push for economic development would give rise to rapacious businesses and banks that would gouge ordinary Americans. The mismatch in the two men's worldviews would, unsurprisingly, lead to a clash between them. While one crucial element of the American System, the Tariff of 1824, passed narrowly in the House, it was clear that without the support of the chief executive, progress would be severely limited.

In the 1824 election, the problem that both Jackson and Clay faced, however, was that they were just two of the four major candidates running for president. At that time, the predominant national party was the Democratic-Republican Party, which had won six consecutive elections. The only other major party, the Federalist Party, which had been the party of Washington and John Adams, had dissolved shortly after Adams lost the 1800 presidential election to his own vice president, Thomas Jefferson. After the Federalist Party melted away, the country entered what was commonly called the Era of Good Feelings, a deceiving nomenclature, as the 1824 election showed. The fact that there was one dominant political party did not mean every Democratic-Republican shared the same outlooks or allegiances. Unlike today's political parties, those in the antebellum era did not simply coalesce around an agreed-upon platform of policies. Instead, they were formed around regional interests and beliefs about whether the Constitution envisioned a strong, effective federal government or a significant realm of state authority over which the federal government had no say.

In 1824, four different men vied for the Democratic-Republican Party's mantle: William Crawford, who had served as Monroe's secretary of war and Adams's Treasury secretary but then suffered a debilitating stroke. His disability was an open secret likely to hinder support from outside his home state of Georgia. John Quincy Adams, the son of President Adams, had served in a series of prestigious public offices; he was the sitting secretary of state, the same office that James Madison had occupied when he was elected president the first time in 1808, and that James Monroe had occupied when he ran in 1816 to succeed Madison. Jackson quit after serving brief stints in both the Senate and the House. Clay, on his way to becoming the longest-serving speaker of the House of Representatives, was widely revered (and castigated) as a visionary and seasoned statesman. A fifth candidate, John Calhoun, secretary of war and the most outspoken defender of slavery on the national stage, competed only for the vice presidency and therefore ensured that he would serve as the vice president for whomever was elected president.

None of the four major candidates seemed to have a good chance at winning the presidency, as none could muster anything more than moderate regional backing. Adams received support in New England and split the Mid-Atlantic region with Jackson but did not win the popular vote. Jackson and Crawford split the popular vote in the South, while Jackson and Clay split it in the Western regions. Jackson claimed a plurality of the national popular vote, but no one won a majority in the Electoral College.

Under the Twelfth Amendment, which had been ratified to prevent any confusion over how electoral votes should be counted for president and vice president, as had occurred in the election of 1800, the House of Representatives decided the outcomes of presidential elections unresolved in the Electoral College. Only the top three candidates in the popular election were eligible to be considered in the House. Because Clay had finished fourth in the popular vote, he was no longer eligible to be a candidate, but as speaker of the House, he was in charge of handling the vote to break the electoral stalemate. He threw his support to Adams—unsurprising given that Adams was the only other candidate who had supported the infrastructure program that Clay favored. Due to Clay's support and influence in the House, Adams became president, and he named Clay secretary of state.

Bitterly disappointed, Jackson threw one of the most famous fits of anger in American history. From the moment the House made Adams president to the 1828 rematch between Jackson and Adams, Jackson denounced wherever he went the arrangement between Adams and Clay as a "corrupt bargain."[71]

When the 1828 election came around, Jackson's grudge against both Adams and Clay was as strong as ever. This time, it was only Jackson and Adams who faced off, since as Adams's secretary of state, Clay was obviously in the president's camp. Nor were there any minor candidates to siphon votes from either of the major candidates. Besides recirculating Eaton's biography, Jackson initiated a style of campaigning that candidates continue to use today, including personal appearances, soliciting backing from newspapers, and reminding voters of Jefferson's endorsement in his earlier run for president.[72] Jackson worked with Martin Van Buren and others to build a new party apparatus called the Democratic Party to replace the deteriorating Democratic-Republican regime.

For his part, Adams was largely tone-deaf when it came to political acumen. Throughout his administration, he had not bothered to use his appointments to solidify support within his administration or Congress, nor had he bothered to curry favor with congressional leaders to get his legislative initiatives enacted. He had little to show for his four years in office except perhaps for his stubbornness and determination not to suffer fools gladly. And this time he faced not only an energized Jackson but a brand-new party.

In the months prior to the election, Jackson, with the help of a small band of close advisers that included Martin Van Buren, had established the Democratic Party, emphasizing its commitment to following the will of a majority of voting Americans. Clay replaced the name of the Democratic-Republican Party, which was all but defunct anyway, adopting the other half of the old party's moniker: he was now the candidate of the National Republican Party.

Jackson's new party destroyed the competition. Jackson won the 1828 election with nearly 56 percent of the popular vote and over twice as many Electoral College votes as Adams had won in 1824. During the 1828 campaign, Calhoun, then the vice president to Adams, offered to serve as Jackson's vice president if he won. Jackson agreed. Many of the people who voted for him were Southern Democrats who also supported Calhoun, and both he and Calhoun opposed federal overreach into domains that, in their opinion, were properly within the jurisdiction of the states.

Everyone expected the 1832 presidential election to be the culmination of the feud between the Jacksonites and Clay men. It was not. Their ideological dispute was not put to rest until after their deaths, Lincoln's reelection, and the end of the Civil War.

Neither Jackson nor Clay anticipated that Vice President John Calhoun would attempt to thwart Jackson's reelection. Jackson and Calhoun had been increasingly at odds throughout most of Jackson's first term, as Calhoun and his allies in the Cabinet belligerently tried to push Jackson toward a more extreme defense of slavery and adoption of the doctrine of nullification (the entitlement of states to disregard any federal laws they considered to encroach upon their autonomy).

In February 1831, with the presidential election more than a year away, Calhoun hoped to sabotage Jackson's reelection by leaking a copy of a letter that President Monroe had written to Jackson back in 1818. The letter seemed to indicate that Monroe had not given Jackson clear authority to take the aggressive measures that he did to help the United States wrest Florida from Spanish control. Clay and other critics of Jackson—who continued to claim that he'd had Monroe's support—seized on the letter as further evidence of Jackson's tyrannical disposition.

Jackson restructured his Cabinet to rid himself of Calhoun's allies as well as the members whose wives had snubbed the wife of Jackson's friend, biographer, and war secretary, John Eaton—a purge seemingly driven more by personal slight than policy. Jackson asked Secretary of State Martin Van Buren, who had suggested the reorganization, to resign so that Jackson could appoint him as minister to Great Britain. To avoid a clash in the Senate, Jackson gave Van Buren a recess appointment as minister in August 1831. When in 1832 the Senate split over the nomination of Van Buren as ambassador, Calhoun, in his capacity as vice president, cast the tie-breaking vote to defeat it. In doing so, he made Van Buren a martyr for Jackson's cause.

As the turmoil in the Jackson administration subsided, Henry Clay tried to outmaneuver Jackson on a different front. Clay decided to turn the national bank—the centerpiece of his American System—into *the* major issue in the upcoming presidential election. Previously, on May 27, 1830, Jackson had vetoed the Maysville Road project.[73] The road would have connected Lexington to Maysville, Kentucky, a sixty-six-mile stretch that would have extended the Cumberland Road, the nation's first interstate highway, built between 1811 and 1837 and designed to extend from Cumberland, Maryland, to the Northwest Territory. Jackson argued that the Maysville project was unconstitutional because it was purely intrastate and therefore a matter to be addressed solely by Kentucky authorities.[74] Clay decided, along with Nicholas Biddle, the director of the national bank, to bring up the rechartering of the bank five years sooner than it needed to be, in order to force Jackson to again show the extent to which he opposed the concept.

Clay underestimated Jackson. Jackson killed the national bank in perhaps the most famous veto message in American history. In spite of the fact that the United States Supreme Court had previously upheld the national bank's constitutionality as a lawful exercise of Congress's authority under the Necessary and Proper Clause (because the law made collection and redistribution of federal money much easier), Jackson, in a message drafted by his then–attorney general Roger Taney, argued that this same clause vested him with independent authority to determine whether a law was "necessary" or not.[75] Jackson concluded that the national bank charter was not. Lambasting the bank as "corrupt," Jackson warned that "if this monopoly were regularly renewed every fifteen or twenty years on terms proposed by themselves, they might seldom in peace put forth their strength to influence elections or control the affairs of the nation." As for the Supreme Court's decision unanimously upholding the bank's constitutionality, Jackson declared that its decision "ought not to control the coordinate authorities of this Government." In a declaration that would guide every subsequent president, including Lincoln, Jackson wrote, "The Congress, the Executive, and the Court must each for itself be guided by its own opinion of the Constitution." The president, he explained, is "independent of both" the Court and Congress, particularly since the president is the only *national* leader elected by the voters. In the upcoming campaign, Jackson men would argue that the bank was corrupt and indeed was responsible already for one national economic downturn, the Crisis of 1819, when banks failed because they overextended their credit and then foreclosed mortgages, forcing people out of their homes and off their farms.

Besides baiting Jackson with the national bank, Clay baited him with barbs, theatrics, and satire every chance he had. He rebuffed Jackson's charge of "bargain and corruption" by producing a letter from James Buchanan, who denied Jackson's claim that Buchanan had told him about the deal struck between Adams and Clay at Jackson's expense. While Jackson's rhetoric was plain, direct, and often profane, delivered much like a sharp jab to the jaw of an opponent, Clay characteristically opted for more rhythmic, dramatic rhetoric, often sprinkled with alliteration or palilalia (repeating the same sentence or word) and rhetorical questions instead of declarative statements, such as when he implored the House to approve the Tariff of 1824 (a protective tariff designed to protect American businesses from cheaper British commodities):

The object of the bill under consideration is to create this home market, and to lay the foundations of a genuine American policy. . . . Are we doomed to behold our industry languish and decay more

and more? But there is a remedy, and that remedy consists in . . .
adopting a genuine AMERICAN SYSTEM. We must naturalize the
arts in our country, and we must naturalize them by the only means
which the wisdom of nations has yet discovered to be effectual—
by adequate protection against the overwhelming influence of for-
eigners.

Jackson rejected flowery language and complex metaphors in
further contrast with Clay, who often indulged in convoluted,
intricate similes and allegories to make his point, as he once did
when, in the Kentucky state legislature, he likened the current capital, Frankfurt, to "an inverted hat" and "penitentiary" so difficult
to navigate that he wondered, "Who that got in, could get out?"

Clay also undertook several efforts during the campaign to bolster his own image and to cast Jackson in a bad light. Believing that
Jackson's veto of the national bank placed him on the wrong side
of federal power, Clay and Biddle authorized the printing and distribution of thirty thousand copies of the text of the veto. Around
the same time, Clay authorized George Prentice to write a campaign biography as a response to the one Eaton had written several
years before about Jackson. Prentice hailed Clay as a man who had
worked his way up from nothing, whose oratory was "the voice of
salvation in the country" and whose story exemplified American
independence and virtue.[76] Prentice made no money from the biography, in spite of the fact that twenty thousand copies were sold. To
help Prentice financially, Clay procured him a job as the editor of
the *Louisville Journal* in 1830.

Dennis Hanks later suggested that Lincoln had read Prentice's
biography in his teens, but that was impossible, for it was not published and widely distributed until 1831, when Lincoln turned
twenty-two.[77] But Lincoln did not need to read the book when it
first appeared to know the details of Clay's life, as he avidly read
the *Louisville Journal,* which reliably celebrated Clay and published
his speeches and many of the same pro-Clay, anti-Jackson stories
that appeared in the Clay campaign biography. Through his daily
reading and political discussions and debates with his friends and

neighbors, Lincoln tightened his embrace of Clay's American System to such an extent that his fidelity to Clay's political vision became obvious to everyone he met.

V

Largely by accident, twenty-two-year-old Lincoln arrived in New Salem, Illinois, in late July 1831. It was a tiny town, with only about a hundred residents. He was on his second trip there when the flatboat he was steering got stranded near a dam. Denton Offutt, who had hired Lincoln to pilot the boat, lent him an auger, which Lincoln used to drill a hole in the boat that allowed the water to drain out, freeing the boat to sail past the dam. Impressed with Lincoln's ingenuity, Offutt offered him a job in his store. Over the next six years, Lincoln would find employment as a shopkeeper (Offutt's store failed within a year, and he turned out to be a con man rather than a legitimate businessman), a shop owner (the shop went belly up, saddling Lincoln with debt that took years to pay off), a soldier (who saw no combat), a hardworking land surveyor tasked with determining the boundaries of several neighboring towns (in the words of one nearby resident, "Mr. Lincoln had the monopoly of finding the lines, and when any dispute arose among the Settlers Mr. Lincolns Compass and chain always settled the matter satisfactorily"), a rail splitter, and a postmaster.[78] None of these jobs captured his imagination. Lincoln disliked physical labor, even when he was good at it. (Lincoln loved to tell friends, "[My] father taught [me] to work but never learned [me] to love it.") Instead, politics captured his interest and shaped his ambitions.

The work did not impress Lincoln much but the people did: He found the residents of New Salem friendly, welcoming a young stranger who had no ties there. He settled into town around the time newspapers were reporting John Calhoun's leaked letter from President Monroe. Lincoln's arrival also coincided with an off-year

election for Congress, set for August 1, 1831. It was the first election in which Lincoln cast a vote. Voting at that time was done
not in secret but by open declaration. Lincoln walked up to the
station set up in the middle of town and announced that he was
voting for James Turney, the pro-Clay, National Republican candidate. It was a brave thing to do, given that the community was
largely Democratic, but Clay's vision of federal government had
enthralled Lincoln.

The man responsible for tabulating the votes was Mentor Graham, the local schoolteacher. Legend has it that Graham asked
Lincoln to help him when he discovered Lincoln could read and
write.[79] More likely, Lincoln hung around the table for most of the
day, chatting with anyone who listened. By the time the day was
over, Lincoln's candidate had lost, but Abe had met most of the
townsfolk.[80]

Becoming known in the community quickly produced a problem for Lincoln. Gangly at six four but not fierce, he seemed ripe
pickings for a local gang, led by a bully, Jack Armstrong. Armstrong was shorter than Lincoln but known for his muscle and
toughness. While reports conflict on what exactly happened between the two, they entered into a wrestling match. Much of the
town is said to have come out to watch the two men wrestle to
a draw (though legend has Lincoln defeating him). Up until that
point, Armstrong, as far as anyone knew, had never lost a match.
Lincoln's strength and confidence impressed the gang and particularly his opponent, who afterward became a lifelong friend.

John Todd Stuart, a prominent Whig lawyer from nearby Springfield, said the wrestling match "was a turning point in Lincoln's
life."[81] It is unclear whether Stuart actually witnessed the event (he
met Lincoln later when he was a land surveyor and again when
they served together in the state militia), nor is it clear exactly what
Stuart meant. In light of Lincoln's later political acumen, however,
the match obviously served as an apt metaphor for Lincoln's canni-
ness in waiting for people to undo themselves by overplaying their
hands, as well as his gift for bringing enemies into alliance.

In New Salem, Lincoln boarded first with one of the town elders, then with Mentor Graham for several months. Almost certainly, Graham later exaggerated his importance to Lincoln's education. He had only rudimentary knowledge of math and was barely literate himself, yet he was the best the town had for a schoolmaster. In all likelihood, Lincoln sharpened his math under Graham's roof and studied other books Graham and others gave him. Graham claimed that, besides teaching Lincoln arithmetic, he persuaded him that a thorough knowledge of grammar was indispensable to an aspiring politician.[82] Graham supposedly told Lincoln, "If you ever expect to go before the public in any capacity, I think it is the best thing you can do."[83] Even if this were the counsel he gave Lincoln, it was unnecessary advice, given Lincoln's studies before this point, but probably on his own volition, Lincoln spent time reviewing Samuel Kirkham's *English Grammar,* a leading textbook of the era, as well as any newspapers he could get his hands on. Indeed, Graham is said to have observed that Lincoln's "text book was the Louisville Journal."[84] This has the ring of truth, for the *Louisville Journal* had become, under the leadership of Clay's man George Prentice, the best-selling and most popular newspaper in the west. It deepened and strengthened Lincoln's allegiance to Clay. John Rowland Herndon, a friend from New Salem, recalled Lincoln's idolization of Clay much as Dennis Hanks remembered. Recounting Lincoln's early life, Herndon later wrote, "Henry Clay was his favorite of all the great men of the nation. He all but worshipped his name."[85]

Jack Kelso, a book lover himself, was another man with whom Lincoln briefly boarded in New Salem. Kelso urged Lincoln to read Shakespeare and Robert Burns, both of whom Abe had encountered earlier when his stepmother had brought William Scott's anthology home. Another New Salem resident said Kelso and Abe "were always together—always talking and arguing."[86] The two would sit for hours on the bank of the Sangamon River and "quote Shakespear."[87]

Lincoln and Burns had similar backgrounds. They both grew up in working-class families, and both had lost their mothers in their formative years. Lincoln adored Burns, sometimes claiming him as his favorite poet. The motifs, patterns, and rhyme schemes of Burns's poetry were ingrained in Lincoln's mind, memorized by him as a youth in Indiana, and recited by him as an adult in New Salem and beyond. Much of Burns's poetry deals with themes of poverty, enlightenment, independence, honesty, and the use of reason. At the 1865 annual banquet of the Washington, D.C., Robert Burns club, Lincoln was asked to make a toast to the poet. He replied, "I cannot. . . . I can say nothing worthy of his generous heart and transcending genius. Thinking of what he has said, I cannot say anything which seems worth saying."[88]

David Herbert Donald suggests that "during his New Salem years [Lincoln] probably read more than at any time in his life."[89] Retreating to the woods, walking through the village with a book tucked under his arm, or sitting by the fire, Lincoln "read a great deal, improving every opportunity, by day and by night."[90] Another friend from New Salem remembered that Lincoln "used to sit up late of nights reading & would recommence in the morning when he got up but 'knew nothing of his reading a novel.'" Instead, "History & poetry & the newspapers constituted the most of his reading."[91] A fellow shopkeeper, William Greene, believed "he never saw anyone who could learn as fast as Lincoln."[92] His abundant reading led more than a few people to complain that Lincoln was lazy, particularly because he was often discovered reading a book rather than working.

Another significant influence on Lincoln's development in New Salem was a man named Bowling Green, whom Lincoln had voted for as the town's justice of the peace in 1831. Green, who'd easily won that election, was much older than Lincoln, rotund, jocular, and a fierce Jacksonian Democrat. Later, the two met as members of a local debating society. At its meetings, residents fenced over political topics, not just of local interest but also state and national. Young men of all kinds joined such gatherings, which were common around the country. (When working with George Wythe, Clay had participated in a Richmond debating society.) Like Mentor Graham, Green encouraged Lincoln to read and loaned him books, including some about the law. Green also let Lincoln come to his court to observe him at work. Initially just for fun, he let his visitor argue some make-believe cases, and rather quickly Green saw Lincoln's potential and encouraged him to study law. Later, in 1839, Lincoln did not support Green for a seat in the General Assembly. When Green died three years later, Lincoln returned to New Salem from Springfield for the funeral, one of the few times anyone saw him cry. Those who knew Lincoln and Green remembered their close relationship. One of them recalled, "Mr. L Loved Mr. Green as he did his father"[93] and said "that he owed more to Mr. Green for his advancement than any other Man."[94]

Less than a year after arriving in New Salem, though not yet gainfully employed, Lincoln felt sufficiently comfortable in the community to follow Jackson's example in both declaring his candidacy for public office and heading into battle. Clay had been too young to fight in the Revolutionary War and then too old and well established in civilian life to fight in any other war, but it was common for (white) American men between eighteen and forty-five years of age to volunteer in the state militias. Lincoln followed other townspeople in signing up for the Black Hawk War, a campaign authorized by President Jackson to rebuff the efforts of Sauk Warrior Black Hawk to bar Americans from settling on traditional tribal lands. Serving under Jackson as a colonel was his friend Zachary Taylor, with whom he later fought against the Seminoles in Florida. In his first monthlong tour of duty, Lincoln was elected captain by the popular vote of his troops. He signed on for two additional short tours. In his last one, he served as a private in the Independent Spy Corps that unsuccessfully tried to track down Chief Black Hawk in southern Wisconsin. It had been at the urging of Zachary Taylor that Lincoln reenlisted as a private, so as to have experience being both a leader and a follower in the war, experiences expected to burnish his credentials for office.

Lincoln took pride in his soldiering (though he enjoyed making fun of his tours by saying the only combat he had was with the mosquitoes) and particularly in his selection by his men as their first captain. In 1859, he told supporters, "I was elected a Captain of volunteers—a success which gave me more pleasure than any I have had since."[95] A year later, after he became the Republican Party's candidate for president, he reiterated that "he has not since had any success in life which gave him so much satisfaction."[96] As a soldier, a Washington or Jackson he was not, but he was "elated"[97] to have had the experience.

Lincoln made several lasting friendships during the Black Hawk War, two of which were significant influences on the rest of his life. The first was with John Todd Stuart. Stuart was only fifteen months older than Lincoln and was a lawyer well known throughout the state for his sharp and crafty courtroom tactics. After graduating from Centre College in Kentucky in 1826, Stuart traveled west to look for a place to settle and to practice law. On October 25, 1828, he moved to Springfield, Illinois, then a small, friendly town of around three hundred people. He opened a solo law practice, which continued to thrive as he added and changed partners over the next several decades.

When Lincoln first met him, Stuart already was a prominent Whig. He was tall, thin, "debonair," and "handsome."[98] He was slick, satirical, but charming—qualities that would be useful in greasing the legislative rails but also in leaving an oily stain on his reputation. Though Lincoln never developed a taste for alcohol or carousing (one legend suggests Stuart introduced Lincoln to prostitutes), both Clay and Stuart were renowned for their abilities to drink, swear, and gamble, and for their reputed sexual affairs.[99]

Though Stuart later outranked Lincoln in the Black Hawk War (he became a major), Stuart initially served under him when Lincoln was captain of a company that included Jack Armstrong and the rest of his New Salem gang. (Stuart had then reenlisted as a private, following, like Lincoln, the advice of Zachary Taylor to young soldiers that they broaden their military experience to include time serving both as a leader and as someone led.) Stuart, whose recollections of Lincoln are widely considered to be among the most reliable, recalled that, while Lincoln was the captain of his men, he "had no military qualities whatever except that he was a good clever fellow and kept the esteem and respect of his men."[100]

Stuart laughed, in recollection, that Lincoln and the others (himself included) tried but failed "to find out where the Indians were," even though "the Indians were all about us, constantly watching our movements."[101]

Another man Lincoln befriended during the Black Hawk War was another prominent Whig lawyer in the state, Orville Browning. Nearly three years older than Lincoln, Browning was Stuart's opposite: taller and stouter, more ponderous in his manner than Stuart, who was quick-witted and sharp-tongued. Stuart was charming, while most of Browning's contemporaries regarded Browning as pompous. Stuart was keen on having a good time wherever he went, while Browning was a homebody whose wife quickly befriended Lincoln as well. Though neither Stuart nor Browning lacked self-confidence, neither much enjoyed the thrust and parry of political campaigns. Browning in particular preferred not to dirty his hands if he could help it. The two men differed in other ways: Browning kept a diary, in which he recorded thoughts, conversations, and events throughout his life, and he liked to write letters, often offering advice or thoughts about contemporary issues. Stuart kept no such records, and his letters rarely engaged in extended political discourse. Yet Lincoln looked to both men for honest, unvarnished counsel. They rarely disappointed.

CHAPTER TWO

FINDING THE PATH TO CONGRESS
(1834–1844)

Within seven months of his arrival in New Salem, Abraham Lincoln announced his first campaign for office. Over the next seven years, he would become the most powerful Whig in the Illinois State House of Representatives.

Lincoln and many other young Whigs supported both the Missouri Compromise and the American System, which he backed until the day he died. Perhaps more than anything else, however, Lincoln was driven by another of Clay's ideas. Andrew Jackson championed the "common man," whom he believed he exemplified—the poor, illiterate, disenfranchised, hardworking men, who were born with nothing but worked with their hands and were the backbone of America, men born in poverty but could rise to the nation's highest elected office. In contrast, Henry Clay had coined the concept of "the self-made man," in 1832, as the centerpiece of his economic vision.[1] Clay's idea was that any man in America, no matter how modest his beginnings, could become economically productive, particularly if the government supported the development of business and internal improvements, such as roads, bridges, and tunnels, that linked the disparate parts of America into one land. It was an ideal that inspired young Whigs like Lincoln to seek to improve themselves through hard work, self-discipline, and social respectability.

In the 1840s, Lincoln declared himself a "self-made man," though he had been expressing the same idea in emphasizing self-reliance in campaign speeches and public pronouncements beginning in the 1830s. He had examples of self-made men all around him, men such as George Washington, Benjamin Franklin, Clay, and even Jackson. Although Lincoln did not win a seat in Washington as quickly as Clay or Jackson, he was not yet forty when he established his own law firm, became a leader in the Illinois Whig Party, and mounted a successful campaign for the U.S. House of Representatives. His chance to make his mark loomed closer.

I

In 1832, both Bowling Green and John Todd Stuart encouraged Lincoln to run for an open seat in the Illinois legislature. Following their advice and his own burning ambition, Lincoln declared his candidacy for the Illinois House of Representatives on March 9, 1832.[2] Clay had begun his political career in the Kentucky General Assembly, and Lincoln looked to start his own in a similar way. Lincoln, however, was three years younger than Clay had been when he first ran for office.

Lincoln's announcement of his first political campaign might not surprise anyone looking back at his life, but it likely surprised more than a few of the townsfolk. He had just turned twenty-three, but to the many who engaged with him, he talked about politics incessantly. Orville Browning recalled that "even in his early days [Lincoln] had a strong conviction that he was born for better things than then seemed likely or even possible." Browning added, "Lincoln's ambition was to fit himself properly for what he considered some important predestined labor or work."[34]

Lincoln's speech to announce his candidacy for the Illinois House was not his best, but it showed he was learning from Clay. According to Clay's 1831 campaign biography, his first campaign speech was brief and to the point: "He told his fellow-freemen that he was, indeed, young and inexperienced, and had neither announced himself as a candidate, nor solicited their votes; but that, as his friends had thought proper to bring forward his name, he was anxious not to be defeated."[5] Clay "gave an explanation of his political views, and closed with an ingenuous appeal to the feelings of the people."[6] From reading that speech, as well as Clay's other speeches or reports on them, Lincoln learned their characteristic flow. Usually, Clay began with some kind of self-deprecation, such as reminding his listeners of his "humble" origins or lack of the superior intellect that others had. He often marked the occasion or context of the speech, where it was happening and why, and praised his adversaries before launching into systematic evisceration— often filled with ridicule and satire—of his opponents' arguments. (Clay did not care about what happened to his speeches once he was done with them. He rarely drafted a speech beforehand; instead, he would write down a few ideas on fragments of paper, which he usually tossed away afterward.)

Clay could build a case as well as any lawyer, but it was his keen sense of humor and colorful images and delivery that helped to set his rhetoric apart. His humor was designed to endear himself and his message to his audience, but he often used humor to mock and belittle his opponents (his followers, for example, called Jackson "jackass" and "King Andrew"), even while professing the greatest respect for them. Lincoln's first speech emulated Clay's early no-nonsense approach and his focus on substance, but it was short on humor. In time, Lincoln would learn to meld the two in winning fashion. In this first speech, Lincoln launched quickly into his purpose, just as Clay would have done. In the short opening paragraph, he declared, "It becomes my duty to make known to you— the people whom I propose to represent—my sentiments with regard to local affairs."[7] His efforts to connect with the crowd were weak because they were too formulaic, and Lincoln would further study Clay's almost invariably successful methods for bonding with his audiences. Yet Lincoln's conclusion was pure Clay in its self-deprecation and expression of humility:

> *Every man is said to have his peculiar ambition. Whether it be true*
> *or not, I can say for one I have no other so great as that of being*

truly esteemed of my fellow men, by rendering myself worthy of their esteem. How far I shall succeed in gratifying this ambition, is yet to be developed. I am young and unknown to many of you. I was born and have ever remained in the most humble walks of life. I have no wealthy or popular relations to recommend me. My case is thrown exclusively upon the independent voters of this county, and if elected they will have conferred a favor on me, for which I shall be unremitting in my labors to compensate. But if the good people in their wisdom shall see fit to keep me in the back ground, I have been too familiar with disappointments to be very much chagrined. [8]

In time, he would learn to begin, as Clay (and classical orators) nearly always did, with what became his trademark expression of humility.

Lincoln voiced support for "the public utility of internal improvements," the core of Henry Clay's American System.[9] Elaborating, he spoke of the need for "roads and canals," a need for "more easy means of communication than we now possess" in Sangamon County, the need to investigate "the expediency of constructing a railroad from some eligible point on the Illinois river," meant to improve the means for navigating the Sangamon River, and a need to outlaw "exorbitant rates of interests" on loans.[10] All of these proposals came from Clay.

So, too, did Lincoln's statement that education is "the most important subject which we as a people can be engaged in."[11] Funding education was to Clay a crucial element of the American System. In declaring that he could "see the time when education, and by its means, morality, sobriety, enterprise, and industry, shall become much more general than at present," Lincoln was delivering a sharp rebuke to his father.[12] Indeed, he was not only demonstrating his support for a program a still-loyal Democrat like Thomas opposed but, in seeking public office, he was publicly seeking a life his father never had, a life like Clay's.

Lincoln enjoyed the rough-and-tumble of the political campaign. At a stop at a sale in the tiny town of Pappsville, Lincoln was about to take the stage when he noticed a friend of his was being heckled. As Lincoln spoke, a fight broke out. Lincoln quickly stepped off the stage, stepped into the middle of the fray, grabbed the main culprit by the neck and trousers, and threw him to the ground. The fighting suddenly stopped. Lincoln calmly walked back up to the stage and recommenced his speech—"Fellow citizens, I am humble Abraham Lincoln."[13]

Whether Lincoln's volunteering for the state militia in the midst of his campaign was simply a means of relatively stable employment after a stretch of professional insecurity or a tactical move to burnish his credentials as a candidate, not long after announcing he headed off to battle. When he returned from the Black Hawk War, the election was only a couple of weeks away. On August 2, 1832, he and the other candidates for the New Salem seat in the Illinois House assembled to give their final speeches before the election on August 6. Drawing on a *Sangamo Journal* story about President Jackson's veto of the national bank's rechartering, along with advice from John Todd Stuart, Lincoln spoke for thirty minutes in defense of the national bank (and how it fit into Clay's broader vision), denouncing Jackson's veto of its rechartering.

It was for naught. Though Lincoln had promoted his candidacy throughout the county, he lost the election, finishing eighth out of thirteen candidates. He took solace in the fact that, although he lost the county, he had won 277 votes out of the 300 cast in New Salem, which was predominately Democratic. Stuart won his election for the Illinois House. Shortly thereafter, Stuart was elected as the floor leader for the Whigs in the House, so while Lincoln had failed in his first campaign for office, he now had a close friend and political compatriot in a position to help him in future campaigns.

Besides doing well as a Whig in a sea of Jackson men, Lincoln had, without realizing it, impressed some important Whigs. Stephen Logan, already one of the state's best trial lawyers, had been in the audience more than once. Logan recalled his first sighting of the candidate, at a political rally at the courthouse in Springfield:

I saw Lincoln before he went up into the stand to make his speech. He was a very tall and gawky and rough looking fellow then . . . But after he began speaking I became very much interested in him. He made a very sensible speech. [Up] to that time I think he had been doing odd jobs of surveying, and one thing and another. But one thing we very soon learned was that he was immensely popular.[14]

The year was far from over. Lincoln returned to the hustings, an activity he had loved ever since he was a little boy delivering funny speeches and stories to his friends. This time, he was on a bigger stage: with the presidential election only a few months away, he visited nearby counties to campaign for Henry Clay, but here too the outcome he had hoped for did not come to pass: Illinois went for Jackson, as did the nation. Calhoun left the vice presidency for the Senate. To replace him, Jackson brought Martin Van Buren back from Great Britain to serve as his new vice president and political heir.

Jackson's triumph over Clay was not the victory for which states' rights enthusiasts had hoped. After the election, the South Carolina legislature passed a law that declared unconstitutional the 1828 and 1832 tariffs that Clay had helped pass to protect American manufacturers from their European competitors. South Carolina declared its entitlement, by virtue of being one of the states that had founded the Union, to disregard, or nullify, any federal enactment it deemed illegitimate. Jackson disagreed. On December 8, 1832, he issued a proclamation declaring that South Carolina did not have the power to nullify a federal law and that such power was "incompatible with the existence of the Union, contradicted expressly by the letter of the Constitution, unauthorized by its spirit, inconsistent with every principle on which It was founded, and destructive of the great object for which it was formed."[15] Jackson had taken a page from Clay (and Clay's rival Daniel Webster) in acknowledging that the Union took precedence over the states and that therefore the states could not undermine it. In agreement, the Illinois governor, a Democrat, issued a proclamation declaring nullification "treasonable."[16]

While Jackson and much of the nation were focused on his rebuttal to South Carolina's "Ordinance of Nullification," Lincoln and Stuart were discussing ways for Lincoln to follow Stuart into the state legislature. Looking back at Lincoln's growing reputation at that time, Stuart said, "Everyone who became acquainted with him in the campaign of 1832 learned to rely on him with the most implicit confidence."[17] In his earnest efforts to help his neighbors by doing all sorts of odd jobs and favors for them and to entertain locals with his stories, Lincoln endeared himself to the voters in his district. He had not abandoned his political aspirations after his defeat, and in this he looked again to Clay for inspiration. Clay, after all, had lost the presidential election in 1824, sat out the 1828 election because he was secretary of state, returned to the Senate in late 1831 to raise his stature and create a perch from which he could try to block Jackson's initiatives, and became the first sitting senator to secure a major party's nomination for the presidency, although Jackson won the 1832 presidential election by a large margin, winning 218 of the 286 electoral votes cast. Those losses had been hard on Clay—how could they not be? After all, elections are measured in a precise and quantifiable manner, and when he'd craved the broadest support, Clay had consistently been liked less than his opponents. Even when he had been in high office, his policy dreams had been muffled, if not sometimes suffocated. And yet such rejection did not deter him. Such resilience was another reason Lincoln revered him.

Inspiration was also more immediately at hand. Stuart believed Lincoln's political career, much like his own, was just beginning, and he encouraged Lincoln to try again.[18] Lincoln had learned from the loss and realized that he had to start earlier and campaign harder.

Lincoln's awed recognition of Clay's fortitude would help him again and again and again. Looking back at the path that he had taken to Congress and later the presidency, he recalled that the 1832 election was the only time "he had ever been beaten by the people."[19] In truth, he would lose eight different elections, but to be fair, six were lost before the general election, and his election to the presidency was not, strictly speaking, a winning popular election but one where the key votes came from electors, not directly from the public. Had he at any time surrendered to the trend, we would likely not know his name today.

II

In 1833, Lincoln had no job and no source of income. John Todd Stuart, Bowling Green, and Orville Browning each stepped up their encouragement for him to study law. Stuart was impressed that Lincoln, then twenty-four, had already acquired a reputation for "candor and honesty," as well as for his ability "in speech-making."[20] Lincoln might not yet be comfortable onstage speaking to large audiences as a candidate, but in smaller settings, where he was speaking to friends or townspeople, he had an ease about him that made people like and trust him. Stuart, as well as Lincoln, thought this boded well not just for a legal career, but also a future in politics. Lawyers needed to write well, study and learn the language of law, and just as important, be able to avoid or settle litigation, protect clients' assets, get along with everyone as much as possible, and be persuasive and compelling in making arguments before judges or juries. The more he refined these skills, the better Lincoln would become as both a lawyer and a politician.

Stuart's law partner in those days, Henry Drummer, recalled that

> Lincoln used to come to our office—Stuart's and mine—in Springfield from New Salem and borrow law-books. Sometimes he walked but generally rode. He was the most uncouth looking man I ever saw. He seemed to have little to say; seemed to feel timid, with a tinge of sadness visible in the countenance, but when he did talk all this disappeared for the time and he demonstrated that he was both strong and acute. He surprised us more and more at every visit.[21]

Even without the encouragement, Lincoln must have been considering it as an option, since so many successful politicians had begun as lawyers. Of the ten men who had been elected to the presidency as of 1836, seven had studied law—Thomas Jefferson, James Madison, James Monroe, John and John Quincy Adams, Andrew Jackson, and Martin Van Buren. Clay was not a president but he, too, was a lawyer. For all these men, the law itself was not the end. It was a stepping-stone to public office. It was a source of income and well-placed contacts who were instrumental for political advancement. Besides his military service and the controversies that he sparked wherever he went, Jackson had also been a legislator and a state judge before becoming president. Clay's national prominence had begun with his law practice, but more important, that work led to his election to Congress, informed and sharpened his arguments and oratory, and facilitated his leadership in the House and Senate. Even Clay's stint as John Quincy Adams's secretary of state was made possible because of the notoriety he had attained through his oratory and other endeavors. As a "self-made" man eager to make his mark on the world, Lincoln knew his path had to be his own, and with each career advancement, he was pushing the negative example of his father further behind him and was coming closer to becoming what his father had never been nor could tolerate—a man like Henry Clay, an accomplished professional and public figure.

Moreover, the law would be meaningful work, likely the best he could expect to find, given the constraints of community and his own education, and it was not the manual labor he detested. Such a station would situate him nicely within the community, and he could make enough money to support a family and his ambition of succeeding in politics. As Stuart well knew, such income could also help Abe pay off the debts he had been trying to settle for years.

The problem was that studying law required both time and money. Lincoln doubted he had enough of either. The time it would likely require to become qualified to practice was at least a couple of years, if not more, especially because, as the junior lawyer, he would have to do all the scut work Stuart didn't want to do himself. Though Lincoln yearned to better himself, he worried that he still did not have the money needed to secure a legal education.

Aware that the son of another villager had earned a law degree from a college in Louisville, Lincoln lamented that he did not have "a better education" that might have allowed him to avoid such tuition.[22] Later, he wrote, seemingly with regret, that he "was never in a college or Academy as a student; and never inside of a college or academic building till since he had a law license."[23]

It being clear to him that full-time pursuit of a law degree was impossible, besides already planning another run for office in 1834, Lincoln needed to find a paying job. From Stuart and Green, he learned that the position of postmaster might be open. The current occupant, Samuel Hill—a friend of Lincoln's—was widely suspected of having committed fraud. Initially, Lincoln demurred when his companions suggested he take the position. He didn't want to become a candidate unless he could be sure he wouldn't be pushing a friend out of the office. Once it was clear that Hill would be ousted because he had neglected his duties, Lincoln allowed his name to be put forward.

Ironically, the person making the appointment was Andrew Jackson. Lincoln did not worry that his vote for Clay would cost him the job. His Democratic friends had vouched for him with the administration, knowing the appointment was going to be made based on their recommendations. It didn't hurt that there was no competition for the position. Over the next three years, Lincoln handled his responsibilities meticulously, as his friends expected of a man they regarded as trustworthy, diligent, and friendly.

III

Less than a year after his loss in his first race for the state legislature and only a month after becoming the local postmaster on May 7, 1833, Lincoln announced his second run for the Illinois House. Sessions were short, usually three to four months long, and paid less than $200 per session. He had turned twenty-four just two months before, but two paying jobs, as postmaster and land surveyor, supported his studying law in his spare time. If he won, he would be beginning his political career and have a third paying job, but more important, he would be on track to make a difference in the world.

This time, Stuart did not leave matters to chance. He took an even greater strategic role in helping Lincoln's candidacy. Both men understood that it had not been effective for Lincoln to just go around the county giving speeches. Instead, he set out on what a friend described as "his hand-shaking campaign, traveling all around the county to talk face-to-face with the voters."[24] Another friend said Lincoln was determined to curry favor with "all persons, with the rich or poor, in the stately mansion or log cabin."[25] Yet another contemporary recalled Lincoln had "great faith in the strong sense of Country People and he gave them credit for greater intelligence than most men do."[26] Lincoln figured, as he had seen in Stuart's campaigns, that personal connections were more important than party. He and Stuart shared Clay's vision of resilient, hardworking people who made their way through the world under their own steam. While he cozied up to the Whigs who had power and money, Lincoln did not forget where the actual votes came from. Bowling Green, a staunch Democrat, encouraged Lincoln to make the second run even though Lincoln was a Whig. At the same time, Browning decided to make a second run for office.

Lincoln's 1834 campaign, however, quickly ran into an unexpected problem. He learned that the Democrats were plotting to defeat Stuart by splitting the Whig vote. Lincoln told Stuart that Bowling Green and other Democrats had told him that they "would drop two of their men and take [Lincoln] up and vote for him for the purpose of beating [Stuart]."[27] Stuart devised a plan almost immediately. He thanked Lincoln for disclosing the plot to him and advised Lincoln that he "had [such] great confidence in [his own] strength" that "Lincoln [should] go and tell [the Democrats who approached him that] he would take their votes."[28] "I and my friends," Stuart recalled, "knowing their tactics, then concentrated our fight against one of their other men . . . and in this

[way] elected Lincoln and myself."[29] Stuart suggested Lincoln's part was to keep his mouth closed on what he and Stuart were planning to do, and Lincoln did. Stephen Logan, later a law partner of Lincoln's, said Lincoln never pretended to be anything but the Whig he was. He believed that "he made no concession of principle—whatever. He was as stiff as a man could be in his Whig doctrine."[30] Yet Lincoln gave no speeches for this election, allowing himself to ride the current of support from his friends on both sides of the aisle. This time, he won—his first victory in elected politics. He learned the lesson that sometimes silence works better than saying too much.

IV

Years later, after Lincoln's death, William Herndon wrote, "His ambition was a little engine that knew no rest."[31] In the next few years, following his first election to the Illinois House, as Lincoln began to rise in Whig leadership in the state legislature, his ambition became more apparent to all around him, as it would simultaneously power his pursuit of a law license and successful completion of his term as postmaster.

As Lincoln's star kept rising and eventually reached the presidency, Stuart was fond of saying, to anyone who would listen, that he (Stuart) would be remembered "as the man who advised Mr. Lincoln to study law and lent him his law books."[32] But while Stuart took credit for Lincoln's formal licensing as a lawyer, there were others, such as Bowling Green, who had helped by allowing Lincoln to observe his work as justice of the peace. Just how much truth there was in Stuart's later claims to have helped Lincoln's education was eventually almost beside the point. Stuart may not have been the only Lincoln friend who crafted his story in a manner most advantageous to his own reputation, just as Lincoln did. John Scripps, who wrote the first published biography of Lincoln, in 1860, said that Lincoln had studied law with "nobody."[33] Lincoln often said so himself to emphasize that he had taught himself law by reading classic legal texts, closely observing lawyers argue their cases in various local courts, and discussing the law with Stuart, Green, and other local attorneys and judges. In 1855, Lincoln responded to a young man asking him about apprenticeship by saying that "I did not read with anyone." He told his correspondent, "Get the books, and read and study them till, you understand them in their principal features, and that is the main thing." Lincoln emphasized "your own resolution to succeed, is more important than any other one thing."[34]

That said, Stuart had indisputably been instrumental in guiding Lincoln in taking several important early steps in law and politics. Stuart found in Lincoln someone whose ambition, intellectual curiosity, and natural intelligence fit well with his need for a partner to both oversee his legal affairs and take up the mantle of his leadership in the Illinois House when he left to make a run for the U.S. House of Representatives. In turn, Lincoln demonstrated his own "resolution to succeed," which drove him to learn not only the law but also the business of practicing law, which he was finally able to do on September 9, 1836, when the justices of the Illinois Supreme Court agreed to admit him to the bar. Lincoln moved to Springfield to begin his practice with Stuart. He was twenty-seven.

In Springfield, the two men spent nearly all their time together. They roomed together, even slept in the same bed for a while, and Stuart introduced Lincoln to the other Whig leaders who lived in Springfield. Several had also served in the Black Hawk War, and one even described Lincoln as "a very decent looking fellow," appropriately dressed in loose trousers, which was then the Whig uniform.[35]

Stuart was grooming Lincoln to take over his responsibilities as the leader of the Whig minority in the Illinois house, so he could devote all of his attention to his own run for Congress. Where Stuart went, Lincoln followed. As Stuart's political partner and protégé, Lincoln became quickly known around Illinois "as one of the most Devoted Clay whigs in all the State."[36]

Stuart did much more than introduce Lincoln to politicians—he introduced him to politics as it was actually practiced. He schooled Lincoln in the art of logrolling—trading favors for votes—so men of differing views or with different agendas could both get what they wanted. Thomas Ford, a Democrat who was governor of Illinois when Lincoln first entered the statehouse, confirmed that the Sangamon delegation was unusually large and included "some dexterous jugglers and managers in politics" and had a "decided preponderance in the log-rolling system in those days."[37] Lincoln once described the plight of the legislator in having to find solutions to a variety of disputes:

> *One man is offended because a road passes over his land, and another is offended because it does not pass over his; one is dissatisfied because the bridge for which he is taxed crosses the river on a different road from that which leads from his house to town; another cannot bear that the county should go in debt for the same roads and bridges; while not a few struggle hard to have roads located over their lands, and then stoutly refuse to let them be opened until they are first paid the damages. Even between the different wards and streets of towns and cities we find this same wrangling and difficulty.*[38]

Yet here Lincoln stood out, as Stuart recalled, for "refus[ing] to be sold. *He never had a price.*"[39]

When Lincoln made proposals of his own or on Stuart's behalf, they almost always followed standard Whig Party policies and therefore aligned with those that Clay championed on the national stage. Indeed, the first bill Lincoln introduced proposed public financing of the Illinois and Michigan Canal. Initially, Lincoln had wanted the canal to be built from the proceeds of sales of government lands (a popular Whig strategy), but he switched strategies when it became clear that his fellow Whigs actually favored having the state pay for the canal. He then worked with his fellow Whigs, as well as Gurdon Hubbard, a former legislator who had pushed hard for the canal in 1832 and failed but who helped Lincoln behind the scenes. After passing the bill, Lincoln dedicated its passage "to the untiring zeal of Mr. Stuart," whose "high minded and honorable way" had secured "the accomplishment of this great task."[40] Hubbard was not happy Lincoln failed to thank him, but Lincoln needed Stuart's help more.

For all the talk of his devotion to Clay, Lincoln did not always follow his lead. Sometimes he followed Jackson instead. In 1834, Andrew Jackson's threat to veto the rechartering of the Second Bank of the United States reopened a debate over establishing state banks in Illinois. Though Democrats believed that Whigs would oppose state banks, as Clay had, Lincoln saw the virtue of a state bank that "could allow the surplus capital of the rich to be invested and available to the industrious poor person so he might get ahead."[41] Lincoln joined a coalition of Whigs and Democrats to send instructions to their two senators back in Washington to remove states' funds from the national bank and place them in state-chartered banks.

Two years later, Lincoln again followed Jackson's lead. This time, he was running for his second term in the Illinois house. Because of reapportionment, the state legislature had increased the number of Sangamon County's representatives to seven. Unsure of how many people were running for the state legislature in 1836, the *Sangamo Journal* invited all the candidates running to "show their hands." Lincoln quickly wrote back, "Agreed. Here's mine!"[42] He then outlined the principles he was running on. Among the first, he said, "I go for all sharing the privileges of government, who assist in bearing its burthens. Consequently I go for admitting all whites to the right of suffrage, who pay taxes or bear arms [serving in the state militia], (by no means excluding females)." In the prior session of the legislature, 1834–1835, Lincoln had supported a successful move to ensure that the right to vote be extended to all white males of the age of twenty-one years and not just to those who owned real estate.[43] Such proposals echoed Jacksonian principles for empowering ordinary Americans with access to voting (even though the state constitution already had extended the vote as Lincoln and others were now lobbying for).

In another important early legislative success, Lincoln joined with a group of eight other legislators known as the Long Nine, a name given to them because they were all at least six feet tall and were Whigs who shared similar political principles. The Long Nine were instrumental in supporting various internal improvements throughout the state in exchange for moving the capital from Vandalia to Springfield, a growing center of business in the state. Such investments in infrastructure could be complex because they involved benefits like roads and canals that were specific to particular areas. Lincoln was disposed to strongly favor them, as such improvements were a central tenet of the Whig philosophy espoused by Henry Clay. Because Lincoln's delegation from Sangamon County was the largest in the state assembly, it had significant leverage when its members voted as a bloc. On January 24, Browning, with both Stuart's and Lincoln's input, took the lead on Springfield's behalf by introducing the bill in the Senate for the legislature to move the capital to a new permanent location. After a few weeks of debate and delay, the Senate approved the bill 24–13.

In February 1837, Lincoln introduced the proposal in the House. The leader of the opposition was a newly elected Democratic member, Stephen Douglas, an ardent supporter of Andrew Jackson. Douglas preferred that the capital stay where it was or move to Jacksonville. With Stuart's help behind the scenes to leverage the sizable Sangamon County coalition, Lincoln and his fellow members of the Long Nine traded votes to ensure that, after four rounds of voting, the legislature formally approved relocating the state capital just before the end of the legislative session. The Long Nine, Douglas said, "used every exertion and made every sacrifice to secure the passage of the bill."[44] As one of the Long Nine, Robert L. Wilson, later recalled,

> In these dark hours, when our Bill to all appearances was beyond recussitation [sic], and all our opponents were jubilant over our defeat, and when friends could see no hope, Mr. Lincoln never for one moment despaired; but, collecting his Colleagues to his room for

consultation, his practical common Sense, his thorough knowledge
of human nature, then made him an overmatch for his compeers and
for any man that I have ever known.[45]

If Wilson's recollections lapsed too much into romanticizing Lincoln's role, Orville Browning, never one quickly to give praise to others, credited the Long Nine, including Lincoln, in less mellifluous prose for "their judicious management, their ability, their gentlemanly deportment, their unassuming manners, their constant and uniting labor."[46]

Throughout, Stuart closely watched as Lincoln observed floor leaders wheeling and dealing. The record indicates further that there was no occasion on which Stuart and Lincoln were both absent from the legislature. He voted independently of Stuart on twenty-six out of one hundred and twenty-six votes, but overall, Lincoln hewed closely to the Whig party line.

Under Illinois law, the new capital would not become official until two years later, when the building projects were to be completed. Originally called Calhoun to honor vice president John Calhoun, the town of roughly 1,300 changed its name to Springfield in 1832 when its namesake fell out of favor because of his increasingly fiery defense of states' rights and slavery. By 1836, the town became a Whig stronghold within a state that leaned Democratic. Unsurprisingly, after the state capital opened there officially in 1839, Springfield secured its place as the center of law and politics in Illinois.

Just as important for Lincoln, Springfield was Stuart's home and was where, in the same year as the vote to relocate the capital from Vandalia, the two friends began their law partnership. Besides the bond that Lincoln and Stuart had formed during the Black Hawk War, they were both from Kentucky. Stuart was a graduate of Centre College and already a fixture in Springfield as its best-known lawyer. He was popular with local judges and juries and instrumental in introducing Lincoln to a wider circle of people who became lifelong friends, supporters, and political allies. The firm—Stuart and Lincoln—had a modest but steady practice involving many trivial legal contests, such as neighborhood quarrels, livestock disputes, crop damage, replevin of large animals, and some divorces.[47] Because Stuart's focus was increasingly on his congressional contest against Stephen Douglas for a seat in the U.S. House of Representatives, Lincoln learned on his own how to interview clients, identify and apply the relevant law, draft legal documents, and collect fees. Lincoln grew comfortable with being his own boss.

With the contest between Stuart and Douglas looming, Lincoln pushed the practice of law aside to help. This provided him with a front-row seat to assess the matchup. Douglas was known as the Little Giant, because he was a man of small stature but gigantic, ruthless ambitions. Stuart often asked Lincoln to substitute for him in debating Douglas throughout the district and to write letters on his behalf to the local newspaper, the *Sangamo Journal,* and to Whig leaders in the district who were critical of Stuart's foe. His deputation was so entrenched that at one point Lincoln joked, "We have adopted it as part of our policy here, never to speak of Douglas at all. Isn't that the best way to deal with such a small matter?"[48]

In the middle of the campaign, Stuart and Lincoln found themselves on opposite sides of a murder case prosecuted by Douglas. The trial and the campaign confirmed their polar opposites in personality. Stuart liked to ridicule his opponents through deftly worded taunts (as well as through anonymous letters he authorized Lincoln and other supporters to publish that attacked Douglas's political views and ethics—or lack thereof). Douglas used words the way other people used fists, to bluntly humiliate and pound his opponents into dust. Sometimes it went beyond words: the debates between Stuart and Douglas occasionally ended in physical confrontations, the last of which included Stuart's grabbing Douglas in a headlock that Douglas broke by savagely biting Stuart's thumb. Stuart proudly displayed the scar for the rest of his life. Lincoln, unsurprisingly, was determined to avoid such confrontations should he ever stand against Douglas.

Douglas had his nickname, and Stuart did, too. He had become so well known for his unctuous politicking, indolence, and under-whelming campaigning (thus the need for him to rely so much on his law partner) that his fellow legislators took to calling him Jerry Sly, a moniker that followed him for the rest of his life. Democrats, unimpressed by the energy of his campaigning, gave Stuart a dif-ferent name, Sleepy Johnny, and enjoyed comparing him to Rip Van Winkle awakening from his long slumber. "The last we saw of him, he was rubbing his eyes open at the corner of the street, with his arms raised above his head, giving a most portentous yawn," the Democratic paper said of him during his campaign against Douglas. "After all of his boasting that he was sure of six thousand majority," it said, "without stirring from home, we marvel much, that he should have had energy to arouse himself from his leth-argy, and sufficient condescension to visit the people at all."[49]

Everyone understood that the immediate subject of their con-test was the economy (though slavery was intertwined with that as it was with virtually everything else). Just a year before, the nation had entered into its first great depression. A likely cause could be traced to one of Andrew Jackson's last acts as president, the Spe-cie Circular, which required that all payments for public land be made in the form of specie, or hard currency (coins, in this case, of gold and silver). The problem was that specie was hard to get, and on May 10, 1837, New York banks, unable to meet continuing demands for it, refused to convert paper money into hard currency in the form of gold or silver. Soon thereafter, the convergence of many factors (including restrictive lending policies in Great Britain and a sharp decline in cotton prices and mortgage payments), pro-duced panic nationwide. More than a third of the nation's banks failed, credit became practically impossible to obtain to start new businesses, cotton prices fell dramatically, and the trade balance with England deteriorated. At the same time, a drought hit Illinois and caused many crops to fail.

Naturally, Democrats blamed Whigs for the economic collapse, and Whigs blamed Democrats. Van Buren, Jackson's self-selected successor, believed that overreach by the federal government was the principal cause of the depression, but another was the Whigs' contempt for republican values, particularly a lack of commitment to civic virtue and to the self-discipline required for saving money and avoiding debt. Arguing that the American people were too self-indulgent, Van Buren proposed to replace the national bank with a system of independent treasuries that would create an institutional choke point between the federal treasury on one side and the states and the private sector on the other.

In the Senate, Clay denounced Van Buren as out of touch with most American workers and his financial plan as ineffective, since it failed to invest in programs and projects that could help the people economically succeed to the point where they would be able to contribute to the solvency of the system as viable economic actors. Following Clay's lead, Stuart and Lincoln themselves argued that the solution to the nation's economic problems was the national bank, which they believed was instrumental to stabilizing the nation's credit and improving the handling of the federal government's financial affairs. Clay and his fellow Whigs in Congress, as well as Stuart and Lincoln on the campaign trail, also derided Jackson's—and now Van Buren's—consolidation of presidential power as usurping the legislative authority vested in Congress by the Constitution.

As is often the case in politics, crisis became an opportunity for finger pointing. Just as Van Buren had blamed Whig ideology, the Whigs capitalized on the economic collapse and Van Buren's inability to sustain Jackson's appeal as the champion of the common man. Lincoln published a series of anti-Douglas letters in Springfield's *Sangamo Journal* as Douglas and Stuart traveled around the district debating each other.

Lincoln later recalled the give and take of the debates, describing from the vantage point of 1854 the thrust and the parry as "a neatly varnished sophism . . . readily penetrated" by Stuart,[50] but recognizing in Douglas's response that "a great, rough non-sequitur was sometimes twice as dangerous as a well-polished fallacy."[51] When the congressional election ended in August 1838, almost everyone expected a Douglas victory, but it did not materialize. Instead, the final tally gave Stuart a narrow victory by thirty-six votes. Douglas complained that Stuart had won because of vote fraud, but he did not press the claim, because the fraud was not likely confined to just one side of the ledger. Stuart and Lincoln also won their murder trial. It was not a good summer for Douglas.

In the first two of his four successive terms in the state legislature, Lincoln voted consistently in line with Clay's positions on infrastructure expansion. Many of the improvements were to be state funded, while Lincoln, as a state legislator, was in the position of voting to instruct the state's senators on the issues that came before them. The votes, particularly those mandating state funding, came back to haunt Lincoln when the 1837 depression hit. With the tightening of credit and extensive foreclosures, the state faced insolvency, and Lincoln had to choose between finding a way to keep the state budget from hemorrhaging and sticking with Clay. He stuck with Clay.

V

Two of Lincoln's speeches from this period show the significant influence of Clay as his mentor. The first was "The Perpetuation of Our Political Institutions," given in 1837 to the Young Men's Lyceum of Springfield, an organization Stuart had been instrumental in bringing to the town. The timing of the speech coincided with several significant developments—the economic fallout; Stuart's upcoming 1838 campaign for the House; Lincoln's repeated attempts in the state legislature to curb slavery, including filing an official protest declaring "that the institution of slavery is founded on both injustice and bad policy" and a failed attempt to amend a pro-Southern resolution cautioning Congress against abolishing slavery in the nation's capital (his amendment would have affirmed the voters' right to abolish slavery);[52] Lincoln's concurrent campaign for reelection to the state legislature; the lynch-mob murder of Elijah Lovejoy, an abolitionist minister and newspaper publisher in Alton, Illinois; and the horrific burning of an African American in St. Louis. While it is customary to consider the speech as a verbose attack on Stephen Douglas, it responded to a theme that was common to all these developments: threats to the rule of law from unruly mobs stoked by populists or, as Lincoln suggested, a tyrant like Stephen Douglas or especially Andrew Jackson.[53] At the same time, the speech was an attempt at something grander than the kinds of newspaper letters and political attacks Lincoln had unleashed against his political opponents.

Early in the speech, Lincoln referred to an "ill-omen" developing within the nation by which, he said, "I mean the increasing disregard for law which pervades the country; the growing disposition to substitute the wild and furious passions, in lieu of the sober judgment of Courts; and the worse than savage mobs, for the executive ministers of justice."[54] (In his Lyceum Address, Lincoln used the terms *mob* or *mobs* eight times.)[55] "This disposition," he argued, "is awfully fearful in any community; and that it now exists in ours, though grating to our feelings to admit, it would be a violation of truth, and an insult to our intelligence, to deny. Accounts of outrages committed by mobs, form the every-day news of the times. They have pervaded the country, from New England to Louisiana."[56] Though "tedious" to recount the "horrors" of what these mobs did, he did recount that in Mississippi "white men, supposed to be leagued with the negroes" and with "strangers" "were seen literally dangling from the boughs of trees upon every road side."[57] Lincoln did not expressly mention Lovejoy's murder; he said without saying. Jackson's base and those who attended his rallies were poor and rowdy, and to his detractors Jackson was King Mob because of the undisciplined and unruly mobs he controlled, yet here too his nickname went unsaid, the allusions clear. No one, at the time or later, mistook that Lincoln was saying Jackson's supporters were responsible for the violence against Lovejoy and other abolitionists.

Lincoln mentioned the rise of tyrants nearly as often as the mobs. The "new reapers" who fomented this violence were "men of ambition and talents" who would "spring up amongst us. And, when they do, they will as naturally seek the gratification of their ruling passion, as others have so before them."[58] Overly ambitious men would not be satisfied with merely "a seat in Congress" or "a gubernatorial or a presidential chair."[59] "What! Think you these places would satisfy an Alexander, a Caesar, or a Napoleon? Never! Towering genius disdains a beaten path. It seeks regions hitherto unexplored. –It sees *no distinction* in adding story to story, upon the monuments of fame, erected to the memory of others."[60] In all likelihood, Lincoln's reference to "towering genius" was a swipe at Stephen Douglas, who was often ridiculed for his short stature but lofty aspirations. Lincoln went further to suggest that the tyrannical disposition, which he obviously thought both Jackson and Douglas had, "*denies* that it is glory enough to serve under any chief. It *scorns* to tread in the footsteps of *any* predecessor, however illustrious. It thirsts and burns for distinction; and, if possible, it will have it, whether at the expense of emancipating slaves, or enslaving freemen."[61]

If "some man possessed of the loftiest genius, coupled with ambition sufficient to push it to its utmost stretch, will at some time, spring up among us," Lincoln warned, "it will require the people to be united with each other, attached to the government and laws, and generally intelligent, to successfully frustrate his designs."[62]

Of course, Lincoln himself was intensely ambitious and well understood the lure of power. The difference was that he understood it through Clay's prism, that its exercise was valid only if used in line with the republican principles of the Founding Fathers. He was also expressing the hope that the people who were inclined to support aspiring despots had the intelligence and the courage to bring them down. They should prefer someone who came from nothing but made his own way by his own labor, someone like himself, a self-made man, just like Clay.

The nation's salvation depended on the public's appreciating that "passion has helped us," for it brought about the American Revolution, but it "can do so no more."[63] Instead, he said "Reason, cold, calculating, unimpassioned reason, must furnish all the materials for our future support and defence.[64] Let those materials be moulded into *general intelligence, sound morality,* and in particular, *a reverence for the constitution and laws,*" which could lead the American people to a point at which they could look back and know that "we improved to the last; that we remained free to the last; that we revered his name to the last; that, during his long sleep, we permitted no hostile foot to pass over or desecrate his resting place; shall be that which to learn that the last trump shall awaken our WASHINGTON."[65] This distinction between passion and reason was important not just to Lincoln but to Madison and the Founders—and likely Lincoln, too—who took it from classical authors Cicero and Seneca. Aristotle was a major influence on the latter two, but while he counseled plainness and directness in writing Lincoln was, at that time, seemingly in the thrall of the ornamentation common to the classical orators Aristotle criticized. Perhaps Lincoln read no Aristotle. More likely, he had not yet settled on the realization that the more plainly he spoke the more the public understood, or took to heart, his message.

Lincoln's Lyceum speech was one of hope for a better future. He was denouncing overly ambitious men but expecting the nation's salvation to depend on finding a new Washington, fearing tyrants but remaining faithful to a single leader who could lead the nation out of its current mess. Lincoln, as Clay had done, was characterizing the project of overcoming slavery, demagoguery, and lawlessness as a return to the values that were the foundation of America and its Constitution. It was a distinctly idealistic objective, which Whigs clearly shared. (The *Sangamo Journal* reprinted the speech so it could be read more widely.) Jackson and his acolytes, Van Buren and Douglas, were promising to decentralize power, give more of it back to the states, and expect less from the nation's capital, but the Whig solution for maintaining the Union was respect for the rule of law and the values enshrined in the grand language of the Constitution.

In retrospect, it is clear that Lincoln was struggling in his Lyceum Address, as he had struggled in his maiden campaign speech, to find his voice. Occasionally he repeated a short phrase and a word—a popular rhetorical device at the time, as reflected in the speeches of Clay and Webster. (It is a rhetorical technique that also appears throughout the Shakespeare corpus, which Lincoln had studied and enjoyed reciting to himself and others.) But that technique was overwhelmed by a greater ambition, his urgent need to make a mark on the world. His remarks were cluttered with the kind of ornamentation common to classical orations and references to Napoléon (twice), the Bible, and the Founders as "a fortress of strength" and "a forest of giant oaks" swept away by "the all-restless hurricane," which "left only, here and there, a lonely trunk, despoiled of its verdure, shorn of its foliage; unshading and unshaded, to murmur in a few gentle breezes, and to combat with its mutilated limbs, a few more ruder storms, then to sink, and be no more."[66] This was the insecurity of a twenty-nine-year-old trying to embellish his message (in this specific case, before a crowd assembled under "academic" pretenses), and the ornaments dangled poorly. He was not unaware that the forced grandiosity and formality poorly suited him. He was searching for language that could straightforwardly, memorably, and movingly capture the Whig project and his own role in advancing it.

Prentice's biography of Clay mentioned his eloquence on nearly every page, and Clay's friends and foes alike often remarked upon that quality. Clay was not stirring, fluent, and memorable in the same ways as his contemporary and rival, Daniel Webster of New England, was in the turning of a phrase or striking declaration. Instead, Clay's reputation was rooted in his humor and skill as a performer—the way he held his body, the way he used his voice and hands, the pauses in his speech, and the timing of his insertion of a jab here or a cutting remark there. It is likely, given the way in which Lincoln viewed Clay, that if the young man had been able to witness his "mentor" (again, Lincoln's term), he might have shed the ponderous attempts to show off in favor of something more honest and open. By the time he finally saw Clay in action, he was already transforming his earlier extrapolations of Clay's style into something all his own.

Lincoln's other signature speech delivered in these years was his December 26, 1839, address on behalf of the Whig candidate for president, William Henry Harrison, who was challenging the incumbent, Martin Van Buren. While Clay was not the candidate, the expectation among Whigs was that Harrison would follow the party line and therefore allow Congress, where Clay reigned, to take the lead in domestic affairs. The arguments for Harrison were, in other words, the same as they would have been if Clay had been the candidate, including discouraging the use of the presidential veto and deferring to the Cabinet and Congress. Perhaps Harrison's most important innovation was in the campaign he ran, including using women to spread his message and the first campaign slogan in a presidential race, "Tippecanoe and Tyler, too," a reference to his prowess as a fighter against Native Americans and to his running mate, a stalwart Democrat, who brought balance to the ticket. Clay's "American System" was no match as a rallying cry.

Michael Burlingame suggests that Lincoln's speech "became the Illinois Whig Party's textbook for 1840."[67] Unlike his Lyceum Address in front of a more detached crowd, the intent here was to mobilize his fellow Whig partisans. Lincoln was more comfortable in these settings than academic ones, perhaps because he was self-conscious about his lack of formal education, or perhaps he could be less self-conscious and more relaxed and candid with his fellow partisans. In any event, this speech demonstrated that Lincoln was evolving toward the rhetorical patterns that had made Clay a legend. First, he did not save his humility for the end as he had done in his first campaign speech but instead began the speech with self-deprecation (a Clay trademark) by noting that the crowd was smaller than it had been for previous speakers. "The few who have attended," Lincoln said, "have done so, more to spare me of mortification, than in the hope of being interested in anything I may be able to say. This circumstance casts a damp upon my spirits, which I am sure I shall be unable to overcome during the evening."[68]

Lincoln then launched into a searing attack on President Van Buren's subtreasury plan (creating independent subtreasuries for the collection and distribution of federal money), which, he said,

would cause "distress, ruin, bankruptcy and beggary" by removing money from circulation.[69] After suggesting that the poor
would be hit the hardest by Van Buren's economic policies, he defended Clay's favorite project, the national bank, which Lincoln
claimed handled money more responsibly than run-of-the mill
government officials did. He proceeded to lambaste Jackson, Van
Buren, and Douglas as spendthrifts, deftly turning the criticism
leveled against proponents of internal improvements—that they
were fiscally reckless—against them. His attacks were unsubtle:
he declared Douglas "stupid" and "deserving of the world's contempt" and his arguments "supremely ridiculous," while Van Buren
was captive to the "evil spirit that reigns" in Washington.[70] The
biblical allusions of the Lyceum speech were now decidedly on the
underside and the prophetic. He described the nation's capital as
hell, with "demons" running amuck and "fiendishly taunting all
those who dare resist [their] destroying course"[71] before casting
himself as heroic and his cause blessed by the Almighty:

> If ever I feel the soul within me elevate and expand to those dimen-
> sions not wholly unworthy of its almighty Architect, it is when I
> contemplate the cause of my country deserted by all the world be-
> side, and I standing up boldly and alone, and hurling defiance at her
> victorious oppressors. Here, without contemplating consequences,
> before high heaven and in the face of the world, I swear eternal
> fidelity to the just cause, as I deem it, of the land of my life, my lib-
> erty, and my love.[72]

Lincoln's speech for Harrison was a paean not only to the candidate but his new profession. It sounded the theme that faith
in law could bring order to the chaos that was the alternative,
a theme that Lincoln reiterated throughout his career, and one
that Stuart, Clay, and Webster all repeated as well. At the same
time, Lincoln's rhetoric was evolving stylistically, his phrasing
was plainer, more succinct, and therefore more memorable. His
fellow Whigs praised the eloquence, passion, and reasoning of
this speech.

This Lincoln was neither shy nor retiring. He was choosing a different path; as he spent more time in the legislature, he was becoming more comfortable with becoming sharply partisan, following Clay's example by destroying the competition before it could destroy him. Lincoln was testing the limits of such fierce attacks. He lived in a community—and a state—dominated by Democrats. First in New Salem and then in Springfield, most of Lincoln's friends and neighbors, even those he worked for and learned from, such as the lawyer Bowling Green and surveyor John Calhoun, were Democrats. Incredibly, Lincoln managed to remain cordial to his friends on the other side. His adept balancing of his friendships with the increasing need for partisanship was evident in December 1839 in a series of debates held in a church in Springfield between leading Democrats on the one side and leading Whigs on the other. As one Lincoln biographer relates, "In Springfield in the winter following, when the legislature was in session, a new form of campaigning sprang up. It was called the Three day debate."[73] This newly fangled debate was informal and lengthy, and yet observed some simple rules—respect for your opponent and no spurious attacks. Among the Whigs who regularly participated in the debates were several of Lincoln's closest friends in the bar, including Edward Baker, Orville Browning, and Stephen Logan. Among the regular, prominent Democratic participants were Stephen Douglas and Ebenezer Peck, who would later become a prominent Chicago lawyer and Republican leader. "The debate was so good natured, informal, and helpful that a request was presented that the format be repeated and similar debates were held in nearby towns in the spring of 1840."[74] Lincoln did more than merely hone his debating skills in these contests. The friendships and trust forged among the regular participants endured in spite of sharp political differences in the ensuing years. Nevertheless, though Lincoln engaged with Democrats, he was actually becoming less tolerant of the spirit of compromise. The more time he spent with devout Whigs, the more Whiggish he became. That would become increasingly evident in the stretch ahead.

VI

In April 1841, John Todd Stuart amicably ended his law partnership with Lincoln. It was a business decision, which was intended to benefit them both. Stuart realized that, given Lincoln's passion for politics, his junior partner might not always be able to cover the firm's work when Stuart was in Washington. He needed someone younger, for whom the law, not politics, was the driving passion. Stuart took on a young, Yale-educated Whig, Benjamin Edwards, who was from Springfield. Stuart suggested Lincoln partner with another Springfield lawyer, the aforementioned Stephen Logan.

Lincoln and Logan already knew each other well. Logan, then a state court judge, heard the first case Lincoln tried with Stuart. He had watched Lincoln's campaign speeches closely. Logan was well known as one of the state's premier legal minds and well respected in the Illinois bar, a reputation upheld despite the fact that he dressed sloppily, never wore a necktie, and dribbled tobacco juice while he spoke in court.[75] He was widely feared, with a reputation for being difficult and demanding. (Logan was once described as "snappy, irritable [and] fighting like a game fowl.")[76]

Lincoln became friendly with Logan while they both rode the circuit together, which involved traveling with a judge and another lawyer or two to handle disputes in the counties comprising a particular region of the state, in this case the First Judicial Circuit of Illinois. Lincoln and Logan were among the lawyers who rode the ten-county First Judicial Circuit until 1839, when Sangamon County was included in the newly created Eighth Judicial Circuit, which covered nine counties. Besides Logan, Lincoln met several other lawyers and judges in those days who remained close friends and political allies over the years, including David Davis, a friend from the state legislature, and Leonard Swett, a fellow lawyer in Springfield. Browning sometimes rode the circuit, as did another young lawyer, Abraham Jonas, the first Jew admitted to the Illinois bar. Jonas had begun his career as an apprentice to Browning.

Logan, as the historian Michael Burlingame has noted, was "a better lawyer" but "a worse politician than Stuart."[77] Certainly Stuart was not alone in thinking that Logan was the best attorney in Springfield. In 1843, the *Sangamo Journal* declared that Logan "is regarded as perhaps the best lawyer in the State."[78] The article noted that, while Logan's "voice is not pleasant," he had "a most happy faculty of elucidating, and simplifying the most obstinate questions."[79] Such illumination was appealing not only to judges and jurors but also to Lincoln.

Logan accepted Lincoln as a partner mostly because he had been impressed with his speaking abilities—a skill, Logan said, "exceedingly useful to me in getting the goodwill of the juries."[80] Yet Logan also quickly realized Lincoln's limitations as a lawyer. Logan could see that although Lincoln had read some legal texts, Lincoln had little meaningful experience in the actual practice of law. Logan learned that Stuart might have taught Lincoln how to sway a jury or negotiate a contract but would not have taught him other important legal skills—how to argue before judges, draft legal documents, and file pleadings. Logan knew Lincoln was "never a reader of law; he always depended more on the management of his case."[81] Indeed, Logan was not surprised to find that, even after a few years of practicing law, "Lincoln's knowledge of the law was very small."[82] However, he knew Lincoln "would work hard and learn all there was in a case he had in hand." In the end, Lincoln became, in Logan's estimation, "a pretty good lawyer though his general knowledge of law was never very formidable."[83]

Under Logan's stern tutelage from 1841 to 1843, Lincoln "tr[ied] to know more and studied how to prepare his cases."[84] Logan instructed Lincoln on how to use the legal materials he had read to make his arguments stronger. While Stuart was skillful at cajoling and charming juries, Logan instead taught Lincoln how to better organize his arguments and to integrate the facts and the law of a case in order to persuade judges and juries. Logan required Lincoln to observe him in court, paying special attention to his arguments before juries. After watching, Lincoln stated "that it was his greatest ambition to become as good a lawyer as Logan,"[85] who was "the best [trial] lawyer he ever saw."[86] Lincoln never praised Stuart in such a manner. He admired how Logan could "make a nice distinction in law, or upon the facts, more palatable to the common understanding, than any lawyer he ever knew."[87] The lessons learned from Logan, including how to frame or adapt arguments to different audiences, would turn out to be important not only in Lincoln's development as a lawyer, but also as a politician.

When the Illinois Supreme Court and federal courts moved to Springfield in 1839, thanks to his partnership with Logan, Lincoln was an ideal position to expand his own practice.[88] As Michael Burlingame notes,

> *Of the 411 Supreme Court cases that Lincoln appeared in during his twenty-four-year legal career, a substantial number were tried during his brief partnership with Logan. In response to the hard times following the Panic of 1837, Congress enacted a short-lived bankruptcy law in 1841 to relieve debtors, many of whom enlisted the services of Logan and Lincoln. They handled seventy-seven such cases, more than any other firm in Springfield and the fourth largest of any firm in the state.*[89]

Lincoln continued to ride the circuit in order to earn additional money, and as he became more familiar with the law's complexities, he, like other lawyers at the time, had to deal with the jarring reality that judges varied in quality. Some judges knew and cared about the law, while many others did not. Outcomes often did not depend on the facts but on a judge's politics. In the nineteenth century, judges rose to the bench because of their political connections, rarely because of their acumen or distinction as lawyers. Their courts were often poorly run and their decisions erratic. Lawyers were representing different parties constantly, so an opponent one day could be an ally the next or vice versa. The legal system was much like the rest of the Old West at that time, where order did not strictly follow the law.

Lincoln was equipped to fare well in such a world. A common description of him as a lawyer in those years was that he was plainspoken, and this quality, along with his natural and well-honed penchant for storytelling, made him more effective with juries than judges. It also made him more effective on the hustings. Logan pushed Lincoln harder to not just repeat the points made by others but to make his arguments in his own words. Lincoln's 1840 textbook critique of Van Buren's fiscal policies demonstrated that he was improving in the clarity and coherence of his political attacks, putting them into plainer language and simpler metaphors that he could more effectively hammer home.

Even as Lincoln earnestly took Logan's counsel to heart, they both understood the extent to which partisan forces could shape outcomes. Perhaps no incident better illustrates this than Lincoln's unsuccessful effort as the Whig minority floor leader in the Illinois House to stop a Democratic initiative to remake the state's highest court in order to favor Democratic objectives. Stephen Douglas, four years younger than Lincoln, led this effort.

In 1839, the Illinois Supreme Court's decision in *Field v. People of the State of Illinois, ex rel. John McClernand*, provoked Democrats in the state legislature to introduce a court-packing plan.[90] Thomas Carlin, a Democrat, was elected governor of Illinois in 1839. Upon assuming office, Carlin nominated John McClernand as secretary of state, even though the office was occupied and had no set term. The current occupant, Alexander Field, was a Whig who had no intention of leaving. The Whigs and a small number of Democrats blocked the nomination on the ground that the governor could not remove Field without the legislature's approval. (A similar argument would be made later by Radical Republicans in response to President Andrew Johnson's dismissal of his secretary of war Edwin Stanton.) Carlin waited for the legislative recess, then named McClernand as the acting secretary of state. Field still refused to leave office and filed a lawsuit to block the governor. The trial judge, a Democrat, ruled against Field, who appealed the judgment to the state supreme court. The state supreme court at that time had four justices: three Whigs and a Democrat. One Whig recused himself, the other two voted to reverse the trial judge, and the Democrat voted to affirm the trial judge's decision.[91]

That is how things stood until 1840 when Democrats increased their control of the Illinois legislature. The Illinois state constitution was unclear on whether foreigners without U.S. citizenship were entitled to vote, but by 1840 more than nine thousand had joined the ranks of the Whigs, while barely a thousand supported the Democrats. The Democrats filed a lawsuit barring the noncitizens in the state in voting in statewide elections and then followed the lead of Stephen Douglas, whom the legislature had appointed secretary of state and who urged the legislature to expand the size of the state supreme court from four to nine. As a result of the 1840 elections, the newly constituted state legislature, with a Democratic majority, would have the power to appoint five new justices. In 1841, it did that, bringing the total number of Democratic appointees on the state supreme court to six against three remaining Whigs. Lincoln and thirty-four other Whig representatives in the state legislature denounced the scheme "as a party measure for party purposes," which manifested "supreme contempt for the popular will."[92] Lincoln's hand in crafting the attack is evident in the characteristic wordplay of the response, the repetition of *party* to underscore the clever use of *supreme* to ridicule what the party did. The Whigs further argued that the Democrats' "party measure" undermined "the independence of the Judiciary, the surest shield of public welfare and private right" and set a "precedent for still more flagrant violations of right and justice."[93] (Here again was Clay-like repetition to underscore the magnitude of what was lost—not just a particular right of the people but a safeguard of all rights.)[94] In April, an anonymous letter, likely written by Lincoln (it was similar in style and content to his public remarks), suggested that the bill probably passed the legislature because one member had delivered his vote in exchange for his appointment as clerk of the state supreme court.[95] The letter went further to ridicule Douglas, who was one of the five new additions to the state supreme court (thereby becoming the youngest person ever appointed to the court), dubbing him a hypocrite for publicly opposing life offices but then accepting one when he was appointed.[96]

With the newly reconstituted supreme court to back him, the

Democratic governor again fired Field. Field appealed the decision, as he had done before, but this time the court was literally stacked against him. He lost the appeal and his job.

It was not the last time that Lincoln witnessed the Democrats use their majority on the state supreme court to ratify the party's power and agenda. In 1843, the Illinois legislature enacted a law that allowed white men who were residents but not citizens of the state to vote in state elections. The Illinois Supreme Court, including Douglas, upheld the policy, this time in a move that seemed to undercut Douglas's and the Democrats' earlier concerns about noncitizens voting. And this time, Lincoln objected, believing that the law was designed to make it easier for Democrats from other states to reside just long enough in Illinois to tip elections in Democrats' favor. He argued that only citizens should be allowed to vote, but simply because he felt the Democrats were trying to manipulate elections. Broadening the entry into citizenship was consistent with Clay's American System, an attempt to maximize the contributions people could make to the productivity of the United States. Lincoln believed that this expansion of the vote was designed for partisan purposes, not democracy and not the economy.

In later years, Lincoln rarely mentioned the threats to judicial independence posed by the partisan court stacking, but it is possible he never felt the need to do so. He agreed with one of the foundations of Jacksonian democracy, the spoils system—the practice of giving plum appointments in return for political favors and campaign donations. As New York Democratic senator William Learned Marcy baldly explained the idea in the Senate in 1832: "They see nothing wrong in the rule that to the victor belong the spoils of the enemy."[97] It was not a new idea to give allies and friends the offices that would have gone to the opposition had it won the election, and Marcy lived by the code through three terms as governor until he finally lost reelection to an ambitious young Whig, William Seward, in 1838. Seward practiced the same philosophy as Jackson and Marcy, distributing rewards to patrons and friends when he came into power, just as Lincoln himself would try to do when the time came.

VII

The 1841–1842 session was Lincoln's fourth and last full term as a representative in the Illinois House. He had a few good reasons for leaving the legislature. The first was that his chances for reelection were becoming increasingly slim. The success of the Democratic Party in Illinois, built on Jackson's popularity and appeal as the champion of the working man, along with some popular policies, such as ending the national bank, likely accounted for the Whigs' and Lincoln's dwindling margins of victory. Aside from riding a wave of support resulting from its policy of allowing resident aliens to vote in state elections, Lincoln and his fellow Whig legislators were running out of ways to help the state avoid insolvency from paying for all the internal improvements that they had gotten the state legislature previously to approve. Lincoln's support in each election was less than in the previous one, and there was no reason to think the trend would reverse.

In leaving the state legislature, Lincoln was following the lead of his former partner and mentor John Todd Stuart, who had abandoned his seat in the Illinois House to run his congressional campaigns. Lincoln wrapped up his work in the state legislature in time to make a run for the Whig nomination for Illinois's Seventh District in the U.S. House of Representatives, but he entered too late and lost his party's nomination to a friend and distant cousin of Mary Todd's, John J. Hardin.

Hardin was a popular, handsome newspaper editor, a rival to Lincoln for leadership of the Whig Party in the district. Lincoln was also indebted to him politically and personally. As Lincoln was completing his service in the statehouse, the Democrats and Whigs were yet again embroiled in heated argument over the fate of the national bank. James Shields, a prominent Democrat who was the state auditor, publicly weighed in against the state bank shortly after the Democrats had swept the statewide elections in 1842. In response, Lincoln followed a tack he had before, publishing anonymous letters (in this case attacking Shields) in the *Sangamo Journal*.

As Sidney Blumenthal relates, "One of the telltale characteristics of Lincoln's writings and speeches throughout his career was his appropriation of the rhetoric of his opponents to turn against them."[98] Lincoln had learned the technique from both Clay and Stuart, but as he soon learned, he had yet to master it. It went one step too far in the way he demeaned Shields.

Shields was greatly offended by the numerous attacks made against him in the anonymous letters. The writer insinuated that Shields supported Mormonism, a new Christian denomination whose ten thousand members had settled in Illinois after being expelled by mobs and militias from their villages in New York and Missouri because of their biblical revisionism, fervent abolitionism, amity with Native Americans, prosperity, and insularity. The letters called Shields a "fool," a "liar," and a bumbling lover bound to marry one of the lovely ladies making fun of him.[99] Shields wanted an apology or a retraction and pressed the publisher of the *Sangamo Journal* to disclose the author of the offending letters. The editor relented.[100] It was Lincoln.

Shields challenged him to a duel. As the man challenged, Lincoln had the choice of weapons. He chose broadswords. He figured Shields was more adept at pistols than he was with swords and that his long reach would give him an advantage over his much shorter challenger. Lincoln even hoped Shields might withdraw from the fight once he realized the disadvantage. But Lincoln didn't know that Shields had trained as a fencer and was quite comfortable—indeed, confident—in a swordfight.

Hundreds of people reportedly gathered to watch the two men square off on the field of battle. There is more than one story about what happened next. The most popular is that, moments before the duel commenced, Hardin and other "would-be pacificators" rode up on their horses and pleaded with both men to put their dispute before a disinterested panel.[101] In another account, Hardin reached both men before weapons were drawn and persuaded them to drop the fight, and both quickly agreed. Whatever the truth, Lincoln subsequently looked back upon the affair only with embarrassment, as a cautionary tale about how far to go in taunting an opponent anonymously in the press. Whenever anyone, even Mary Todd, later referred to the matter, Lincoln refused to discuss it and quickly changed the subject.

Much to Lincoln's chagrin, Hardin won the general election for the congressional seat in 1842. Afterward, Lincoln persuaded other Whig Party leaders in the state to adopt "rotation in office," which Andrew Jackson and the Democrats had introduced at the federal level in 1828. In every election or appointment cycle, a political party would rotate new men as candidates for each office. Jackson defended the practice as implementing the will of the electorate, and Lincoln adapted it to ensure broader participation and inclusion of party loyalists in elections.

When Hardin secured his party's nomination for the House seat he occupied, he had appeased his fellow Whigs by agreeing to take the seat on the condition that he would rotate out of it in 1844 to allow another Whig to compete for the nomination that year. Unfortunately for Lincoln, Edward Baker, a friend but an equally ambitious Whig, took the nomination for the House seat next, won the general election in 1844, and served in the congressional seat until he resigned in 1846 to enlist as an officer in the Mexican War. The resignation became necessary to avoid a conflict with the Constitution's incompatibility clause, which bars an "officer of the United States" from serving in Congress.[102] Baker was a colonel in the local militia and therefore was technically an army officer, an "officer of the United States." When Baker resigned his seat, it became open for Lincoln to compete to fill.

VIII

Lincoln's politicking in the late 1830s and early 1840s did not interfere with his courting eligible women in Springfield. He was popular in Springfield social circles, as a young "self-made man" on the rise, and on November 4, 1842, he married Mary Todd. She was ten years younger than Lincoln and was soon expecting their first child, Robert Todd Lincoln, who was born on August 1, 1843.

Neither Stuart nor Browning expressed love, or much if any like, for Mary Todd. Both opposed the match, and neither ever changed his mind. We cannot know what, if anything else, either man said to Lincoln when they must have spoken in person about Mary Todd. We do not even know how often they did. From correspondence and observations of Stuart, Browning, and Joshua Speed, whom Lincoln had befriended when they both lived in Springfield, we can gather that all three men knew that Lincoln's relationship with her was often tempestuous and unstable, even before they married. After once breaking off his engagement with her, Lincoln wrote to Stuart, "I am now the most miserable man living," adding, "If what I feel were equally distributed to the whole human family, there would not be one cheerful face on the earth. Whether I shall ever be better I cannot tell; I awfully forbode I shall not. To remain as I am is impossible; I must die or be better, it appears to me."[103] Though Lincoln was sad other times, Speed felt obliged "to remove razors from his room [and] take away all the knives and other such dangerous things."[104]

Speed warned Lincoln that he would die unless he pulled himself together. Lincoln responded that he was unafraid to die but for his regret "that he had done nothing to make any human being remember that he had lived" and that he had not yet done anything to make the world a better place.[105] More than a year later, Lincoln still could not decide whether he should marry Mary Todd. "Before I resolve to do the one thing or the other," Lincoln confided to Speed, "I must regain my confidence in my own ability to keep my resolves when they are made."[106] Lincoln took his own advice to heart; he was characteristically slow and deliberate in making decisions, but once he made them, he stuck by them. As Mary Todd years later remembered, he was "a terribly firm man when he set his foot down—none of us—no man no woman Could rule him after he had made up his mind."[107] It was a rigidity bound to make things worse at home, since unlike Abraham, Mary had an aristocratic background and usually got her way. But his stubbornness would ultimately provide crucial ballast on a much greater stage.

Though Lincoln went on to do what he thought best, eventually marrying Mary Todd, Stuart and Browning each continued to talk of her as untrustworthy, histrionic, and difficult, and they both described Lincoln as unhappy on the day of his marriage. (Lincoln reputedly said, in response to a question about what he was about to do, that he was headed "to hell."[108]) Stuart and Browning believed that Lincoln's difficult, turbulent relationship with his wife might have explained why he spent so much time away from home riding the circuit and working on campaigns. Stuart and Browning also believed Mary Todd was more ambitious for Lincoln than even Lincoln was, though it seems reasonable to assume that Lincoln welcomed a wife who shared his ambitions or had even grander ones for him than he might have imagined for himself. In their opinion, however, she was the aggressor in the relationship, and possibly had seduced Lincoln on the eve of their marriage as a way to make it impossible for him to escape. (Robert Todd Lincoln, their first child, was born slightly less than nine months after the date of their wedding.)[109]

For Lincoln, there was another likely incentive: Henry Clay was a friend of the Todd family, a fact that undoubtedly would have pleased Lincoln. Mary Todd's father, Robert Todd, had been a law student of Henry Clay's at Transylvania University in Lexington, Kentucky, and later a business partner and political ally of Clay's. Mary Todd had supposedly met and socialized with Clay when she was younger and was so loyal to Clay that she became known as "a violent little Whig." For all of her faults, Mary Todd was fiercely in Lincoln's corner, calling their marriage "our Lincoln party." If Lincoln's confidence lagged, and it did, she was there to refuel their joint ambitions.

On January 16, 1844, Charles Dresser, the minister who had performed their wedding ceremony, sold Lincoln and Mary Todd a one-and-a-half-story, five-room cottage at Eighth and Jackson Streets. Jackson was one of five Springfield streets named for former presidents. Every day Lincoln took his short walk from his home to his office at Sixth and Adams, the State Capitol building at Fifth and Adams, or both, he almost certainly would have thought of the nation's early presidents and their ongoing presence in his and the nation's life.

While Lincoln was settling into married life in 1844, he ended his two-year law partnership with Stephen Logan and began a new one with a younger partner, William Herndon. Lincoln's impending family responsibilities and his interest in running for Congress explain why he chose to partner with a younger lawyer—he needed someone else to run the office while he campaigned for the House. As Lincoln learned from working with both Stuart and Logan, a younger partner could be given more of the firm's work, freeing the senior partner to drum up more business or plan a political run. According to Henry Clay Whitney, who rode the circuit with Lincoln, Lincoln had explained to Herndon that he had taken him "in partnership on the supposition that he was not much of an advocate, but that he would prove to be a systematic office lawyer; but it transpired, contrary to his supposition, that Herndon was an excellent lawyer in the courts and as poor as himself in the office."[110]

IX

On June 8, 1845, Andrew Jackson died. On his deathbed, he forgave his political enemies, including Clay. His final words were to his family, "Be good children, all of you, and strive to be ready when the change comes."[111] (Legend has it that Jackson had a parrot, which erupted in profanity the moment Jackson died.) At the time of his death, Democrats hailed his legacy as one of America's strongest presidents, an American hero who opposed corruption and an overreaching federal government and was the relentless champion of democracy and the common man.

The Whigs were not inclined to forgive Jackson for anything.

Daniel Webster, who had aligned with Jackson in opposing secession, was the only prominent Whig leader to eulogize Jackson. In
a speech at the New-York Historical Society, he called Jackson a
man "of dauntless courage, vigor, and perseverance" who sometimes had shown "wisdom and energy."[112] Clay said nothing. Yet
again following Clay's lead, Lincoln was silent.

Like Clay, Lincoln considered Jackson a tyrant, whose twelve
vetoes were more than those of any other president up until that
time. His dismissals of his Cabinet and of Whigs throughout the
government to serve his own political whims and his appointments
of friends and allies to replace Whigs whom he had dismissed had
seriously damaged the American Constitution. Clay and Lincoln
believed that Jackson should have been held accountable, even in
death, for his bad acts, including deliberately using inflammatory
rhetoric to stoke vicious and frenzied actions by his supporters.
They likely would have agreed with the assessment of Jackson
made by the visiting French diplomat Alexis de Tocqueville, who
in his monumental two-volume book *Democracy in America* declared, "General Jackson is the majority's slave; he yields to its
intentions, desires, and half-revealed instincts, or rather he antic-
ipates and forestalls them."[113] On his travels throughout the United
States, Tocqueville had closely observed Jacksonian democracy in
action, famously deriding it as nothing but the tyranny of the majority.[114] Lincoln and his fellow Whigs agreed.

Another likely reason that Clay and Lincoln said nothing positive in reacting to the news of Jackson's death is that, although
the former president was gone, the worst parts of his legacy were
still alive, including the man now in the White House. Jackson's
protégé James K. Polk, newly into his first term, gave every indication that he was prepared to be the same kind of president in
terms of policies, vicious partisanship, and constitutional outlook.
"Young Hickory," as those who supported Polk called him, fully
commanded the Whigs' attention. Besides being something for
which they each might have once wished, Jackson's death was almost an afterthought when Polk took the oath of office in 1845,
such was Polk's ideological fidelity.

Clay and Lincoln remained, however, shocked that it was not Clay in the Oval Office. In 1844, Clay had run against Polk as the Whig candidate for president; it was his third run as a major-party candidate for the nation's highest office. Lincoln had been selected as an elector for Clay in the Electoral College, and the entire Whig Party believed that Clay's chances had never looked better.

True, in 1840, the innocuous and bland William Henry Harrison beat out Clay to become the first Whig president, but he died a month into office, elevating to the presidency his vice president, John Tyler, who had left the Democratic Party to be Harrison's running mate. Whigs didn't trust him, and Democrats hated him for helping the Whig Party win the presidency.

The Whigs' distrust of Tyler turned out to be for good reason. Even though as a senator he had harshly criticized Jackson for his tyrannical behavior, as president he acted a lot like his former target—vetoing infrastructure investments and tariffs, and defending states' rights at every turn. Clay led the movement to oust Tyler from the Whig Party.

Tyler saved his most outrageous act for the end. As a lame duck (both parties hated him), he was seriously considering taking the initiative on perhaps the biggest issue confronting the country. Mexico continued to be perceived as a threat to the Union, since it claimed Texas on the basis of the original Spanish explorations by Alonso Álvarez de Piñeda, Álvar Núñez Cabeza de Vaca, Francisco Vásquez de Coronado, and Luis de Moscoso de Alvarado, the area rightly passing to Mexico upon independence in 1821. The Mexican government maintained it would go to war if the United States tried to take it. Americans who had become leaders in Texas asked for its incorporation into the Union, and Democrats like Jackson and Tyler looked favorably upon the request because its admission would add an additional slave state. From the sidelines, Jackson, still the most powerful voice in the Democratic Party, encouraged Democrats to take it. "Texas must be ours," he proclaimed. "Our safety requires it."[115]

Clay did not yet know who the Democrats might nominate to oppose him in the early months of 1844, but he was aware that

Martin Van Buren, who had lost the presidency to Harrison in 1840, was hoping to become the Democratic nominee again. Clay wanted to take a stand on the Texas issue before Van Buren could, and on April 17, 1844, with the election nearly six months away, he made the fateful decision, as his biographer Robert Remini wrote, to write "the letter on Texas that ultimately destroyed his presidential bid."[116] Clay began the letter by reviewing the history of the region. Originally, the territory of Texas was part of the land that was included in the Louisiana Purchase in 1803. But according to Clay, that area had been given back to Mexico in the Adams-Onis Treaty, negotiated in 1819, several years before he became John Quincy Adams's secretary of state. Hence, in Clay's judgment, it was absurd, "if not dishonorable," he wrote, to attempt to resume title to Texas as if it had never ceased being a part of the United States.[117] Claiming title to it would be an act of war, he predicted: "Of that consequence there cannot be a doubt. Annexation and war with Mexico are identical."[118]

Clay understood that Jacksonians were not averse to going to war, but "I regard all wars as great calamities," he wrote, "to be avoided, if possible, and honorable peace as the wisest and truest policy of this country."[119] While some Democrats believed that defeating Mexico in a war would not be difficult, Clay cautioned that Great Britain or France might come to its aid because each was "jealous of our increasing greatness, and disposed to check our growth" and eager to find a way to "cripple us."[120] Even if for some reason Mexico agreed to allow the United States to annex Texas, Clay argued that its annexation would be opposed by a "considerable and respectable portion of the Confederacy."[121] (*Confederacy* was a word that the framers' generation had used to mean the union, or compact, of states comprising the United States.) Hence, the annexation of Texas would produce discord and turmoil within the nation and possibly endanger the Union. He expected the likely Democratic nominee, Martin Van Buren, to also oppose annexation, and added, "We shall therefore occupy common ground."[122]

Clay's letter appeared in the *National Intelligencer* on April 27, 1844, the same day that the *Washington Globe*, the Democratic newspaper begun with Andrew Jackson's blessing and led by Francis Blair, published a letter from Van Buren to Congressman William Hammett of Missouri expressing opposition to the annexation.[123] No one knew how Clay could have anticipated Van Buren's position, but the simultaneous publications and nearly identical content of the two letters quickly became problematic for Van Buren. The similarities produced widespread concern that Clay had once again struck a "corrupt bargain," this time to attain the presidency. Jackson was one of the first to predict that the letter and an editorial Clay wrote in its defense would destroy Clay's bid, noting that they made Clay "a dead political Duck."[124] But he also said that, upon reading Van Buren's letter that "it was impossible to elect him."[125] Consequently, Jackson gave his support for the Democratic nomination to his protégé James Polk, who had been the governor of Tennessee after having served four years in Clay's previous position as the speaker of the House of Representatives. Clay had easily secured the Whig Party's nomination in April 1844 before his letter appeared, while Polk became the surprise winner on the ninth ballot for the Democratic nomination.

In an attempt to mollify the increasing number of voters in favor of annexation, Clay tried to help himself by writing a series of letters to clarify his position. The more he wrote, the worse it got, and as he kept trying to stand on both sides of the Texas question the more his prevarications played into the hands of Democrats who used it to show that Clay's ambition was out of control. As the campaign neared its conclusion, Clay wrote to the publisher of the *Washington National Intelligencer* on October 1, 1844. His letter reaffirmed his opposition to the annexation of Texas and complained that he was being misunderstood around the country and said that he would no long speak publicly on national issues until after the election.

That left a month in which Clay fell (largely) mute while the Democrats relentlessly hammered him for his persistent shifts, supposed hypocrisies, and overabundant ambition for the presidency. Whigs tried to counter by using many of the tactics they had used effectively in 1840 to get Harrison elected, including putting on numerous events to entertain prospective voters and plastering Clay's name on nearly anything that could be given away. They thought it clever to keep asking "Who is James K. Polk?" as a constant refrain to underscore his mediocrity and anonymity.[126] But their candidate was effectively nowhere to be seen.

In the end, it was a close election: Neither Polk nor Clay received a majority of the popular vote, though Polk had a slightly higher plurality, but only 105 electoral votes went to Clay as opposed to 170 for Polk. Clay won eleven states, but Polk won fifteen, including Indiana and Illinois, the two states where Lincoln had campaigned for Clay. Yet the election was even closer than it appeared. Clay lost New York by only 5,100 votes, and a win there would have made the difference between Clay as president and Clay as a three-time loser.

Lincoln had genuinely expected Clay to win this time and doubted the result, at least for a while. Less than a year after the loss, Lincoln wrote an acquaintance, "If the Whig abolitionists of New York had voted with us last fall, Mr. Clay would now be president, Whig principles in the ascendant, and Texas not annexed; whereas by the division, all that either had at stake in the contest, was lost."[127] Of course, it could also be said that if Clay had not kept shifting his position on Texas during the election, he might have been president. He also might have won if he had he given any thought on how to handle the third-party candidacy of James Birney of Michigan, who ran as the Liberty Party candidate, committed to abolition. He could not have kept him off the ballot, but he could have devised a strategy that might have prevented or minimized the damage it caused by siphoning votes away from Clay in key Northern states.

Lincoln never forgot the lessons of the 1844 presidential campaign: it was the closest Clay ever would come to winning the presidency, and he lost the office he most coveted through a series of mistakes and oversights, as well as through the inability of many Whigs to see beyond the moment. If, for example, Whig abolitionists had backed Clay, a lifelong opponent of slavery who owned slaves, they would have had a president much friendlier to the cause. If Clay had allowed his career and particularly his party to speak for him rather than publish letters where he said more than he had to and kept exposing himself to more trouble, he might have been president. If Clay had disposed of the Liberty Party or the appeal it had to abolitionist voters, he might have been president. If Clay had not compromised himself by shifting positions on the most important issue of the day, he might have won. Ironically, the man famous for his oratory was brought low by his own carelessness with words.

Later, as a candidate for the House and still later for the presidency, Lincoln would be a model of self-control, relentlessly staying on message and otherwise saying nothing, while party leaders, the party faithful, and Lincoln's surrogates reassured constituents that he was their best bet. Clay's mistakes would be among the most lasting lessons Lincoln learned from his mentor.

The Constitution gave the president-elect a five-month transition period between the election in November and inauguration in March. (The Twenty-Second Amendment, adopted in 1933, shortened the time between election and presidential inauguration from March to January 20.) True to character, President Tyler decided not to be idle during those five months. Working with his secretary of war, John Calhoun, the lame duck president developed a plan to get both houses of Congress to approve a treaty that Calhoun had negotiated with Texas for its annexation. Once they did, all that would be left to be done would be for Congress to admit Texas as a new state and for the next president to sign the bill authorizing Texas's admission into the Union. The ensuing battles, which carried over to the newly installed Polk administration, would shape Lincoln's presidency and years in Congress.

CHAPTER THREE

CLAY MAN IN THE HOUSE
(1844-1850)

Henry Clay's loss to Polk in the 1844 presidential contest was devasting. It meant much more than the end of his quest for the presidency and much more than a political defeat for the Whig Party. It was a constitutional defeat for the nation.

Jacksonian Democrats viewed the president as the central constitutional actor; he gave the orders, and it was Congress's duty to follow them. Whigs like Clay and Lincoln saw this as a distortion of the proper constitutional order, a seizure of power at the expense of Congress. They viewed the legislative branch as the locus for the great debates on the Constitution and the future of American democracy; in Congress, the great issues were to be deliberated on and resolved. Once resolved through policy, it became the president's duty to implement the policy formulated by Congress. Democrats, on the other hand, saw the president, and particularly Jackson, as the embodiment of democracy and the most legitimate servant of the popular will. Whigs countered that presidents should defer to their Cabinets and that Jackson's dismissal of his was a flagrant abuse of power. Democrats believed that presidents should *direct* their Cabinets and that Jackson's blanket dismissal was his prerogative.

Henry Clay, "the Great Compromiser," embodied the great spirit of democracy at work in Congress and, in the perspective of the Whigs, the country. With Clay at its helm, Congress could set the terms of national debate (not just Whigs, in theory) could shape the priorities of the nation, and thus rise to the challenges the framers had left this generation to handle. Yet with the only Whig elected president dying ridiculously early in his administration, the members of the Whig Party had yet to see their vision ever put fully into practice.

From the time that Lincoln first cast a ballot in a presidential election, in 1832, to his vote for Clay in 1844, only once had he backed the winning candidate. At thirty-five, he had experienced only a single month of a Whig presidency. There had been a long string of Democrats—Jackson followed by Van Buren, Tyler (whom no one mistook for a Whig), and now Polk—all destroying Clay's and Lincoln's shared vision of constitutional ideals. Theirs was a gloomy view: Jackson's eight years as King Mob, who tried to dominate Congress, had been followed by four years of Van Buren bumbling through the nation's first depression in a failed effort to extend that legacy. Harrison never had a chance to stifle the tidal wave of Democratic control, while Tyler had realized the Whigs' worst fears, turning out to be a staunch Jacksonian. Tyler and Clay had once been friends, but they were foes by the time Tyler left office.

If Henry Clay were president, he might have been able to restore the balance of power that his Democratic predecessors had upended, but of course he was not. Now Lincoln watched from afar as yet another Democrat, Polk, prepared to lead the nation for another four years in exactly the wrong constitutional direction.

Lincoln's interest in running for Congress was thus motivated by concerns more important than merely satisfying his personal ambitions. True, he was ambitious, and election to Congress was another step on a path to achieve national fame, but this would have been equally true for all of Lincoln's contemporaries who were no less ambitious and aspired to the same offices. Lincoln ran for the House because he desperately needed to be a part of the solution, which included the larger debate on the great constitutional issues of the day, to assert the Whig conceptions of presidential and congressional power and national unity, and to push back against—if not thwart—Jacksonian domination of the presidency and, thereby, of the entire federal government, including Congress. He did not run merely for fame or fortune or even for rewards to his district. He was heeding Clay's call. He ran to secure Clay's American System.

But, on March 4, 1845, it was James K. Polk who took the oath of office as the eleventh president of the United States. His rise to power marked a corresponding decline in the influence of the Whig Party. Polk became president with solid Democratic majorities in both the House and the Senate, yet his single four-year term turned out to more momentous than he ever dreamed. It coincided with the most serious military conflict that Americans had been involved in since the War of 1812. As a candidate and member of Congress, Lincoln attentively studied how a president actually handled a war and its aftermath, coming to believe, like Clay and so many other Whigs, that Polk had abused his power in starting the war, misleading Congress in the process.

In 1847, Lincoln joined what was called a "president-making Congress," because it coincided with the 1848 presidential election and many of its members were eyeing the presidency for themselves or their party. From his desk near the back of the chamber, and in the hallways and rooms of the Capitol, Lincoln watched as the most prominent politicians of the day vied to become (or to control the selection of) the next president, so consumed with their own ambitions they missed what was happening on the floor of the House in front of them. Many Democrats and Republicans who fought in Congress from 1847 to 1849 were still battling a decade later—some on the battlefield—over the fates of the Union and slavery. Jefferson Davis was in the Senate, as Clay returned for a platform to fight for at least one last time for the Whig nomination for president and the preservation of the Union. Initially, Lincoln aligned with Clay, but he soon felt compelled to choose between backing Clay or the same vision championed by a different man, Zachary Taylor, a Whig who had a much better chance of being elected president in 1850. He chose Taylor.

I

James K. Polk justly earned his nickname, "Young Hickory."
Though he was a half foot shorter than Jackson and thicker around
the middle than his sinewy mentor, no one was more loyal to Jackson than Polk. Jackson's temperament had been forged in war,
while Polk's had been forged in more refined, less violent venues,
the halls of state legislatures, the House of Representatives, and the
Tennessee governor's mansion. Though Polk lacked Jackson's fiery demeanor, he was no less a partisan, and—like Jackson—never
forgot a slight. Jackson exploded in anger; Polk quietly seethed and
plotted revenge.

Polk was born in North Carolina in 1795, grew up in central
Tennessee, and attended college at the University of North Carolina. After graduation, he went back to Tennessee, where family connections and his background as a college debater earned
him a law apprenticeship with a powerful Tennessee Democrat
and attorney, Felix Grundy. With Grundy's help, he became clerk
to the Tennessee Senate in 1819. Four years later, he was elected
to the Tennessee House. Once there, he increasingly sided with
Andrew Jackson, who was beginning in earnest his campaign for
the presidency, instead of Grundy, in skirmishes over what instructions the Tennessee state legislature should have been giving its
senators in Washington on such issues as the national bank and
land reform. Polk married into a well-connected political family,
for whom Jackson was a close friend and was affectionately known
as Uncle Andrew. In 1823, Polk successfully led an effort to break a
deadlock in the Tennessee legislature over Jackson's appointment
as a senator; Polk's intervention helped to tip the balance in favor
of Jackson, who was then able to add the title, if not the experience,
of U.S. senator to his military accomplishments. In 1825, at twenty-
nine, Polk was elected to the U.S. House of Representatives. His
first speech, proposing to replace the Electoral College with the
popular vote, fell largely on deaf ears. He had greater success in advising Jackson in the run-up to the 1828 presidential election, after

which President Jackson never missed a chance to assist Polk's rise in the party and in Congress.

In Jackson's second term, he was so grateful for Polk's loyalty and his ability to calmly but firmly advance his policies in Congress that in 1833 Jackson placed Polk in charge of the congressional battle over the national bank's future. Jackson arranged for Polk to be appointed chair of the House Ways and Means Committee, which meant that any issue relating to the national bank would have to go through him. Polk promptly directed investigations into corrupt practices of the bank's president, Nicholas Biddle, and wrote a minority report approving of Jackson's transferring federal funds from the national bank to state banks as a way to thwart Biddle's control. Polk supported Jackson's opposition to the bank and to Clay's beloved internal improvements, while Jackson reciprocated by rallying support for Polk to win election as speaker of the House in 1835. (The two men must have been delighted to have Polk now in the position that Clay once held in the House.) As speaker, Polk was instrumental in supporting Jackson's and Van Buren's fiscal policies and in 1836 implementing the controversial "gag rule." The Constitution guarantees to citizens the right to "petition the government for a redress of grievances," and in the first few decades of the nineteenth century, Congress was receiving thousands of petitions, most of them sponsored by the Anti-Slavery Society. In response to these petitions, the House adopted the gag rule—a series of resolutions barring the House from hearing or taking any action on any of these petitions. The rule stayed in effect until former president John Quincy Adams, who, after leaving office, had been a member of the House in 1831, eventually assembled a coalition of Northern and Southern Whigs and Northern Democrats to get it repealed in December 1844.

After seven terms in the House, Polk faced a turning point. He was concerned how he could fulfill his own presidential ambitions, and staying in the House felt like a handicap, as no speaker had ever been elected president. Instead, he ran for governor of Tennessee. As it turned out, Polk served only a single term before being defeated in the Whig wave of 1841 in response to the nation's first great depression, which had begun on Van Buren's watch and torpedoed his presidency.

Neither Jackson nor Polk forgot the importance of Jackson's support and mentoring in Polk's career. Particularly as a presidential candidate, Polk frequently consulted Jackson. After his victory in the 1844 election, Polk exchanged letters with Jackson on appointments and the new administration's priorities. In January 1845, Polk traveled to Jackson's home to speak personally with the former president before heading to Washington for his inauguration. Jackson was pleased that Polk intended not only to have a geographical diversity of Cabinet officers but also to secure a promise from anyone serving in his Cabinet to forgo any presidential ambitions while serving Polk as president. Aware that he might be viewed as merely Jackson's tool, Polk made clear to the party, congressional leaders, and the public that he intended not just to keep anyone else or Congress from hijacking his administration (as Calhoun had tried to do with Jackson), but also to prevent Jackson from doing the same. More than once, Polk declared that he alone would be responsible for everything his administration did.

As a candidate, Polk shrewdly made another vow—that he intended to serve only a single term. Harrison had been the first president to pledge serving only a single term but died long before he could complete even those four years. Polk and Harrison had nothing else in common, but such an affirmation made sense for them both: Harrison could appease voters concerned about a possible Whig tyrant in the White House, Polk's lame duck status immediately distinguished him from Jackson, who had run in three successive elections, and from Clay, who in 1844 was making his third run for the presidency. Thus, Polk reassured undecided voters that as president he would pursue what he believed to be the right policies and not just the expedient ones that would have been good for him or, at least in theory, his chosen successor.

Polk distinguished himself further from Jackson—and all previous presidents—by announcing only four ambitious goals as president. In both the campaign and in his Inaugural Address, Polk declared his plans (1) to lower tariffs (and thereby avoid funding or supporting the internal improvements favored by Whigs); (2) to complete the acquisition of the Oregon territory; (3) to acquire from Mexico the Western territories of California, New Mexico, and Texas; and (4) to reestablish the independent subtreasury system that Van Buren had championed.[1] Polk's concerns about the Oregon territory and those that he wanted to secure from Mexico reflected his overriding determination to realize the nation's "manifest destiny" (a term that editor John Louis Sullivan had coined in an unsigned editorial in *The United States Magazine and Democratic Review* in the summer of 1845) to control as much of the continent between Mexico and Canada as possible. Yet acquiring total control of the Oregon territory (comprising the present-day states of Oregon, Washington, and Idaho, along with parts of Montana, Wyoming, and British Columbia) would not be easy, since the United States and Great Britain had signed a treaty in 1818 providing them both with "joint occupation," a settlement that lasted until 1846. Meanwhile, Mexico laid claim to the lands of California and New Mexico, as well as Texas, in spite of a declaration of independence by the Republic of Texas in 1836. Polk prioritized the quest to control the Oregon territory, whose northern boundary was the latitude line 54°40′, memorialized the slogan "Fifty-Four Forty or Fight."

Acquiring Texas was complicated. It was unclear what if any diplomatic mechanism the United States could use to annex Texas legitimately. A treaty seemed unlikely because of Mexican intransigence—perhaps through some other agreement, since a portion of Texas had proclaimed its independence from Mexico, and therefore Mexico's assent to its acquisition was unnecessary. As a candidate, Polk expressly approved Tyler's annexation of Texas and had even helped behind the scenes during the transition to secure the passage of the annexation resolution. Tyler teed up the issue nicely for Polk by publishing his plan on the annexation of Texas on the evening before Polk's inauguration, though resistance persisted; Democrats, such as John Calhoun and Jefferson Davis, made clear they supported the acquisition because Texas would likely be admitted into the Union as a slave state, tipping the balance of power in Congress in favor of the proslavery forces. Whigs would never consent to any such thing.

In his Inaugural Address (the second longest after Harrison's), President Polk characteristically left no doubt where he and the country stood. He declared that two states "have taken their positions as members . . . within the last week,"[2] referring to Florida and Texas. He emphasized that he was as committed as Jackson had been to maintaining the Union. "Every lover of his country," he proclaimed, "must shudder at the thought of the possibility of its dissolution, and will be ready to adopt the patriotic sentiment, 'Our Federal Union—it must be preserved.'"[3] These last words had been taken verbatim from Andrew Jackson's toast given at the annual Democratic Jefferson Dinner on April 13, 1830, as a retort to John Calhoun's nullification efforts. In sealing the divide between the two men, Calhoun had responded with his own toast, "The Union, next to our liberty, most dear. May we always remember that it can only be preserved by distributing equally the benefits and burdens of the Union."[4]

Still, after using Jackson's phrase, Polk followed with a robust defense of slavery. "It is a source of deep regret," he declared, "that in some sections of our country misguided persons have occasionally indulged in schemes and agitations whose object is the destruction of domestic institutions existing in other sections—institutions which existed at the adoption of the Constitution and were recognized and protected by it."[5] Polk then returned to the Texas question, repeating points made by Tyler and Calhoun: "Texas was once a part of our country—was unwisely ceded away to a foreign power—is now independent, and possesses an undoubted right . . . to merge her sovereignty as a separate and independent state in ours."[6] Without mentioning Tyler, Polk offered to "congratulate my country that by an act of the late Congress of the United States the assent of this Government has been given to the reunion."[7] He expressed equally steadfast support and recognition of "the right of the United States to that portion of our territory which lies beyond the Rocky Mountains."[8] Knowing that Britain laid claim to the Oregon territory and that its ambassador was in the crowd, Polk repeated the pledge of the Democratic platform: "Our title to the country of the Oregon is 'clear and unquestionable,' and already are our people preparing to perfect that title by occupying it with their wives and children."[9] Polk reminded constituents that to his administration "belongs the duty of protecting them adequately wherever they may be upon our soil."[10] Echoing Jackson's declaration less than a decade before, he concluded that "in his official action he should not be the President of a part only, but of the whole people of the United States."[11]

Polk's messages, then and while at the White House, were clear (though not always trustworthy, in Lincoln's judgment), and so was his determination. He intended to work hard, and he did: He personally reviewed every unit of the government, including every department, and carefully monitored all his appointees to ensure they were sticking to his policies. His approach to Cabinet selection helped to ensure allegiance within his administration to him and his priorities, though the exception was Polk's appointment of James Buchanan as his secretary of state. Jackson opposed the appointment, because he thought Buchanan had been in league with Adams's "corrupt bargain," which had denied him the presidency in 1824. Polk did not trust Buchanan, even though Buchanan had served as Jackson's minister to Russia. Polk, however, respected Buchanan's experience in foreign affairs (which also included serving as chairman of the powerful Senate Committee on Foreign Affairs). Even more important, Polk wanted to lower the tariff and needed Buchanan's support in Pennsylvania, a state that favored protective duties for manufacturing and mining operations. Though Buchanan initially favored Polk's appointing him to the Supreme Court to fill a vacancy Tyler had failed to fill before the end of his term, Buchanan eventually relented and agreed to become Polk's secretary of state. It came as no surprise that the most difficult relationship Polk had with any Cabinet officer was with Buchanan, whose allegiance always appeared to be in service to his own rather than the president's ambitions.

For much of his first year in office, Polk tried to avoid being drawn into war on two fronts: one on the western coast against the British over the Oregon territory and another in Mexico over California, New Mexico, and Texas. Polk had declared in his Inaugural Address that the United States' claim to the entire Oregon territory was "clear" and "indisputable," and in his end-of-the-year message to Congress in 1845, he requested a joint resolution approved in both chambers to notify the British of the termination of the joint occupancy agreement. Not surprisingly, these bold declarations angered the British. Knowing that such a resolution would bring the two nations closer to war and that Britain's naval power was far superior to that of the United States, Congress debated the issue for months. Eventually, in April 1845, Congress settled on a relatively mild resolution calling upon the parties to settle the matter amicably. Even so, Polk welcomed the result, which, he believed, strengthened his negotiating position. With most of its ships on the eastern seaboard, Britain did not relish the hardships of moving the bulk of its force to the opposite coast nor the likely war that might ensue if it did. Fourteen months later, on June 18, 1846, the Senate ratified a treaty that Buchanan had negotiated with the British to transfer the Oregon territory into American hands and establish its northern boundary at the 49th parallel, which had become Polk's fallback once it was clear the British would never agree to the 54th. (Slogans were designed to win campaigns, not bind a president once in office.)

In the meantime, Polk was discovering that avoiding war with Mexico was much trickier than it had been with the British. Though Polk worked tirelessly on each matter, the job of annexing Texas presented far more problems. Securing congressional approval of the acquisition of Texas—something he desperately wanted—was one thing, but finishing the job turned into a bloody drama.

By the end of 1845, Texans had voted overwhelmingly in favor of annexation, which Congress had approved as well. While Texas planned a constitutional convention on the matter, Mexican authorities refused to budge. Polk then arranged for John Slidell, who spoke Spanish and was a loyal Democratic supporter of Polk in the House, to travel to Mexico in December 1845 to offer $25 million in exchange for Texas. Mexico had been notoriously unstable since the country had secured its independence from Spain in the 1820s. While the government initially refused to receive Slidell, his arrival coincided with a successful revolution by nationalist forces. The new government, led by General Mariano Paredes y Arrillaga, was even less receptive to Slidell's overtures to purchase Texan independence and more determined to prevent Texas from becoming part of the United States.

Next, Polk hit upon the idea of trying to turn the instability of Mexico's government to his advantage. He arranged safe passage for Mexico's deposed president, General Antonio López de Santa Anna, to travel from exile in Cuba into Mexico, where Santa Anna promised that, in exchange for $30 million for himself, he would arrange for Mexico to sell all contested property to the United States at a reasonable price. Nevertheless, once successfully returned to Mexico in August 1846, Santa Anna reneged on his promise to Polk and instead declared his intention to lead Mexican forces to defend against U.S. aggression.

In the meantime, Polk's success in convincing Texas to take steps to support American annexation brought war closer. Polk was aggressive not just in his rhetoric, but also in his use of power, particularly his use of the military. After Polk accepted Texas's claim of the Rio Grande as its boundary with Mexico, Mexican leaders threatened to attack the Texas frontier. Having promised to protect Texas as soon as they had accepted annexation, Polk dispatched a naval squadron along the Gulf Coast and moved several thousand troops from the Louisiana border to the northern edge of the disputed boundary zone, granting permission to the commanding general to move south if he thought necessary. General Zachary Taylor did just that.

In choosing Taylor to lead the United States' defense against Mexican aggression, Polk bypassed several more-senior officers, including Winfield Scott, the commanding general of the U.S.

Army. His reasoning was with a less exotic battlefield in mind: Polk distrusted Scott because he was an unapologetic Whig. Taylor, commander of the army's Western Division, appealed to Polk because he had a long-standing reputation as apolitical. Perhaps more important, Jackson had recommended Taylor to Polk. Jackson had grown close to Taylor and developed great respect for his leadership when he had served as a commander under Jackson in fighting the Seminole tribe in Florida.

Zachary Taylor had been a soldier all his adult life. Born in 1784 to relatively wealthy landowners in Virginia, he grew up in Kentucky and joined the army in 1808, a year before Lincoln was born. For the next several decades, Taylor rose steadily in the ranks. He commanded troops as a captain in the war of 1812, which made Jackson famous. He was a colonel in the Black Hawk War in 1832 and a brigadier general in the Second Seminole War in 1837. In 1840, he was assigned to a post in Louisiana, where he settled on a large estate, with more than one hundred slaves, in Baton Rouge. His Southern heritage and support for slavery made him popular in the South—and with Polk. All along the way, Taylor's men revered him for many distinctive qualities—keeping his head under fire, always being willing to listen to and trust his officers and troops in the heat of combat, his ingenuity and undefeated record in major battles, and his honest and unassuming nature. His soldiers dubbed him Old Rough and Ready based on his gruff language and preference to dress plainly during battle rather than in uniform.

As Taylor and his army moved deeply into the disputed territory between the Rio Grande and Nueces River, he heard rumors of possible attacks coming from both north and south of where his troops were placed. Taylor decided to investigate. He sent one group of soldiers farther south to determine whether a threat was coming from that direction. The group reported back that there was none. Taylor then sent other troops north under the command of Captain Seth Thornton, who encountered Mexican troops who had crossed the Rio Grande. The Mexicans attacked his men. They retreated quickly and sent word of the attack to Taylor. In turn,

Taylor relayed the news to Polk, who informed Congress of an attack on American forces, one that he considered unprovoked.

As Polk prepared to ask Congress for a declaration of war, Taylor and his army of roughly four thousand men found themselves under assault. As they had done in attacking Thornton's units, Mexican troops again crossed the Rio Grande, this time to directly challenge Taylor's forces. The American army decisively defeated Santa Anna's forces on two successive days in the battles of Palo Alto (May 8) and Resaca de la Palma (May 9). On May 13, 1846, Congress agreed, at Polk's request, to declare war against Mexico. Polk's Cabinet wanted him to order American forces to take all of Mexico, but Polk rejected their advice. He defined the American objective as securing Texas.

For the victories in Palo Alto and Resaca de la Palma, Taylor received a brevet promotion to major general and a formal commendation from Congress. Back in the states, he became a popular hero and was promoted to the full rank of major general. The national press began comparing Taylor to both George Washington and Andrew Jackson, whose status as military heroes became stepping stones to the presidency, but he quickly rejected the comparison, saying, "Such an idea never entered my head, nor is it likely to enter the head of any sane person."

Taylor did not rest on his newly won laurels. He led his troops south across the Rio Grande and advanced toward the city of Monterrey. They captured the city on September 22–23, and Taylor, on his own initiative, then granted the Mexican army an eight-week armistice.

This grant of respite infuriated Polk, who was already disturbed by Taylor's growing popularity. He pressed Taylor to push his advantage harder, but Taylor angered Polk further by writing a letter, which found its way into the press, criticizing both the president and his secretary of war, William Marcy, for their handling of the conflict. In response, Polk ordered Taylor to confine his actions to those necessary for defensive purposes and transferred Taylor's best troops to the army led by Winfield Scott, relenting on his earlier decision to bar any Whig commanders for the sake of electoral victory.

In February 1847, Taylor learned that Santa Anna was mobilizing an army to attack his diminished forces. Taylor marched his troops south into a narrow pass that made an attack by Mexican forces difficult. As Taylor was ordering his men forward, the Mexican army attacked. Santa Anna had intercepted an American letter acknowledging Taylor's depleted forces and tried to press the advantage against the smaller American contingent. In the ensuing Battle of Buena Vista during February 22–23, 1847, Taylor's troops won a significant victory over a Mexican army that outnumbered the Americans nearly four to one.

The headlines praising Taylor for his unexpected victory at Buena Vista were the last straw for Polk. He was angrier at Taylor than ever before. He considered that his order to Taylor to assume only a defensive position meant that Taylor should no longer take the initiative in the fight against Mexico. Polk relieved him of his command. Taylor spent the next few months in Mexico waiting for leave to return home, which came in November. His victory in the Battle of Buena Vista was his last battle.

Scott oversaw several more victories against Mexican forces, which brought the Mexican government to the bargaining table and the war to its end. The Mexicans agreed to settle the dispute through the Treaty of Guadalupe Hidalgo, signed on February 2, 1848. It granted to the United States more than 500,000 square miles of new territory, including land that now makes up part or all of eight Western states—California, Texas, Arizona, Utah, Nevada, Colorado, New Mexico, and Wyoming. With that one stroke, Polk expanded the United States nearly one-third in size. In return for the lands Mexico ceded to the United States, the United States paid Mexico $15 million and agreed to assume $3.25 million in debts that Mexico owed to American citizens.

Taylor returned to the United States a hero, but many did not come back. Nearly 14,000 Americans lost their lives, the largest number of casualties that the United States suffered in any military conflict until the Civil War.

II

As Polk was struggling to avoid war with the British on the west coast and to end the war with Mexico, Abraham Lincoln's attention was elsewhere. He was intent on going to Congress.

Ron Keller suggests, in his study of Lincoln's years in the Illinois House, that "something awakened in Lincoln in 1839 and 1840. His stature as a Harrison presidential elector, his visibility and attention as a statewide spokesman for Whig policy, and his leadership position in the state legislature instilled in him a certain consciousness."[12] Whether the interest in higher office came earlier, later, or at that time, Lincoln undoubtedly had it. Many years later, Herndon agreed that by 1840, Lincoln "had begun to dream of destiny."[13] Lincoln's runs for the state legislature, beginning in 1832, suggest that his "little engine" of ambition (as Herndon called it) had been changing hard for some time.

Oratory was instrumental to Lincoln's success, as it had been for Clay's. Since Lincoln had been a boy, he had worked tirelessly on his delivery. He was not just parroting Clay and Webster, another of America's greatest orators, but identifying what worked best for each of them and adapting their techniques and language to fit his needs. Beyond the debates he'd had with Stephen Douglas in Stuart's run for Congress and later during the 1840 presidential campaign as a Whig elector, he constantly honed his speaking style when campaigning across the state. After delivering what he considered to be a subpar performance in one debate with Douglas, he urged the organizers to give him a second chance. Witnessing the next debate between the two men, Lincoln's friend Joseph Gillespie recalled, "I never heard and never expect to hear such a triumphant vindication as he then gave Whig measures or policy. He never after to my knowledge fell below himself."[14]

At another Whig rally in 1840, an observer noted that Lincoln "discussed the questions of the time in a logical way, but much time was devoted to telling stories to illustrate some phase of his argument, though more often the telling of these stories was resorted to for the purpose of rendering his opponents ridiculous."[15] At yet another campaign event, a reporter observed that Lincoln was "highly argumentative and logical, enlivened by numerous anecdotes, [and was] received with unbounded applause."[16] Even some Democrats recognized the power of his delivery, as one did in observing that Lincoln "always replies [jokingly] and in good humor . . . and he is therefore hard to foil."[17] Robert Wilson, who studied Lincoln as he studied others and would have a bright political future himself, said that Lincoln "seemed to be a born politician. We followed his lead; but he followed nobody's lead. It almost may be said that he did our thinking for us."[18]

While there is no doubt Lincoln was blessed with considerable natural talents, he made it all look easy because he had studied classical speeches and Clay's oratory for so long and, having diligently practiced his techniques, had begun mastering the art of adapting them to suit his purposes. By 1846, Lincoln was convinced that his turn for national office had finally come: his cousin-in-law John Hardin had served a term in Congress from 1843 to 1845, after which his competitor Edward Baker had served most of a two-year term in the House. If the Whig Party followed the Jacksonian practice of rotation, which Lincoln repeatedly urged, 1846 was his year.

Lincoln left nothing to chance. He had learned the hard lesson more than once that politics was do or die and early entry into a race was essential for victory. The first thing Lincoln had to do was to secure the Whig nomination, which he did not expect to be difficult as long as Hardin deferred to the practice of rotation. But while Lincoln liked the idea of rotating after a single term, Hardin did not, and he told everyone, including Lincoln, that he objected to following it in this election cycle. He argued that the party should back the most deserving man, who he thought was himself.

Hardin had several advantages over Lincoln. He had gained notoriety as the commander of five hundred state militia troops who had restored law and order in the Utah territory after the murder of Mormon prophet Joseph Smith. (In 1844, Orville Browning successfully defended five men charged with Smith's murder.) And of course, Hardin had previously defeated Lincoln and Logan for the Whig nomination for the U.S. Senate in 1845.

Lincoln proceeded to use some of the same tactics and wiliness that he had learned from Stuart to outmaneuver Hardin. Stuart had been ruthless in his victory over Stephen Douglas in 1838, and Lincoln now followed suit. He wrote to several newspapers to push Hardin's candidacy for Illinois governor to get him out of the way for the congressional seat. When Hardin read the papers, he announced his refusal of the invitation and blamed Lincoln for the ploy. Once Lincoln's friend, Hardin was now his rival. Hardin proposed a direct primary of Whig voters in the district with the candidates restricted to electioneering only in their home counties. Lincoln objected and instead stood by the convention system, "the old system," as he wrote Hardin.[19] Under this system, Whigs gathered in each district to nominate their preferred candidates. He had early experience with this system and knew how to lobby the delegates in each district, so he could ensure that, by the time a general nominating convention was held, most districts would be supporting his nomination. He knew most of the likely attendees in each district anyway and felt confident he could persuade them to adopt the practice of rotation, which would work to his benefit. At the same time, Lincoln did what he and Stuart had done before, rallying the support of friendly newspaper editors in the district as well as reminding Whig elected officials, who would serve as convention delegates, "Turn about is fair play,"[20] by which he meant that rotation, giving someone else a chance to win the office, was the right thing to do. Hardin angrily wrote Lincoln that he had never consented to a deal for rotation and defended his proposal for a direct primary. Lincoln, rather disingenuously, responded that he had not been trying to force Hardin out of the race and that Hardin's accusations against him were an "utter injustice."[21]

As they argued back and forth, Lincoln continued to work the conventions throughout the district. As the voting in each convention began to be tallied, it was clear that Lincoln had the requisite support sewn up, and Hardin grudgingly withdrew his name in February 1846. In the Whig convention on May 1, each of the

district delegations pledged its vote to the nominee whom a majority of its delegates had supported. With Hardin presiding, the
delegates from every district cast their votes for Lincoln. The convention then adopted a platform for supporting a strong tariff to
fund internal improvements. It did not mention either the Oregon
territory negotiation with Britain or the mounting tensions over
Texas.

As Lincoln was wrapping up his party's nomination for the
House, Democrats were still scrambling for a candidate. Eventually, they settled on Peter Cartwright, a Methodist preacher who
was an ardent supporter of Jackson and his policies.

Thirteen days after the Whig convention nominated Abraham
Lincoln as its candidate for the House, Congress declared war on
Mexico. While questions about the cost and purpose of the war
were debated throughout much of the country, they were of less
concern in Illinois. A number of Lincoln's friends and associates
enlisted, including both Hardin and Baker as colonels. Rather
than focusing on Lincoln's opposition to the war, Cartwright and
his fellow Democrats leveled against Lincoln the same kinds of
charges that Polk and the Democrats had successfully directed
against Clay in the 1844 presidential election: They charged him
with immorality and even infidelity, a man of no religion and no
principle. Lincoln countered by traveling throughout the district,
meeting voters, telling stories whenever possible, and pushing the
need for a tariff to fund domestic improvements. He barely mentioned the war.

Shortly before the election, Lincoln responded to Cartwright's
constant charges of immorality by adopting a strategy he had employed before. In Whig newspapers, he published a handbill in
which he denied that he had ever been critical of religion and declared that he had great respect for it.[22] In fact, Lincoln's friends
knew he had questioned religion generally and Christianity in particular, but during the election they supported the stance he was
taking.

Lincoln and Cartwright crisscrossed the district, and at one
revival meeting that he was leading, Cartwright spotted Lincoln

in the crowd. (Lincoln enjoyed attending opponents' rallies, both to rattle them and to study them.) From the lectern, Cartwright pointed his finger and shouted at Lincoln, "If you are not going to repent and go to heaven, Mr. Lincoln, where are you going?" Without missing a beat, Lincoln responded, "I am going to Congress, Brother Cartwright."[23] As was true for Clay, Lincoln's quick wit was invariably his best asset.

In response to Cartwright's persistent charge that he was a man of no religion and no principles, Lincoln published a handbill in league with abolitionists—who were, in Cartwright's opinion, responsible for the unrest and turmoil throughout the nation. Instead of publicly engaging with the charge, Lincoln agreed to be interviewed by two abolitionists. They were pleased with his answers and his record defending people harboring fugitive slaves. They spread the word that he was sympathetic to their cause.

On August 3, 1846, Lincoln won the congressional race by the largest margin that a Whig had ever captured in the district, 6,340 votes to Cartwright's 4,829, with a smaller number going to a third-party candidate. Lincoln was finally headed to Washington.

III

Only thirty-seven when he won election to the House, Lincoln was already well known as Old Abe among his friends and neighbors. For the past ten years, as he walked the path, nearly daily, from his home to his law office or the capitol, he appeared to them as a dotty old man. With his victory in hand, Old Abe was spotted yet again in the streets, mulling over the issues likely to come before him. He had to make the most of his short term, since he expected to be rotated out in two years.

While Stuart had been especially helpful to Lincoln in securing election in the past, he was planning to run for a seat in the Illinois Senate, and—opening a breach with Lincoln that would intermittently separate them from each other for the next several years—Stuart had no time to help Lincoln ready himself for Congress. Nor did he have to. Through his eight years in the Illinois House, Lincoln had already learned what he needed to know to succeed in the U.S. House, already understood from firsthand experience and Stuart's tutelage the importance of logrolling and working within the party system for advancement. From his law practice with Logan and his successes in campaigning for the state and national legislatures, Lincoln had developed increasing confidence in being able to tutor himself on the issues that he knew had to be mastered. He also had plenty of time to prepare himself, as there was a long hiatus between the date of his election to the House on August 3, 1846, and his swearing in more than a year later on December 6, 1847.

The Mexican War was fought and won before Lincoln stepped into the House, but the peace had yet to be brokered, and many of the dead had yet to be buried. The losses were felt keenly in Lincoln's world. Among the local heroes brought back to be buried in Illinois was John Hardin, who had died leading a counterattack at the Battle of Buena Vista. Many of Lincoln's fellow Whigs in Illinois had thought Hardin, not Lincoln, had the greater promise to become a leader on the national stage. Instead, it was Lincoln who would serve from 1847 to 1849 as Illinois's only elected Whig in the nation's capital. Of Illinois's representatives in the House, all seven were Democrats except for Lincoln, and the two senators, Stephen Douglas and Sidney Breese, were Democrats.

As the sole Illinois Whig in the Thirtieth Congress, Lincoln was alone, but he had the self-assurance he needed to do the job. In July 1847, he made his first trip to Chicago as congressman-elect to speak at the River and Harbor Convention, where about 2,500 delegates, mostly Whigs, had gathered to protest Polk's 1846 veto of an appropriations bill for rivers and harbors, most in the Great Lakes region. This would be the largest crowd Lincoln had ever addressed. They assembled under a large pavilion, about a hundred feet square, near the center of downtown Chicago. Many of the Whig Party's most prominent leaders gathered there, including Edward Bates, a St. Louis lawyer, who was chosen as the convention president. Others in attendance were Horace Greeley, the editor of the *New York Tribune,* a staunch critic of Jackson and an ally of Henry Clay, and two other notable New Yorkers—the political boss Thurlow Weed and his protégé, William Seward, New York's governor from 1839 to 1842. Lincoln was undaunted, though newspapers and even some fellow Whigs made fun of his appearance. His brief speech made a small but positive impression on Greeley, who reported that "in the afternoon, Hon. Abraham Lincoln, a tall specimen of an Illinoisan, just elected to Congress from the only Whig district in the State, was called out, and spoke briefly and happily in reply to" David Dudley Field, a prominent Democrat who had braved the convention to speak against internal improvements.[24]

While Lincoln's brief speech confirmed his credentials as a Clay Whig, his mentor was not there. He was secluded at his estate in Ashland, Kentucky. The old, defeated warrior, just a few months before, had received the shattering news of the death of his son, Henry Clay Jr., in the Mexican War.

IV

One question that has intrigued students of Lincoln is whether he and Henry Clay ever met in person. Historians generally think the answer is no or, if so, only briefly and in passing. There is reason to believe they might have met once, though there is better reason to think the claim that they did is suspect. In the spring prior to his move to Washington, Lincoln received a copy of a book, *The Life and Speeches of Henry Clay,* with an inscription written in Clay's hand, reading "To Abraham Lincoln: With constant regard to friendship H. Clay Ashland 11 May, 1847."[25] There is no correspondence, nor any other record, indicating whether the two men had met before Clay sent him the volume; every indication is that they had not.

Lincoln was, however, in Clay's presence at least once. In November 1847, before Lincoln and his family traveled to Washington, they stopped in Lexington, Kentucky, to visit Mary Todd's family. While there, Lincoln attended a speech given by Henry Clay. Lincoln's father-in-law, Robert Smith Todd, a former student and longtime friend of Clay's, brought both Lincoln and Mary Todd to Clay's speech. With Lincoln in the crowd, Clay sat on the stage next to Todd. As vice chairman of the event, Todd introduced Clay, who then gave a long-awaited speech heralding his return to the national stage. The subject was Polk's war.

The speech was delivered nearly nine months after Clay's son had died during the Battle of Buena Vista. Young Clay's death must have been on the old man's mind as he set forth his case against the Mexican War, in what became known as the Market Street Speech, because of its location. (Clay's bitterness over the death of his son was surely compounded by Polk's insensitivity in not sending any condolence to the grief-stricken family.)

Clay's speech was remarkably long, even for him, taking more than two and a half hours to deliver.* At the outset of the speech, Clay characteristically played down the occasion by saying that it was nothing more than his civic duty as a private citizen to voice his concerns about the war. Everyone, including Lincoln, would have thought that Clay was considering, if not already committed to, another White House run. Indeed, shortly after receiving the news of his son's death, Clay had written to a friend, "Up to the Battle of Buena Vista, I had reason to believe that there existed a fixed determination with the mass of the Whig party, throughout

---

* At seventy, Clay must have appreciated the fact that, as he stood in the cold, his speech was longer than the ninety-minute Inaugural Address given by the first Whig president, William Henry Harrison, in the icy rain that led to the pneumonia that, along with typhoid fever, killed him.

the U.S., to bring me forward again. I believe that the greater portion of that mass still cling to that wish, and that the movements
we have seen, in behalf of [General] Taylor, are to a considerable
extent superficial and limited."[26] Clay was further stung by the be-
trayal of his former political ally and fellow Kentucky senator John
Crittenden, who was already backing Zachary Taylor in the upcoming presidential election. Lincoln did not need to know Clay's
private thoughts to know the direction of the old man's ambitions.

Lincoln must have listened closely to Clay's speech. Having studied Clay's oratory all his life, he would have quickly recognized
that its structure was classic Clay, beginning with a comment on
the occasion itself, a "dark and gloomy" day, for it was overcast and
raining when he spoke. Clay likened the day to "the condition of
our country, in regard to the unnatural war with Mexico."[27] This
war, he said, was not like other wars the country had fought, even
the Revolutionary War: "This is no war of defence, but one of unnecessary and offensive aggression. It is Mexico that is defending
her fire-sides."[28] Clay made no direct reference to the death of his
son, but rather raised a startling rhetorical question, asking, "Who
have more occasions to mourn the loss of sons, husbands, brothers, fathers, than Whig parents, Whig wives and Whig brothers,
in this deadly and unprofitable strife?"[29] He reminded his audience
that the crucial defect of the war was that it did not derive proper
authorization from Congress, as it should have in the Whig conception of separation of powers, but rather from the president.
"Who," he asked, "in the free government is to decide upon the
objects of a War, at its commencement, or at any time during its
existence? Does the power belong to the Nation, to the collective
wisdom of the Nation in Congress assembled, or is it solely vested
in a single functionary of the government?"[30]

Again characteristically, Clay proceeded systematically to lay
out the problems with the war and its supposed rationale. First,
he complained that Congress had not set forth the objective of the
war as it should have. Second, he rejected the conquest of Mexico
as a legitimate basis for waging war. Third, he worried that there
had not yet been a settlement of the war. Clay expected the United

States to be paid money for its expenses, though it was not until early the next year that the United States would receive a lot of territory and money from Mexico in exchange for ending the war. Fourth, Clay denounced "any desire, on our part, to acquire any foreign territory whatever, for the purpose of introducing slavery into it."[31] Fifth, Clay reminded his audience of the "unmixed benevolence" of turning to the project of "gradual emancipation," which he, as a charter member of the American Colonization Society, had long advocated as a solution to the problem of slavery.[32] These resolutions included a commitment: "That we do, positively and emphatically, disclaim and disavow any wish or desire, on our part, to acquire any foreign territory whatever, for the purpose of propagating slavery, or of introducing slaves from the United States, into such foreign territory."[33] Under this plan, the federal government would assist with purchasing the freedom of African American slaves and arranging for them to relocate "back to their homelands" in Africa. Clay concluded with eight resolutions designed to emphasize the right and duty of Congress to investigate the origins of the Mexican War—"to determine upon the motives, causes, and objects of any war, when it commences, or at any time during the progress of its existence."[34] This commitment was a restatement of a proposal made on August 6, 1846, by Representative David Wilmot, a Pennsylvania Democratic member of the House, to ban slavery in any of the territory acquired from Mexico in the Mexican-American War. Wilmot introduced his proposal as a rider to a $2 million appropriations bill intended for the final negotiations to settle the war. The House passed the bill on August 6, 1847, but it failed in the Senate. The proposal became known as the Wilmot Proviso. The congressman repeatedly tried to attach it as a rider to each new appropriations bill for the settlement of the war, but each time it failed in the Senate.

Lincoln never offered an opinion, public or private, on the Market Street Speech. There are, however, reports that after the speech, he spoke briefly with Clay, who, one person alleges, invited him to dinner at his Ashland estate near Lexington. Many

years later, Usher Linder, a Democrat who had sometimes practiced law with Lincoln on the circuit, recalled details of the dinner. He said that Lincoln had told him that

> *though Mr. Clay was most polished in his manners, and very hos-*
> *pitable, he betrayed a consciousness of superiority that none could*
> *mistake. [Lincoln] felt that Mr. Clay did not regard him, or any other*
> *person in his presence, as, in any sense, on an equality with him. In*
> *short, he thought that Mr. Clay was overbearing and domineering,*
> *and that, while he was apparently kind, it was in that magnificent*
> *and patronizing way which made a sensitive man uncomfortable.*[35]

Sidney Blumenthal notes that Alexander McClure, a prominent
Republican supporter of Lincoln's, suggested in his biography of
Lincoln that at the dinner, "Clay was courteous, but cold . . . Lincoln
was disenchanted; his ideal was shattered."[36]

Clay was well known for being arrogant and full of himself (his
opponents always chastised him for being elitist), but he was also
renowned for being a charming host, though he might not have
been that evening, given the recent death of his son, his preoc-
cupation with the upcoming presidential election, or both. Moreover, while Linder was a friend of Lincoln's before he entered
Congress, he later became a Democratic ally of Stephen Douglas,
and his characterization of Clay aligns perfectly with the Democratic critique directed successfully against Clay in the 1844 presidential campaign. Also, Linder's recollections portray Lincoln as
a simpleton who was incapable of developing nuanced appraisals
of the men he was dealing with. Lincoln knew that between him
and Clay the one of them who had a political future in 1847 was
likely the incoming congressman from Illinois and not the former
speaker. (Linder's son fought for the Confederacy, which suggests
a further affinity on Linder's part to construct a negative image of
Lincoln or the man whom he idolized, Clay.)

Lincoln revered Clay's oratory and career, but he never thought
of Clay as perfect. At that point, in 1847, he considered Clay a

three-time loser in seeking the presidency and past his prime. Lincoln was clear-eyed in his appraisal of men, not someone to be put off by the charm or demeanor of a host or ally. Clay's speech probably confirmed that Clay's best days were behind him; it was not Clay's finest by a long shot. The humility seemed disingenuous, as when he proclaimed near its beginning, "I have come here with no purpose to attempt a fine speech, or any ambitious oratorical display. I have brought with me no rhetorical bouquets to throw into this assemblage." It was too late in Clay's career to lower the crowd's expectations on the one thing everyone knew as Clay's greatest strength, his oratory, and his long technical critique of how Polk, not the Mexicans, had started the war likely surprised no one in attendance. Lincoln, who had closely studied Clay's rhetoric, would have recognized the flaws in Clay's performance.

Lincoln was always closely watching people and learning from them. Sometimes, he learned the most by observing the failures of others. Clay's strengths had molded him, but Lincoln's genius in selecting his mentors was in his capacity to distinguish the deficiencies of the admirable and the admirable traits of the deficient. Lincoln could learn from all of them. He despised much of Jackson's despotic conduct, but he still found several elements in Jackson's strong leadership worth emulating. Clarity was one of them; consistency, another. It was not in Lincoln's nature to follow someone mindlessly or blindly but rather to learn what he could later put to his own purposes.

Less than a month after Clay's Market Street Speech, Lincoln was sworn in to Congress. He soon would use many of the same arguments Clay had made in Lexington to denounce Polk and the Mexican War on the floor of the House. One of Clay's tragic flaws, Lincoln knew, was he had trouble seeing how others saw him or how they could sometimes see through his artifice, a fault that was on display early in the Market Street Speech when he referred to the support that he naïvely thought he still had within the Whig Party. Lincoln knew Clay had no such support, because a rising star in the party already had it.

V

When Lincoln arrived in Washington, in the winter of 1847, it was his first visit to the nation's capital. Five years earlier, Charles Dickens had declared Washington a "City of Magnificent Intentions," with "spacious avenues that begin in nothing, and lead nowhere; streets, mile-long, that only want houses, roads, and inhabitants; public buildings that need but a public to complete."[37] Another British writer, Alexander MacKay, said that "at best, Washington is but a small town, a fourth-rate community."[38]

On approaching the Capitol itself, Lincoln saw "an immense lantern, towering over the dome of the rotunda," six feet in diameter inside an eight-foot mast.[39] That impressive rotunda was lined with paintings telling the story of America—from John Vanderlyn's *The Landing of Columbus* (just installed in January 1847) to John Trumbull's magnificent depictions of the Second Continental Congress's reception of the Declaration of Independence, Lord Cornwallis's surrender at Yorktown, and General Washington's resigning his commission. When Lincoln and other House members walked into the Hall of Representatives, they passed through a door with a portrait above of the folk hero Daniel Boone fighting a tomahawk-wielding Native American. Elsewhere within the Capitol was the Supreme Court library and the nation's largest collection of books, the Library of Congress, which would give Lincoln opportunities to advance his knowledge. Marble busts of American leaders—George Washington, Thomas Jefferson, John Marshall, Andrew Jackson, and even Martin Van Buren, among others—stood on pedestals throughout the room. Lincoln could not have helped but notice the absence of any important Whig among them.

Lincoln arrived three days late for the Thirtieth Congress, which had convened on December 6, 1847. It had taken seven days for Lincoln, Mary Todd, and their two sons to trek from Springfield to Lexington to Washington as a family, a break with the traditional practice that members of Congress left their families back home. Once in the capital, Lincoln was eager to get to work.

Initially, the family stayed at the city's most storied hotel, Brown's Indian Queen Hotel, though it lacked whatever grandeur it had once had. It had been the site of the inaugurations of James Madison, James Monroe, and John Tyler. For nearly thirty-five years, it had been the place where the members of the Supreme Court boarded, including Chief Justice John Marshall, during each term of the Court.

Finding Brown's too expensive, Lincoln moved his family to a more affordable boarding house managed by Mrs. Ann Sprigg, the widow of a clerk of the House of Representatives, and near the home of Duff Green. In 1827, Jackson had asked Green to start a partisan newspaper in Washington, the *United States Telegraph*, defending his administration, and Green became a member of President Jackson's band of unofficial advisers, which his opponents called the "kitchen Cabinet." Green often ate at Mrs. Sprigg's.

Within a few weeks after taking his seat, Lincoln sent his family back to Springfield. He told them they "hindered me some in doing business."[40] Mary Todd was not unhappy, because she felt bored and alone in Washington. Later, Lincoln wrote to her that he missed her and wished she and the children were with him, but they never returned while he was in Congress.[41]

Lincoln was the youngest of the members of Congress in his boarding house. He befriended them all, regardless of party. They debated the issues before the House, often finding common ground on many of them. Late into the evenings, Lincoln entertained them with his storytelling and countless humorous asides. He forged especially close relationships with three of the men, each of whom would have a major impact on his term in Congress and career afterward.

One was Joshua Giddings, an Ohio Whig, who would push Lincoln to oppose slavery altogether. Orlando Ficklin, a Democrat from Ohio, recalled that "Lincoln was thrown in a [boarding house] with Joshua R. Giddings," described as a "tall man, of stout proportions, with a stoop in his shoulders, the face marked, and the hair gray." Ficklin suggested that it was in this company that Lincoln's "views crystallized, and when he came out from such association he was fixed in his views on emancipation."[42] In his two-year term, Lincoln consistently sided with Giddings against the extension of slavery. Less than three weeks after Lincoln was sworn in to the House, he cast one of his first votes in support of Giddings's motion to refer an antislavery petition to the Judiciary Committee. In July and August, Lincoln voted with Giddings on thirteen of fourteen roll call votes on the question of allowing slavery in the territories. In the one deviation, Lincoln supported the suspension of House rules to permit consideration of a joint resolution declaring it expedient to establish civil government in New Mexico, California, and Oregon. Giddings opposed the resolution because he worried that New Mexico might be forced to unite with Texas, which was strongly proslavery. The two men disagreed further on the need for extremist tactics in fighting against the slave power, Giddings disposed to support any measure in opposition no matter how radical but Lincoln inclined to compromise and to oppose any resistance to the rule of law, no matter how wrong the law.

Another friend at the boarding house was Pennsylvania's David Wilmot, who was as virulently antislavery as Giddings. Wilmot's reputation as a fierce abolitionist grew each time he tried to attach his proviso as a rider to any appropriations pertaining to the territories acquired in the Mexican War.

Lincoln proclaimed that he had voted for the Wilmot Proviso "at least" forty times in his single term in the House, but in fact he had voted for it or its equivalent only about five times.[43] The exaggeration came in handy for Lincoln when he was battling for the Republican nomination for president against fiercer opponents of slavery, including Seward of New York and Salmon Chase of Ohio. In 1847, however, Lincoln's moderate position on slavery— opposing its extension but not its continuation—was enough to lump him together with Giddings and Wilmot so that their boarding house became known as Abolition House.

Another new friend who lived nearby and hung out with Lincoln and his housemates was "a little slim, pale-faced, consumptive man," Alexander Stephens, a congressman from Georgia and a fellow Whig. Stephens and Lincoln formed a lasting bond, rooted in friendship, mutual antipathy for the Mexican War, hatred of Polk, and a shared interest in forging a compromise on slavery that would keep the country unified. Stephens was one of the few people Lincoln trusted as a confidant, even from the beginning. Stephens said that "he was as intimate with Lincoln as well as with any man except perhaps" Robert Toombs, one of Georgia's two senators.[44] Toombs and Stephens remained Whigs as long as they could before the national divisions over slavery pushed them both to side with secession. Lincoln respected Stephens, his favorite Southern Whig, and his respect was reciprocated. On February 2, 1848, Lincoln wrote Herndon that Stephens, with a voice that reminded him of Logan, "has just concluded the very best speech, of an hour's length I ever heard. My old, withered, dry eyes, are full of tears yet."[45] In it, Stephens shredded the basis for the Mexican War. He declared, "The principle of waging war against a neighboring people to compel them to sell their country, is not only dishonorable, but disgraceful and infamous."[46] Lincoln and Stephens joined in looking for a promising Whig to take back the White House in 1848, as well as for a way out of the bloody civil war they both wanted to avoid.

In terms of his pre-Washington experience, Lincoln was not alone in the House. Two hundred other representatives were also new in town. Two-thirds of the House members had served in their state legislatures. Shortly after being sworn in, he wrote Herndon,

> As to speech-making, by way of getting the hang of the House, I made a little speech two or three days ago, on a post office question of no general interest. I find speaking here and elsewhere about the same thing. I was about as badly scared, and no worse, as I am when I speak in court. I expect to make [another speech] within a week or two, in which I hope to succeed well enough, to wish you to see it.[47]

The focus of Lincoln's first speech was on a matter he well understood as a former postmaster. It involved a dispute over a postal contract for the Great Southern Mail, which carried mail by rail through Virginia to Washington but charged outrageously high rates for its service. Once its contract expired, the U.S. Post Office opted for a less expensive carrier, but Congressman John Botts of Virginia, the chair of the House Committee on Post Offices and Roads (of which Lincoln, too, was a member), introduced a bill to force the postmaster general to renew the contract with the Great Southern Mail. Lincoln's humor and grasp of the facts were immediately apparent. He demonstrated how under the contract the postmaster

> took the most expensive mail coach route in the nation. He took the prices allowed for coach transportation on different portions of that route and averaged them, and then built his construction of the law upon that average. It came to $190 per mile. He added 25% of that rate and offered the result to this railroad company. The gentleman from Virginia says this was wrong [for the Postmaster General to do]: I say it was right.

It was not a huge sum, but it was the principle of gouging the public that animated Lincoln, who insisted the carrier was entitled to "just compensation" but not to a rate that exceeded the one for traveling across the state of New York on a steamboat or the one for traveling between Cincinnati and Louisville. His humor was aptly employed. When confronted with the fact that he was out of order to reference the committee proceedings on the issue, he laughed and said he never could stay in order for long. Even the *Congressional Globe* recorded the fact that there was a "laugh" when he referred to "the lawyers in this House (I suppose there are some)."[48] In the evening he joked with his housemates about it. One guest later wrote, "I recall with vivid pleasure the scene of merriment at the dinner after his first speech in the House of Representatives, occasioned by the descriptions by himself and other of the Congressional mess, of the uproar in the House during its delivery."[49]

Lincoln supported every internal-improvement measure proposed, including not just the first bill he spoke about on the House floor but also the resolutions upholding all the measures that had been proposed at the Chicago River and Harbor Convention to improve navigation on the nation's lakes and rivers.

Lincoln noticed two significant differences from his prior legislative experience. In the Illinois state legislature, leadership mattered; people usually followed what their party leader told them to do. In the House, it mattered less. Lincoln was a loyal party man, which is what the House leadership cared about most, but he was, after all, expected to serve only a single term, and none of the leaders had any leverage over how he voted. Generally, he voted the party line, but not always. When Lincoln was not speaking or working behind the scenes on drafting legislation and crafting coalitions, he was studying his colleagues. (He was present for 97 percent of House votes, compared with the House average of 74 percent.)

In the vote for speaker, Lincoln supported Robert Winthrop while Giddings stayed out of the selection process so he could avoid being held responsible for its result. Winthrop was not a Clay Whig. He was a protégé of Daniel Webster, one of Clay's fiercest competitors for the heart and soul of the Whig Party. Winthrop had no patience or interest in Lincoln's penchant for hanging around the House post office to entertain people with his stories. The new congressman lacked a college education like Winthrop, who had attended Harvard, or Webster, who had studied at Dartmouth. In Illinois, Lincoln had been one of the more literate people, but in Washington he was not.

More significant, Winthrop had voted for the Mexican War, which placed him and Lincoln at sharp odds. Lincoln was faithful to the Whig conception of executive power, which included the president deferring to Congress and to the Cabinet. Though he opposed the war, Lincoln made clear his support for the troops in the field.

As Lincoln knew, the Whig Party was divided into regional camps. Northern Whigs tended to favor more internal improvements, because they would benefit their states more. Southern Whigs were more concerned with stifling executive tyranny but often disagreed about opposing slavery. In Congress, these differences were readily apparent, and they weakened the Whigs, then destroyed the party less than a decade after Lincoln left the House.

No one knows precisely why Lincoln became such a determined, persistent, and vocal critic of the Mexican War. Back home, Democrats relentlessly attacked him for his stand, which one might have thought would have endeared him to ardent Whigs, but it didn't, because in his district so many had fought in the war or had family or friends who did, and to them it seemed a just cause. Lincoln may have been haunted by the deaths of Henry Clay Jr., John Hardin, Daniel Webster's son Edward, or the more than thirty-five thousand other soldiers and civilians on both sides who died of combat, battlefield diseases, and collateral damage. At any rate, something led him to question the lawfulness of the war. He might have thought it was simply good Whig politics or perhaps a way to emulate, if not ingratiate himself with, Clay, as he would likely have seen in Polk's push for war the same kind of abuse of power he and Clay had seen in Jackson, particularly in his slaughter of American natives and efforts to kill the national bank. As Lincoln fashioned a censure of Polk for his misleading the nation into war, his model was Clay's 1834 censure of Jackson for illegally transferring federal deposits from the national bank in an effort to destroy it. The Senate's later expungement of the resolution in January 1837 did not erase its passage from the memories of Clay and his supporters.

Lincoln's first order of business, upon his arrival in the House, was to follow through on Clay's critique of the war. Barely a month after hearing his idol denounce the Mexican War for more than two hours, Lincoln did the same on the House floor. According to Polk, Mexican forces on American land had provoked the United States into war by firing and spilling American blood first. On December 22, 1847, with Mary Todd in the balcony, Lincoln introduced eight resolutions to demand from Polk the exact "spot" of "soil" where "the blood of our citizens was so shed."[50] Lincoln's spot resolutions were legalistic in their fixation on the precise location Mexico started the war, as if Lincoln figured that all he had to do to defeat Polk was call attention to the weakest spot in his argument. Though the failure of these resolutions was often used to taunt Lincoln, on January 3, 1848, only six weeks after Clay's speech in Lexington, the House approved a resolution not unlike Lincoln's declaring that the Mexican War had been begun "unnecessarily and unconstitutionally."[51] Lincoln voted in favor of the resolution, which barely passed 85–81. When House Democrats tried to expunge the House's censure resolution of Polk, as the Democrat-controlled Senate had expunged Clay's censure of Jackson a decade before, the House rebuffed their efforts 105–95. Polk thus became the only American president to be, in effect, censured twice by the House.

Before that second vote, however, on January 12, 1848, nearly two months to the day since Lincoln had listened to Clay in Lexington, Lincoln took to the floor of the House to deliver a major speech denouncing Polk's war.[52] His main purpose was to respond to Polk's end-of-the-year message in December 1847 defending his order for American forces to take the initiative. In his Market Speech, Clay had described Polk's "order for the removal of the army," which placed it in harm's way, as "improvident and unconstitutional."[53] Lincoln made the same point in simpler, more direct language.

In Lexington, Clay had focused his attack on Polk's displacing Congress from its "right and duty" (a phrase he repeated more than once for emphasis) to determine the objects of the war, a position that aligned perfectly with the Whig conception of separation of powers.[54] But Clay framed the attack within broader discourses on both separation of powers and the history of war. Lincoln left out a disquisition on war and the nature of government and instead focused on the abuse of presidential authority, particularly Polk's duplicity and incompetence. Sometimes, Lincoln spoke like the lawyer that he was, repeatedly crafting his arguments as if they were being made in a court of law, referring to the need for "evidence" to support Polk's shifting justifications for the war.[55] At other times, Lincoln sounded like the partisan he also was, even as he dismissed that he or others criticizing the war were engaged in "mere party wantonness."[56] Clay cultivated his oratory in the halls of Congress, where he cast his rhetoric to fit the occasion and the audience. Lincoln cultivated his oratory not just in the courtrooms of Illinois but also in diligently refining arguments down to their basics for an audience of farmers and laborers. Clay rarely distilled his argument down to a single memorable sentence. His message came through the overall flow of his speech, but the same could not be said of Lincoln. Lincoln made his points directly, unvarnished, and crystal clear: "I propose to try to show," he declared on the floor of the House, that "the whole of this—issue and evidence—is, from beginning to end, the sheerest deception."[57] Indeed, in the paragraph in which this line appears, Lincoln three times refers to Polk's "deception."[58] The rhetorical trick of repeating the word or idea that the speaker wishes his audience to take away did not originate with Clay, but he was among those whose mastery of the technique Lincoln followed.

Lincoln, following Clay's lead, focused on Polk's inconsistent, disingenuous statements about the objectives of the war and particularly for indemnifying the conflict. "How like the half insane mumbling of a fever-dream, is the whole war part of his late message!" Lincoln exclaimed rhetorically.[59] While Clay's Mexican War speech lacked his usual caustic asides or analogies, Lincoln inserted his relentlessly: "The President is resolved under all circumstances to have full territorial indemnity for the expenses of the war; but he forgets to tell us how we are to get the excess after those expenses shall have surpassed the value of the whole of the Mexican territory."[60] Lincoln continued, "So, again, he insists that the separate national existence of Mexico, shall be maintained; but he does not tell us how this can be done after we shall have taken all her territory. Lest the questions I here suggest be considered speculative merely, let me be indulged a moment in trying to show they are not."[61]

But here Lincoln had gone too far, undoubtedly emboldened with the verbal thrashings he had been using in campaigns over the preceding decade. The harsh attack on character was a tendency Lincoln indulged but had to break or his prospects for future office might suffer. In trying to outdo Clay in the chamber where he served for eleven years, almost all of which were as speaker, Lincoln managed to do the opposite—lose crucial support back home. He was already thinking, early in his term, of retaining the office "if nobody wishes to be elected," but he squandered his chance by insulting his Democratic friends who backed Polk and by denouncing a war many of his own constituents supported.[62] Nevertheless, to his credit, any loss in popularity back home did not deter him from speaking out.

Lincoln also stuck with the oratory and humor that got him to the House. Just as Clay often did, Lincoln routinely incorporated stories into his speech to illustrate his points, stories that he must have tested on his friends in the boarding house and the House post office. (Mrs. Spriggs's home offered him a similar opportunity in Washington as he had back in Springfield where he roomed with friends and allies.) Lincoln remembered to work the stories into his speech:

> *I know a man, not very unlike myself, who exercises jurisdiction over a piece of land between the Wabash and the Mississippi; and yet so far is this from being all there is between those rivers, that it is just one hundred and fifty-two feet wide, and no part of it much within a hundred miles of either. He has a neighbor between him and the Mississippi—that is, just across the street, in that direction— whom, I am sure—he could neither persuade nor force to give up his habitation; but which, nevertheless, he could certainly annex, if it were to be done, by merely standing on his own side of the street and claiming it, or even sitting down and writing a deed for it.*[63]

He inserted another analogy to underscore the president's duplicity: "I have sometimes seen a good lawyer, struggling for the client's neck, in a desperate case, employing every artifice to work round, befog, and cover up, with many words, some point arising in the case, which he dared not admit, and yet could not deny."[64] Lincoln concluded by asserting that "after all this, this same President gives us a long message, without showing us that, as to the end, he himself has even an imaginary conception. As I have said before, he knows not where he is. He is a bewildered, confounded, and miserably perplexed man." In these partisan broadsides, Lincoln was delivering in plain, simple, direct language the essence of the problem before the nation, a president who lied, and was vindictive and out of his depth.

In some ways, Lincoln was repeating the mistakes of his Lyceum Address, trying too hard to impress his audience through volume and parlance, and thus having trouble finding the right tone. In a paragraph that later came to haunt him, Lincoln told the House:

> *Any people anywhere, being inclined and having the power, have the right to rise up, and shake off the existing government, and form a new one that suits them better. . . . Any portion of such people that can, may revolutionize, and make their own, of so much territory as they inhabit. More than this, a majority of any portion of such people may revolutionize, putting down a minority, intermingled with, or near about them, who may oppose their movement. Such minority, was precisely the case, of the tories of our own revolution. It is a quality of revolutions not to go by the old lines, or old laws; but to break up both, and make new ones.*[65]

As Michael Burlingame explains, "Lincoln may have been trying to curry favor with Southern Whigs resentful of Northern congressmen, like John Quincy Adams, who had denied the legitimacy of the Texas revolution of 1836."[66] Among those closely listening was his friend Alexander Stephens, who was already helping Zachary Taylor, a fellow Southerner and the hero of the Mexican War, win the Whig Party's nomination for president.

Despite Lincoln's oratorical growing pains, Stephens, thinking back to that speech and others Lincoln delivered in the House, said, "Lincoln always attracted and riveted attention of the House when he spoke," because "his manner of speech as well as thought was original."[67] It might have been Lincoln's effort to make his speech plainer, less adorned with the high-sounding rhetorical flourishes of Henry Clay, that captured listeners' attention. In Stephens's judgment, Lincoln "had no model."[68] In fact, Lincoln had his models; he just did not follow them robotically or thoughtlessly.

Certainly on the policy front, Lincoln followed Clay in supporting "compensated emancipation," the American Colonization Society's goal of purchasing the freedom of African American slaves and transporting them back to the countries of their origins.[69] This plan was intended to compensate the Southern slave owners but did not include any provision to compensate the people enslaved for their labor or suffering. Nor did it provide an option for the enslaved in America to become citizens or to obtain any of the property they worked to build. Yet Lincoln did follow Clay, as well as Giddings and Wilmot, in opposing the extension of slavery. Historian Kenneth Winkle notes that, in "his first year in Congress, Lincoln's voting record on slavery adhered closely to the statement of principles that he had enunciated a decade earlier," as a member of the Illinois house and on the hustings helping Stuart, other Whigs, and of course his own elections. "He supported every antislavery measure that came before the House, most of which called for the abolition of slavery or the slave trade in the District of Columbia."[70] Though Giddings thought Lincoln somewhat "timid" in opposing slavery in his early days in the House, Lincoln joined in voting to remove from the agenda and table all the pro-slavery measures.[71] He was a consistent supporter of Whigs' efforts to stop slavery from spreading westward.

However, in the second year of his term, Lincoln broke with his friends Giddings and Wilmot, who were plotting to "blow the Taylor party sky-high."[72] The two men brooked no compromise on slavery, whereas Lincoln, by temperament, training, and emulation of Clay, favored compromise on this most difficult, divisive issue. In the judgment of Giddings and Wilmot, slavery was immoral and therefore had to be stopped. Lincoln knew it was wrong, but as a pragmatist, like Clay, he had not concluded that law and morality must be one and the same in this case. He saw the law more as a policy to be incrementally walked back. It might be less than perfect but could be (re)shaped, step-by-step, into something better with the support and consensus of the voting public.

Giddings was disappointed that Lincoln had voted with a major-ity of the House to table a motion to abolish the slave trade alto-gether in the District of Columbia. Lincoln went against Giddings again shortly thereafter, but this time he had Wilmot on his side, in opposing an initiative introduced by Giddings to require a vote to decide the fate of slavery in the District of Columbia. Again, Lincoln was on the winning side. His preference when torn be-tween following Clay and extremists, like his housemates, was to follow Clay, who regarded the "extension" of slavery as the most immediate problem facing the country. Indeed, after returning to Congress in 1848, "Lincoln never again voted to support discussion of abolition in the District." He did support the Wilmot Proviso, though not as much or as often as he claimed.[73]

Another inspiration for Lincoln was not far from his seat in the back of the House—John Quincy Adams, the former president and longtime ally of Clay who was now in his seventeenth year in Congress. Adams had made a mess of his presidency by not caring to rotate out of his administration disloyal Democrats who backed Jackson or his initiatives. (He did not take the time and did not have the temperament or interest to do so.) Adams was a staunch critic of slavery and repeatedly condemned the Mexican War as being waged by slaveholders so they could extend slavery into the territories. Adams agreed with Lincoln's vigorous attacks on Polk and the war.

On February 21, 1848, in the midst of a debate on honoring army officers who had served in the Mexican War, Adams collapsed at his seat from a massive cerebral hemorrhage. Because Lincoln sat in the farthest row in the back, he was near where Adams fell, and he likely was among the first House members who rushed to the former president's aid. Adams died two days later. Speaker Win-throp acknowledged the political alliance between Lincoln and Adams by naming Lincoln as a member of the House committee responsible for making the arrangements for the funeral.

Three days later, on February 24, 1848, Congress held a joint meeting of the House and the Senate to honor Adams. Lincoln, Stephens, and Howell Cobb, who would soon become the speaker, were among the House members present, while Jefferson Davis, Hannibal Hamlin, and Andrew Johnson were among the senators attending. Stephen Douglas was there, too, having entered the Senate as Illinois's newest senator less than three months after Lincoln had been sworn into the House. Lincoln, John Calhoun, Thomas Hart Benton, and Chief Justice Roger Taney were among the pallbearers. Clay was unusually silent, though he and Adams had long been political allies and Clay had served with distinction as his secretary of state, not to mention being the man whose support gave the presidency to Adams in 1824. Adams was one of the few people Lincoln met who had known the Founders personally. Adams had believed that the principles of the Declaration of Independence were the foundation of the Constitution and that slavery violated those principles, and, among those carrying him to the Congressional Cemetery to be laid to rest, only Lincoln was in the position to pick up the mantle Adams would no longer carry.

VI

From the moment Lincoln entered the House of Representatives, he was immersed in the 1848 presidential election, as was nearly every other member of Congress. Joshua Giddings described it as "a President-making Congress," because the upcoming contest overshadowed everything else being done in the House.[74] Lincoln had not backed a winner in a presidential election since William Henry Harrison in 1840; he was desperate to do so now, and it was clear to him who could win this time around (Zachary Taylor)— and who could not (Clay). Even the formerly staunch Jacksonian Duff Green backed Taylor. Green told Lincoln that Taylor would have the support of not only the Whigs but also Democrats who, like himself, had preferred Calhoun over Jackson because of Calhoun's much stronger support for the rights of states over the federal government on questions relating to slavery. Lincoln was also approached by John J. Crittenden, one of Kentucky's two Whig senators and a longtime friend of Clay's. Crittenden had frayed their relationship when he backed Taylor early for the 1848 presidential election. Crittenden had served as a member of both the House and the Senate and as attorney general for presidents Harrison and Tyler. He was governor-elect of Kentucky in 1848 but was promoting Taylor this time, to Clay's never-ending condemnation. Even though Clay came to Washington in 1848 to solicit support for yet another run, Lincoln, too, had already cast his lot with Taylor.

In fact, Lincoln was a Taylor man before he arrived in Washington. On August 30, 1847, Whig leaders, who were attending a state constitutional convention, gathered at the home of Ninian W. Edwards (father of Stuart's younger partner) to discuss the upcoming presidential campaign. Lincoln explained to the group that the purpose of the meeting was to choose "some other man than Henry Clay as the standard bearer of the Whig party." Lincoln suggested Taylor was the man and urged "the necessity of immediate action," because, "if the Whigs did not take Taylor for their candidate" for president, then "the Democrats would," because Taylor had appeal as a war hero. If this sounded as if victory was the main thing that mattered to Lincoln, it was, because that is what he had learned by watching Clay repeatedly fail in his bids for the White House. Lincoln reportedly told the group that "the Whig party had fought long enough for principle, and should change its motto to success."[75]

After the Mexican War, Taylor was often compared to Washington and Jackson, which boded well for his chances, but he also differed from them in important ways. He bore little physical resemblance to either of them; both were tall, while Taylor was only five eight, with a thick, powerfully built frame, long arms, short bowed legs, and an angular face. He was not known for his eloquence, but his men adored him for his candor and courage under fire. From the time he had become a captain and commander of Fort Knox in Kentucky, he developed a knack for outmaneuvering the enemy. In the War of 1812, Taylor led the defense of Fort Johnson and the first land victory of the war and thereby earned

Jackson's respect and gratitude. More than thirty years later, he continued to lead his troops successfully against the odds. Washington had not only been the commanding general of the army but the presiding officer at the U.S. Constitutional Convention. Jackson had at least been a member of both the House and Senate, a judge, a member of his state's constitutional convention, and an experienced politician, not to mention a three-time nominee for president. Taylor had had no career other than the military (except as an occasional land speculator and owner of a large plantation).

Taylor was among the first to acknowledge that he had never been involved in politics, indeed had never bothered with it before. The absence of any record, particularly any that indicated affinity for the Whig Party, turned off party leaders early in the campaign. Caleb B. Smith of Indiana said that he expected Taylor would have no success among Northern Whigs; Senator Willie Mangum of North Carolina agreed.[76]

One of the bonds between Lincoln and Stephens was their shared confidence that Taylor would win the presidency in 1848. Stephens liked the fact that Taylor was a slaveholder and was therefore expected to be sympathetic to the interests of slaveholders, while Lincoln found Taylor's apolitical history appealing: he could not be attacked, as Clay had been, for shifting positions to suit the current needs, but he could instead be sold as being above politics. Together, Stephens and Lincoln formed the first Congressional Taylor Club, which was dominated by Southerners. They called themselves the Young Indians, corresponded with Whigs around the country, and gave speeches on behalf of Taylor, both on the floor of the House and wherever else they were needed and could go.[77] The Young Indians agreed that the fact that Taylor had not been a lifelong politician distinguished him from Clay as well as Polk or whomever else might become the nominee of the Democratic Party. Lincoln and Stephens worried that Polk might reconsider serving for only a single term, but they believed that Taylor's record made him a more compelling figure than either Clay or Polk.

The Young Indians shared plenty of advice with Taylor, perhaps too much—Taylor hated being lectured to and treated as though he knew nothing of the world. Lincoln suggested that Taylor should announce his intention to endorse a national bank if Congress were to pass a bill establishing one, recommend a higher protective tariff to fund internal improvements, pledge not to use his veto power, and seek to acquire no territory from Mexico "so far South, as to enlarge and aggravate the distracting question of slavery."[78] In April 1848, Taylor made the decision to publicly identify himself as a Whig, then went further to denounce wars of conquest (even agreeing that the Mexican War had been unconstitutional) and proclaim his willingness to sign Whig economic measures into law if they were enacted by Congress.

At the Whig national convention held in Philadelphia on June 7, 1848, Lincoln attended as a delegate for Taylor. It was one of the quickest nominating conventions in history. Conventions usually lasted a few days, but this one met for only a single day, choosing Taylor as its candidate for president on the fourth ballot. Clay finished a distant second. The Whigs endorsed no platform after the delegates recognized that Taylor could be hurt only if he allowed himself to be pinned down on the issues. The delegates chose a longtime faithful Whig, New York congressman Millard Fillmore, as their vice presidential candidate.

All of this was in dramatic contrast to the Democratic convention a month before. Polk's strategy not to include presidential hopefuls in his administration worked relatively well for maintaining unity and support within that circle, but it did not help the Democrats. Polk's determination to serve only a single term left the incumbent out of the 1848 presidential election and no obvious successor. In the end, the Democratic Party settled on Lewis Cass, who had served as a brigadier general in the War of 1812, governor of the Michigan Territory, Jackson's secretary of war, and Polk's floor leader for three years in the Senate. The nomination split the party. Cass was a strong proponent of popular sovereignty—the notion that each state's voters should decide for themselves whether their states would be slave or free, but Democrats who opposed slavery opted to back Martin Van Buren, who had emerged as the presidential candidate for the new Free Soil Party, formed as an alternative to the Whigs and the Democrats after the latter refused to endorse the Wilmot Proviso at their convention. Recoiling from their party's endorsement of popular sovereignty, the radical faction known as Barnburners (who opposed extending slavery) joined with antislavery Whigs and members of the Liberty Party, which had supported abolition, to form the new party. Its major principle was steadfast opposition to the extension of slavery into the Western territories.

Shortly after the Whig Party nominated Taylor as its presidential candidate in 1848, Lincoln took to the House floor to support the nomination and destroy Cass. He defended Taylor's promise to use the veto power sparingly, a pledge that had become part of Whig orthodoxy to distinguish their candidates from Jackson, who had used it to thwart the national bank. Lincoln praised Taylor's willingness to defer to Congress, because it aligned with "the principle of allowing the people to do as they please with their own business."[79] He expressed the hope that Taylor would oppose "the extension of slavery" into the territories and sign any bill with the Wilmot Proviso.[80]

Throughout the speech, Lincoln exhibited a growing mastery of Clay's tools of gesticulation and ridicule, yet he also demonstrated an improved alliance of barb and instruction. His humor and storytelling set him apart from the other, more somber members of Congress, and he relished the attention it brought him. Lincoln's "sparkling and spontaneous and unpremeditated wit" entertained Daniel Webster, when they met occasionally for breakfast on Saturdays, as well as other "solid men of Boston" in Congress.[81] When Maine's senator Hannibal Hamlin came to the House chamber and asked the newspaper man Ben Perley Poore who the speaker was that was entertaining the House and the galleries, Poore said that it was Abe Lincoln, known as "the champion story-teller of the Capitol."[82]

For much of the speech, Lincoln stuck again with what had brought him to the House. He ridiculed the Democrats and their candidate mercilessly. Responding to the claim made the day before by a Georgia congressman that the Whigs had "deserted all our principles, and taken shelter under General Taylor's military coat-tail," Lincoln accused the Democrats of having used "the ample military coat tail" of Andrew Jackson:

> *Like a horde of hungry ticks you have stuck to the tail of the Hermitage lion to the end of his life; and you are still sticking to it, and drawing a loathsome sustenance from it, after he is dead. A fellow once advertised that he had made a discovery by which he could make a new man out of an old one, and have enough of the stuff left to make a little yellow dog. Just such a discovery has General Jackson's popularity been to you. You have not only twice made President of him out of it, but you have had enough stuff to make Presidents of several comparatively small men since; and it is your chief reliance now to make still another.*[83]

Lincoln satirized nearly everything about Cass—his military record, which Lincoln suggested was comparable to his own experience in the Black Hawk War dodging mosquitoes; his waffling on the Wilmot Proviso; his financial records when he was governor of the Michigan Territory from 1813 to 1831; and especially his corpulence.[84] Lincoln ridiculed the Democratic candidate's "wonderful eating capacities," which enabled him to consume "ten rations a day in Michigan, ten rations a day here in Washington, and near five dollars worth a day on the road between the two places!"[85] He warned his colleagues never to stand between Cass and food.[86]

After Congress adjourned on August 14, 1848, Lincoln stayed in Washington to help the Whig Executive Committee of Congress organize the national campaign. It was Lincoln's first chance to see inside the operations of a national campaign, overseen by Clay's onetime friend Senator Crittenden of Kentucky.

Under the direction of Crittenden, Lincoln corresponded with party leaders and distributed copies of his speeches and those by other Whigs in defense of Taylor. He instructed young Whigs back home to take the initiative, to get involved and push for Taylor: "You must not wait to be brought forward by the older men," he wrote during the campaign, "For instance, do you suppose that I should ever have got into notice if I had waited to be hunted up and pushed forward by the older men[?]"[87] It was a telling instruction from Lincoln. He had learned from his own political experience not to be overly dependent on others but rather to depend primarily on himself to advance his own interests and those of his party. Here was his foundational self-made man proposition through a civic filter. At the same time, Lincoln persistently counseled the candidate and his surrogates to stay on message, avoiding Clay's folly in opining on nearly everything (often in contradictory ways), instead emphasizing that Taylor leaned in the direction of the Whigs and their basic principles but was no zealot.[88]

Over the next two months, Lincoln followed his own advice to the young Whigs. He went out among the voters and stumped for Taylor. Besides writing letters and (usually anonymous) opinion pieces and helping to organize support from Washington, Lincoln rallied supporters in Maryland, New England, and Illinois. In Massachusetts, he shared the stage with one of New York's senators, William Seward. As someone who had vied with Fillmore to control the Whig Party—and its spoils—back home, Seward could not have been happy to see his rival on the national ticket at his own expense. Nonetheless, he gave a rousing speech in opposition to slavery. But Seward was not impressed with Lincoln's performance, criticizing to a correspondent Lincoln's "rambling storytelling speech, putting the audience in good humor, but avoiding any extended discussion of the slavery question."[89] Lincoln was more complimentary in return. "I have been thinking about what you said in your speech," Lincoln told Seward after their joint appearance. "I reckon you are right. We have got to deal with this slavery question, and got to give much more attention to it hereafter than we have been doing."[90]

Throughout the campaign, Taylor's doubtful allegiance to Whig principles troubled party leaders, especially when he accepted a nomination for president from a group of dissident South Carolina Democrats, which had formed their own mini-convention in protest over the party's nomination of Cass. Thurlow Weed, the powerful Whig boss of New York and Seward's mentor, threatened to call a mass meeting of New York Whigs to denounce their party's candidate. Fillmore wrote Taylor directly in mid-August to point out the dangers of accepting support from the opposition party. On September 4, Taylor replied to Fillmore in a letter much like one that he had written previously to his brother-in-law Captain John S. Allison of Louisville, Kentucky, who had shared the letter with the public. The first missive, dated April 22, 1848, was prompted by the need for Taylor to push back an effort by Clay to claim the party's nomination. In it, Taylor acknowledged that he was not sufficiently familiar with many public issues to pass judgment on them. He said, "I reiterate [that] I am a Whig but not an ultra Whig. If elected, I would not be the mere president of a party—I would endeavor to act independent of party domination, & should feel bound to administer the Government untrammeled by party schemes."[91] He then promised, in good Whig fashion, to limit his vetoes to "cases of clear violation of the Constitution," since "the personal opinion of the individual who may happen to occupy the executive chair ought not to control the action of Congress upon questions of Domestic policy."[92] This statement meant he would follow Congress on questions of the tariff, currency, and internal improvements. The letter achieved its purpose of reassuring Whig voters of Taylor's commitment to their party's basic principles.

In the second letter that Allison shared with the public, Taylor complained that people had not properly understood what he had been trying to say in the first. He pointed out that all who had served with him in the Mexican War knew that he was a Whig in principle. Moreover, even while a commanding general in Mexico, he had been nominated for president by informal, popular assemblies of Whigs, Democrats, and Native Americans but had declined the endorsements in order to avoid appearing to be partisan. Taylor continued to insist that he was not a partisan candidate but would be the president of all the people, promising not to impose indiscriminate, politically motivated personnel changes nor to coerce Congress with vetoes of constitutional legislation. He wrote separately to reassure Crittenden that this would be the last letter he intended to write during the campaign. The correspondence held the party in line, at least through election day.[93]

The split within the Democratic Party nearly guaranteed Taylor a victory in the general election, but his final margin of victory was thin, with 1,360,000 popular votes to 1,220,000 for Cass and 291,000 for Van Buren. Taylor's margin over Cass in the Electoral College was more decisive, 163–127. Van Buren did not carry a single state, but his 120,000 votes at home in New York provided Taylor his victory margin there. Taylor carried all of New England except Maine and New Hampshire, plus the three Middle Atlantic states and the three border ones. In the South, he carried five (Kentucky, Louisiana, Florida, North Carolina, and Georgia). He won four states that Clay had lost—Georgia, Louisiana, New York, and Pennsylvania, but in the Midwest he lost Michigan, Indiana, Missouri, and Illinois. He carried no Western states, and the Democrats controlled a majority of seats in both the House and the Senate. For the fifth straight time in five presidential elections, Abraham Lincoln had yet to deliver Illinois to his preferred candidate.

VII

The end of Lincoln's single term in the House coincided with Zachary Taylor's inauguration. In the five months between election day in November 1848 and Taylor's inauguration on March 5, 1849, Lincoln reaffirmed his strong attachment to Clay's American System in his support for internal improvements and opposition to slavery. But whatever hope he had to retain his place in Congress was firmly dashed when Herndon wrote to inform him that Lincoln's friend and former partner, Stephen Logan, wanted the seat.[94] Lincoln stood down. Democrats tightly controlled Illinois's Senate seats, so Lincoln looked elsewhere. He told several friends, perhaps in an effort to save face and appear still to be politically relevant, that he had declined an offer to serve as the head of the Land Office in the newly created Department of the Interior, even though the position paid the handsome salary of $3,000 annually.[95]

For one of the few times in his political career, Lincoln was indecisive, unsure of what to do. He wrote Mary Todd that "having nothing but business—no variety—[Washington] has grown exceedingly tasteless to me." Worrying about his sons, he asked her, "Don't let the blessed fellows forget father."[96] He felt her beckoning him home—"How much, I wish instead of writing, we were together this evening"—but Lincoln stayed in Washington.[97]

With Taylor's inauguration speedily approaching, Lincoln realized that there was still a vacancy in the position of leading the Land Office, which oversaw the administration of federally owned lands throughout the nation and the territories.[98] Whoever ran the Land Office would have a significant say over the extent to which the United States allowed or barred slavery in federal territories.

Throughout the first several months of 1849, Lincoln, in his capacity as a member of Congress, forwarded names for the administration to consider for the job. On March 11, he and Edward Baker, with whom he had long competed for leadership of the Sangamon County Whigs, visited the office of Secretary of the Interior Thomas Ewing, an Ohio Whig who had once been close with Henry Clay. One object of the meeting was to secure the commissionership of the Land Office for an Illinois candidate, but neither Lincoln nor Baker made a recommendation for either of the two leading candidates—Cyrus Edwards, a lawyer who once ran for governor of Illinois, or J.L.D. Morrison, a Mexican War veteran and Democratic member of the Illinois house—to be chosen. Several of Lincoln's friends urged him to break the deadlock by competing for the office himself, but he declined, telling them that he refused to compete for the appointment unless Taylor denied it to Edwards, a friend who was also the brother of Ninian Edwards, the husband of Mary Todd's sister.[99] The stalemate broke when another candidate, Justin Butterfield of Chicago, said he wanted the office. Lincoln knew Butterfield as an accomplished lawyer and fellow Whig but an active partisan for Clay, not Taylor. Butterfield's lack of efforts on Taylor's behalf prompted Lincoln to write Ewing that "[Butterfield] is my personal friend, and is qualified to do the duties of the office but of the quite one hundred Illinoisians equally well qualified, I do not know one with less claims to it."[100] Lincoln thought it absurd that Taylor would give the position to someone who had neither backed the Taylor campaign nor worked for it, as Lincoln had done, and he was offended when Ewing said Butterfield was his choice for Land Office commissioner.[101]

At this point, Lincoln decided to compete for the office himself; perhaps he had been planning to all along. He sent appeals to his friends in Illinois and surrounding states, asking them for support and urging them to contact Taylor personally.[102] Taylor and Ewing made clear that they wanted the office to go to a Clay man, and Clay backed Butterfield. Lincoln was displeased, particularly with the administration's seemingly perverse interest in rewarding not those who had served the campaign, but rather those who had served past party leaders. Ewing instead offered Lincoln the prestigious governorship of the Oregon Territory. Lincoln declined.

In fact, he wanted the position. John Todd Stuart had encouraged Lincoln to pursue the opportunity, since it likely meant that once Oregon became a state, Lincoln would be assured, as so many other territorial governors had been, of returning to Congress as one of the new state's two senators. Cass, for example, had once briefly been the governor of the Michigan Territory before his congressional career.

The opposition to the move came from Mary Todd. The Oregon Territory was a dangerous place, which she didn't want to visit, much less move to. Indeed, John Gaines, the man whom Taylor appointed to the spot Lincoln had turned down, lost two daughters to sickness as they were traveling to Oregon from Kentucky.

Lincoln, however, never expressed regret about moving back to Springfield. As the only Whig in Illinois's national delegation, he had a special role to play back home. Indeed, he had explained in letters asking friends to back him for the Land Office job that such concern had held him back before deciding to apply late for the position.

But there may have been another reason for Lincoln's turning down the assignment. Lincoln had watched how Jackson had used patronage to unify his party and administration and how Adams's mismanagement of it had doomed his presidency. Now it seemed that Taylor was abandoning the Jackson strategy in a hopeless attempt to placate his opponents. Lincoln confessed to his friend Joshua M. Lucas, a clerk in the Land Office, however, that he was personally hurt because the Taylor administration flattened his wishes "in the dust merely to gratify" Clay and his followers.[103] Lincoln had been a Clay man all his adult life, but he didn't follow Clay mindlessly, as his support of Taylor made clear. Instead, he learned from Jackson's success and Clay's failures. Jackson and Van Buren had invented the spoils system as a way to reward their allies and supporters. Jackson had promised that system as a candidate and used it to win a second term in the White House. Lincoln had told friends that Butterfield's appointment was "an egregious political blunder," because of the negative repercussions he believed it would have on loyal Whigs who expected patronage in exchange for their support.[104] As former Whig Committee chairman Dr. Anson G. Henry had asked rhetorically, "Who ever heard of Butterfield as a Whig, until the fight was over?"[105]

In public and in communications with the Taylor administration, Lincoln was careful to keep his complaints to himself (or close friends). He wanted to be a good party man, and so he put on a brave front and threw his support behind the appointment of Butterfield. He knew that was what his fellow Whigs expected, and what he often pleaded with them to do, and that the needs of the floundering Whig Party in Illinois were of greater urgency than infighting over how Taylor handed out appointments. Even when he learned that Secretary Ewing had likely removed two letters of recommendation from his file in an effort to weaken his candidacy, Lincoln stood by the appointment of Butterfield and the administration. As he told David Davis, then an Illinois state judge, "I hope my good friends everywhere will approve the appointment of Mr. B. in so far as they can, and be silent when they cannot."[106] A fractured party had kept Cass out of the White House in 1848, done the same to Clay and the Whig Party in 1844, while a unified party had kept Jackson in charge of it. If Taylor was not careful, Lincoln worried, the Whigs would lose the power that he and his fellow ardent supporters had won for them in 1848.

Of course, it was sadly ironic that Taylor wanted a Clay man to get the position of leading the Land Office, given that Lincoln had turned away from his mentor for the campaign. Lincoln had expected that his service to Taylor would have counted as the most important thing in his appointment, but in spite of his protestations that he was a genuine, long-standing Clay man, Lincoln was not considered enough of one to appease either the wounded Clay or the victorious Taylor.

Besides staying for Taylor's inauguration, Lincoln attended one of the major inaugural balls on the evening of March 4, 1849. He spoke briefly with Taylor's former son-in-law Jefferson Davis, now remarried. We know little about whom else he talked to, but among the other guests were Robert E. Lee, who had served on General Winfield Scott's staff in Mexico, and an unhappy President Polk. After initially resisting meeting President-Elect Taylor, Polk welcomed him to the White House and held a dinner in his honor. The former president left town the day after the inauguration for his first vacation in years.

Unfortunately, it did not end well. The work of the presidency had taken a toll on him, and within three months of leaving office, Polk died, his body exhausted after four hard years in office and vulnerable to the cholera that killed him. Less than a decade before, sixty-eight-year-old William Henry Harrison, at the time the oldest person ever elected president, died barely a month into office. Over the span of a few weeks, he had been weakened by pneumonia and ultimately succumbed to typhoid fever. Polk, who had been the youngest person elected president, was now the youngest former president to have died. He was fifty-three. Clay greeted the news of Polk's death in the same way he had greeted news of Jackson's—he said nothing. Following suit, Lincoln remained silent.

Taylor's inauguration was the first that Lincoln ever attended. He had no idea if he would ever attend another or whether he would ever return to Washington. The knowledge that there was another Whig in the White House was of little solace to him. A presidential victory that depended on the thinnest of margins of victory in a state—New York—that Whigs should have had firmly in their column was cause for concern, not celebration. While a Whig presidency should have brightened his future, clouds had swept in. Essentially a political neophyte, Taylor was an enigma to Whigs and Democrats alike. Taylor could barely stay on script during the general election. The prospect that Seward and Weed would write the only script he might follow in the future did nothing to relieve Lincoln's concerns or those of most Whig loyalists.

The fragile coalition that brought Taylor into office was further cause for concern. As historian Kenneth Winkle noted, "Lincoln clearly recognized the strange Whig brew [electing Taylor] that included free soil Democrats, writing 'all the odds and ends are with us—Barnburners [an antislavery faction in New York], Native Americans, Tyler men, disappointed office seeking locofocos [a radical faction opposed to any financial policies they deemed antidemocratic], and the Lord knows what.'"[107] Keeping that coalition together or forging a more solid one to ensure Taylor's reelection was likely impossible. It could not be done without a compelling vision of the future that no one in the party had yet put together. Lincoln was not sure how to do that. Before he could chart that larger course, he had to do something else, something he had not done since he walked into New Salem—find a path that could take him from obscurity to political relevance.

CHAPTER FOUR

LEARNING FROM FAILURE
(1849–1856)

If a man can learn from his failures, he can go far. Lincoln did.

On returning home, Lincoln had much to be proud of. From humble origins, he had risen in eighteen years to significant heights—serving four terms in the Illinois House, becoming a Whig leader in Illinois in all but name, and serving a term in the U.S. House when the nation elected its second Whig president. In that span, Lincoln met two presidents (Polk and Taylor), traded stories with Daniel Webster, debated the Democrats' rising star Stephen Douglas more than once, and stood on the floor of the House to make speeches that made that grand old institution shake with laughter. He had been friendly with the last giant of the founding era, John Quincy Adams, and had stood shoulder to shoulder with such Democratic luminaries as John Calhoun, Thomas Hart Benton, Chief Justice Taney, and Jefferson Davis. He had a volume of Henry Clay's speeches inscribed by the man himself, and he had even seen Clay in person. He'd made a reputation in Washington and Illinois as a storyteller extraordinaire, and now he had more than a handful of impressive encounters to recount.

Nevertheless, Lincoln's failures were mounting. His effort to secure a second term in the House had come to naught, and he was returning to a community in which he had managed, through his strident partisanship, to alienate many Democratic friends and old Whig allies. He had made some useful friends in Washington, but none among the party's leadership. To add insult to injury, back to practicing law just before he left the capital, he argued his only case before the Supreme Court, a dispute in which Lincoln represented the defendant, who argued that Illinois law barred an action against him brought by a nonresident of the state. In an opinion by Chief Justice Taney, the Court ruled 6–1 against Lincoln's client. The only vote Lincoln got came from John McLean, a Jackson appointee who had many Whiggish sympathies. Several years later, Lincoln would try in vain to get the Republicans to nominate McLean as its presidential candidate. Lincoln had many fences to mend in Springfield, besides trying to revive a law practice that Herndon had managed to keep afloat in his absence. Herndon recalled that, upon his return to Springfield, Lincoln was despondent that he had not done more: "How hard—Oh how hard it is to die and leave one's Country no better than if one had never lived for it!"[1]

From nearly half a continent away, Lincoln watched the nation's leaders fumble in their efforts to find solutions to the mounting problems of nativism—a movement among the "native born" (those born in the United States) against new immigrants (as well as actual natives)—and slavery that were dividing the nation. Yet Lincoln never fully disappeared from the national stage in the 1850s. When he made his bid to take center stage in 1859 and 1860, he was not the same man who had returned to Springfield ten years before. He was still Abe Lincoln, the father, husband, storyteller, and loyal Whig, but this reconstructed Lincoln was more moderate, more deliberate, more contemplative, more disciplined, less biting in his wit, and more eloquent. Like Clay and Jackson, he never quit, but he went further than either of them to work on himself and find his voice and a vision for the nation's future that picked up where Clay's had ended.

I

It is unknown exactly when the people closest to Lincoln began noticing he was cold and ruthlessly ambitious. There is a point in every great history of Lincoln when this side—perhaps his core—is noted, but ambition is always retrospectively obvious when the subject is a president. Lincoln's intense craving for higher office may have become most apparent in the 1850s, but it is likely to have been there all the time, and his brief stint in Washington likely made him more eager than ever to be at the center of the political action.

Among Lincoln's friends and mentors, there was surprising consensus on what they perceived the adult Lincoln to be. Herndon said of Lincoln in the 1850s, "Mr. Lincoln never had a confidant, and therefore never unbosomed to others. He never spoke of his trials to me or, so far as I knew, to any of his friends."[2] After Lincoln's death, Herndon wrote, "Even after my long and intimate acquaintance with Mr. Lincoln I never fully knew and understood him. [He] was the most reticent and mostly secretive man that ever existed; he never opened his own soul to one man . . . even those who [were] with him through long years of hard study and under constantly varying circumstances can hardly say they knew him through and through."[3] In short, Herndon said, "He never touched the history or quality of his own nature in the presence of his friends."[4] Leonard Swett, a fellow lawyer in Springfield, agreed that "beneath a smooth surface of candor and an apparent declaration of all his thoughts and feelings," Lincoln was a private man, who "handled and moved men remotely as we do pieces on a chessboard."[5] He added that Lincoln was a "remorseless trimmer with men; they were his tools and when they were used up he threw them aside as old iron and took up new tools."[6]

John Todd Stuart, who had known Lincoln all his adult life, agreed as well. He said, "L[incoln] did forget his friends. There was no part of his nature which drew him to acts of gratitude to his friends." He observed as well that there was in Lincoln "his want of passion—Emotion" that accounted for Lincoln's "peculiar constitution—this dormancy—this vegetable constitution."[7] The word "peculiar" appears in the assessments of many associates and family members. David Davis, who traveled the law circuit with Lincoln and later led his presidential campaign, said,

"Lincoln was a peculiar man. [He] never asked my advice on any question. . . . [Lincoln] had no Strong emotional feelings for any person—Mankind or thing. He never thanked me for any thing I did."[8] Lincoln's sister-in-law Elizabeth Edwards said, "I knew Mr L well—he was a cold man—had no affection—was not Social—was abstracted—thoughtful."[9] Herndon's experiences, too, confirmed that "Lincoln was undemonstrative" and "somewhat cold and yet exacting."[10]

Many other allies, from as far back as New Salem and later in Washington, spoke of Lincoln's circumspection. Gustave Koerner, the leader of the large German American population in southern Illinois, supported Lincoln all his adult life but thought he was not "really capable of what might be called warm-hearted friendship."[11] Pennsylvania journalist Alexander McClure wrote, "Mr. Lincoln gave his confidence to no living man without reservation. He trusted many, but he trusted only within the carefully-studied limitation of their usefulness, and when he trusted, he confided, as a rule, only to the extent necessary to make that trust available."[12] After years of working with Lincoln, McClure concluded, "Neither by word nor expression could anyone form the remotest idea of his purpose, and when he did act in many cases he surprised both friends and foes."[13] John Bunn, who knew Lincoln in his Springfield years, recalled that Lincoln "had his personal ambitions, but he never told any man his deeper plans and few, if any, knew his inner thoughts. What was private and personal to himself he never confided to any man on earth. When men have told of conversations with Lincoln in which they represent him as giving out either political or family affairs of a very sacred and secret character, their tales may be set down as false."[14] A fellow chess player observed that

While playing chess [he] seems to be continually thinking of something else. Those who have played with him say he plays as if it were a mechanical pastime to occupy his hands while his mind is busy with some subject. He plays what chess-players call a "safe game."

Rarely attacking, he is content to let his opponent attack while he concentrates all his energies in the defense—awaiting the opportunity of dashing in at a weak point or the expenditure of his adversary's strength.[15]

There may have been no man who was closer to Lincoln than Orville Browning. Like Stuart, he had known Lincoln all his adult life. Contrary to Herndon's assessment, Lincoln often confided with Browning, indeed, perhaps more with him than anyone else, with the likely exception of Mary Todd. On looking back over his long relationship with Lincoln, Browning said, "Our friendship was close, warm, and I believe sincere. I know mine for him was, and I never had reason to distrust his for me. Our relations to my knowledge were never interrupted for a moment."[16] Yet Browning also saw Lincoln's ambition and cunning.

True, many of these critical appraisals of Lincoln seem like sour grapes, the negative reactions of people who may not have gotten all they had wanted from Lincoln, or perhaps attempting, after Lincoln's death, to bring him down a peg or two. Yet these comments remain credible because they came from people who thought of themselves as Lincoln's allies and friends. They might have felt betrayed because they were not as important to Lincoln as they had hoped or because Lincoln had not confided in them as much as they would have liked as he paved his path to the presidency. They wished to be remembered for their own impact on history.

Many of Lincoln's closest associates, perhaps all, missed the fact that Lincoln was fundamentally a pragmatist. Principles, history, ideas, people—he thought of them all as tools. Lincoln's hero, Clay, had been the same, earning his most common nickname, the Great Compromiser. Yet it would be wrong to say that the only thing Lincoln refused to compromise was his own career prospects. His moral imperative, particularly when it came to opposing the extension of slavery, remained his compass. The surprise for many was how fiercely he pushed others out of the way on his relentless quest for power.

II

Lincoln was ever mindful of his failures and limitations. In 1850, he began a lecture to young law students with the candid acknowledgment (reminiscent of Clay's trademark self-deprecation) that "I am not an accomplished lawyer. I find quite as much material for a lecture in those points wherein I failed, as in those wherein I have been moderately successful."[17] He thought, too, of how Stephen Douglas, younger than he, had surpassed him in Illinois and national politics. In 1852, he acknowledged, "Douglas has got to be a great man, and [be]strode the earth. Time was when I was in his way some; but he has outgrown me and [be]strides the world; and such small men as I am, can hardly be considered worthy of his notice; and I may have to dodge and get between his legs." Four years later, he was still thinking of Douglas, remembering that

> twenty-two years ago Judge Douglas and I first became acquainted. We were both young then; he a trifle younger than I. Even then, we were both ambitious; I, perhaps, quite as much so as he. With me, the race of ambition has been a failure—a flat failure; with him it has been one of splendid success. His name fills the nation; and is not unknown, even, in foreign lands. I affect no contempt for the high eminence he has reached.[18]

Lincoln wanted such eminence for himself. He put in the hard work on behalf of a cause bigger than himself for the good of the country and acclaim seen through the prism of Lincoln's faith in the self-made man. He was not going to quit because he had yet to achieve such eminence. Jackson did not despair in 1824 that he had lost his chance to be president. To the contrary, he redoubled his efforts and became the standard of success for other presidents to measure themselves. Though Clay had lost the presidency three times, he never quit, either. As Lincoln was leaving Washington, Clay was returning to Washington to try, in spite of his frail health, for at least one more chance to lead the Senate and make another run for the presidency.

Though Lincoln was back in Springfield, he had not lost his ambition. As Browning noted, Lincoln was "always a most ambitious man."[19] In Browning's judgment, Lincoln hoped "to fit himself properly for what he considered some important predestined labor or work . . . , that he was destined for something nobler than he was for the time engaged in."[20]

In the last paragraph of the first speech Lincoln gave announcing his arrival on the political stage, he had declared, "Every man is said to have his peculiar ambition. Whether it be true or not, I can say for one that I have no other so great as that of being truly esteemed of my fellow men, by rendering myself worthy of their esteem. How far I shall succeed in gratifying this ambition, is yet to be developed." For the rest of his life, he reminded audiences of his "humble" origins ("I was born," he said, "and have ever remained in the most humble walks of life."[21]) while acknowledging his "ambition" to serve. In his 1838 speech to the Young Men's Lyceum in Springfield, Lincoln denounced the hazards of political ambition, which enticed men to become tyrants. Years later, as president, he understood the importance of braving those hazards for the greater good. As he counseled General McClellan, "If we never try, we shall never succeed."[22]

The most common theme of Lincoln's counsel to others in the 1850s was that success required relentless determination on behalf of a noble cause. These are what drove men like Jackson, Clay, and Lincoln to make an enduring mark on the world. Failure was not going to stop Lincoln's "little engine" of ambition. Not trying was, for Lincoln, the greatest failure of all.

A yearning for something better, some grander objective, was deeply engrained within him. In 1850, Lincoln further suggested to young law students, "The leading rule for the lawyer, as for every man of every other calling, is diligence. Leave nothing for tomorrow which can be done today."[23] In 1855, Lincoln counseled Isham Reavis, who had written for advice on becoming a lawyer: "If you are resolutely determined to make a lawyer of yourself, the thing is more than half-done already."[24] Nearly three years later, he wrote another aspiring lawyer, William Grigsby, "If you wish to be a lawyer, attach no consequence to the place you are in, or the person you are with; get books, sit down anywhere, and go to reading for yourself. That will make a lawyer of you quicker than any other way."[25] In 1858, James Thornton wrote to Lincoln seeking his assistance in training John Widmer, who was aspiring to practice law even though he was older than the usual young man starting the study of the law. Lincoln declined the chance "to be a suitable instructor for a law student." His advice for Widmer was that "he reads the books for himself without an instructor. That is precisely the way that I came into the law. Let Mr. Widmer read Blackstone's Commentaries, Chitty's Pleadings—Greenleaf's Evidence, Story's Equity, and Story's Equity Pleadings, get a license, and go to the practice and keep reading."[26] Lincoln told Reavis, "I did not read with anyone."[27] (So much for John Todd Stuart, Bowling Green, and Stephen Logan.)

Lincoln's reading always extended beyond the law. In the 1850s, he reread the poetry and other books he loved best. John Hay, one of Lincoln's secretaries when he was president, recalled that Lincoln "read Shakespeare more than all the other writers together."[28] As president, Lincoln told the actor James Hackett, "Some of the plays I have never read; while others I have gone over perhaps as frequently as any unprofessional reader. Among the latter are Lear, Richard Third, Henry Eighth, Hamlet, and especially Macbeth."[29] Lincoln read *Macbeth* aloud when the mood suited him, and also the somber, sad poetry of Robert Burns, *Pilgrim's Progress,* and William Knox's *Mortality* (sometimes called by its most famous line, "Oh Why Should the Spirit of Mortal be Proud?").

Pilgrim's Progress was a perrennial Lincoln favorite. Its hero, Christian, finds salvation only after surmounting the challenges of corruption run wild in the world and the countless temptations that routinely bring men down—most of all, the sin of pride. Lincoln also loved *Hamlet* and the *Henry* plays, but one reason he might have preferred *Macbeth* was that its actual hero does not die in the end. Macbeth is an antihero whose ambition leads to his downfall. In the end, it is "the good Macduff," the quiet man who is respected when he speaks and is devoted to his country above all else, who prevails. Lincoln also loved Shakespeare's *Julius Caesar,* another tragedy in which an overambitious main character dies. Brutus says, "As he was ambitious, I slew him."[30] There were lessons in these literary masterpieces, and Lincoln relished not only their language, but also their precepts.

In the 1850s, Lincoln scoured newspapers daily, perhaps more voraciously than ever before. He was rarely home, spending most of his time in his law office, reading, writing briefs, arguing cases in court, and traveling the circuit. Sometimes, Herndon thought, he was too wrapped up in his own thoughts and business. Herndon had to hear everything Lincoln read, too: "Lincoln never read any other way but aloud," he complained. "This habit used to annoy me beyond the point of endurance."[31] Herndon recalled that, when he arrived at work at seven every morning, he found Lincoln reading newspapers. "Lincoln's favorite position when unraveling some knotty law point was to stretch both of his legs at full length upon a chair in front of him," wrote Herndon, and "in this position, with books on the table nearby and in his lap, he worked up his case."[32] Herndon was also annoyed when Lincoln's "brats," Tad and Robert, came to visit the office. They tore books, newspapers, and legal materials apart, and even peed on the floor.[33]

Others noted Lincoln's absorption in the written word. "He would pick up a book and run rapidly over the pages, pausing here and there," remembered a clerk, "at the end of an hour—never, as I remember, more than two or three hours—he would close the book, stretch himself out on the office lounge, and with hands under his head, and eyes shut, he would digest the mental food he had just taken."[34]

One of the few books Lincoln read in its entirety in the 1850s was Euclid's classic work on geometry, an odd choice for most people, but Lincoln believed it would sharpen his mind, making his thinking more logical, rigorous, and organized as he figured out the next steps he had to take in order to return to the nation's capital. Given that the former land surveyor thought of others as objects to be moved and replaced, the study of angles and congruencies might have offered an interesting, if literally tangential, amusement.

III

William Herndon was few people's idea of a good lawyer. In Lincoln's earlier associations, he had been the junior partner to older and more experienced men—John Todd Stuart and Stephen Logan. Stuart was gone for much of the time, serving in Congress while Lincoln ran both the law office and Stuart's campaigns. With Logan, Lincoln again ran the law office, but the partnership foundered in part because both of them wanted to run for Congress. Herndon was different. He was as surprised as anyone when Lincoln invited him to be his partner. He came from a long line of opiniated Jacksonian Democrats; worse, he was an angry drunk and notoriously untactful. He alienated Mary Todd for life when in 1837 he first met her at a ball where he asked her to dance but told her that she "seemed to glide through the waltz with the ease of a serpent." She never forgave him for the comparison.

Lincoln chose Herndon because he was "a laborious, studious young man . . . far better informed on almost all subjects than I have ever been."[35] He loved books as much as Lincoln did and had one of the best private libraries in Springfield, filled with law books; the works of English historians; translated writings of great Western philosophers, such as Kant; works on political economy by John Stuart Mill and Henry Carey, who had built the economic underpinnings of Clay's American System; and great literature, including the works of Shakespeare and everything that the essayist Ralph Waldo Emerson and the preacher Henry Ward Beecher, among others, had published. It is unclear how much of the library Lincoln read, though, later as president, he was evidently familiar with Carey's economics and Beecher's sermons. Lincoln and Herndon were opposites who in theory complemented each other: Lincoln believed in "cold, calculating, unimpassioned reason," while Herndon was intuitive, disposed, in Lincoln's estimation, to "see the gizzard of things."[36] Herndon claimed that he could predict the future in his bones, leading Lincoln to joke regularly upon seeing him first thing in the morning, "Billy—how is your bones philosophy this morning?"[37] Herndon knew how to keep the books and, perhaps most important, was eager to serve Lincoln's every need.

The First Judicial Circuit, which Lincoln had crisscrossed numerous times as a young lawyer, had been merged with the Eighth Circuit, which consisted of fifteen counties. Lincoln was the only lawyer who rode the entire territory. His old friend David Davis, who had become a judge in 1848, oversaw the circuit and did almost all the judging in it. The other lawyers who frequently rode with Lincoln—Leonard Swett, Nathan Judd, Ward Hill Lamon, and sometimes Stephen Logan and Orville Browning—were lifelong friends and fellow Whigs. (John Stuart Todd sometimes rode the circuit as well, though his political leanings were shifting, and he was increasingly aligning more with the Democrats, including his onetime rival Stephen Douglas.)

Lincoln enjoyed the travel and the camaraderie, and his companions came as close as any group to being Lincoln's kitchen Cabinet. Nevertheless, every evening Lincoln kept up an active correspondence. His work took him away from Springfield and his family for nearly six months of the year: three months each spring and each fall. Looking back at that time many years later, Davis said, "Lincoln was as happy, as happy as he could be."[38]

Lincoln's law practice was varied. Some cases were much bigger than others, some clients had more money than others, some cases were more interesting than others, and Lincoln immersed himself more deeply into some cases than others. He represented masters seeking the return of their slaves and slaves who had escaped their bondage. By the late 1850s, Lincoln started avoiding fugitive-slave cases, though in 1856 or early 1857 he agreed to help a woman whose son faced enslavement in New Orleans by raising money to secure the young man's freedom. During the 1850s,

Lincoln and his partner "appeared in at least 133 cases concerning railroads—sometimes representing the roads, and sometimes opposing them. The most famous of these cases involved the Illinois Central Railroad; Lincoln & Herndon, as attorneys for the railroad, received what was then the enormous fee of $5000 for their services. It, like all other fees, was divided equally between the partners."[39] They also represented small banks, debt collectors, spouses in divorce cases, and once Orville Browning, who had tripped on a Springfield sidewalk and broken his leg. (Lincoln took Browning's case all the way to the Illinois Supreme Court, which ruled for Browning because the city had a duty to keep its streets safe and well maintained.)

Almost 10 percent of Lincoln's cases were in the federal courts, including the one Supreme Court case Lincoln argued, which he lost. Lincoln's practice also included murder trials. In one, he sharply questioned a witness's certainty in identifying the defendant on the night of the murder, successfully casting doubt by presenting an almanac that showed that there was very little moonlight on the evening in question. He won another murder trial, shortly before he secured his presidential nomination, by convincing a jury that his client had killed another man in self-defense.

Lincoln's practice with Herndon also included advising clients on all sorts of matters not involving litigation, including writing deeds, registering land, paying taxes, and drafting contracts and wills. In all, over the course of a legal career extending from 1837 until shortly before he left for his inauguration in 1861, Lincoln handled more than five thousand cases. Despite their many hours together, Lincoln's preoccupations about politics, law, and literature confounded Herndon. Herndon was an inveterate optimist, who believed "in the universal progress of all things, especially of man's up going."[40] Lincoln agreed, but he was far more contemplative. Though he often broke his silence with stories and laughter, these were not enough to put Herndon at ease. He found Lincoln "incommunicative—silent, reticent, secretive—having profound policies—and well laid—deeply studied plans."[41]

Everyone, including Lincoln, agreed that he did his best work with juries. Otherwise, the lawyers who practiced with Lincoln regarded him as a good lawyer but not a great one. For example, his friend Henry Clay Whitney, who rode the circuit with him, said that Lincoln "was not more than ordinarily successful for a first-class lawyer."[42] One court observer compared Lincoln to Norman Purple, who served on the Illinois Supreme Court from 1845 to 1848, by saying that Purple,

> *in intricate questions, is too much for [Lincoln]. But when Purple makes a point, which cannot be logically overturned, Lincoln avoids it by a good-natured turn, though outside the issue. Lincoln's chief characteristics are candor, good nature, and shrewdness. He possesses a noble heart, an elevated mind, and the true elements of politeness.*[43]

Another friend said that Lincoln "did not stand at the head of the bar, except as a jury lawyer."[44] Herndon, too, did not consider Lincoln to be a first-rate lawyer, believing he was "very deficient" in some ways because he "never thoroughly read any elementary law book" and "knew nothing of the laws of evidence—of pleading or of practice. [He] was purely and entirely a case lawyer—nothing more."[45]

Later, when Lincoln was considering the old Pennsylvania pol Simon Cameron for his Cabinet, he said, "I suppose we could say of General Cameron, without offence, that he is not 'Democrat enough to hurt him.' I remember people used to say, without disturbing my self-respect, that I was not lawyer enough to hurt me."[46] Likening himself to swine scavenging for acorns in a forest, Lincoln described himself as "only a mast-fed lawyer."[47] According to one of the residents Lincoln visited when he rode the circuit, Lincoln was "aware of his inferiority as a lawyer" and was always ready to acknowledge it "with a smile or a good-natured remark."[48]

Herndon saw weakness in Lincoln's inability to be more deeply philosophical in his reasoning. In describing how to confound Lincoln, Herndon said, 'If you wished to be Cut off at the knee, just go at Lincoln with abstractions—glittering generalities—

indefiniteness—mistiness of idea or expression." In response to abstract thinking or arguments, Lincoln would "become vexed and sometimes foolishly so."[49] Yet, Lincoln chided Herndon, "Billy don't shoot too high—shoot low down, and the common people will understand you."[50] Rather than a defect, crafting his rhetoric to be understood by "the common people"—reminiscent of both Jackson's oratory, direct and unvarnished, and Clay's, which employed humorous and enlightening analogies—was one of Lincoln's defining strengths.

Lincoln's limitations as a lawyer were, however, dramatically exposed in two of his most important cases. In the first, *Todd Heirs v. Wickliffe*, Lincoln represented his father-in-law, Robert Todd, in an 1848 lawsuit. Todd claimed that Robert Wickliffe had illegally taken the property of Todd's cousin, Polly, after she had become Wickliffe's second wife. Polly's father had left her his vast estate, and her first husband and her son had died before Polly married Wickliffe. When she died, Todd claimed that he was the rightful heir to her estate under her father's will, which stipulated that if she had no living heirs, the estate would be split among the descendants of her father's brothers, which included Todd. The will, however, had disappeared. Lincoln represented the Todds, who maintained that Wickliffe had coerced Polly into marrying him and giving her estate to him in exchange for the right to purchase the release of her family's two slaves. (As a married woman, she had no right to purchase or sell property herself.) It appeared to be an open secret that one of the two slaves was in fact Polly's son, who would have been an heir to her estate but for the fact that as an African American slave he was not recognized as a person under Kentucky law, let alone having any of the rights or privileges of a propertied white man, including the right of inheritance. Lincoln tried mightily to prove the existence of the will, but in spite of testimony from John Todd Stuart's father that he had seen the document, the Kentucky courts, including the Kentucky Supreme Court, ruled in favor of Wickliffe as the heir to Polly's fortune. Lincoln knew that the case broke Robert Todd's heart, and did not speak of it for years.

In the other case, Lincoln had the rare opportunity to measure his talents against one of the nation's most famous and highly respected lawyers, Kenyon College–educated Edwin Stanton of Pittsburgh. In 1855, the Great Reaper Trial, as it was known, pitted a nearly penniless inventor from Rockford, Illinois, John Manny, and his partners against the wealthy industrialist Cyrus McCormick, Chicago's largest employer. Both Manny and McCormick manufactured agricultural reapers, and both held several patents, although the foundational patent on the McCormick reaper had expired, and therefore the original invention had entered the public domain and was free for anyone to use. McCormick sued Manny in federal court in Chicago, seeking to put him and his partners out of business. The Manny team decided it needed a lawyer who knew the local judge and the local law, and they hired Lincoln as their counsel. However, the case was eventually moved for the judge's convenience to Cincinnati, and Manny's team, who no longer had as much need for Lincoln's limited utility, brought in Edwin Stanton, later Buchanan's attorney general, as their main counsel. No one told Lincoln. Because it was a high-profile dispute and Manny's team had promised Lincoln one of the largest remunerations he was ever promised as a lawyer, $5,000, he spent considerable time on the matter, and was excited to travel to Cincinnati to make the closing arguments in the case. When Lincoln arrived, Stanton took one look and asked an associate, "Where did that long-armed baboon come from?"[51] Lincoln was told his services were no longer needed. He remained to watch Stanton argue the case. So impressed with Stanton's command of the law and the facts was he that Lincoln told his co-counsel, Ralph Emerson, "I am going home. I am going home to study law."[52] Emerson pleaded, "Mr. Lincoln, you stand at the head of the bar in Illinois now! What are you talking about?"[53] Lincoln responded, "I do occupy a good position there, and I think I can get along with the way things are done there now. But these college-trained men, who have devoted their whole lives to study, are coming West, don't you see? And they study their cases as we never do. They have got as far as Cincinnati now. They will soon be in Illinois."[54]

After a pause, he added, "I am as good as any of them, and when they get out to Illinois I will be ready for them."[55]

Lincoln's varied clientele reflected his pragmatism to earn his living however he could. Whereas Stephen Douglas was perfectly aligned with the interests of big business, Lincoln's practice showed him how the law worked on the ground, its effect on everyday citizens, not just elite businesses. All of this deepened his ability to identify with the common man, because he did legal work for common men nearly every day. It also sensitized him to how status often drove the application of the law, as he saw firsthand that women and slaves were not afforded the Constitution's promise that all would be treated equally.

Lincoln's law practice kept him busy—so busy that he claimed he did not have time to travel a hundred miles to attend the funeral of his father, who died on January 17, 1851. Lincoln's stepbrother had urged him to see Thomas before he died, as well as to come to the funeral, but Lincoln demurred. "Say to him that if we could meet now, it is doubtful whether it would not be more painful than pleasant." In his life, Lincoln never had a kind or positive word to say about his father and, in the years after his death, spoke of Thomas only in ways that elevated his own image of himself as a "self-made man" and denigrated his father as squandering his own chances to make something of himself.

The skills Lincoln refined as a lawyer were as important for his political career as they were for his legal practice. In 1850, he advised young law students, "Discourage litigation. Persuade your neighbors to compromise whenever you can. Point out to them how the nominal winner is often the real loser—in fees, expenses, and waste of time. As a peacemaker the lawyer has the superior opportunity of being a good man. There will still be business enough." He stressed, "Never stir up litigation. A worse man can scarcely be found than one who does this. Who can be more nearly a fiend than he who habitually overhauls the register of deeds in search of defects in titles, whereon to stir up strife, and put money in his pocket? A moral tone ought to be infused into the profession which should drive such men out of it."[56] In 1842, Lincoln had told the Springfield Washington Temperance Society, "When the conduct of men is designed to be influenced, persuasion, kind, unassuming persuasion, should ever be adopted. It is an old and true maxim that a 'drop of honey catches more flies than a gallon of gall.' So with men. If you would win a man to your cause, first convince him that you are his sincere friend."[57]

Such advice was not as obvious as it might seem. Litigation was almost universally understood as the path for a lawyer to achieve prominence in his community or state, and thus it was quite tempting to treat the other side as the enemy. A focus on mutual accommodation clashed with the combative nature of the court system and couldn't yield the thrill of winning and crushing your opponent. Lincoln told young law students about the importance of both persuasion and preparation, two skills crucial to success in law and politics. In 1850, he explained, "Extemporaneous speaking should be practiced and cultivated. It is the lawyer's avenue to the public. However able and faithful he may be in other respects, people are slow to bring him business if he cannot make a speech."[58]

One observer said, "He never considered anything he had written to be finished until published, or if a speech, until it was delivered."[59] Lincoln also "habitually studied the opposite side of every disputed question, of every law case, of every political issue, more exhaustively, if possible, than his own side. He said that the result had been, that in all his long practice at the bar he had never once been surprised in court by the strength of his adversary's case—often finding it much weaker than he had feared."[60]

The advice Lincoln gave in 1850 applied to everything he said and did in politics and law, both before and especially later—to be a "peacemaker," to speak with "a moral tone," to find "compromise" whenever possible, to listen to what others had to say, to learn from his failures, to study opponents' arguments for their strengths and weaknesses, to persuade people with "a compliment," and to make friends of your enemies. This was the creed of Clay.

IV

In 1850, Henry Clay looked at the first year of Zachary Taylor's presidency and concluded, "I have never seen such an administration. There is very little co-operation or concord between the two ends of the avenue. There is not, I believe, a prominent Whig in either house that has any confidential intercourse with the Executive."[61] Lincoln agreed. There was no prominent Whig leader in the Cabinet, either. Taylor left filling vacancies within the administration to his Cabinet heads, but they felt little loyalty to Taylor or his policies. The ensuing disorder was compounded by Taylor's refusal to abide by one of the central tenets of the Whig Party—presidential deference to the will of both Congress and the Cabinet. In one of his few acts as president before he died, William Henry Harrison had rejected that practice as well, arguing that he, not they, was elected to office and their job was to advise him, not the other way around. Taylor followed suit, and, like Harrison, found himself at odds with his own Cabinet.

Taylor's next move infuriated the Whig faithful further. As a presidential candidate, Taylor had gone to great lengths to assure loyal Whig voters that he shared their principles of governance. In the second of the letters that he had written to his brother-in-law John Allison, he had reemphasized that "I am not prepared to force Congress, by coercion of the veto, to pass laws to suit me or to pass none."[62] Though Taylor had made no reference to those principles in his first public statement following his election, many Whigs were reassured by his declaration in his Inaugural Address that "it is for the wisdom of Congress itself, in which all legislative powers are vested by the Constitution, to regulate [various] matters of domestic policy."[63] He went further, at that time, to say, "I shall look with confidence to the enlightened patriotism of that body to adopt such measures of conciliation as may harmonize conflicting interests and tend to perpetuate the Union which should be the paramount object of our hopes and affections."[64]

However, in Taylor's first—and, as it turned out, only—Annual Message to Congress (delivered at the end of 1849), the fears of his Whig constituents were fully realized: rather than wait for any lead or signal from Congress, he laid out the bold proposal for Congress to admit California and New Mexico separately as new states into the Union and leave each of them to decide how they would handle the issue of slavery. While Taylor recognized that Congress had complete discretion to condition the admission of a new state on any basis it chose, he made clear that his proposal should be the first and only order of business in Congress. Everyone knew that if Taylor's plan were followed, it would tip the balance of power in Congress in favor of antislavery forces, because both California and New Mexico were disposed to endorse antislavery constitutions and the Senate was at that time evenly split between slave and free states. Many Whigs liked the idea of weakening the slaveholders' power in Congress, but they liked even less that Taylor was demanding that they do as he directed. Taylor stuck by his proposal because he believed it would avoid, rather than provoke, a nasty fight in Congress over extending slavery into the territories. He thought the plan had the further advantage of respecting popular sovereignty, because it would have allowed each territory to choose for itself in its constitution whether to allow or prohibit slavery. Most members of Congress, including Stephen Douglas (who considered himself the principal champion of popular sovereignty), objected to Taylor's plan because they either disagreed with it substantively or objected to his making demands of Congress rather than following its will. House leaders refused to take any action on his plan, while Senate leaders refused to act on hundreds of his nominations to positions requiring confirmation. Taylor then set a record for making the most recess appointments by any president till then.

New Mexico responded to the president's plan immediately by applying for statehood under an antislavery constitution. Texas authorities had other ideas. To expand the domain of slavery, they threatened to acquire, by force if necessary, all the New Mexico land east of the Rio Grande, including Santa Fe. They declared that it belonged to them and threatened civil war if the United States tried to stop them.

The prospect of war didn't deter Taylor; indeed, it strengthened his resolve. In February 1850, he met with Southern leaders in Congress and warned them that anyone "taken in rebellion against the Union, he would hang . . . with less reluctance than he had hanged deserters and spies in Mexico."[65] He sent federal troops to Santa Fe and directed the colonel in charge to prepare his men to rebuff any invasion of New Mexico. These soldiers kept Texas forces at bay. Taylor made clear that if Texas made any aggressive move to capture any portion of New Mexico, he would lead federal troops in response.

Taylor tried repeatedly but unsuccessfully to persuade Democrats and Southern Whigs that his plan was the best possible compromise because it gave "the North substance of the Wilmot Proviso but without forcing the South to swallow it as a formally enacted principle."[66] The fact that Taylor's chief defender in the Senate was Andrew Jackson's old Democratic ally, Thomas Benton of Missouri, revealed how much Taylor's leadership violated Whig principles. Not only that, but Southern Whigs, led by Henry Clay, responded with their own proposal that included a fugitive slave law. Whereas Clay favored a compromise that helped the slave power, Taylor did not, objecting that it would have drawn the federal government into supporting slavery and would have ripped the Union apart. Southern Whigs, including Clay, were outraged by Taylor's threatened veto of the compromise because they believed, in accordance with Whig orthodoxy, that a president should veto only measures that are clearly unconstitutional, and since the Constitution at that time recognized slavery (for example, in calculating the populations of congressional districts), their legislation did not exceed that threshold. Accordingly, on May 21, 1850, Clay formally broke with Taylor, arguing that Taylor, "entertaining that constitutional deference to the wisdom of Congress which he had professed, and abstaining from any interference with its free deliberations, ought, without any dissatisfaction, to permit us to consider what is best for our common country."[67]

Taylor again warned Southern Democrats that they would be worse off if they failed to support his proposal. He argued that their opposition ran the risk of motivating Congress to approve the Wilmot Proviso to ban slavery in any of the territory acquired from Mexico in the Mexican-American War, which, he made clear, he believed was constitutional. In response, several Southern Democrats, including Mississippi senator Jefferson Davis, declared their opposition to Taylor's plan because it enabled antislavery forces to become a majority in the Senate—after already controlling the House—and thus provided a back door through which to enact the Wilmot Proviso. When other Southern Democrats, including John Calhoun in his last statement on the floor of the Senate, threatened secession rather than accept Taylor's plan, the president issued his own threat—to use military force to stop any secession movement. He was ready to stop Texas aggression *and* Southern secession.

By the spring, with war threatening on two fronts, Taylor's problems with his Cabinet worsened. On one front, Taylor had managed, in his lame efforts to secure geographical balance, to exclude anyone from the Northeast. Thus the only contingent that actually supported his plan, the Northern Whigs, were absent from his team. At the same time, a scandal of unprecedented proportions threatened to rip Taylor's administration apart. His attorney general, Reverdy Johnson, had authorized Treasury Secretary William Meredith to pay the full amount of the interest on a claim that the Galphin family had made against the U.S. government for wrongfully seizing control of their family estate in Georgia in 1773. When it became known that just before Taylor took office Congress had enacted a law directing that the interest should be five times the size of the principal and that half of the principal and half of the interest were owed to Taylor's war secretary, George Crawford, for his legal services on behalf of the Galphin family, a public outcry arose. The matter festered for months, while the House considered censuring not only Cabinet members Johnson, Crawford, and Meredith but perhaps also Taylor. Under intense pressure from Congress to get his administration in order, Taylor considered firing his entire Cabinet to remove any appearance of

corruption within his administration. Not satisfied with that response from Taylor, some House leaders considered initiating an
impeachment inquiry against Taylor for allowing such corruption
to fester in his administration.

With a stalemate in Congress over the admission of the two new
states and a threat of impeachment hanging over him, Taylor reluctantly made plans to reorganize his administration. It included
dismissing his entire Cabinet. Taylor knew Jackson and Tyler had
each removed their Cabinets entirely, so neither he nor his able
attorney general, Reverdy Johnson, had any doubts that he had
the power to do the same thing. As Taylor prepared to go public
with his plans, he died unexpectedly from either a stomach virus
or cholera on July 9, 1850.

Back in Springfield, Abraham Lincoln was as stunned as most
Whigs to read about the turmoil in Taylor's Cabinet and the im-
passe over admission of California and New Mexico. Now Taylor's
death left nearly all of them speechless—all but Lincoln. He was
one of the few prominent Whigs who took the opportunity to eulogize the late president. He put aside his disappointment in not
securing an appointment with the Taylor administration, the debacle of Taylor's Cabinet appointments, and the anger over Taylor's
break with Clay. Long overshadowed by the tribute that he would
offer his idol Henry Clay two years later, this eulogy reveals Lincoln's significant affinities for his subjects—a fondness sculpted by a
great deal of selective recall. In its fourth sentence, Lincoln notes
that Taylor's "youth was passed among the pioneers of Kentucky,
whither his parents emigrated soon after his birth; and where his
taste for military life, probably inherited, was greatly stimulated."[68]
Lincoln said nothing of the time Taylor spent in any other state,
particularly Louisiana, where he had owned a plantation with
slaves.[69]

Zachary Taylor came into prominence and the presidency because of his military career, and Lincoln's eulogy was devoted almost entirely to that period of his life. Yet the fact that Polk picked
Taylor as his initial commanding general in Mexico went without
comment.[70] Nor did Lincoln mention that Polk had removed Tay-

lor from command in Mexico.[71] Instead, Lincoln recalled the fallen heroes in that "last battle" of Taylor's, including Henry Clay's son, as well as John Hardin, his onetime friend and rival. "Passing in review, General Taylor's military history, some striking peculiarities will appear."[72] For Lincoln, the first was this:

> *No one of the six battles which he fought, excepting perhaps, that of Monterey, presented a field, which would have been selected by an ambitious captain upon which to gather laurels. So far as fame was concerned, the prospect—the promise in advance, was, "you may lose, but you can not win." Yet Taylor, in his blunt business-like view of things, seems never to have thought of this.*[73]

Lincoln found most significant the fact that "it did not happen to Gen. Taylor once in his life, to fight a battle on equal terms, or on terms advantageous to himself—and yet he was never beaten, and never retreated. In *all*, the odds was greatly against him; in each, defeat seemed inevitable; and yet *in all*, he triumphed."[74] Lincoln did not have to mention the race for the presidency, since that turned out just as every other battle in Taylor's life did, with Taylor prevailing in the end. "Wherever he has led," Lincoln noted, "while the battle still raged, the issue was painfully doubtful; yet in *each* and *all*, when the din had ceased, and the smoke had blown away, our country's flag was still seen, fluttering in the breeze."[75]

Though Lincoln had never seen, much less participated in, an actual battle, he recognized the greatness in Taylor as a military commander. Lincoln declared, "General Taylor's battles were not distinguished for brilliant military maneuvers; but in all, he seems rather to have conquered by the exercise of a sober and steady judgment, coupled with a dogged incapacity to understand that defeat was possible." Here was Lincoln delivering his greatest acclamation for Taylor and most aspirational for himself and the country. "His rarest military trait," Lincoln said of Taylor, "was a combination of negatives—absence of excitement and absence of fear. He could not be flurried, and he could not be scared."[76] At the precise time in Lincoln's life when he had reason to be scared that he might never win another campaign or achieve the fame he desperately desired, Taylor's capacity to be unafraid of failure was inspiring.

> *It is perhaps enough to say—and it is far from the least of his honors that we can truly say—that of the many who served with him through the long course of forty years, all testify to the uniform kindness, and his constant care for, and hearty sympathy with, their every want and every suffering; while none can be found to declare, that he was ever a tyrant anywhere, in anything.*[77]

The "tyrant" was a not so subtle reference to the difference between Taylor and the Democratic presidents who preceded him. He was not, in other words, disposed to be a Jackson, a Tyler, or a Polk. Lincoln did not yet know all of the men who would look back with gratitude at Taylor's "uniform kindness" as a leader and mentor, but on the night of Taylor's inauguration, he had likely met two of them—Robert E. Lee and Jefferson Davis.

While Lincoln was serving in the Black Hawk War, Taylor's daughter, Sarah, had met and fallen in love with Davis, who was a lieutenant under Taylor's captaincy. Taylor opposed the marriage because he thought the life of a military wife would be too hard for her. Davis then resigned from the service, and the two were married with Taylor's blessing in 1835. For their honeymoon, Davis brought her back to his family's plantation in Mississippi, where she contracted malaria and died just a few months later. Taylor vowed never to forgive Davis, but after nearly a decade of not speaking to each other Davis returned to the army, the two men reconciled, and Davis served with distinction under Taylor during the Mexican War. Later, shortly after Taylor's election, Taylor told Davis to follow his personal and constitutional convictions without fear of losing Taylor's respect. In turn, Davis was one of the three senators who planned Taylor's inauguration, though he vigorously opposed his policies. The two kept in touch, though they never discussed politics. Davis was at Taylor's bedside when he died, and he persuaded House leaders to put aside the movement to censure Taylor after his death. In his eulogy, Davis defended Taylor's proposals on California and New Mexico as the only way to preserve the opportunity for Congress to peaceably settle the boundaries of Texas and New Mexico.

Lincoln could only stand in awe of a man who could earn the allegiance of a fierce proslavery senator like Davis *and* a fierce abolitionist like William Seward, who was widely believed to be Taylor's closest confidant. Taylor was the model of a man who could separate politics from the personal in order to maintain bridges across the chasm of political differences defining his time.

Having lauded Taylor for his military prowess and lack of any pretensions or arrogance, Lincoln moved next to the "point of time" when "Taylor began to be named for the next Presidency."[78] He noted, "The incidents of his administration up to the time of his death, are too familiar and too fresh to require any direct repetition."[79] Thus Lincoln was able to gloss over most of the chaos of Taylor's fifteen months in office. After all, Lincoln said, "The Presidency, even to the most experienced politicians, is no bed of roses; and General Taylor like others, found thorns within it."[80] In apparent acknowledgment of the hostile House he faced at the time of his death, Lincoln observed, "No human being can fill that station and escape censure. Still I hope and believe, when General Taylor's official conduct shall come to be viewed in the calm light of history, he will be found to have deserved as little as any who have succeeded him."[81]

Of Taylor's death, Lincoln could not help but wonder "what will be its effect, politically, upon the country."[82] Lincoln knew, as did the nation, that Taylor's death elevated to the presidency an old-line Whig—his vice president, Millard Fillmore. "I will not pretend to believe," Lincoln expressed hopefully, "that all the wisdom, or all the patriotism of the country, died with General Taylor."[83] Yet as a close student of the news printed in the Whig papers that he religiously read, Lincoln expected Fillmore to be hard pressed by Clay, Douglas, and others to bend too far in favor of the slave power to spare the country from a civil war. "I fear," Lincoln then said, "the one great question of the day, is not now so likely to be partially acquiesced in by the different sections of the Union, as it would have been, could General Taylor have been spared to us."[84]

This was as far as Lincoln would go to opine on the choices facing the nation, but he knew whom he hoped would come up with the answer. "Yet, under all the circumstances, trusting to our Maker, and through his wisdom and beneficence, to the great body of our people"—meaning, in Lincoln's parlance, the Congress— "we will not despair, nor despond."[85]

Before Lincoln closed with a quotation from the Gospels, a hymn from Isaac Watts (the "Godfather of English hymnody"), and several stanzas from one of Lincoln's favorite poets, William Knox,[86] he reminded the audience of its "duty." He repeated the word three times,[87] emphasizing that he expected "the American people" and their leaders to undertake it now that Taylor was dead.[88] In closing, Lincoln said,

> The death of the late President may not be without its use, in reminding us, that we, too, must die. Death, abstractly considered, is the same with the high as with the low; but practically, we are not so much aroused to the contemplation of our own mortal natures, by the fall of many undistinguished, as that of one great, and well known, name. By the latter, we are forced to muse, and ponder, sadly.[89]

The prospect of "duty and death" bracketed not just Taylor's life but Lincoln's own.

V

Millard Fillmore was not much better known in 1850 than he is today. Taylor had barely given a second thought to the selection of his vice president, either at the convention or once they were in office. Their differences defined their relationship, or lack of one. At six feet, Fillmore towered over the short, weather-beaten ex-soldier. As a young man, Fillmore was regarded as strikingly handsome with brown wavy hair. Now his hair was white, and he had gained nearly fifty pounds. Prior to his selection as a compromise choice to be Taylor's running mate, Fillmore had chaired the powerful House Ways and Means Committee. He tried but failed to win the House speakership in 1841 and New York's governorship in 1844. He arrived at the convention as New York's comptroller, a particularly unimpressive credential, but his nomination appealed to the delegates because he came from a rival wing of the party to that of Seward and Weed, who were already suspected of having positioned themselves to wield enormous influence within the administration if Taylor won. Thus Fillmore's addition to the ticket was not only supposed to broaden Taylor's support within the party but check the oversized influence of Seward and Weed.

The plan failed. Taylor ignored Fillmore. Taylor didn't listen to him; indeed, he barely let Fillmore say anything in his presence.

Fillmore knew Lincoln but was unimpressed. As a modestly successful lawyer from the West, Lincoln offered little of interest to the new president as a one-term Whig congressman who told entertaining stories. Thurlow Weed, ever the self-interested matchmaker, arranged the first meeting between the two men in Albany, New York, on September 24, 1848. Weed had been instrumental to Taylor's nomination, and he was the force behind William Seward's rise in American politics. As someone who appeared aligned with Seward, Lincoln knew he could expect little if anything from Fillmore. Whatever was discussed at their meeting, it led nowhere. Lincoln never bothered to apply for any government post while Fillmore was president. The two men did not meet again in person until after Fillmore left office.

Even before Taylor died in July 1850, Fillmore had told Clay that he intended, if he got the chance, to cast the tie-breaking vote to approve a compromise bill. Taylor had been angry over the news, for Fillmore seemed disposed to accept *any* compromise with the slave power, not just the one Clay forged. On the day that Fillmore became president, he told Daniel Webster, then a key proponent for compromise in the Senate, that he was withdrawing Taylor's plan and was willing to accept any reasonable agreement approved by Congress. On Fillmore's second day as president, the entire Cabinet resigned in protest over his pledge to Webster. Fillmore promptly accepted the resignations and underscored them by appointing Webster as secretary of state. Webster accepted the job, correctly realizing that his selection was a confirmation of Fillmore's intention to approve any legislative compromise. Others in Congress read it the same way.

Meanwhile, Clay was trying to craft an agreement through a series of separate bills, each appeasing a different constituency in Congress. Nearly six months before Taylor died, he began introducing these bills in a set of speeches that would eventually be remembered as among his greatest. Clay ended the first of them with a clever piece of theater. He said a man had come to his hotel earlier that day and given him "a precious relic."[90] Clay paused, and then produced it: "It is a fragment of the coffin of Washington."[91] He rhetorically asked if this relic was a bad omen for the Union and answered, "No, sir, no."[92] It was instead a warning for Congress "to beware, to pause, to reflect before they lend themselves to any purposes which shall destroy the Union which was cemented by his exertions and example."[93] The story never happened, but it served Clay's purposes.

Two months later, Clay delivered one of his longest and most memorable speeches, on February 5, 1850, to plead for a compromise to save the Union. Warning that disunion was an imminent threat, he begged his fellow senators, from both the North and the South, to "pause" before they took the final steps to destroy the Union through bloody civil war. He proposed a plan that had three goals: to settle once and for all every question arising from the problem of slavery; to craft a compromise that required neither side to sacrifice its core principles; and to ask the opposing sides to make concessions, "not of principle," but "of feeling, of opinion."[94] He called for mutual forbearance from both parties, saying that flexibility would not be easy for either side, but asking each to overcome their distrust of the other or face the destruction of all they held dear.

The next day, Clay returned to the floor of the Senate to continue pressing his case. He again predicted that secession—as threatened by John Calhoun and Jefferson Davis—meant civil war. Staring at Fillmore, who was sitting as the presiding officer of the Senate, Clay declared,

> *I am directly opposed to any purpose of secession or separation. I am for staying within the Union, and for defying any portion of this confederacy to expel or drive me out of the Union. I am for staying within the Union, and fighting for my rights, if necessary, with the sword, within the bounds and under the safeguard of the Union. . . . Here I am within it, and here I mean to stand and die.*[95]

He then concluded his two-day plea:

> *I implore gentlemen, I adjure them, whether from the South or the North, by all that they hold dear in this world—by all their love of liberty—by all their veneration for their ancestors—by all their regard for posterity—by all their gratitude to Him who has bestowed on them such unnumbered and countless blessings—by all the duties which they owe to mankind—and all the duties they owe to themselves, to pause, solemnly to pause at the edge of the precipice, before the fearful and dangerous leap is taken into the yawning abyss below. . . .*[96]

Clay took one final pause, again looking directly at Fillmore. "I implore, as the best blessing which Heaven can bestow upon me, upon earth, that if the direful event of the dissolution of the Union is to happen, I shall not survive to behold the sad and heart-rending spectacle."[97]

On March 7, 1850, Daniel Webster joined the debate with one of his finest speeches—some think the greatest he ever gave—declaring at the outset that "I speak today for the preservation of the Union."[98] After pleading for compromise between the contending sides, he concluded,

We have a great, popular, constitutional government, guarded by law and by judicature, and defended by the affections of the whole people. No monarchial throne presses these States together, no iron chain of military power encircles them; they live and stand under a government popular in its form, representative in its character, founded upon principles of equality, and so constructed, we hope, as to last forever.[99]

These words foreshadowed an even more troubling declaration he would make later, after Taylor's death, which would effectively acknowledge the legitimacy of secession.

Less than a week later, Seward denounced the slave power on the floor of the Senate in the harshest terms possible. He acknowledged that the Constitution provided for the recapture of fugitive slaves. "But," he proclaimed, "there is a higher law than the Constitution. God's law made slavery immoral and illegitimate, and God's law commanded Christians to disobey laws, which they deemed unjust. Slavery subverted democracy."[100] Seward scolded his colleagues, "I confess that the most alarming evidence of our degeneracy which has yet been given is found in the fact that we even debate such a question."[101] He dismissed threats of secession as mere bombast. Inflaming the public did not bother him; he dared Congress to do the only sensible, principled, moral thing to do—end slavery. "Whatever choice you have made for yourselves," he suggested, "let us have no partial freedom; let us all be free."[102]

At the end of March 1850, South Carolina's John Calhoun died of tuberculosis. Earlier that month, he had foreseen the kinds of arguments Seward and others would make and had asked a colleague, James Mason of Virginia, to read what became Calhoun's last statement on the floor of the Senate. Characteristically, it was a zealous defense of both slavery and secession. The prospect of war did not bother Calhoun. "What is it that has endangered the Union?"[103] Calhoun had Mason ask rhetorically. The answer, for Calhoun, was the persistent meddling from outsiders with the "equilibrium between" the North and the South on the institution of slavery at the time of the founding.[104] The movement to admit California into the Union threatened to create "disequilibrium" in the Union. "If you admit her under all the difficulties that oppose her admission," Mason read, "you compel us to infer that you intend to exclude us from the whole of the acquired territories."[105] Calhoun argued that slavery was sanctioned in the original Constitution and therefore was indissoluble. The "agitation" over slavery portended disunion, and Calhoun wrote that the only protection against such disunion was to guarantee slavery in the acquired territories.[106] He went further to call for a constitutional amendment to restore to the South "in substance the power she possessed of protecting herself before the equilibrium between the sections was destroyed by the action of this government."[107] He ended by suggesting that it was entirely up to the North, not the South, to decide if and how the "great questions" could be settled.[108] He emphasized that it should all be done on the South's terms: "If you who represent the stronger portion" of the Union "cannot agree to settle" these questions "on the broad principle of justice and duty, say so; and let the states we represent agree to separate and part in peace."[109] But, he warned at the end, "If you are willing we should part in peace, tell us so, and we shall know what to do when you reduce the question to submission or resistance."[110]

When Calhoun died, several senators praised his legacy, while many others denounced it. Henry Clay rose to honor Calhoun as a long-serving Senate colleague. Calhoun and Clay had battled against each other more than once for the presidency, but they had been allies early in their careers in agreeing on the need for internal improvements to connect the states more tightly together in one Union. "He has gone!" Clay cried, and lamented further,

> No more shall we witness from yonder seat the flashes of that keen and penetrating eye of his, darting through this chamber. No more shall we be thrilled by that torrent of clear, concise, compact logic, poured out from his lips, which, if it did not always carry conviction to our judgment, commanded our great admiration.[111]

Clay cleverly used words beginning with hard *c* to subliminally reinforce a connection between adjective and subject. Webster

praised Calhoun's "undoubted genius,"[112] while Democratic senator Thomas Hart Benton warned his colleagues, "He is not dead,
sir—he is not dead. There may be no vitality in his body but there
is in his doctrines. Calhoun died with treason in his heart and on
his lips. Whilst I am discharging my duty here, his disciples are
disseminating his poison all over my state."[113]

But, in the weeks immediately after Taylor's death, compromise
was elusive, even though Fillmore was now in the White House.
Fillmore was dull but a true Clay Whig, who was disposed to follow the lead of Congress. Clay's health continued to deteriorate,
and on July 22, he rose for the last time to speak in his beloved
Senate. Though physically drained, Clay held the floor for more
than four hours. He did not begin with his usual dramatic flourish
but instead peppered his comments with harsh asides directed at
opposing senators. His tone was patronizing and angry because
Southern senators had made no concessions to save the Union but
instead offered fiery defenses of slavery and their right to maintain
it and extend it into U.S. territories. Defending the omnibus bill that
he had offered as the only option that could bridge the gulf between
the contending sides, Clay said, "There is neither incongruity in the
freight nor in the passengers on board of our 'Omnibus.' . . . We
have no Africans or Abolitionists in *our* 'Omnibus,' no disunionists
or Free Soilers, no Jew or Gentile. Our passengers consist of Democrats and Whigs," who had abandoned their customary antago-
nisms to confront the nation's crises like patriots.[114]

At one point, Clay condescendingly asked, "What is a compromise? It is a work of mutual concession—an agreement in which
there are reciprocal stipulations."[115] Uncharacteristically, but desperate for compromise, Clay defended slave-owners as benign
masters, not monsters, and depicted abolitionists as the genuinely
bad actors "who would go into the temples of the holy God and
drag from their sacred posts the ministers who are preaching his
gospel for the comfort of mankind,"[116] and who, "if their power
was equal to their malignity, would seize the sun of this great
system of ours, drag it from the position in which it keeps in order the whole planetary bodies of the universe, and replunge the

world in chaos and confusion to carry out their single idea."[117] Yet he also accused the extremists in the South of inviting war by arbitrarily interpreting the Constitution to suit their own interests. He pleaded: "All we want is the Constitution."[118] These extremists, too, had lost the ability to listen to the other side, he said, and their desire to carry slaves westward to the south of the Missouri Compromise line exposed the fundamental and hopeless contradiction at the heart of their position: "You cannot do it without an assumption of power upon the part of Congress to act upon the institution of slavery; and if they have the power in one way, they have the power to act upon it in the other way."[119]

Not even Clay knew that he was making the point that years later Lincoln would push Douglas to acknowledge in their great debates. In this debate, Clay asked (as Lincoln would almost a decade later), "What more can the South ask?" The compromise Clay was struggling to forge would have killed the Wilmot Proviso, strengthened the Fugitive Slave Law, and barred abolition in the District of Columbia. His omnibus bill remained, in his judgment, everyone else's best option; it "was the vehicle of the people, of the mass of the people."[120] Without the bill, Clay warned, there would be war not only in Texas and New Mexico but throughout the country, for "the end of war is never seen in the beginning of war."[121] Americans wanted no war, he declared. "The nation . . . pants for repose, and entreats you to give it peace and tranquility."[122] Reaching for one final metaphor, he declared, "I believe from the bottom of my soul, that the measure is the re-union of this Union. I believe it is the dove of peace, which, taking its aerial flight from the dome of the Capitol, carries the glad tidings of assured peace and restored harmony to all the remotest extremities of this distracted land."[123] He collapsed in his seat as the galleries erupted in tears and applause.

Nevertheless, the speech failed to garner a majority for any of the bills that Clay had introduced to save the Union. Dejected and sick, Clay left Washington for a desperately needed break.

At that point, Stephen Douglas, the Senate's youngest member, jumped into the center of the national stage. Clay had tried for half a year to move the Senate to compromise, but Douglas, chair of the powerful Senate Committee on Territories, needed only a few days to broker the deal that the Senate approved. It was not his speech that saved the compromise, though he had spoken for two days in March to assert his solution to the dilemma facing the country—popular sovereignty, letting a majority of white men in each territory and state decide whether to allow or bar slavery. Rather, it was his indefatigable work behind the scenes, tirelessly lobbying as the younger Clay had done, stitching together the different Senate coalitions that eventually supported each of the five bills that formed the historic Compromise of 1850. Clay, having briefly returned to Congress, worked by Douglas's side to help House leaders overcome opposition from Northern Whigs to approve the Compromise of 1850. With this success, the thirty-seven-year-old Douglas had established himself as a force to be reckoned with.

There were two essential steps left to put the Compromise of 1850 into effect. First, Fillmore signed each of the five bills into law—admitting California as a new state, abolishing the slave trade in the District of Columbia, organizing New Mexico and Utah as new territories, resolving the border dispute between Texas and New Mexico, and approving the Fugitive Slave Act of 1850, which required that all escaped slaves, upon capture, be returned to their masters with the cooperation or assistance of officials and citizens of the free states. Together, Fillmore declared, these bills provided "a final settlement of the dangerous and exciting subjects which they embraced."[124]

Now law, the compromise required a second element, no less important, to go into effect: enforcement. Fillmore, as well as Secretary of State Webster, promised to vigorously enforce each provision, including the Fugitive Slave Act. When nine Northern states enacted personal-liberty laws later in 1850 and in 1851, forbidding state officials from enforcing the Fugitive Slave Law or using their jails in fugitive slave cases, both Fillmore and Webster defended the law and denounced any such resistance as treacherous and no different from nullification and secession, both of which were unconstitutional. Fillmore even promised to send federal forces to Boston to put down riots against the law. In May 1851, the president and his Cabinet took the first train from New York City to the shores of Lake Erie to celebrate completion of the Erie Railroad. Along the way, Webster made side trips to defend the Fugitive Slave Law in Syracuse, Buffalo, and Albany. In Syracuse, he denounced the refusal to abide by federal law as treason.[125] In Buffalo, he used the metaphor of a "house divided" to stress the need to "preserve the Union of the States, not by coercion—not by military power—not by angry controversies . . . but by the silken chords of mutual, fraternal, patriotic affection."[126] He reminded his audience that the Constitution, through its supremacy clause, made federal law supreme over state resistance, and he promised "to exert any power I had to keep that country together."[127]

In June 1851, Webster went a step too far in his argument. In Virginia, he likened the Constitution to a compact, in which no party had the freedom to ignore a provision that the parties had originally consented to. "A bargain cannot be broken on one side, and still bind the other side," he said.[128] "I am as ready to fight and to fall for the constitutional rights of Virginia as I am for those of Massachusetts. . . . I would no more see a feather plucked unjustly from the honor of Virginia than I would see one so plucked from the honor of Massachusetts."[129] Naturally, slaveholders took his language to mean that Webster supported secession, inferring from the Constitution's barring any federal interference with slavery before 1808 as tacit recognition of its legality. Webster spent the remainder of his life trying to explain that he never intended that interpretation and that his wording, though infelicitous, was nonetheless consistent with his support of the Union.

The secession question was intertwined with the issue of the extent to which the Constitution permitted the federal government to regulate slavery or required protecting it. Back in Illinois, Lincoln followed the great debate in newspapers and correspondence. Lots of people, including Whigs like Lincoln, read Webster's comments as accepting the legitimacy of secession and confirming what Lincoln and many other Whigs had suspected for some time—that there could be no real compromise possible between those who demanded abolition and those who demanded the protection and expansion of slavery. As early as 1850, John Todd Stuart had told Lincoln that he predicted that soon all men would have to choose between abolitionism and the Democratic Party.[130] Stuart leaned in favor of joining the latter, while Lincoln agreed the choice had to be made but added, "in an Emphatic tone" that, "when that time comes my mind is made up. The Slavery question can't be compromised."[131]

VI

Henry Clay never returned to the Senate. Too ill to go home to Lexington, he died of tuberculosis in Washington on June 29, 1852. Rutgers College president Theodore Frelinghuysen, a former senator and Clay's running mate in 1844, delivered his eulogy in Washington. In Congress, members of each chamber rose to pay homage to Clay, and there was an outpouring of eulogies around the country.

Eight days after Clay's death, Abraham Lincoln delivered his. Eulogies are notoriously unreliable, for they tend to accentuate, if not overstate, the positive. (Clay's for Calhoun was a perfect example.) This was no doubt as true of the eulogies given by former colleagues and rivals of Clay as it was of Lincoln's. His eulogy was noteworthy because it was his highest-profile address since leaving Congress, and he had arranged, with editors he'd known in Illinois and met in Washington, for the eulogy to be printed in newspapers all over the country.

Today, people read Lincoln's eulogy of Clay for how it illuminates Lincoln's vision of himself. At the time he delivered and distributed it, his tribute reminded Whigs that he was still alive and well and one of them. Speaking at a podium at the front of the Hall of Representatives in the Illinois state capitol, he could not have asked for a more dramatic setting, and if anyone had previously missed Lincoln's persistent declarations of fealty to Clay, they could not miss them now.

Lincoln began, as Clay and classical funeral orations characteristically did, with an acknowledgment of the circumstances. Just a few days before, the nation had celebrated Independence Day, and Lincoln recognized that Clay's life and the life of the United States had nearly been identical; Clay was born one year after independence from Britain. As Lincoln remarked, "The infant nation, and the infant child began the race of life together. For three quarters of a century they have travelled hand in hand. They have been companions ever."[132] He reminded his audience of the crucible that the nation had been fused in then, perhaps not unlike those that forged Clay's character in public life. "The nation has passed its perils, and is free, prosperous, and powerful. The child has reached his manhood, his middle age, his old age, and is dead. In all that concerned the nation the man ever sympathized; and now the nation mourns for the man."[133]

Lincoln knew that the Whig Party, which Clay had built and Lincoln had long supported, was splintering under the stress of the Compromise of 1850. It had always been Clay's greatest aspiration to place the country's needs above his own and those of his party. Lincoln cleverly elaborated on that theme by quoting from "one of the public Journals, opposed to him politically."[134] What followed (the longest quote from another source in the eulogy) underscored Clay's patriotism.

> Ah, it is at times like these, that the petty distinctions of mere party disappear. We see only the great, the grand, the noble features of the departed statesman. . . . Henry Clay belonged to his country—to the world; mere party cannot claim men like him. His career has been national, his fame has filled the earth, his memory will endure to the last syllable of recorded time.[135]

Lincoln quoted the journal's description of the distinctive attributes of Clay's patriotism, noting that his "character and fame are national property."[136] This portion echoed the epitaph that Clay had written for his tombstone: "He knew no North, no South, no East, no West, but only the Union, which held them all in its sacred circle, so now his countrymen will know no grief, that is not as widespread as the bounds of the confederacy."[137]

Lincoln, drawing his words from the same source, recalled Clay's remarkable career of public service, trying to bring peace whenever and wherever he could, through deeds and words: "'His eloquence has not been surpassed. In the effective power to move the heart of man, Clay was without an equal.'" In the fights that threatened to rip the Union apart, he "'has quelled our civil commotions, by a power and influence, which belonged to no other statesman of his age and times.'"[138]

Lincoln then began to sketch in his own words the course of Clay's life. He remarked that "Mr. Clay's lack of a more perfect early education, however it may be regretted generally, teaches at least one profitable lesson: it teaches that in this country, one can scarcely be so poor, but that, if he will, he can acquire sufficient education to get through the world respectably."[139]

He proceeded to review Clay's career, beginning with his legal studies, his law practice, election to the Kentucky state legislature, election to the U.S. Senate, reelection to the Kentucky House of Representatives, selection as the speaker of the Kentucky House, service again for the remainder of an open term in the Senate, election to the U.S. House of Representatives, selection as speaker there, commissioner for negotiating an end to the war with Britain in 1814, reelection to the House, reselection as speaker, selection as secretary of state, his return to the practice of law, and reelection to the U.S. Senate more than once. Through that remarkable public career, Lincoln suggested, "there never has been a moment since 1824 till after 1848 when a very large portion of the American people did not cling to him with an enthusiastic hope and purpose of still elevating him to the Presidency. With other men, to be defeated, was to be forgotten; but to him, defeat was but a trifling incident."[140]

Lincoln found Clay as averse to quitting as Taylor (and of course himself). "Even those of both political parties, who have been preferred to him for the highest office, have run far briefer courses than he, and left him, still shining, high in the heavens of the political world. Jackson, Van Buren, Harrison, Polk, and Taylor, all rose *after,* and set long before him."[141] (Lincoln did not bother including Tyler or Fillmore, neither of whom had been elected; they were accidents.) Clay, unlike any other man in Lincoln's estimation, "was surpassingly eloquent; but many eloquent men fail utterly; and they are not, as a class, generally successful. His judgment was excellent; but many men of good judgment, live and die unnoticed. His will was indomitable; but this quality often secures to its owner nothing better than a character for useless obstinacy."[142] Taken together, these qualities "are rarely combined in a single individual; and this is probably the reason why such men as Henry Clay are so rare in the world."[143] Emulating Clay meant refining several attributes, not just one; a great and inspiring leader like him led not only through example, but through excellence in judgment, eloquence, and determination. Clay had shown Lincoln— and now Lincoln was trying to show his fellow Whigs—that party was only part of a man, that party came second, after allegiance to the nation and its perpetuity. The Whig Party could fracture, but the nation had to endure.

Clay's eloquence required further comment. Webster's excellence as an orator was based on his beautiful declarations, while Calhoun's oratory was based on the remorseless logic of his arguments. But Clay's rhetoric, Lincoln suggested,

> *did not consist, as many fine specimens of eloquence do, of types and figures—of antithesis, and elegant arrangement of words and sentences; but rather of that deeply earnest and impassioned tone, and manner, which can proceed only from great sincerity and a thorough conviction, in the speaker of the justice and importance of his cause.*

In fact, as many had concluded, Clay's eloquence was a matter of theatrics. Lincoln nonetheless suggested that Clay stood out as an orator because "no one was so habitually careful to avoid all sectional ground. Whatever he did, he did for the whole country."[144] Even if this was not entirely true of Clay, Lincoln understood that a great orator seeks to cast his rhetoric on a higher plane for a higher purpose than mere partisan interest. In the case of Clay, Lincoln said that higher purpose was "a deep devotion," like Clay's, "to the cause of human liberty—a strong sympathy with the oppressed everywhere, and an ardent wish for their elevation."[145]

Where there was division, Clay relentlessly looked for unity. Lincoln surveyed Clay's uncanny knack at working out deals to avert disaster and achieve compromise. Lincoln brought up the decades-earlier controversy about the admission of Missouri into the Union as a slave state, which would have thrown off the equilibrium between proslavery and antislavery forces in Congress. He recalled Thomas Jefferson's remembrance that "'this momentous question, like a fire bell in the night, awakened, and filled me with terror. I considered it at once as the knell of the Union.'"[146] Just starting his storied career in Congress at that point, Clay forged the Missouri Compromise, which allowed for the admission of Maine (a free state) with Missouri (a slave state) at the same time. The deal also provided that, except for Missouri, slavery was to be excluded from the Louisiana Purchase lands above an imaginary line drawn by Congress at 36°30′ north latitude.

Lincoln saved the most difficult subject—slavery—for the last several paragraphs of his eulogy. He knew that Clay had arranged for his own slaves to be gradually released after his death and that he was committed to gradual emancipation all of his life. Indeed, Lincoln said, Clay "did not perceive, that on a question of human right, the negroes were to be excepted from the human race."[147] Lincoln suggested that even though Clay owned slaves, he "did not perceive, as I think no wise man has perceived, how it could be at once eradicated, without producing a greater evil, even to the cause of human liberty itself."[148] Lincoln said Clay had the virtue of not being at either extreme in the slavery debate, while it was the extremists at both ends who raised the specter of disunion.[149] No one missed the obvious fact that, in 1852, Lincoln still thought of Clay's vision—an indissoluble Union and gradual emancipation—as his own.

Without naming his target, Lincoln took direct aim at the proslavery theologian Alexander Campbell, who had sneered at the "declaration that 'all men are created free and equal'" and dismissed it as not being in his Bible.[150] Lincoln identified that position with Calhoun and others who had contempt for "republican America. The like was not heard in the fresher days of the Republic,"[151] and he contrasted such hateful rhetoric "with the language of that truly national man, whose life and death we now commemorate and lament."[152] He quoted from a speech given in 1827 by Clay to the American Colonization Society, of which Clay had long been president. In it, Clay responded to the critics of the society who defended slavery and opposed their efforts to return enslaved African Americans to their native lands. Lincoln quoted Clay: "If they would repress all tendencies towards liberty, and ultimate emancipation, they must do more than put down the benevolent efforts of this society. They must go back to the era of our liberty and independence, and muzzle the cannon which thunders its annual joyous return. They must renew the slave trade with all its train of atrocities."[153] Worse, he said,

> they must blow out the moral lights around us, and extinguish that greatest torch of all which America presents to a benighted world— pointing the way to their rights, their liberties, and their happiness. And when they have achieved all those purposes their work will be yet incomplete. They must penetrate the human soul, and eradicate the light of reason, and the love of liberty. Then, and not till then, when universal darkness and despair prevail, can you perpetuate slavery, and repress all sympathy, and all humane, and benevolent efforts among free men, in behalf of the unhappy portion of our race doomed to bondage.[154]

Lincoln could not match Clay's eloquence in his final two paragraphs, so he did not try. Instead, he returned to Clay's hope for "a glorious consummation" when slavery could be abolished.[155] "And

if, to such a consummation, the efforts of Mr. Clay shall have con-
tributed, it will be what he most ardently wished, and none of his
labors will have been more valuable to his country and his kind."
Lincoln ended by reminding his audience—thanks to the pending
distribution of his speech, an audience well beyond that in front of
him—that the nation still was "prosperous and powerful" in part
because of Henry Clay.[156] "Such a man," he declared, "the times
have demanded, and such, in the providence of God was given us.
But he is gone. Let us strive to deserve, as far as mortals may, the
continued care of Divine Providence, trusting that, in future national emergencies, He will not fail to provide us the instruments
of safety and security."[157]

Lincoln concluded with repeated references to the divine, putting both Clay and himself on the side of the angels. Lincoln never
mentioned the enormous impact Clay had on him, at least not in so
many words, nor did he quote from Clay's more recent speeches,
particularly his last. Instead, he quoted most extensively Clay's earlier speeches, no less great than his later ones, to show the longev-
ity and consistency of Clay's thoughts. Those, of course, had been
the speeches that Lincoln had studied and recited for years.

On October 24, 1852, four months after Clay passed away, Daniel Webster died. The "great triumvirate," Calhoun, Clay, and
Webster—the three men who had dominated national discourse
for decades—were no more. Though Lincoln admired (and often
modeled) Webster's oratory, he made no public eulogy for Webster
as he had done for Taylor and Clay. Lincoln knew Webster and
respected him, but he never felt the ideological kinship to him that
he had felt for Clay. Besides the fact that Webster was from Massachusetts and the other two from his home state, Webster had
been more equivocal over secession than either Taylor or Clay had
been. Clay and Taylor had always opposed secession, and while
Clay had supported a fugitive slave law, he did so in the spirit of
compromise, without the zeal with which Webster had defended
it. Webster's ambiguous rhetoric over secession and his over-the-
top support for the Fugitive Slave Act of 1850 confirmed Lincoln's
reluctance to honor him. Silence would be Lincoln's farewell.

VII

As the presidential election of 1852 approached, Lincoln was aware that the Whig Party was nearly defunct. Regional differences had weakened it, but the Compromise of 1850 finished the job once and for all. It divided the Whigs into proslavery and antislavery camps, with fault lines so deep they made Fillmore the first sitting president to fail to receive his party's support for another term. Instead, the party eventually agreed on its fifty-third ballot to nominate the old general Winfield Scott for president. Scott's long-standing opposition to slavery discouraged support anywhere in the South, while the Whig Party's discrepant decisions not to embrace the Compromise of 1850 and not to denounce slavery in its platform cost it support throughout the North. That left Scott only one option—to lose, which he did, to a lackluster former senator, Franklin Pierce of New Hampshire. Pierce likened himself to Jackson and Polk, though unlike either of them, he had a drinking problem so severe that his wife had forced him to leave the Senate to deal with it. It was the last time the Whig Party nominated a presidential candidate.

Besides his drinking problem, Pierce had other distinctions, none good. He had never sponsored any bill in his two terms in the House or his single term in the Senate. He had been a brigadier general in the Mexican War but was discharged early after he was injured when his horse fell on him. When informed her husband had won the Democratic Party nomination for president, Pierce's wife fainted. She was convinced that if he won the general election, the pressure of the presidency would lead him to start drinking again. Though Pierce called himself Young Hickory of the Granite Hills to invoke the notion that he was Andrew Jackson reincarnated, his most notable attribute was that he was a "doughface," a proslavery Northerner.

As Pierce took the oath of office, Lincoln was still practicing law in Springfield and traveling the circuit, but he watched with consternation as Stephen Douglas, Jefferson Davis, and now President

Pierce, yet another pretender to Jackson's legacy, pushed a scheme that brought the nation closer to civil war.

It began with a constitutional conundrum that Pierce largely made for himself and had to confront. Strict constructionists, like Pierce, who claimed to read powers-granting provisions of the Constitution narrowly, had argued that Congress lacked the power to restrict slavery in the territories, but as a candidate Pierce had promised to uphold the Compromise of 1850, which, in reauthorizing the original Missouri Compromise, had barred slavery from the federal territories it covered. Kansas and Nebraska had been included in the land that the French sold the United States in the Louisiana Purchase, and by 1854, farmers, ranchers, and prospectors were moving out west to seek their fortunes. The surge intensified the pressure for organizing territorial governments in Kansas and Nebraska to the extent that it became impossible for Pierce and Congress to ignore it. Abolitionists wished for the two areas to be free, while their opponents wanted to extend slavery into both, but the Missouri Compromise stood in their way, and although Pierce urged vigorous enforcement of the Fugitive Slave Law, he did not want to revisit the Missouri Compromise. He left the crafting of a solution to Congress, meaning the Senate Committee on Territories.

The committee's chair, Stephen Douglas, devised a plan to promote western expansion and facilitate construction of a transcontinental railroad. (As a lawyer for the rail lobby, he received sizable payment for his support.) Douglas figured the vast plains west of the Missouri could be broken into two new federal territories, Kansas and Nebraska. The most controversial part of the original plan was his proposal to organize the new territories in accordance with the principle of popular sovereignty, which he believed had the greatest promise of averting civil war.

In pushing his plan, Douglas initially tried to avoid saying anything about repealing the Missouri Compromise. He hoped to report out of his committee a bill giving settlers in Kansas and Nebraska the right to draft their own state constitutions at the time of statehood. Southern Whigs and Douglas's fellow Democrats told him, however, that they would not support the proposed bill unless it allowed the local residents of both Kansas and Nebraska to vote on the slavery question during the territorial years. This required repealing the Missouri Compromise, which had forbidden the extension of slavery west of Missouri.

Until then, neither Pierce nor his Cabinet knew about the negotiations over Douglas's bill. Douglas pushed a reluctant Pierce to meet with his Cabinet on Saturday, January 21, 1854, to discuss whether the Missouri Compromise should be repealed. With the backing of a majority of his Cabinet, Pierce agreed to bring the question to the Supreme Court, which he expected, given that a majority of its members had been appointed by Democratic presidents (including himself), to declare the Missouri Compromise unconstitutional on the ground that stripping slave-owners of their property (slaves) when they traveled through the territory violated the Fifth Amendment's ban on seizing property without due process of law. This way, Pierce could let the Court take the heat for dismantling the Missouri Compromise.

Later on January 21, Douglas consented to a repeal of the Missouri Compromise to maintain the support of Southern Whigs and Democrats for his planned Kansas-Nebraska bill. Because he had to present the amended bill on Monday or have the bill take a backseat to other pressing legislative business, he realized that he had to meet Pierce the next day, Sunday, January 22, 1854. But Pierce had vowed, after becoming president, not to do any business on Sunday. It was a decision prompted by tragedy. When Pierce, his wife, and their son, Bennie, were traveling in New Hampshire before the inauguration, their train car derailed, and, as it fell off an embankment, Pierce and his wife watched with horror as their only son was crushed to death in front of them. Pierce's wife swore never to forgive him, and Pierce promised to attend church services and spend his time contemplating spiritual matters and doing penance on Sundays. To get a meeting then, Douglas had to find some way—or some person—to persuade the president to make an exception to his rule.

Early on Sunday morning, Douglas went to the one man he believed could persuade Pierce to do business on a Sunday, Pierce's

secretary of war, Jefferson Davis. Davis had become Pierce's closest and most trusted confidant. Douglas brought a group of Southern Democrats with him to Davis's residence, where they met with
Davis and stressed the need to move as quickly as possible on the
Kansas-Nebraska Act. They persuaded Davis to intercede with
Pierce and arrange a meeting with him for later that same day.
Democrats had the numbers in both the House and the Senate to
get the bill passed, but they needed Pierce's support to ensure that
it would become law. If Pierce were inclined to keep his promise to
abide by the Missouri Compromise, Douglas and Davis knew they
did not have the numbers to muster the two thirds necessary to
override his veto. Moreover, Democrats held only a bare majority
in the House, and they needed every vote to get the bill through.
Davis and the group then went to the White House, and Davis met
privately with Pierce to urge that he meet with them. After some
hesitation, Pierce agreed.

Douglas and Davis took charge of the meeting. They explained
to Pierce that the bill was consistent with the constitutionally protected rights of states and slaveholders and the ideal of popular
sovereignty. Pierce agreed to support their bill. Determined that
Pierce not change his mind, Douglas took the extraordinary step
of asking him to write out in his own hand the portion of the bill
repealing the Missouri Compromise. Pierce agreed.

The wheels in motion, Pierce did everything he could to get
the law approved in both chambers of Congress. The Democratic
majority was so large in the Senate that passage was a virtual certainty, but Pierce made support for the bill a test of loyalty in the
House, vowing to withhold patronage and other favors from any
Democrat who opposed it. When the dust settled, a coalition of
more than half the Northern Democrats and most Southerners
approved the bill 35–13 in the Senate and 113–100 in the House.
Eight days later, on May 30, 1854, Pierce signed it into law.

The Kansas-Nebraska Act instantaneously transformed the
constitutional landscape. By repealing the Missouri Compromise,
Pierce and Congress were rejecting one of Henry Clay's greatest
achievements, which had been predicated on the principle that had

been a fixture of American law since Monroe's administration—
that Congress had the authority to bar slavery in the territories.
The new law was based on the entirely different constitutional
principle of popular sovereignty. This new principle was largely
untested; it worked in Nebraska, where the people eventually voted
against slavery, but Pierce, Douglas, Davis, and the majority of
each chamber in Congress were betting that popular sovereignty
would solve the fight over slavery in Kansas.

The bet was a bust of monumental proportions. Southern Democrats and the people of Nebraska were content to leave the slavery question to the people of Kansas, but the Democratic Party
suffered huge losses in the midterm elections. In the congressional elections, Democrats lost in every antislavery state except California and New Hampshire. Losing more than fifty seats in the
House, the Democrats went from having a solid majority in the
first two years of Pierce's administration to a minority in what
would be its last two years. While Democrats actually increased
their number of seats in the Senate, the gains were illusory: The
coalition that had brought Pierce to the White House was shattered, and Democrats who opposed slavery would flee the party.

Lincoln did not know all the machinations that had brought
the new law into being, but even from as far away as Illinois, he
knew the Kansas-Nebraska Act was a disaster for everything that
he, Henry Clay, and the Whigs had worked to attain over decades.
Just two years before, Lincoln's eulogy for Clay had placed the
Missouri Compromise that he had forged in 1820 at the center of
his legacy. Now, two years later, the Whig Party and the Missouri
Compromise lay in ruins. It was unclear what or who would take
their place. A new antislavery party, the Republican Party, had
been established in Ripon, Wisconsin, on March 20, 1854, but it
was too soon to tell whether it would have any more success than
the Free Soil and Know-Nothing parties.

Still thinking of himself as a Whig, Lincoln would not let the
destruction of one of Clay's greatest legacies go unaddressed. On
October 3, 1854, Douglas appeared in the House of Representatives hall at the Illinois state capitol to defend the Kansas-Nebraska

Act. Lincoln waited in the wings as Douglas spoke and shouted at Douglas once he finished that he wished to offer a rejoinder the next day on the same stage. Douglas reluctantly agreed.

Lincoln arrived well-prepared, reading his well-researched speech, dissecting Douglas's arguments one by one. Douglas sometimes interjected, but the interjections did not disrupt Lincoln's flow, establishing a pattern they would repeat during their 1858 contest for the Senate. On this occasion, as he would twelve days later in Peoria, Illinois, when Douglas repeated the same speech, Lincoln meticulously explained his objections to popular sovereignty and the Kansas-Nebraska Act, defended the Missouri Compromise, and explained his moral objections to slavery. As he did so, Lincoln did not mince words; the very opening of his speech reflected his awareness of the damage just done to a rightfully valued centerpiece of Clay's legacy.

He began, "The repeal of the Missouri Compromise, and the propriety of its restoration, constitute the subject of what I am about to say."[158] He laid out the foundations of the Missouri Compromise, which he said had been based on the Northwest Ordinance, a law enacted by the Continental Congress that prohibited slavery in the new territories that were eligible for admission into the Union as new states. Lincoln explained how the Northwest Ordinance had been fashioned in 1787 by Thomas Jefferson, "the author of the Declaration of Independence, and otherwise a chief actor in the revolution; then a delegate in Congress; afterwards twice President; who was, is, and perhaps will continue to be, the most distinguished politician in our history."[159] Seventeen when Jefferson died in 1826, Lincoln was drawn to Jefferson's political philosophy before becoming a fan of Clay. Indeed, Lincoln rarely thought of one without the other, Jefferson having crafted the vision that Clay and then Lincoln followed. "All honor to Jefferson," Lincoln declared later in 1859:

> a man who, in the concrete pressure of a struggle for national independence by a single people, had the coolness, forecast and capacity to introduce into a merely revolutionary document, an abstract

truth, applicable to all men and all times, and so to embalm it there,
that today, and in all coming days, it shall be a rebuke and a stum-
bling block to the very harbingers of reappearing tyranny and op-
pression.[160]

Back in Peoria in 1854, Lincoln did not need to tell his audience that Jefferson was the same man whose political vision
Henry Clay had always argued he was attempting to champion.
Lincoln said it was "with Jefferson" that "the policy of prohibiting
slavery in new territory originated"[161] and that the Missouri Compromise followed the example of the Northwest Ordinance, which
the Continental Congress adopted on July 13, 1787. "The Missouri
Compromise," he reminded his audience, and Douglas, "had been
in practical operation for about a quarter of a century, and had received the sanction and approbation of men of all parties in every
section of the Union."[162] Lincoln then recounted the history of that
landmark agreement, which had been fashioned by "Henry Clay,
as its prominent champion," and argued that popular sovereignty
could not supersede the Northwest Ordinance and the Missouri
Compromise.[163] Lincoln conveniently left out of his history that
the fugitive slave clause in the original Constitution had first appeared in the last article of the ordinance.

If the North and South were locked into positions on slavery
that they could not easily or naturally abandon, Lincoln wondered,
what national solution to the problem was feasible? He confessed
that he did not know the answer, even while maintaining that
owning slaves was immoral: "When southern people tell us that
they are no more responsible for the origin of slavery, than we; I
acknowledge the fact. When it is said that the institution exists;
and that it is very difficult to get rid of it, in any satisfactory way, I
can understand and appreciate the saying. I surely will not blame
them for not doing what I should not know how to do myself. If all
earthly power were given me," he confessed, "I should not know
what to do, as to the existing institution."[164] Lincoln acknowledged
further the problems with some proposed solutions: "My first impulse would be to free all the slaves, and send them to Liberia,—to

their own native land. But a moment's reflection would convince me, that whatever of high hope (as I think there is) there may be in this, in the long run, its sudden execution is impossible."[165] He explained that "if [the slaves] were all landed there in a day, they would all perish in the next ten days; and there are not surplus shipping and surplus money enough in the world to carry them in many times ten days."[166] Unable to go beyond what he thought the people of the state could accept, he asked, "What next?"

> *Free them and make them politically and socially, our equals? My own feelings will not admit of this; and if mine would, we well know that those of the great mass of white people will not. Whether this feeling accords with justice and sound judgment is not the sole question, if indeed, it is any part of it. A universal feeling whether well or ill-founded, cannot be safely disregarded. We cannot, then, make them equals. It does seem to me that systems of gradual emancipation might be adopted; but for their tardiness in this, I will not undertake to judge our brethren of the south.*[167]

Nevertheless, try as he might not to be critical of Southerners as a people (he had many close friends from the South, including Alexander Stephens), Lincoln had gently suggested that the likeliest solution to the problem was the one that Clay had championed— gradual emancipation—for which Lincoln had praised Clay at the end of his eulogy[168] but which conflicted with the desires of Southern leaders to protect slavery, not to do away with it.

Lincoln went further to dismiss the disingenuous arguments Douglas had made that conditions in Kansas and Nebraska were somehow not hospitable to the entry of slavery; it was a poison that Lincoln knew would threaten to consume these territories if given the chance, and Douglas had given them that chance. Lincoln acknowledged, "The doctrine of self-government is right— absolutely and eternally right—but," he added,

> *it has no just application, as here attempted. Or perhaps I should rather say that whether it has such just application depends upon*

whether a negro is not or is a man. If he is not a man, why in that case, he who is a man may, as a matter of self-government, do just as he pleases with him. But if he is a man, is it not to that extent, a total of destruction of self-government, to say that he too shall not govern himself? When the white man governs himself that is self-government, but when he governs himself, and also governs another man, that is more than self-government—that is despotism.[169]

Lincoln attacked the morality of slavery itself, just as Henry Clay had done and he had lauded Clay for doing. He argued that the slaves were people, not animals, and consequently possessed certain natural rights. "If the negro is a man, why then my ancient faith teaches me that 'all men are created equal'; and that there can be no moral right in connection with one man's making a slave of another."[170] He continued, "No man is good enough to govern another man, without that other's consent. I say this is the leading principle—the sheet anchor of American republicanism."[171]

It followed, then, that the extension of slavery into the territories and, prospectively, "to every other part of the wide world, where men can be found inclined to take it," was equally wrong.[172] So was Douglas's "declared indifference, but as I must think, covert real zeal for the spread of slavery."[173] Lincoln had arrived at the core of his political and constitutional belief, derived from the Declaration of Independence, that "all men are created equal."[174] He explained that the Founders understood that slavery was wrong.[175] For practical reasons they could not outlaw it altogether at the time of the founding, but instead they "hedged and hemmed it in to the narrowest limits of necessity."[176] Indeed, they did not allow the word *slavery* in the Constitution but permitted only indirect references to it, "just as an afflicted man hides away a wen or cancer, which he dares not cut out at once, lest he bleed to death; with the promise, nevertheless, that the cutting may begin at the end of a given time."[177]

Lincoln added, "The Missouri Compromise ought to be restored. For the sake of the Union, it ought to be restored."[178] Whether it be the Whigs or whatever party took their place, Lincoln was urging his fellow citizens "to elect a House of Representatives which will vote its restoration. If by any means, we omit to do this, what follows?"[179] Lincoln predicted it would not be just the possibility of slavery being approved in Kansas, but something worse—the loss of "the SPIRIT of COMPROMISE; for who after this will ever trust in a national compromise? The spirit of mutual concession—that spirit which first gave us the constitution, and which has thrice saved the Union" (by the Northwest Ordinance, the Missouri Compromise, and the Compromise of 1850), the spirit of Henry Clay, would be lost again.[180] Lincoln denounced slavery again for its immorality:

> Slavery is founded in the selfishness of man's nature—opposition to it, is his Love of justice. These principles are in eternal antagonism; and when brought into collision so fiercely, as slavery extension brings them, shocks, and throes, and convulsions must ceaselessly follow. Repeal the Missouri compromise—repeal all compromises— repeal the declaration of independence—repeal all past history, you still can not repeal human nature. It still will be the abundance of man's heart, that slavery extension is wrong; and out of the abundance of his heart, his mouth will continue to speak.[181]

Lincoln devoted much of the rest of the speech to exposing the fallacies of Douglas's claims that the principle of popular sovereignty developed from or was perfectly consistent with the principles of the earlier compromises over slavery. (Nearly every one of Clay's great speeches had a list of reasons for opposing any alternative to Clay's proposals.) Douglas claimed that the Compromise of 1850 established the precedent for the new law, but Lincoln argued that "the North consented to" allowing Utah and New Mexico to decide whether to come into the Union "with or without slavery as they shall then see fit,"

> not because they considered it right in itself; but because they were compensated. . . . They, at the same time, got California into the Union as a free State. This was far the best part of all they had

struggled for by the Wilmot Proviso. They also got the area of slavery somewhat narrowed in the settlement of the boundary of Texas. Also, they got the slave trade abolished in the District of Columbia. For all these desirable objects the North could afford to yield something, and they did yield to the South the Utah and New Mexico provision.[182]

The Kansas-Nebraska Act, in contrast, gave the North nothing in exchange for its support.

A major problem Lincoln had with the principle of popular sovereignty was his fervent belief that some things were not negotiable and should not be subject to majority rule or popular decision, including the morality of slavery, which a growing number of Americans believed was wrong. Another problem was that popular sovereignty "enables the first FEW, to deprive the succeeding MANY, of a free exercise of the right of self-government."[183] It was not just bad that Douglas and the Democrats were arguing that popular majority could decide who was human and who was property, but that once those popular majorities had their way, they could keep others subjugated.

Next, Lincoln considered "whether the repeal, with its avowed principle, is intrinsically right."[184] He likened the fight over the extension of slavery to a fight in which the South considered any compromise a defeat. Reverting to a useful metaphor, Lincoln explained, "It is as if two starving men had divided their only loaf; the one had hastily swallowed his half, and then grabbed the other half just as he was putting it to his mouth."[185] He further illustrated the injustice and absurdity of the South's position by pointing to how the South wanted both to allow jurisdictions to permit slavery but to bar jurisdictions from keeping slaveholders out. In this way, the South could never lose and the North could never win.[186]

At the end, Lincoln contested Douglas's claim that Clay and Webster were not in agreement with Lincoln's side of the argument:

They were great men; and men of great deeds. But where have I assailed them? For what is it, that their life-long enemy, shall now make profit, by assuming to defend them against me, their life-long friend? I go against the repeal of the Missouri compromise; did they ever go for it? They went for compromise of 1850; did I ever go against them? They were greatly devoted to the Union; to the small measure of my ability, was I ever less so? Clay and Webster were dead before this question arose; by what authority shall our Senator say they would espouse his side of it, if alive? Mr. Clay was the leading spirit in making the Missouri compromise; is it very credible that if now alive, he would take the lead in the breaking of it? The truth is that some support from whigs is now a necessity with [Douglas], and for thus it is, that the names of Clay and Webster are now invoked. His old friends have deserted him in such numbers as to leave too few to live by.[187]

Never before had Lincoln reached such rhetorical heights, and never before had he focused so clearly and forcefully on the immorality of slavery. He would return to these themes throughout the remainder of the decade, time and again defending and aligning himself with Clay's legacy of compromise and long-held belief that the framers did not design the Constitution to protect slavery but rather to allow the federal government to regulate, even abolish, slavery.

Douglas stayed for the entire Peoria speech and quickly charged onto the stage the moment it ended. In front of hundreds of people, Douglas challenged Lincoln to a debate. Lincoln surprised him by immediately asking Douglas to debate him in Peoria on October 16. After some hesitation, Douglas agreed to speak the same day as Lincoln but not at the same time; he spoke in the afternoon, before the evening, when Lincoln was scheduled to speak. In Peoria, Lincoln gave the same speech he had given in Springfield, but this time he wrote it out in full for publication over a week's issues in the *Illinois State Journal*.[188] After Peoria, he delivered the same speech in Urbana. The speeches reminded the voters of Illinois that Lincoln was a political force to be reckoned with. They belied any notion that he had retired from politics. Indeed, he had never left it.

CHAPTER FIVE

BECOMING PRESIDENT
(1856-1860)

There was no dramatic moment when Lincoln suddenly became the man who would be the mythic, beloved president he became. It is tempting to think there must have been some epiphany, such as when in the 1850s Lincoln awoke with a start to tell his friend Judge Dickey, "This nation cannot exist half slave and half free." But Lincoln was not a man of fits and starts. He was invariably cautious, deliberate in his actions, probing issues from every angle until he was content that he fully grasped them. The 1850s were no exception.

For much of the nation, the biggest and most sudden political surprise of the 1850s was Abraham Lincoln. The split between North and South had been coming for decades. Pierce's actions led to violence between abolitionist and proslavery forces in Kansas. This conflict known as "Bleeding Kansas" was an intermittent five-year guerrilla war begun when proslavery militias sacked the abolitionist town of Lawrence, burning down the Free State Hotel and destroying the presses of the two newspapers. (One of the raiders suffered the only known death, killed by a piece of the collapsing hotel.) The violent strife was a precursor of the bloodletting that would spread outside the state's borders and culminate in the Civil War.

Meanwhile, in the 1850s, a new generation of leaders fought their elders to take control of each of the major parties. Stephen Douglas's star continued to rise, but it was older Democrats, like James Buchanan of Pennsylvania (a man Clay dismissed as one of the "subordinates of Democracy" unworthy of his respect), Clay's former friend John Crittenden of Kentucky, and New Jersey's William Dayton, who were Whigs who later became Republicans. As the Whig Party collapsed, William Seward, Salmon Chase, Edward Bates, and Orville Browning were other prominent former Whigs intent on establishing a new party devoted to the abolition of slavery. Both of the major parties traced their origins to Thomas Jefferson, Democrats taking their name from half of Jefferson's Democratic-Republican Party, while part of the Whig diaspora claimed the other half.

Few gave a second thought to Lincoln. He was in Illinois, practicing law, while the man who outmaneuvered Douglas to win the presidency in 1856, James Buchanan, was hastening civil war. Buchanan had snatched the Democratic Party's nomination from Pierce, but like the man he'd defeated, he backed slave-owners' interests over those of abolitionists, placed federal power on the side of slavery, and blamed abolitionists for the nation's troubles. The spirit of compromise had died with Henry Clay.

In Washington, all eyes were on Douglas. Democratic leaders saw him as a lock on the 1860 presidential nomination as long as he won his reelection campaign in 1858. They saw no reason for him to be worried about reelection, but Douglas did. He was acutely aware—and well informed—that Lincoln was still a popular Whig leader in their home state and Lincoln was planning a run against him.

In declaring himself a "flat failure," Lincoln had lowered any expectations that he would ever be returning to the national stage.[1] Yet those closest to Lincoln—David Davis, Orville Browning, William Herndon, Leonard Swett, to name a few—knew that lowering expectations served Lincoln's political purposes. His self-deprecation reinforced his "humble" image as a "self-made man." This was, of course, fully in line with Clay's presentation of himself, a braid of himself and a lot of tactics. Drawing on one of Aesop's most famous fables, Lincoln was the tortoise in this race; the others, the hares, bounding ahead to the audition. Few saw Lincoln coming. Douglas did. They both knew that, in a nation that was tearing itself apart, only the man in the middle could mend it.

I

In the aftermath of the violent fallout from the Kansas-Nebraska Act and Pierce's strong backing of slavery interests in Kansas, Lincoln faced two immediate challenges. The first was to decide what, if any, role he expected to play in helping to establish a new political party to replace the Whigs. Lincoln's second challenge was figuring out his future in politics. Surmounting both challenges was crucial for Lincoln's newest ambition—a run for the Senate.

In making his decision, Lincoln was following the examples set much earlier by both Jackson and Clay. With the Whig Party dead, Lincoln had to find a new political home. "The man who is of neither party is not—cannot be, of any consequence," Lincoln said of Clay in his eulogy.[2] Jackson, too, showed that the path to higher office could be traveled only with a unified party behind a candidate with a clear constitutional vision that voters could rally around.

As Leonard Swett recalled, Lincoln "believed from the first, I think, that the agitation of Slavery would produce its overthrow, and he acted upon the result as though it was present from the beginning. His tactics were, to get himself in the right place and remain there still, until events would find him in that place."[3] John W. Bunn, a fellow Whig partisan and a merchant who funded Lincoln's campaigns, found that "Lincoln was a practical politician, but he was not altogether like many other practical politicians. He had his personal ambitions, but he never told any man his deeper plans and few, if any, knew his inner thoughts."[4] In the absence of such disclosures, Lincoln can best be judged on the basis of what he did; his actions revealed his plans. He recognized that he needed the support of a party system, so it was to the party that he knew best that he next turned: the remains of the Whig Party apparatus and the party faithful in Illinois.

Perhaps by design, Lincoln managed not to be in Springfield in October 1854, when the newly formed Republican Party held its convention there. Its platform urged an end to slavery in all federal territories and a repeal of the Fugitive Slave Act of 1850. The Republicans, including Browning, designated Lincoln as a member of the state central committee. Ever sensitive to keeping the different factions within the party as happy as possible, Lincoln pointedly neither accepted nor declined membership on the committee. He likely shaded the truth when he told a friend on the committee, "I have been perplexed some to understand why my name was placed on that committee. I was not consulted on the subject; nor was I apprized [sic] of the appointment, until I discovered it by accident two or three weeks afterwards."[5] Thinking about his run for the Senate the next year, Lincoln explained, "I supposed my opposition to the principle of slavery is as strong as that of any member of the Republican party; but I had also supposed that the extent to which I feel authorized to carry that opposition, practically, was not at all satisfactory to that party."[6] Lincoln still saw himself as closely aligned with the policies of Clay, as he made clear in his Peoria speech, where he had declared that he was not opposed to the elimination of slavery in all the territories but that he still accepted the Fugitive Slave Act (as long as it was narrowly enforced), even expressing sympathy for Southerners. While Democrats who opposed slavery were turning their backs on Pierce, Buchanan, and Douglas, they were still nominally Democrats, who were nonetheless interested in leaving the party for a more sympathetic base. Lincoln was trying to walk a narrow path that could win old-time Whigs, former Whigs who called themselves Republicans, and Democrats, as well as those who were aligned with the anti-immigration, anti-Catholic Know Nothing Party. He retook a seat in the Illinois House to remind the legislators that he was one of them but perhaps alienated some of his constituents when he resigned it after only twenty-two days to focus on joining Douglas in the Senate.

The new Illinois state legislature, assembled on January 1, 1855, would select the state's next senator. Lincoln told Herndon that he thought he had twenty-five members committed to his candidacy for the Senate. His difficulty was that he needed twenty-five more to get the majority needed from the assembly to secure the open seat, but he was unsure where he could find the requisite support. It would be difficult, given that almost half the general assembly were Democrats who likely supported the incumbent congressman James Shields, an old rival. Lincoln enlisted support from Judge David Davis and Stephen Logan, who had been elected to the Illinois House of Representatives; they estimated on the day of the election in the legislature that Lincoln was only three votes away from the majority he needed to win. What they did not count on was the support enjoyed by Lyman Trumbull, who had bolted the Democratic Party in opposition to the Kansas-Nebraska Act and was currently a member of the U.S. House of Representatives.

On the initial ballot, Lincoln had forty-five votes to Shields's forty-one; Trumbull had five votes, and one member went for Governor Joel Mattison. After six ballots, nothing changed, but on the seventh, the Democrats who supported Shields shifted their support to Mattison, and by the ninth ballot, Lincoln's support had dwindled to fifteen, Trumbull's had increased to thirty-five, and Mattison's forty-seven was only three away from the majority he needed for election to the Senate. Lincoln, still loyal to his Whig roots, made the snap judgment to ask his supporters to vote for Trumbull on the tenth ballot. They did, and Trumbull handily won the seat. Lincoln later confessed, perhaps with false modesty, that "a less good humored man than I, perhaps would not have consented to it."[7] Privately, Lincoln was angry and so, too, was David Davis, who made known that he distrusted Trumbull as "a Democrat all his life—dyed in the wool—as ultra as he could be."[8] Mary Todd was so outraged that she refused to speak to Trumbull's wife, who once had been a friend of hers.

Lincoln learned from this defeat, as he had learned from every one of the ups and downs in his career. If Clay, Jackson, and Taylor had anything in common besides their strong fidelity to the Union, it was the fact that they were always planning their next move. Lincoln had said as much in his eulogies for Taylor and Clay, but he had once again moved too slowly in corralling support. He had begun hustling for the Senate seat a year earlier, but it was not early enough. Taking this lesson to heart, Lincoln did what he had not done before: he began moving quickly and decisively to position himself well in advance to run for the state's other Senate seat in 1858. On the night after Trumbull won his seat, the Anti-Nebraska Democrats (those opposed to allowing slavery by popular sovereignty), who were gratified that Lincoln had made an appearance that same evening to show his support for his former foe, pledged in return to support him in the next Senate race. Lincoln was also able to get two other Anti-Nebraska Democrats, Norman Judd and John Palmer, both from Chicago, to pledge their future support. Each had previously bankrolled successful Whig candidates.

Thus backed, Lincoln focused on challenging Douglas's reelection bid in 1858. Lincoln had more than two years to plan, but he understood that victory required him to choose his party as soon as possible. Jackson first ran for the presidency as a Democratic-Republican in 1824, while Clay first ran as the candidate for the National Republicans in 1832. In 1833, a year after he had run against Jackson, Clay founded the Whig Party as a foil to Jackson and a base for future runs for the presidency. With the Whig Party in ruins, the Republican Party was the logical place for Lincoln to go, but in 1855 and 1856 it had not yet become the home for all the opponents of slavery.

Lincoln pondered his options, as revealed in a letter to his friend and fellow former Whig Joshua Speed of Kentucky. Speed told Lincoln of his strong opposition to slavery and his view that the Union ought to be dissolved if Kansas declared itself proslavery, and his hope—against all the evidence to the contrary—that Kansas might still find a way to vote itself a free state. Lincoln struck a pragmatic tone in response. He wrote that he thought of the Kansas-Nebraska Act "not as a law, but as violence from the beginning,"[9] a brazen effort to force the spread of slavery. He disagreed with Speed's view that the men enforcing the law were the problem; Lincoln believed that "the way it is being executed is quite as good as any of its antecedents. It is being executed in the precise way which was intended from the first; else why does no Nebraska man express astonishment or condemnation?"[10] Not yet ready to fully commit to the newly minted Republican Party, Lincoln answered Speed, who'd asked where he stood. "I think I am a whig; but others say there are no whigs, and that I am an abolitionist."[11] He reminded Speed, "When I was in Washington I voted for the Wilmot Proviso as good as forty times, and I never heard of anyone attempting to unwhig me for that. I now do more than oppose the extension of slavery."[12] In fact, Lincoln voted for the Wilmot Provision far fewer times, but his support for it was consistent. Next, he ruled out the Know Nothing Party. Indeed, he had hosted Fillmore when he came through Springfield in June 1854. Fillmore was then considering his third-party run for the Know Nothing Party's presidential nomination, but Lincoln had no interest in joining a party that did not stand on the same principles on which the Whig Party had been founded. As Lincoln explained to his friend Speed in 1855,

> I am not a Know-Nothing. That is certain. How could I be? How can any one who abhors the oppression of negroes, be in favor of degrading classes of white people? Our progress in degeneracy appears to me to be pretty rapid. As a nation, we begin by declaring that "all men are created equal." We now practically read it "all men are created equal, except negroes, and foreigners, and Catholics." When it comes to this I should prefer emigrating to some country where they make no pretense of loving liberty—to Russia, for instance, where despotism can be taken pure, and without the base alloy of hypocrisy.[13]

On February 22, 1856, Lincoln and Herndon secured invitations as two nonjournalists to attend the conference of Anti-Nebraska newspaper editors who were planning for the upcoming presidential election later that year. With Lincoln's input, the conference drafted a declaration that called for restoring the Missouri Compromise, upholding the constitutionality of the 1850 Fugitive

Slave Law, and promising noninterference with slavery in the states where it currently existed. It is little wonder that Lincoln would fit in so comfortably with the group; they were endorsing Clay's compromises of 1850. At the same time, the group endorsed Free Soil doctrine, recommending that freedom be guaranteed in federal districts and territories but not abolished by force in slave states. Free Soilers urged religious toleration and opposed restrictive changes in immigration laws. Though the conference avoided calling itself Republican, it was in all but name, and it planned at a statewide convention in Bloomington, Illinois, on May 29, 1856, to formalize the establishment of the Republican Party in Illinois. On the night of the final banquet for the program, the editors toasted Lincoln "as the warm and consistent friend of Illinois, and our next candidate for the U.S. Senate."[14]

Also, in May 1856, Herndon, who was a member of the Anti-Nebraska state committee at the editors' gathering, had published a call for a meeting of Sangamon County residents opposed to the Kansas-Nebraska Act so they could select delegates for the Bloomington convention. With Lincoln's knowledge, Herndon signed both Lincoln's name and his own as potential delegates. Reputedly, when the signatures became public, an irate John Todd Stuart stormed into Lincoln's law offices to ask whether Lincoln had actually signed the form. Lincoln was not around, but his partner Herndon, who was, said he had done it without consulting Lincoln, to which Stuart replied, "Then you have ruined him."[15] Stuart did not believe that a Republican, especially a radical one (and he thought all Republicans were radicals), could win a statewide election in Illinois.

Herndon and Lincoln thought otherwise, but the former had anticipated that Lincoln might have wanted to try to have it both ways—to be able to take advantage of aligning with the party growing in popularity but at the same time appear not to be taking a leading role or sanctioning its major activities. When he telegraphed Lincoln to alert him that he had signed him up as a delegate to the Republican convention, and that conservative Whigs like Stuart were not happy with his new radicalism (in 1856, Stuart campaigned for Fillmore in the hopes of thwarting "Black Republicans," those within the party who supported giving the vote to African Americans, which, he said, would "array the North against the South"), Lincoln responded briefly, "All right; go ahead. Will meet you—radicals and all."[16]

On May 29, 1856, Lincoln was one of around 270 delegates to attend the Bloomington convention, which formally recognized the formation of the Republican Party in Illinois. Whigs of all stripes were there, as were Anti-Nebraska Democrats and abolitionists. Lincoln's friend John Palmer, a former Democrat, was the presiding officer. Orville Browning was there, too, representing conservative Whigs. Browning's plan was to move the old Whig Party in the state, as he told Lyman Trumbull, "under the control of moderate men, and conservative influences, and if we do so the future destiny of the State is in our own hands—victory will inevitably crown our exertions. On the contrary if rash and ultra counsels prevail all is lost."[17] Recognizing upon his arrival that there had been few advance plans, Browning took the initiative to undertake one of the most important functions there: drafting a platform for the new party. This was a delicate task, the kind that required tact and coordination and finding consensus and common ground. It was easy to think Browning might not be well suited for the task, since his self-assurance and tendency to take himself too seriously might have rubbed more than a few people the wrong way. But this was a job for a good lawyer and astute politician, and Browning was both in spite of whatever other limitations he had. He understood this was his moment, and he shined. He called fifteen to twenty delegates to his room to get their input and find out what they could each accept and not accept. Then he prepared two platform resolutions that everyone, including Lincoln, could endorse: that the Constitution and the nation's institutions guaranteed that "we will proscribe no one, by legislation or otherwise, on account of religious opinions, or in consequence of place of birth,"[18] and that Congress

possesses the full power to prohibit slavery in the territories; and that while we maintain all constitutional rights of the south, we

also hold that justice, humanity, the principles of freedom as ex-
pressed in our Declaration of Independence, and our national con-
stitution, and the purity and perpetuity of our government, require
that the power should be exerted to prevent the extension of slavery
into territories heretofore free.[19]

On the afternoon of May 29, Browning made two speeches to
the convention, each emphasizing the values of compromise and
moderation. He was there to speak to the "old Clay-Whigs" and
he did. He told the delegates that they could choose no better role
model than Henry Clay. As Browning's biographer Maurice Baxter
describes the speech,

> *He read extracts from the speeches of Henry Clay from his first en-*
> *trance upon public life to the close of his career, all of which proved*
> *him to have been steadfastly and uniformly opposed to the spread*
> *of slavery into free territory, and that had he been upon the na-*
> *tional stage when his great measures of pacification—the Missouri*
> *Compromise—was ruthlessly violated, his voice and vote would*
> *have been the same in 1854, that they were in 1820.*

Baxter surmised that "Browning's emphasis of old-line Whig tra-
ditions [was] cogently and eloquently expressed and made a strong
impression on his colleagues."[20]

It was no accident that Browning looked to Clay as the model
for the new party. He knew—nearly everybody did—that Clay was
Lincoln's idol and the idol, in all likelihood, of most of the people
in attendance. Browning had met Clay in 1844, and as he noted
in his diary, "I was never more charmed with a man. So plain, so
unaffectedly kind, so dignified, so unaustatious [*sic*], so simple in
his manners and conversation, that he is irresistibly fascinating."[21]
This meeting apparently arose shortly before the 1844 presidential election, at which time Clay might well have been at his most
charming—and in need of support among old-line Whigs like
Browning, John Todd Stuart, and Lincoln. Ostensibly, as Browning recalled, no introduction was required—Clay knew who he

was and where he was from. As Baxter describes the meeting, "This evidence of personal interest reinforced Browning's belief that Clay had all the personal qualities with which he had been credited. He appeared younger than Browning had expected, as he was in good health, and above all he was not the least bit egotistical. Undoubtedly he ought to be President of the United States." Browning's perception of Clay is more consistent with what we know about Clay than Linder's description of Lincoln's meeting, when Clay was described as obnoxious and pretentious. Browning's view is also consistent with what we know about *him;* much more than Lincoln, he would have been receptive to such flattery and attention.

Browning was determined to revive the spirit of Clay for the convention. If "compromise" and "moderation" were the hallmarks of a Republican, as Browning told the delegates, Lincoln fit that bill. Indeed, Browning often assumed Lincoln was a conservative like himself, prone to upholding internal improvements funded by tariffs and restrictions on slavery but not to undertake more radical notions, such as complete abolition. Lincoln did nothing to dissuade Browning of that impression.

Though Lincoln had little role in organizing the convention, the delegates called him as the last major speaker. Everyone knew Lincoln had his eye on the Senate. He gave a short preview of the positions he expected to take in the upcoming election. As Judge John Scott, who witnessed the speech, recalled, Lincoln had "an expression on his face of intense emotion seldom if ever seen upon any before. It was the emotion of a great soul. Even in statu[re] he appeared great. A sudden stillness settled over the body of thoughtful men as Lincoln commenced to speak. Everyone wanted to hear what he had to say." Scott concluded that this was "the speech of his life in the estimation of many who heard it. [It] was a triumph that comes to few speakers. It was an effect that could be produced by the truest eloquence."[22] Such effusive praise was possible not only because of Lincoln's passionate delivery (while he was sometimes reserved in personal conversation, once onstage he came alive, particularly in front of a friendly audience) but also the content—

content that Lincoln, unlike that of his other speeches, did *not* want to reach a wide audience. This became the "lost speech," which Lincoln purposely had not written down but suppressed, because he and party leaders thought it too radical for publication and nationwide distribution. Lincoln had learned from Clay's mistakes of often speaking too much and inconsistently to appease a broad constituency, and he and his supporters were careful not to allow anything but moderation to define Lincoln.

What made the speech so touchy was that Lincoln identified slavery as the principal cause for the nation's problems, defended the idea of a union that opposed the extension of slavery, and closed by reiterating the declaration that Daniel Webster famously had given in 1830 in response to the South Carolina nullification movement, which maintained states had the authority to nullify or refuse to follow federal laws they did not like: "Liberty and Union, now and forever, one and inseparable."[23] This was the Webster whom Lincoln preferred to remember. In beginning his life as a Republican, Lincoln reminded those listening, and those later reading reports about his remarks in friendly newspapers, that while he might have been newly repackaged as a Republican, he remained, contrary to what Douglas said in 1854, faithful to the commitment of Clay and Webster to the Union.

II

While Lincoln was maneuvering for the Illinois Republican nomination for the Senate, Pierce's plans were falling apart. Kansas was in turmoil. Even before the Kansas-Nebraska Act had gone into effect, proslavery residents of Missouri had flooded into Kansas. They congregated mostly in the southern part of the territory, where, on March 30, 1855, they voted to select a proslavery legislature. That legislature quickly passed a statute outlawing antislavery activities. Meanwhile, antislavery residents had congregated in the northern portion of Kansas, where they formed a government of their own, which they called the Topeka Constitution. With the state divided into two halves and both sides beginning to engage in physical confrontations and violence, Pierce publicly sided with the proslavery faction and announced he would send federal forces into the territory if necessary to enforce their claims. He blamed Kansas's problems on the "inflammatory agitation" of outsiders, code for abolitionists.[24] He also declared that the Constitution protected the rights of slaveholders and agreed to station federal troops at Forts Leavenworth and Riley to serve as needed by the territorial governor.

Several violent outbreaks further grabbed national attention, one in the U.S. Senate and others in Kansas. On May 19–20, 1856, Massachusetts senator Charles Sumner delivered what he believed was the most important speech of his career. He was right, but for the wrong reason. He not only spoke of a widespread conspiracy involving the Pierce administration to force slavery on the prospective new state of Kansas, but he directed insults—including vulgar sexual imagery—against Douglas and particularly South Carolina senator Andrew Pickens Butler. Two days later, Congressman Preston Brooks, a cousin of Senator Brooks, marched into the Senate and confronted Sumner at his desk. Without warning, he repeatedly beat Sumner with his walking stick. Sumner was stunned and blinded by the first few blows, after which he wrenched his desk from its mooring and fell onto the Senate floor. Several senators watched him bleeding profusely and unconscious on the floor but did nothing, having been told to back off by Brooks's gun-waving accomplices, two other Southern representatives. By the time some senators stopped the beating, Sumner was nearly dead. Although reelected in 1857, the damage from the beating kept him out of the Senate until 1859. As for Brooks, an investigating committee recommended his expulsion from the House, but instead he was merely censured. Brooks resigned from the House but was reelected.

Back in Kansas, on May 21, 1856, proslavery forces ransacked the city of Lawrence, which had been settled largely by antislavery forces from Massachusetts. In response, a rabid abolitionist named John Brown led a closely knit band of followers who killed five pro-slavery settlers north of the Pottawatomie Creek during the night of May 24 and early morning of May 25. From there, Brown led his antislavery forces at two other battles in Kansas. They wreaked havoc wherever they could, culminating in an attack on a federal armory in Harper's Ferry, Virginia. Within thirty-six hours, a Marine force led by Robert E. Lee captured Brown. Brown was tried and convicted of treason and hanged on the spot. Democrats used Brown as the symbol of the radical abolitionism they said was destroying the country.

III

Bleeding Kansas was the central issue in the 1856 presidential election. On the Democratic side, Stephen Douglas made his first serious effort to grab the presidential nomination, as did three other prominent contenders, including Pierce, Lewis Cass of Michigan, and Polk's secretary of state, James Buchanan. At the Democratic nominating convention held in Cincinnati, Ohio, in 1856, Pierce struggled to keep his candidacy alive for as long as he could, but he withdrew his name from contention as his support fell precipitously in the late rounds of balloting. In being denied renomination, Pierce became the first elected president not to be renominated for a second term in office. Douglas's candidacy lasted until the seventeenth ballot, but he ultimately withdrew to avoid a contest with Buchanan that would have amplified internal tensions within the party and hurt its chances to keep the White House in the fall. Douglas's decision was made easier because, at forty-three, he expected to be a viable candidate in the next election. Buchanan, who had been out of the country during Pierce's administration, serving as the ambassador to Great Britain, had the advantage of not having been involved with any of the administration's decision making on the Kansas-Nebraska Act or the civil war in Kansas.

The Republicans held their first presidential nominating convention in Philadelphia, Pennsylvania. Republicans, in the judgment of Lincoln and Orville Browning, were looking for a candidate who was not conservative or at least not perceived as one, and both men supported John McLean, who had served Monroe and John Quincy Adams as postmaster general and whom Andrew Jackson had appointed to the Supreme Court in 1829. (The American Party, which was merely the nativist Know Nothing Party under a different name, nominated Millard Fillmore, who still had great appeal to conservatives in both of the major parties.) Lincoln told Trumbull that McLean's nomination "would save every whig, except such as have already gone over hook and line" to the Democrats. He explained, "I am in, and shall go for any one nominated unless he be 'platformed' expressly, or impliedly, on some ground which I may think wrong."[25] Lincoln had never failed to back his party's presidential nominee, but for the first time, he kept the door open to withholding support from the nominee. The most important thing was to do nothing that could hurt his chances for the upcoming Senate election.

The nomination did not go to McLean, who was actively campaigning in spite of the fact that he was still sitting as a justice on the Supreme Court. Nor did the nomination go to either Seward or the newly elected governor of Ohio, Salmon Chase; as strident abolitionists, neither man held any appeal with the conservative wing of the Whig or Republican Parties. Instead, the nomination went to John Frémont, a former soldier and explorer. In 1848, he had been court-martialed for mutiny and insubordination in a dispute over who was the rightful governor of California, but Polk, in his last full year as president, commuted his sentence and reinstated him to his rank as major in the army so he could resign without disgrace. Frémont had led five expeditions into California, earning him the nickname the Pathfinder. He had also been U.S. senator from California. His appeal derived in part from his having been a Democrat until he resigned from the party in protest over the

Kansas-Nebraska Act. A dashing figure himself, he had by his side his wife, Jessie, renowned as the beautiful, fiery daughter of Jacksonian Democrat Thomas Hart Benton. Drawing on the appeal of Frémont's views and persona, the party adopted as its slogan for the presidential campaign, "Free speech, free press, free soil, free men, Fremont and victory!"

Having chosen Frémont to lead the ticket, the delegates looked for a solid Whig as vice president. The early frontrunner was former New Jersey senator William Dayton, but when Illinois delegates complained that the party was overlooking the middle of the country, they arranged for John Allison of Pennsylvania to put Lincoln's name into consideration for vice president because he was "the prince of fellows, and an Old-Line Whig."[26] Illinois delegate William Archer seconded the nomination, saying that he had known Lincoln for thirty years and had always found him "as pure a patriot as ever lived."[27] Lincoln's friend John Palmer added his endorsement, saying, "We [in Illinois] can lick Buchanan any way, but I think we can do it a little easier if we have Lincoln on the ticket with John C. Fremont."[28]

By the time Lincoln was nominated for vice president, more than half the delegates were already committed to other candidates. In fact, Lincoln was not even present; he was riding the circuit. Dayton eventually won the contest with 253 votes, but the 110 votes cast for Lincoln placed him second in a crowded field of fifteen candidates. When David Davis told him the news that he had been nominated for vice president, Lincoln joked, "I reckon that ain't me; there's another great man in Massachusetts named Lincoln, and I reckon it's him."[29] Yet Lincoln felt the sting once again of beginning a campaign too late as he had done in prior congressional races, especially since this time, without any effort, he had finished second within his party for its nomination for the second-highest office in the land. With effort, he could improve vastly on that.

As the 1856 general election approached, Pierce tried to manage Bleeding Kansas in a way that would not hurt his party's nominee, Buchanan. This meant he continued to put all the force of the national government behind the proslavery forces and enforced their selection of a proslavery constitution for Kansas. In response, Republicans focused on only a single issue: that the Democrats and their attachment to slavery were fanning the flames of war. Democrats argued that Pierce was enforcing the principle of popular sovereignty only when it favored slavery and Buchanan would simply continue to maintain the same policy. When the dust settled, the arguments of both parties did not matter: The election split almost entirely between free states and slave states. Buchanan won seventeen states, including all but one of the slave states, while Frémont won only nine states and received no electoral votes in ten of the fourteen slave states. Buchanan won the electoral vote, 174–114.

In Illinois, Republicans did better than expected, winning four congressional districts, more than the Whig Party ever had in a single election. Lincoln and Browning were vindicated in their belief that a former Democrat had a better chance than a former Whig at winning an election against a Democrat when their candidate for the House, William Bissell, won.

Lincoln had grown experienced in counting votes for logrolling in the state legislature and later in nominating conventions and general elections. In 1856, the Democrats had won the presidential election again in Illinois, but the margin between Buchanan and Frémont was less than 4 percent in the popular vote. By Lincoln's estimate, the results in Illinois and the nation were equally promising for the Republicans: Buchanan had won in both because the opposition vote was split between Frémont and Fillmore. Fillmore received over 15 percent of the popular vote in Illinois, nearly four times the margin separating the two major candidates there.

After the election, in December 1856, Lincoln told a gathering of Chicago Republicans that the path to the White House was clear—if all the factions that opposed Buchanan could "let [their] past differences, as nothing be" and could agree that the proposition that "all men were created equal" was "the 'central idea' in our political public opinion," then the Republicans could win the next presidential election.[30] This might have sounded to many as obvious but hard to do, but for Lincoln, the essential thing that winning required was maintaining party unity, a theme he had been stressing since Clay lost in 1844. For that strategy to work, Lincoln believed only a moderate could draw enough support to win in 1860. But the political landscape could change a lot over the next four years. And it did.

IV

As a lawyer, Lincoln well understood that Supreme Court appointments were among the most important legacies of a president. Once on the Supreme Court, justices—appointed for life—decided the great constitutional questions of the day and would continue to do so for decades thereafter. They were beyond any political retaliation, and if one shared the same constitutional outlook as the president who nominated him, he would entrench that view into the fabric of American constitutional law for many years after that president left office. The Constitution empowers every president to nominate justices—and everyone in the Senate with the authority to confirm or reject them based on their merit or outlook.

When Lincoln was a child and until his early twenties, the man who presided over the Court was John Marshall, who had studied law with the same man whom Clay had studied with. Marshall came to the Court appointed by the last Federalist president, John Adams, and remained as its leader long after Adams's Federalist Party died. In his nearly thirty-five years as chief justice, Marshall wrote many of the Court's landmark opinions upholding the Federalist vision of a strong national government. Among these, as Lincoln and Douglas knew, was the opinion in 1819 upholding the national bank, a centerpiece of Clay's American System. Marshall died in 1835 renowned as the Great Chief Justice for having maintained comity on the Court and having raised its stature among the grand institutions of the federal government. To replace Marshall, Jackson appointed his closest political adviser and attorney general, Roger Taney. Taney had written Jackson's famous veto against Clay's national bank in 1832.

Now, in a case that began in a small courtroom in St. Louis, the Court had to make the biggest decision it had ever confronted, and the nation knew and watched. At issue in the case, called *Dred Scott v. Sandford,* was the constitutionality of Clay's other singular achievement, the Missouri Compromise. Rumors swirled through Washington that, in preparing for his inauguration, Buchanan had written the two Pennsylvania justices on the Court—John Catron and Robert Grier—asking them to side with the slave-owners challenging the agreement Clay had forged in Congress. Taney assured Buchanan, both before his election and on the day of his inauguration, that he had the case well in hand and that Buchanan and the Democratic Party should expect a welcome outcome. The decision in *Dred Scott* came down on March 6, 1856, just two days after Buchanan was sworn in. The timing confirmed the widespread suspicion that the Court's majority was conspiring to take the heat off Buchanan by solving the slavery debate on its own.

At stake in the case was the fate of Dred Scott, a Missouri slave, who had been taken by his owner, army surgeon Dr. John Emerson, first to Rock Island, Illinois, whose constitution prohibited slavery and which, as Lincoln repeated in more than a few speeches, was covered by the Northwest Ordinance, which prohibited slavery. From Illinois, Emerson took Dred Scott to Fort Snelling, in the Minnesota Territory, where slavery had been barred by the Missouri Compromise. After returning to Missouri, Emerson died. Scott found a lawyer—former Jacksonian Democrat Montgomery Blair, the son of Francis Blair, who had helped Jackson found the Democratic Party and had run the newspaper that became Jackson's mouthpiece while he was in office. (The entire Blair family left the Democratic Party in protest over the Kansas-Nebraska Act.) Before the Supreme Court, Montgomery Blair argued that Scott had been made free as a result of having traveled through Illinois and the Missouri Territory, both of which had stripped him of whatever slave status he had and regarded him as a free man.

Though each of the nine justices wrote an opinion, Taney wrote the official opinion for the Court, joined by six others. First, the Court ruled that Scott was not entitled to sue, because only citizens of the United States could bring a lawsuit in federal court and as a slave (and descendant of Africans), he was not eligible to be a citizen of the United States. Taney declared that the framers never intended for Negroes to be citizens of the United States, that, at the time of the founding, enslaved Negroes were considered "so far inferior, that they had no rights which the white man was bound to respect," and the framers had not included them in either the Declaration of Independence or the Constitution.[31]

Second, the chief justice ruled that traveling through the Wisconsin Territory did not transform Scott into a free man because the Missouri Compromise was unconstitutional. On behalf of the majority, Taney explained that slaveholders had a constitutional right to own slaves under the Fifth Amendment of the Constitution, which protected their property from being deprived without "due process of law."[32] Taney said the law did just that, and so he undid another centerpiece of Clay's legacy.

If there was anything novel in what the Court did, it was the decision holding that the Constitution affirmatively protected slavery. But, in terms of reasoning, there was little new in the opinion insofar as Lincoln was concerned. He knew the arguments against the Missouri Compromise well; he had studied that law and followed the congressional debates on its constitutionality for more than two decades. He had also discussed it at length in his eulogy for Clay and again in his speeches in Springfield and Peoria in 1854. Well versed in the arguments that slave-owners and Democratic senators like John Calhoun and Jefferson Davis had been making for years about the rights of slave-owners to own slaves, Lincoln saw no reason to rehash these arguments now. Much as he had once joked to a friendly audience, with respect to the Kansas-Nebraska Act, he said that he "could not help feeling foolish in answering arguments which were no arguments at all."[33]

On the merits, Lincoln agreed with the two dissenting opinions. One was written by Justice John McLean, whom Lincoln and Browning had supported more than once for president. They knew McLean supported the Missouri Compromise, so it was no surprise that he dissented. Jackson never said much about the Missouri Compromise after it had been signed into law by President Monroe in 1820, but everyone presumed his silence meant he supported it. As a Jackson appointee, McLean was a living reminder of the complexity of Jackson's legacy.

The other dissent came from Benjamin Curtis, a Fillmore appointee. Lincoln agreed with his argument that slavery was wrong and violated the promise of the Declaration of Independence. Curtis had taken the dramatic step, after issuing his dissent, of resigning in protest of the decision, but he merely enabled Buchanan to replace him with Nathan Clifford, a virulently proslavery zealot whom the Senate approved 26–23, the closest Senate confirmation vote up until that time.

The *Dred Scott* decision placed the Court at the center of national attention. Lincoln, too, closely followed the case. As a lawyer, he was disposed to be respectful of the Court, even when he knew it was wrong. Indeed, he had previously defended the Court as the ultimate arbiter of disputes over slavery. During the 1856 presidential campaign between Buchanan and Frémont, Lincoln said, "The Supreme Court of the United States is the tribunal to decide such questions," and he pledged for the Republicans that "we will submit to its decisions; and if [the Democrats] do also, there will be an end to the matter."[34]

Lincoln did not publicly discuss the decision until Douglas gave him the opportunity. In June 1857, Douglas returned to Illinois to defend the "honest and conscientious" justices in the majority and to condemn any criticism of the Court as a "deadly blow at our whole republican system of government."[35] He heartily agreed with Taney's claim that African Americans belonged to "an inferior race, who, in all ages, and in every part of the globe . . . had shown themselves incapable of self-government."[36] It was not uncommon for people who defended slavery to claim it kept white women safe from African American men or for the people who owned slaves to rape and terrorize them, and Douglas, true to form, warned his constituents that Republicans favored the "amalgamation, between superior and inferior races."[37]

On June 26, 1857, Lincoln delivered a speech at the State House in Springfield, responding to Douglas's defense of the *Dred Scott* decision. He began, as expected, by declaring that the decision was "erroneous. We know the court that made it, has often over-ruled its own decisions, and we shall do what we can to have it over-rule this. We offer no resistance to it."[38] As he had in the past, Lincoln was expressing the classical respect for a Supreme Court decision that might have been wrongly decided; there was a right way to undo it and a wrong way. The wrong way was to disobey it. Clay would never have sanctioned flouting the rule of law, and Lincoln would not go that far either. Instead, Lincoln was reminding his audience that the Constitution provides legitimate ways to overrule or undo erroneous decisions, including persuading the justices that they erred. Another, but not one mentioned in Lincoln's speech, was appointing justices who would move the Court in a different direction.

Lincoln knew that Douglas, once the beneficiary of the Illinois Democrats stacking the state supreme court to rule as they would like, was being hypocritical in his praise for the Court. Rather than being guilty of any such hypocrisy himself, Lincoln instructed his audience on how weak the opinion was and built the case for its overruling. In January 1856, Lincoln acknowledged that, if the Court had decided that Dred Scott was a slave, he "presumed, no one would controvert its correctness."[39] Now, in June, he went further: "If this important decision had been made by the unanimous concurrence of the judges, and without any apparent partisan bias, and in accordance with legal public expectation, and with the steady practice of the departments throughout our history," it would be "factious, nay, even revolutionary," not to accept it.[40] But that was not this case. When a majority of the justices—overruling numerous precedents and ignoring Justice Curtis's historical evidence showing many states had recognized African Americans as citizens—extended their ruling to an entire race, it was wrong. Thus, the decision lacked the attributes of a decision commanding respect from the other branches and the American people. Without saying so, Lincoln was questioning *this* Court's legitimacy.

Lincoln did not end his speech there. He was especially troubled by Chief Justice Taney's claim that neither the Declaration of Independence nor the Constitution was ever intended to include African Americans. Lincoln declared that Taney was doing "obvious violence to the plain unmistakable language of the Declaration," which used to be thought by Americans to include everyone.[41] In this, Lincoln agreed with Clay that the Declaration's great pronouncements were intertwined with the Constitution. But the Declaration, on Taney's reading, "is assailed, and sneered at, and construed, and hawked at, and torn, till, if its framers could rise from their graves, they could not at all recognize it."[42] Not only was Lincoln making it clearer that the decision lacked legitimacy, but he never again spoke of the Taney Court with any respect; indeed, he largely ignored it.

The legitimacy of the Court's decision, Lincoln argued, was eroded further by Taney's appearing to be in league with Douglas and the Democratic Party. For many Radical Republicans, this was the heart of the matter, though it took Lincoln time to get there. He charged that Taney and Douglas had allied to oppress Negroes and conspired to perpetuate and extend slavery. Lincoln argued that Douglas tried to make the oppression tolerable by suggesting Republicans wanted to have sex with black women. Lincoln rejected "that counterfeit logic which concludes that, because I do not want a black woman for a slave I must necessarily want her for a wife."[43] The authors of the Declaration of Independence never intended "to say all were equal in color, size, intellect, moral developments, or social capacity," but they "did consider all men created equal—equal in 'certain inalienable rights, among which are life, liberty, and the pursuit of happiness.'"[44]

In the end, this was not a radical speech, though many would charge that it was. Instead, it was Lincoln's return to the familiar ground that he shared with Clay (and the old-line Whigs he was wooing) that the Constitution must be understood in light of the promises of the Declaration of Independence.

V

Lincoln was determined in 1858 not to repeat the mistake he'd made too many times before, as when he'd last delayed entering the Senate race. Now he wasted no time. Two years before the Senate election, he hustled to consolidate support within the Republican nominating convention in Illinois. In August 1857, he began encouraging his fellow Republicans to do something "now," in letter after letter, to take control of the Illinois state Senate. It was imperative Republicans capture the Senate because it would be selecting whoever took Douglas's seat.[45]

Clay had never been subtle in his campaigns. Regardless of whether he was running for the House, Senate, or presidency, he let the world know his views loudly, if not clearly. It was not always a winning strategy for Clay; he peaked too soon in every presidential race he ran. Particularly with respect to securing his party's nomination for the Senate, it would be better, Lincoln thought, to consolidate support within his party while the opposition was preoccupied with smoothing the path for its nominee—this time, Douglas, of course—to win the general election. "Let all be so quiet that the adve[r]sary [Douglas] shall not be notified," Lincoln advised his supporters.[46]

It came as some surprise to Lincoln, however, that continuing violent instability in Kansas transformed the upcoming midterm election. Lincoln characterized what unfolded next as "the most exquisite farce ever enacted."[47] President Buchanan wanted to rush the admission of Kansas through Congress, but Free Soil voters in Kansas decided not to participate in the selection of a state Constitution because they thought it was rigged against them. As a result, only about 2,200 voters out of the registered 9,000 showed up at the state convention held in Lecompton, Kansas, which was charged with drafting the new constitution for Kansas. Unsurprisingly, the delegates drafted a proslavery constitution, which guaranteed not only that roughly two hundred slaves already in Kansas would remain in bondage but that their offspring would also be slaves. The new constitution further provided that it could not be amended for seven years. Then the delegates rejected Buchanan's advice that they should ratify the constitution they had just drafted. Instead, they arranged for a referendum on the question of whether more slaves could be introduced into the state.

Eager for the Kansas crisis to be settled, Buchanan preemptively kept pushing for the convention to ratify a new constitution. When the delegates produced the proslavery constitution he had been pushing, their Lecompton Constitution, Buchanan sent it to Washington for Congress's approval.

To nearly every Democrat's surprise, Douglas split with Buchanan and decided to oppose the Lecompton Constitution. Because it was increasingly likely he would face Lincoln in the Senate race set for the next year, he understood that Lincoln would press him mercilessly on the defects of the drafting of the document—particularly on the failure to follow the prescribed path for admission, which required a statewide referendum on the new constitution. Douglas was already losing public support over the Kansas-Nebraska Act, Bleeding Kansas, and the *Dred Scott* decision, each becoming an albatross he had to shake in order to keep his seat and begin his presidential campaign.

The Lecompton Constitution violated Douglas's principle of popular sovereignty because the inhabitants of the Kansas Territory had not actually exercised their right to choose their own form of government. It was a constitution foisted on the people of the state rather than one they had approved themselves. Douglas knew that—and publicly acknowledged as much. He vowed to lead the Senate fight against the Lecompton Constitution. He denounced it as "a flagrant violation of popular rights in Kansas" and a violation as well of "the fundamental principles of liberty upon which our institutions rest."[48] He stressed that he took issue not with the proslavery constitution itself but rather with the process by which it was adopted.

The announcement permanently estranged Douglas from Buchanan, who began to systematically remove all Illinois patronage from Douglas's control. However, much to Lincoln's chagrin,

Douglas's opposition to the Lecompton Constitution pleased
Republicans nationwide, and Senator Trumbull went further to
suggest that, despite the fact that Douglas was a Democrat, the
Illinois Republicans nominate him as their candidate for the Senate. When Republicans from outside the state appeared to rally
around the idea, Lincoln and his supporters pushed back hard. In
the meantime, Democratic newspapers in Illinois proclaimed Lincoln unelectable and touted the possible candidacy of "Long John"
Wentworth, a former congressman and editor of the *Chicago Democrat* newspaper, for the Senate.

  Lincoln responded to Wentworth's threat as he had done to Hardin's efforts years before to derail his candidacy for the House.
There were eighty-seven seats up in the state legislature, and
Lincoln had to find a way to secure at least a majority of the Republicans. With Lincoln's approval, his supporters went to county
conventions to secure support for his nomination to the U.S. Senate. With that in hand, they arranged, for only the second time
in American history, to have a statewide convention held for the
purpose of nominating a candidate for the Senate. Lincoln had not
been moved to do so by any principle but rather, as he said, "more
for the object of closing down upon this everlasting croaking about
Wentworth, than anything else."[49]

  When Republicans convened at the statehouse for their convention on June 16, 1858, the outcome was preordained. First, because
Lincoln and other Republicans approved the platform Browning
had drafted for the prior convention establishing the party, they
asked him to draft an almost identical platform for this one. After
nominating candidates for state treasurer and superintendent of
education, they turned to the business of deciding on a nominee to
challenge Douglas. The Lincoln forces quickly played their hand:
state legislator Norman Judd and his Chicago delegation unfurled
a banner declaring, COOK COUNTY IS FOR ABRAHAM LINCOLN. As the
delegates applauded, a member from the Peoria delegation moved
for the convention to adopt the motto, "Illinois Is for Abraham Lincoln." The resulting momentum crushed Wentworth's chances,
and the convention moved unanimously to nominate Lincoln

as "the first and only choice of the Republicans of Illinois for the United States Senate, as the successor of Stephen A. Douglas."[50]

Lincoln secured the nomination at five o'clock on June 16, 1858. The convention scheduled Lincoln's acceptance speech for three hours later. He had been working on his draft for some time, and now he read the draft to Swett, Herndon, Palmer, and other campaign advisers. They all agreed on one thing—the speech would end Lincoln's political career. Herndon thought it was powerful but was delivering the wrong message at the wrong time. Years later, Leonard Swett blamed the speech for Lincoln's defeat: "Nothing could have been more unfortunate or inappropriate; it was saying first the wrong thing, yet he saw it as an abstract truth, but standing by the speech ultimately would find him in the right place."[51] Herndon agreed that the speech proved, in spite of what he thought, to be helpful to Lincoln in the long run: "Through logic inductively seen, Lincoln as a statesman, political philosopher, announced an eternal truth—not only as broad as America, but covers the world."

Lincoln rejected the advice to modify his message or give a more palatable one. He told them, "The proposition [set forth in it] is indisputably true . . . and I will deliver it as written. I want to use some universally known figure, expressed in simple language as universally known, that it may strike home to the minds of men in order to rouse them to the peril of the times."[52] Lincoln had found the self-assurance to speak in his voice. He could not merely compromise for the sake of compromise. Even Clay had understood that there had to be inviolable values—the Union was one, and opposing the extension of slavery was another. Clay did not write his speeches to be read but to be delivered. Lincoln was writing his speech to be both delivered and read later in newspapers. His message had to be simple and direct so anyone reading in a newspaper or reciting it aloud could experience the power of his words. So confident was Lincoln, he invited reporters to cover the speech and spread its message wherever their papers were sold. It soon became known as the House Divided Speech.

Lincoln arrived at the Illinois State Capitol at eight o'clock on

June 16, 1858. It was a familiar venue where he had spoken dozens of times. He began with an homage to Daniel Webster. No one delivered more powerful opening lines than Webster, and Lincoln knew every word of Webster's famous reply to Senator Robert Hayne of South Carolina, the defender of nullification. Rising from his desk in the old Senate chamber, Webster had opened his rebuttal with an elegant metaphor:

> When the mariner has been tossed for many days in thick weather, and on an unknown sea, he naturally avails himself of the first pause in the storm, the earliest glance of the sun, to take his latitude, and ascertain how far the elements have driven him from his true course. Let us imitate this prudence, and before we float farther, refer to the point from which we departed, that we may at least be able conjecture where we are now.[53]

Lincoln adapted that same opening for his midwestern audience, in an early but significant sign of his mastery of simplifying flowery declarations and complex arguments. He wasn't speaking to other senators but to the people of his state. He wasn't aiming to reach the educated elite but the farmers and laborers he'd spoken to for more than two decades in countless campaign rallies. Fancy images were inauthentic. If his message reached them, it could move them to move their representatives and party leaders in Lincoln's favor.

Lincoln's opening thus did not mince words: "If we could first know where we are, and whither we are tending, we could better judge what to do, and how to do it."[54] From there, he reminded his listeners that "we are now in the fifth year, since a policy was initiated, with the avowed object, and confident promise, of putting an end to slavery agitation."[55] However, under the Pierce and Buchanan policy of appeasing the slave power,

> that agitation has not only, not ceased, but has consistently augmented. In my opinion, it will not cease, until a crisis shall have been reached, and passed. "A house divided against itself cannot

*stand." I believe this government cannot endure, permanently half
slave and half free. I do not expect the Union to be dissolved—I do
not expect the house to fall—but I do expect it will cease to be divided. It will become all one thing, or all the other.*[56]

It was common for Lincoln to try out his speeches and arguments
on different audiences and keep tinkering with his message until
the last moment. The metaphor of a house divided was not new, either for Lincoln or his audience. For those who had read Aesop's fables, it was familiar. For those who read the Bible, it was even more
so. As David Herbert Donald suggests in his biography of Lincoln,
the phrase "was familiar to virtually everybody in a Bible-reading,
churchgoing state like Illinois; it appeared in three of the Gospels."[57]
Lincoln had used the image as early as 1843 in urging party solidarity among the Whigs, and abolitionist Wendell Phillips had used it
in his speeches condemning slavery in the 1840s and later. The idea
behind the metaphor as he now used it, that slavery and freedom
were incompatible, had been a standard part of the abolitionists' argument for decades. Webster, too, had used the phrase. As Donald
determined, "As early as 1855, after his first defeat for the Senate,
[Lincoln] raised the question with a Kentucky correspondent, 'Can
we, as a nation, continue together permanently—forever—half
slave and half free?'" During the Frémont campaign the next year,
he used the same phrase again, and in December 1857 Lincoln used
it in another speech he was drafting. The persistent use was clever
rhetorically, for it immediately made his audience feel smart and
identify Lincoln as one of them.

Having shared that powerful message at the outset, Lincoln then
launched into a broadside against the Democrats. Just as he had
done in his response to Douglas on *Dred Scott,* Lincoln returned
to his theme that the Democrats likely were conspiring as their
next step in protecting slavery to get a Supreme Court opinion that
extended the logic of the decision to bar any state from keeping
someone entering with his slaves. "But when we see," he told his
fellow Republicans, "a lot of framed timbers, different portions of
which we know have been gotten out at different times and places

and by different workmen—Stephen, Franklin, Roger, and James, for instance—and when we see these timbers joined together, and see they exactly make the frame of a house or mill, all these tenons and mortices exactly fitting, and . . . not a piece too many or too few," it was impossible not to think the four men had worked from the same plan.[58] With that, Lincoln accused Douglas, Pierce, Taney, and Buchanan of working in concert to strengthen and extend the slave power. He predicted, "Put that and that together, and we have another nice little niche, which we may, ere long, see filled with another Supreme Court decision, declaring that the Constitution of the United States does not permit a state to exclude slavery from its limits. [Such] a decision is all that slavery now lacks of being alike lawful in all the States."[59]

VI

By 1858, Lincoln and Stephen Douglas had been debating each other for more than two decades. They had done it before large crowds, as in Peoria, and smaller ones, as when Lincoln substituted for Stuart in 1838. They had debated in taverns and at conventions. Lincoln had watched Douglas debate John Todd Stuart throughout the district in 1838, and he followed Orville Browning's debates with Douglas in their 1843 contest for the House. In 1838, Stuart had bested Douglas, barely, while five years later Browning had lost, albeit by a respectable margin. In debates, Stuart matched Douglas's combative style with his own brand of sarcasm and taunting, while Browning, with considerably thinner skin than either Stuart or Lincoln, had reached a different agreement beforehand with Douglas "not to violate with each other the courtesies and proprieties of life; and not to permit any ardor or excitement of debate to betray us into coarse and unmanly personalities; [and] the compact was well and faithfully kept on both sides . . . Not one unkind word or discourteous act passed between us."[60]

Lincoln and Douglas had met so often on the battlefield of politics that they had developed a long-standing respect for each other. When Lincoln received the Republican nomination for senator, Douglas told a newspaper man, "I shall have my hands full. He is as honest as he is shrewd."[61] Despite the stinging rebukes Lincoln directed at Douglas in the aftermath of the Kansas-Nebraska Act and Bleeding Kansas, he openly acknowledged Douglas outshone him:

> *Senator Douglas is of world-wide renown. All of the anxious politicians of his party, or who have been of his party for years past, have been looking upon him as certainly, at no distant day, to be the President of the United States. They have seen, in his jolly, fruitful face, post offices, land offices, marshalships and Cabinet appointments, chargeships and foreign missions, bursting and sprouting forth in wonderful exuberance, ready to be laid hold of by their greedy hands. On the contrary, nobody has ever expected me to be President. In my poor, lean, lank face nobody has ever seen that cabbages were sprouting out.*[62]

Elevating Douglas while exuding humility about himself was perhaps tongue-in-cheek, but it was a persistent note Lincoln sounded, inspired by Clay's frequent use of the same device. Herndon agreed with Lincoln's assessment of Douglas:

> *I always found Douglas at the bar to be a broad, fair, and liberal-minded man. Although not a thorough student of the law his large fund of good commonsense kept him in the front rank. He was equally generous and courteous, and he never stooped to gain a case. I know that Lincoln entertained the same view of him. It was only in politics that Douglas demonstrated any want of inflexibility and rectitude, and then only did Lincoln manifest a lack of faith in his morals.*[63]

Lincoln considered Douglas "a very strong logician, that he had very little humor or imagination; but where he had right on his side very few could make a stronger argument; that he was an

exceedingly good judge of human nature, knew the people of the
state thoroughly and just how to appeal to their prejudices and was
a very powerful opponent, both on and off the stump."[64] Joseph
Gillespie recalled that Lincoln "always admitted that Douglass [sic]
was a wonderfully great political leader and with a good cause to
advocate he thought he would be invincible."[65]

Yet Lincoln hesitated to meet Douglas in debate because he
feared that Douglas would stack the crowds with his supporters.
With encouragement from Browning, Herndon, Judd, Swett, and
others in his kitchen Cabinet, Lincoln warmed to the idea when he
realized that standing on the stage with Douglas would improve
his own stature and that reporters from Republican-friendly papers would report favorably on his performance. Lincoln saw his
advantage. He extended an invitation in writing to Douglas, who
initially resisted because Lincoln would tower over him and the
debate might raise Lincoln's profile, but the prospect of statewide
and national coverage persuaded him to accept.

Even after Douglas accepted the invitation and the two men
scheduled debates in seven sites around the state, Lincoln knew
he had little chance of winning. With Douglas's help, Democrats
in the state legislature had reapportioned seats to enable greater
representation from the Southern, more Democratic districts.
Douglas thus entered the contest in a strongly favorable position;
he just had to keep the Democratic districts in line, while Lincoln
had the nearly impossible task of not just carrying the legislators
from his districts but somehow snatching a few from Democratic
ones.

Lincoln meticulously examined the results of the past election
district by district, which indicated where he should focus his energies. He gave only four speeches in the northern portion of Illinois,
four in the south, and otherwise spent his time rallying voters in
the central part of the state, where he hoped to generate significant
support. He thought his best chance to keep the old Whigs in his
camp was to remind them that he was a Henry Clay Whig, as past
election patterns made it clear Clay played well in many of the districts he would be traveling through.

The problem was that Douglas was claiming the mantle of Henry Clay for himself. When Lincoln discovered that John Crittenden, the powerful Kentucky senator who had been Clay's protégé, had followed Clay in joining the National Republican Party in 1828, and was openly encouraging people to support Douglas, Lincoln wrote him. Lincoln had worked closely in the 1848 presidential campaign with Crittenden, whom he thought was as devout a party man as himself and Clay. Crittenden responded that in fact the report was true and that he felt a Douglas reelection was "necessary as a rebuke to the Administration, and a vindication of the great cause of popular rights and public justice."[66] Crittenden was no friend to him or to Clay's memory.

Because of the reapportionment in the state, Douglas had everything to lose in the election. On the one hand, if defeated, Lincoln would be in no worse position than he was now—out of office trying to find his way back in, but likely to have enhanced his reputation and gained national stature by going toe-to-toe with such a daunting and powerful opponent. Douglas was fully aware he could not let his guard down; no one else had more experience debating Douglas than Lincoln.[67] Lincoln never let his guard down, either. Whatever his respect for Douglas may have been, he distrusted his opponent, whom Lincoln regarded as dangerous, unprincipled, and underhanded.

In the seven debates, the two men covered many familiar subjects, ranging from popular sovereignty to slavery to Douglas's charge that Lincoln and his party were dangerous radicals. They were fighting for the middle, and that meant they were fighting over who had claim to Clay's legacy. Douglas claimed that he was Clay's true heir, since Clay and Douglas had both declared themselves devotees of Jefferson, and Douglas had worked with Clay to fashion the Compromise of 1850. Lincoln scoffed at the idea, and the outsize influence of Clay, particularly in Lincoln's thinking, was central in every debate. At the first debate, in Ottawa, Illinois, Lincoln quoted Clay more than forty times, more than he cited any founder or prior president. Together, the two combatants quoted and mentioned Clay nearly a hundred times. These numbers do not include the many times Lincoln was talking about an idea or concept he learned from Clay. Six years after Lincoln delivered his eulogy of Clay, championing his legacy was crucial to the future of his campaign and the country. Proclaimed Lincoln,

> *Henry Clay, my beau ideal of a statesman, the man for whom I fought all my humble life. [Clay] once said of a class of men who would repress all tendencies to liberty and ultimate emancipation, that they must, if they would do this, go back to the era of our Independence, and muzzle the cannon which thunders its annual joyous return; they must blow out the moral lights around us; they must penetrate the human soul, and eradicate there the love of liberty; and then, and not till then, could they perpetuate slavery in this country![68]*

Clay had been one of the first party standard bearers to insist that following the Constitution meant keeping faith with the Declaration of Independence, a position he regarded as the conservative one, derived from Thomas Jefferson, designed to keep the Union intact, and to preserve the ideals of both texts. (George Prentice rammed this point home in his 1830 campaign biography of Clay.) In repeatedly re-sounding that same theme, Lincoln hoped to cast Douglas and other Democratic leaders such as Taney and Buchanan as the radicals bent on destroying the promises and ideals of the nation's founding documents. Rather than intend to protect slavery, the framers had drafted a Constitution that gave the federal government the power to regulate it, Lincoln argued. It was Lincoln and the Republican Party that took the conservative position to follow the original scheme of the Constitution and preserve its original ideals and promises; it was Douglas and his cohorts who were willing to destroy the country's founding commitments for the sake of appeasing slave-owners.

In the second debate, held in Freeport, Illinois, Lincoln said,

> *Yet as a member of Congress, I should not with my present views, be in favor of endeavoring to abolish slavery in the District of Co-*

lumbia, unless it would be upon these conditions: First, that the abolition should be gradual. Washington, Jefferson, and Clay had all endorsed the principle of gradual emancipation. Second, that it should be on a vote of the majority of qualified voters in the District; and third, that compensation should be made to unwilling owners.[69]

These conditions were familiar to many people in the crowd who remembered Clay, who had pushed for them in 1850.

Douglas answered that "Clay was dead, and although the sod was not yet green on his grave, this man [Lincoln] undertook to bring into disrepute those great Compromise measures of 1850, with which Clay and Webster were identified."[70] Indeed, Douglas pointed out,

up to 1854 the old Whig party and the Democratic party had stood on a common platform so far as this slavery question was concerned. You Whigs and we Democrats differed about the bank, the tariff, distribution, the specie circular, and the sub-treasury, but we agreed on this slavery question and the true mode of preserving the peace and harmony of the Union. The Compromise measures of 1850 were introduced by Clay, were defended by Webster, and supported by Cass, and were approved by Fillmore, and sanctioned by the National men of both parties.[71]

No one had to remind listeners that Lincoln was back in Springfield practicing law when this was happening. Everyone knew it was Douglas, not Lincoln, who had made the compromise a reality. "Thus," Douglas said,

they constituted a common plank upon which Whigs and Democrats stood. In 1852 the Whig party, in its last National Convention at Baltimore, indorsed and approved these measures of Clay, and so did the National Convention of the Democratic party, held that same year. Thus, the old line Whigs and the old line Democrats stood pledged to the great principle of self-government, which

guarantees to the people of each Territory the right to decide the
slavery question for themselves.

Now Douglas twisted the knife:

In 1854, after the death of Clay and Webster, Mr. Lincoln, on the
part of the Whigs, undertook to Abolitionize the Whig party, by
dissolving it, transferring the members into the Abolition camp
and making their train under Giddings, Fred Douglass [who had
escaped slavery to become one of the nation's most eloquent and out-
spoken advocates for eradicating slavery], Lovejoy, Chase, [Hiram]
Farnsworth [of Kansas], and other Abolition leaders.[72]

This back-and-forth did not impede Lincoln's strategy in the second debate. Following the advice of *Chicago Tribune* managing editor Joseph Medill, Lincoln pressed Douglas to answer four loaded
questions: First, would Douglas favor the admission of Kansas
before it had the requisite number of inhabitants as specified in
the law controlling the admission of new states? Second, could the
people of a territory, such as Kansas, "exclude slavery from its limits prior to the formation of a state Constitution?"[73] Third, would
Douglas follow a Supreme Court decision declaring that the states
could not exclude slavery from their limits? Fourth, did Douglas
favor acquisition of new territory "in disregard of how such acquisition may affect the nation on the slavery question?"[74]

Douglas dodged most of Lincoln's questions, but it was the second one that Lincoln and his cohort thought was key, and Douglas
took the bait. He answered that the passage of "unfriendly legislation" could keep slavery out of any federal territory because "slavery cannot exist a day or an hour anywhere, unless it is supported
by local police regulations."[75] He added that "the people of a Territory had the lawful power to exclude slavery, prior to the formation of a [State] Constitution."[76] This was a full embrace of his
principle of popular sovereignty, and Lincoln and the Republicans
would use it relentlessly as a wedge to divide Douglas from Buchanan and other proslavery Democrats.

Lincoln also jumped on Douglas's defense of *Dred Scott*. His first rejoinder came in response to Douglas's assertion that he was prepared not to comply with the *Dred Scott* decision. Lincoln pressed Douglas to take a position on the issue that *Dred Scott* contradicted Douglas's principle of popular sovereignty. After ruling in *Dred Scott* that the federal government could not bar slavery from the territories, the next likely step for the Court would be to forbid states from outlawing slavery, presenting Douglas with the dilemma of choosing either the decision *or* his principle of popular sovereignty. Something had to give. Forcing Douglas into a corner, Lincoln argued that "there is nothing that can divert or turn him away from this decision. It is nothing to him that Jefferson did not so believe. I have said that I have often heard him approve of Jackson's course in disregarding the decision of the Supreme Court pronouncing a national bank constitutional. He says, I did not hear him say so . . . though it still seems to me that I heard him say it twenty times."[77]

Lincoln cast Douglas as lacking any principled fidelity to the Supreme Court or the law. He reminded those in attendance that Douglas had endorsed the Democratic Party's 1856 platform that opposed Jackson's stance on the national bank. Because the Supreme Court had upheld the constitutionality of the national bank, Jackson's opposition placed him at odds with the Court. But then Lincoln called attention to the 1840s when Douglas took the lead in Illinois to overturn the "decision of the Supreme Court of Illinois, because [Democrats] had decided that a Governor could not remove a Secretary of State."[78] Lincoln pointedly added, "I know that Judge Douglas will not deny that he was then in favor of overslaughing that decision by adding five new Judges, so as to vote down the four old ones. Not only so, but it ended in the Judge's sitting down on that very bench as one of the five new Judges to break down the four old ones."[79]

Lincoln returned to this theme in the fourth debate, at Charleston, Illinois. He pressed his audience not to forget "the fact that [Douglas] was one of the most active instruments at one time in breaking down the Supreme Court of the state of Illinois, because it had made a decision distasteful to him—a struggle ending in the remarkable circumstance of his sitting down as one of the new Judges who were to overslaugh that decision—getting his title of Judge in that very way."[80] Douglas ignored the taunt. Instead, he reiterated his position that Supreme Court decisions are final, and his duty was to follow them, regardless of whether he agreed with them or not.

In the fifth debate, held in Galesburg, Lincoln reminded his audience of the ideals Clay had fought for all of his life, saying, "I can express all my views on the slavery question by quotations from Henry Clay." He proceeded to do that, once again recalling

> that Mr. Clay, when he was once answering an objection to the Colonization Society, that it had a tendency to the ultimate emancipation of the slaves, said that "those who would repress all tendencies to liberty and ultimate emancipation must do more than put down the benevolent efforts of the Colonization Society—they must go back to the era of our liberty and independence and, so far as in him lies, muzzling the cannon that thunders its annual joyous return—they must blot out the moral lights around us—they must penetrate the human soul, and eradicate the light of reason and the love of liberty.[81]

Lincoln was repeating portions of his eulogy but to good effect with the old Clay Whigs in his audience.

In the sixth debate, held in Browning's hometown of Quincy (though Browning's law practice had taken him out of town), Lincoln again pressed the point that he, not Douglas, was the true heir of Clay. "I wished to show," he said, "but I will pass it upon this occasion, that in the sentiment I have occasionally advanced upon the Declaration of Independence, I am entirely borne out by the sentiments of our old Whig leader, Henry Clay, and I have the book to show it from; but because I have already occupied more time than I needed to do on the topic, I pass over it."[82] Lincoln held the book of Clay speeches in his hand, his personal bible. In responding to Douglas's opposition to thinking of the Declaration of Independence as setting forth the promises and ideals that the Constitution was designed to implement, Lincoln said,

> The Judge has taken great exception to my adopting the heretical statement in the Declaration of Independence, that "all men are created equal," . . . [but] I have only uttered the sentiments that Henry Clay used to hold. Allow me to occupy your time a moment with what he said. Mr. Clay was at one time called upon in Indiana, and in a way that I suppose was very insulting, to liberate his slaves, and he made a written reply to that application, and one portion of it in these words,

which Lincoln then quoted,

> What is the foundation of this appeal to me in Indiana, to liberate the slaves under my care in Kentucky? It is a general declaration in the act announcing to the world the independence of the thirteen American colonies, that "men are created equal." Now, as an abstract principle, there is no doubt of the truth of that declaration, and it is desirable in the original construction of society, and, in organized societies, to keep it in view as a great fundamental principle.[83]

Douglas responded with a lengthy protest that he had been consistently attached to both Clay and his principle of popular sovereignty. In 1850, he "was supported by Clay, Webster, Cass, and the great men of that day" when he included within the Compromise of 1850 provisions that allowed for the entry of California into the Union as a free state but created the new territories of Kansas and Nebraska, which would decide for themselves whether to be slave or free. Thus, he said, he held on to the same principles "in 1854, and in 1856, when Mr. Buchanan was elected President." His audience no doubt thinking of the eventual break between Buchanan and Douglas over the Lecompton Constitution, Douglas continued, "It goes on to prove and succeeds in proving, from my speeches in Congress on Clay's Compromise measures, that I held

the same doctrines at that time that I do now, and then proves that
by the Kansas and Nebraska bill I advanced the same doctrine that
I now advance."[84]

Held before a largely Republican audience, the final debate
featured yet another struggle for each man to show he was more
faithful to Clay's legacy. Douglas, Lincoln said, now "brings forward part of a speech from Henry Clay—the part of the speech of
Henry Clay which I used to bring forward to prove" that Clay's
Whigs were not radical abolitionists. The audience laughed. Lincoln paused, and then said, "I am somewhat acquainted with Old
Line Whigs. I was with the old line Whigs from the origin to the
end of that party; I became pretty well acquainted with them, and I
know they always had some sense, whatever else you could ascribe
to them." Again, the audience howled in laughter. Lincoln then
read an even broader excerpt from Clay's speech on the Declaration and slavery than he had at previous debates. "'That declaration, whatever may be the extent of its import, was made by the
delegations of the thirteen states,'" Lincoln quoted, continuing,

> In most of them slavery existed, and had long existed, and was es-
> tablished by law. It was introduced and forced upon the colonies by
> the paramount law of England. Do you believe, that in making that
> declaration the States concurred in it intended that it should be
> tortured into a virtual emancipation of all the slaves within their
> respective limits? Would Virginia and other Southern states have
> ever united in a declaration which was to be interpreted into an
> abolition of slavery among them?[85]

Lincoln's objective was to cast Clay—and thereby himself—as
no radical on abolition. Rebutting any claim that either he or Clay
was radical, he quoted Clay further:

> I desire no concealment of my opinions in regard to the institution
> of slavery. I look upon it as a great evil, and deeply lament that we
> have derived it from the parental Government, and from our ances-
> tors. I wish every slave in the United States was in the country

of his ancestors. But here they are; the question is, how can they be best dealt with? If a state of nature existed, and we were about to lay the foundations of our society, no man would be more strongly opposed than I should be, to incorporating the institution of slavery among its elements.[86]

It could be no surprise to Lincoln that later Frederick Douglass, who had escaped slavery to become a renowned abolitionist, proclaimed Lincoln completely complicit with the slave-owners. Friends like Giddings and Wilmot also looked away. But their extremism would not win Lincoln this election—or the next he had his eyes on. Only moderation could.

Yet, as Lincoln saw it, moderation did not mean complicity. He reminded the audience of "the real issue in this controversy," the conflict "on the part of one class that looks upon the institution of slavery as a wrong, and of another class that does not."[87] He concluded,

That is the issue that will continue in this country when these poor tongues of Judge Douglas and myself shall be silent. It is the eternal struggle between these two principles—right and wrong—throughout the world. They are the two principles that have stood face to face from the beginning of time; and will ever continue to struggle. The one is the common right of humanity and the other the divine right of kings.[88]

The unmistakable inference was that the framers' legacy ran straight through Jefferson to Clay and to Lincoln himself. And in referencing the distinction between "the common right" of people and that of kings, Lincoln was returning to a notion that Clay had made so many times that it earned him another nickname, the Great Commoner. Lincoln began with Clay and ended with him.

Douglas held nothing back. He attacked Lincoln's assertion that he was an old-line Whig. "He was not," Douglas flatly declared. "Bear in mind that there are a great many old Clay Whigs down in this region. It is more agreeable, therefore, for him to talk about the old Clay party than it is for him to talk Abolitionism."[89] Douglas pointed out that Lincoln said nothing about being an old-line Whig when he was campaigning in Democratic districts. Douglas gleefully asked listeners if they had read a speech from General James Singleton, who was widely known as a friend of Clay's. The audience said, "Yes, yes," and cheered. "You know," Douglas said, "that General Singleton was for twenty-five years the confidential friend of Henry Clay in Illinois, and he testified that in 1847, when the Constitutional Convention of this State was in session, the Whig members were invited to a Whig caucus at the house of Mr. Lincoln's brother-in-law, where Mr. Lincoln proposed to throw Henry Clay overboard and take up General Taylor in his place, giving as his reason, that if the Whigs did not take up General Taylor the Democrats would." The crowd cheered more loudly, as Douglas warmed to his point:

> Singleton testifies that Lincoln, in that speech, urged, as another reason for throwing Henry Clay overboard, that the Whigs had fought long enough on principle and ought to begin to fight for success. Singleton also testifies that Lincoln's speech did not have the effect of cutting Clay's throat, and that he (Singleton) and others withdrew from the caucus in indignation. He further states that when they got to Philadelphia to attend the National Convention of the Whig Party, that Lincoln was there, the bitter and deadly enemy of Clay, and that he tried to keep him (Singleton) out of the Convention because he insisted on voting for Clay, and Lincoln was determined to have Taylor.

The crowd again laughed and applauded. "Singleton says that Lincoln rejoiced with very great joy when he found the mangled remains of the murdered Whig statesman lying cold before him. Now, Mr. Lincoln tells you that he is an old line Clay Whig!" The cheers and laughter got louder. "General Singleton testifies to the facts I have narrated, in a public speech which has been printed and circulated broadcast over the State for weeks, yet not a lisp have

Abraham Lincoln relied heavily on books and his mentors for guidance or support, as shown here in a lighter moment in a photograph taken in the midst of the Civil War (1863). *Alexander Gardner*

Lincoln was ten at the time of this first-known portrait of Henry Clay, then a member of the House of Representatives. *Transylvania University*

John Todd Stuart in his prime as a Whig leader and successful lawyer. *Northern Illinois University*

MAJ. JOHN T. STUART.

Cartoon from 1832 election lampooning Andrew Jackson for acting like a king trampling the Constitution (1832).
Library of Congress, LC-DIG-ppmsca-15771

Jackson subduing Clay in the 1832 election and sewing his mouth shut (1834).
Library of Congress, LC-DIG-ds-00856

No. 26.   *Respecting the Nullifying Laws of South Carolina.*

PROCLAMATION

BY ANDREW JACKSON, PRESIDENT OF THE UNITED STATES.   Dec. 10, 1832.

WHEREAS a convention assembled in the State of South Carolina, have passed an ordinance, by which they declare, " That the several acts and parts of acts of the Congress of the United States, purporting to be laws for the imposing of duties and imposts on the importation of foreign commodities, and now having actual operation and effect within the United States, and more especially," two acts for the same purposes, passed on the 19th of May, 1828, and on the 14th of July, 1832, " are unauthorized by the Constitution of the United States, and violate the true meaning and intent thereof, and are null and void, and no law," nor binding on the citizens of that State, or its officers; and by the said ordinance, it is further declared to be unlawful for any of the constituted authorities of the State, or of the United States, to enforce the payment of the duties imposed by the said acts, within the same State, and that it is the duty of the legislature to pass such laws as may be necessary to give full effect to the said ordinance:

1828, ch. 55.
Vol. iv. p. 270.
1832, ch. 227.
Vol. iv. p. 583.

And whereas, by the said ordinance, it is further ordained, that, in no case of law or equity decided in the courts of said State, wherein shall be drawn in question the validity of the said ordinance, or of the acts of the legislature that may be passed to give it effect, or of the said laws of the United States, no appeal shall be allowed to the Supreme Court of the United States, nor shall any copy of the record be permitted or allowed for that purpose, and that any person attempting to take such appeal shall be punished as for contempt of court:

And, finally, the said ordinance declares that the people of South Carolina will maintain the said ordinance at every hazard; and that they will consider the passage of any act, by Congress, abolishing or closing the ports of the said State, or otherwise obstructing the free ingress or egress of vessels to and from the said ports, or any other act of the Federal Government to coerce the State, shut up her ports, destroy or harass her commerce, or to enforce the said acts otherwise than through the civil tribunals of the country, as inconsistent with the longer continuance of South Carolina in the Union; and that the people of the said State will thenceforth hold themselves absolved from all further obligation to maintain or preserve their political connection with the people of the other States, and will forthwith proceed to organize a separate government, and do all other acts and things which sovereign and independent States may of right do:

And whereas the said ordinance prescribes to the people of South Carolina a course of conduct in direct violation of their duty as citizens of the United

Jackson's 1832 proclamation against South Carolina's threatened nullification and secession. *Law Library of Congress*

Portrait of Jackson
by Edward Dalton
Marchant (1840).
*Courtesy of the Union
League Legacy Foundation*

Cartoon depiction of Jackson thrashing his would-be assassin (1835).
*Library of Congress, from "Shooting at the President!: The Remarkable Trial of Richard
Lawrence, for an Attempt to Assassinate the President of the United States"*

Portrait of William Henry Harrison by Thomas Wilcocks Sully (1840).
Courtesy of the Union League Legacy Foundation

Portrait of Clay by
John Neagle (1843).
*Courtesy of the Union League
Legacy Foundation*

Clay's inscription on a set of
his speeches given to Lincoln.
*Courtesy of Ashland, the Henry
Clay Estate, Lexington, Kentucky*

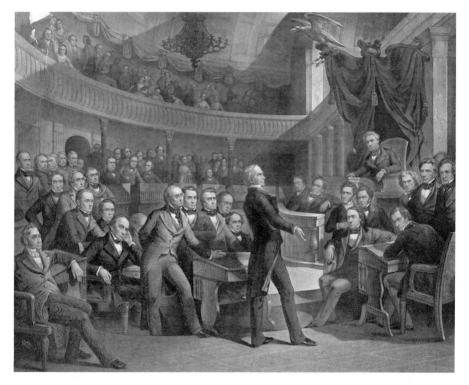

Famous depiction of Clay enthralling the Senate with his defense of the Compromise of 1850, with Millard Fillmore presiding as president of the Senate (1855). *Library of Congress, LC-DIG-pga-05850*

Portrait of Zachary Taylor by Robert Street (1850).
Courtesy of the Union League Legacy Foundation

Portrait of Fillmore by unknown artist (1850).
Courtesy of the Union League Legacy Foundation

POLITICAL INTELLIGENCE.

The Illinois papers come to us filled with reports of the Douglas and Lincoln debates. The audiences are of the largest kind—ten, fifteen, and even twenty thousand people gathering together to witness the sparring, if they cannot hear it, between the Judge and his antagonist. The last great debate came off on Wednesday at Quincy, and so vast was the collection of people that the town was overflowing, the hotels crowded, and many private houses completely filled with strangers. Senator Douglas seems to have made a regular triumphal march from Augusta to Quincy. At Camp Point, on the route—a small town of about one thousand inhabitants—he was met by a cavalcade of military, bands of music, and citizens gathered from that and the adjacent towns. In front of the station-house a splendid bonfire was flaming, and hundreds of torches were carried in the streets. Every house in the town was illuminated, presenting altogether one of the finest spectacles witnessed during the campaign. He arrived at Quincy in the evening, and was received there by a large torchlight procession. On either side of the immense procession by which Senator Douglas was escorted to his hotel—the Quincy House—stood in line hundreds of men holding up to view appropriate and gorgeous transparencies. The evening reception was large and brilliant. Upon the day of the speech the people came into Quincy displaying hickory poles and flags, until the town looked like a forest of hickories. There were present at the meeting upwards of fifteen thousand people, consisting of men of all parties, Democrats and Republicans. But the enthusiasm is by no means all on one side—the Lincoln men are equally as hopeful and determined as their opponents, and make just as vigorous exertions.

A report on the Lincoln-Douglas debates printed on October 23, 1858, in the *National Intelligencer*, the Republican-leaning and leading newspaper published in the nation's capital. *National Intelligencer*

Painted to show the widespread support of national leaders for the Compromise of 1850, this group portrait did not originally include Lincoln. On the eve of the Civil War, it was redone to insert Lincoln at the center in place of John Calhoun but kept Clay, who had died nearly a decade before, seated directly to Lincoln's right to reflect his significant influence on the new president (circa 1861).

U.S. Senate Collection

The two known photographs of Orville Browning, one taken in the late 1850s or early 1860s *(left)*, and the other when he was a senator from Illinois *(right)*. *Courtesy of the Lincoln Museum, Fort Wayne, Indiana. Reference Number: 2578* (left). *Library of Congress, LC-DIG-cwpbh-01588* (right).

Browning's audacious September 17, 1861, letter to President Lincoln. *Library of Congress, Manuscript Division, Abraham Lincoln Papers*

A drawing of Lincoln showing his draft of the Emancipation Proclamation
to his Cabinet, with the official portrait of Jackson in the background (1864).
Library of Congress, LC-DIG-pga-02502

Portrait of Lincoln
by Edward Dalton
Marchant (1863).
*Courtesy of the
Union League Legacy
Foundation*

Drawing of Taylor
(circa 1848).
Library of Congress,
LC-USZ62-71730

Photograph of Ulysses
Grant (June 1864).
Library of Congress,
LC-USZ62-1770

Lincoln's October 24, 1864, meeting with the abolitionist Sojourner Truth, who had waited for hours to meet the president and recalled of Lincoln, "I never was treated by anyone with more kindness and cordiality than were shown to me by that great and good man." *Library of Congress, LC-USZ62-16225*

Lincoln's second inaugural, with John Wilkes Booth among those looking down upon Lincoln from a White House portico over Lincoln's left shoulder. *Library of Congress, LC-USA7-16837*

we heard from Mr. Lincoln on the subject, except that he is an old line Whig."[90]

Douglas went in for the kill:

> What part of Henry Clay's policy did Lincoln ever advocate? He was in Congress in 1848–9, and when the Wilmot Proviso warfare disturbed the peace and harmony of the country, until it shook the foundation of the Republic from its center to its circumference. It was that agitation that brought Clay forth from his retirement at Ashland again to occupy his seat in the Senate of the United States, to see if he could not, by his great wisdom and experience, and the renown of his name, do something to restore peace and quiet to a disturbed country. Who got up that sectional strife that Clay had to be called upon to quell? I have heard Lincoln boast that he voted forty-two times for the Wilmot proviso, and that he would have voted as many times more if he could.

The crowd laughed. "Lincoln is the man, in connection with Seward, Chase, Giddings, and other Abolitionists, who got up that strife that I helped Henry Clay put down." The crowd erupted in tremendous applause. Douglas could have ended there, but he did not.

> Henry Clay came back to the Senate in 1849, and saw that he must do something to restore peace to his country. The Union Whigs and the Union Democrats welcomed him the moment he arrived, as the man for the occasion. We believed that he, of all men on earth, had been preserved by Divine Providence to guide us out of our difficulties, and we Democrats rallied under Clay then, as you Whigs in nullification time rallied under the banner of old Jackson, forgetting party when the country was in danger, in order that we might have a country first, and parties afterwards.

The record indicates the crowd proclaiming, "Three cheers for Douglas."[91]

The outcome of the election was never in doubt. The Republican newspapers all applauded Lincoln for having done more than hold his own with the Little Giant. Even so, on a cold election day in November 1858, Republicans won the popular vote, but because of the apportionment scheme they did not take control of the state senate. Because of that scheme, as David Donald explains, "Republicans, who received about 50 percent of the popular vote, won only 47 percent of the seats in the house, while the Democrats with 48 percent of the popular vote gained 53 percent of the seats."[92] In the election within the state legislature on the choice of Illinois's next senator, held on January 5, 1859, Douglas was the clear winner. He had 54 votes to Lincoln's 46. Douglas was headed back to the Senate, and in an ideal position to launch a serious presidential bid just two years away in 1860.

After the debates, Lincoln reviewed transcripts to provide edited versions that sympathetic newspapers ran. He excised the three times he had used the N-word for the parts of the country that tended toward abolition and made other edits to ensure readers in more conservative regions got the versions that fit their politics.

Beyond Illinois, Lincoln boosted his stature, while the harder Douglas kept harping on his close alliance with Clay, the more it weakened his support among Democrats. Democrats had never been a particularly harmonious party, but those who had not yet fled to the Republican Party or others were largely strong advocates for the maintenance and extension of slavery. John Todd Stuart, for example, had become a Democrat by the time Lincoln was in Congress. In 1856, he had supported Buchanan for president. Nevertheless, as the 1860 presidential election neared, he was growing increasingly frustrated with the party's pandering to the slave-owners. Lincoln was not going to get his vote (which went to third-party candidate John Bell), but neither would Douglas. It was clear to both Douglas and Lincoln that as 1858 turned to 1859 and 1860, Democrats like Stuart were wasting their votes or flocking to the Republican Party. Either way, the Republican nominee would be the beneficiary of the exodus.

VII

After the debates, Lincoln told a friend that they "gave me a hearing on the great and durable question of the age, which I could have had in no other way; and though I now sink out of view, and shall be forgotten, I believe I have made some marks which will tell for the cause of the civil liberty long after I am gone."[93] He told another friend, "The fight must go on. The cause of civil liberty must not be surrendered at the end of one, or even, one hundred defeats."[94] If the great question of the day was the future of slavery, and if Douglas was the likely Democratic nominee for president, Lincoln knew—and anyone reading newspapers reporting the debates around the country knew—that everyone could see there was only one Republican in the country who had stood on the same stage as Douglas for seven straight debates and given as good as he got. It was unimportant that Lincoln was not in the Senate to debate Douglas. He had already more than held his own with Douglas in public, while the other contenders for the 1860 presidential election had not done as well when they had the chance in Congress.

Notwithstanding the themes he had sounded in his debates with Douglas, the Lincoln of 1858 and 1859 was not a starry-eyed follower of Clay, nor was he unmindful of the genuine challenges facing his party and the country. He had learned from not only Clay's successes but his failures. As far back as 1852, Lincoln suggested that the "signal failure of Henry Clay, and other good and great men, in 1849, to effect anything in favor of gradual emancipation in Kentucky, together with a thousand other signs, extinguishes that hope utterly." He added, "Not a single state" had abolished slavery since the founding era. "That spirit," he said, "which desired the peaceful extinction of slavery has itself become extinct. [The] Autocrat of all the Russias will resign his crown, and proclaim his subjects free republicans sooner than will our American masters voluntarily give up their slaves." As for the ultimate fate of slavery, Lincoln said, "The problem is too mighty for me." He said "peaceful, gradual emancipation" was no longer a viable option in the United States.[95]

Lincoln the pragmatist would not say this out loud in his debates with Douglas or in public. If he had, it would have ended all hope of his appealing to anyone who did not want to embrace slavery as the most outspoken Southerners did. The Kansas-Nebraska Act, Bleeding Kansas, and the splintering of the Democratic Party presented the newly established Republican Party with an opening it could exploit—and Lincoln planned to do so.

Rather than back away from pushing for the extension of slavery for the sake of another last-minute compromise to save the Union, Jefferson Davis did the opposite. On July 6, 1859, he proclaimed, "There is not probably an intelligent mind among our own citizens who doubts either the moral or legal right of the institution of African slavery."[96]

A little more than two months later, Lincoln removed doubt about where he stood on the great issue of the day, fully casting aside whatever despair he had in 1852. In a speech on September 16, 1859, to a largely pro-Chase audience in Columbus, Ohio, Lincoln again relied on Clay as his guide, reusing one of his favorite quotes of Clay telling "an audience that if they would repress all tendencies to liberty and ultimate emancipation, they must go back to the era of our independence and muzzle the cannon which thundered its annual joyous return on the Fourth of July; they must blow out the moral lights around us." This imagery plainly appealed to Lincoln, who now adapted it to the task at hand of calling

> attention to the fact that in a preeminent degree these popular sovereigns are at this work; blowing out the moral lights around us; teaching that the negro is no longer a man, but a brute; that the Declaration has nothing to do with him; that he ranks with the crocodile and the reptile; that man, with only body and soul, is a matter of dollars and cents. I suggest to this portion of Ohio Republicans, or Democrats [that] there is now going on among you a steady process of debauching public opinion on this subject.[97]

Here Lincoln might well have been intentionally doing something far more pragmatic—he may have been saying different things to different people, tailoring his message to appeal to his audience (as Douglas had charged in the debates). Lincoln could have been testing the waters, feeling out who else might share this bleak opinion. He sounded conservative to Browning and Stuart but not to Giddings and Wilmot. He was creating a big enough tent of supporters to include not just the old-line Whigs but the growing masses who opposed slavery. Lincoln was not without principle. He drew a line at secession; Clay always had opposed it, just as Jackson did in 1832. He found the bridge that connected the two.

With Jackson and Clay as his inspirations, Lincoln set his sights squarely on the presidency. More nationally prominent, better-known national figures than Lincoln, such as Seward, Chase, and former Missouri attorney general Edward Bates, were maneuvering to secure the Republican Party's nomination for president in 1860. With the date of the mid-May convention fast approaching, the leading contenders gave barely if any thought to the rangy Westerner who had never impressed them in person. Among party leaders, he was widely regarded as a second-tier candidate at best.

However, losing the Senate race to Stephen Douglas made Abraham Lincoln a national figure. Lincoln knew how Jackson, Taylor, and Clay had each made of their failures and built their presidential campaigns by rallying the support not just of the public but also party leaders and the press. He began following—if not perfecting—that path immediately after his debates with Douglas, mailing copies of his speeches and debate transcripts and highlights around the country to friendly newspapers, old friends, and political contacts he was keen to nurture.

The object of Lincoln's efforts was to insert himself into the presidential race, already well underway, beginning with his speech at the Cooper Union Institute in New York on February 27, 1860. Lincoln had stumped for Republican candidates throughout the North, and he was hopeful, after Republican successes in state and local races in key midterm elections, that his candidacy for the presidency held greater promise. The Cooper Union appearance (part of a series of lectures that winter) gave Lincoln the opportunity to move from a second-level candidate to the front ranks. The speech held the prospect of enabling him to secure the support of the Republican elite in New York City, as well as to audiences all over the Northeast and New England through the favorable newspaper coverage that Lincoln was carefully cultivating at the same time.

In the biggest race of his life, Lincoln projected his moderate self. He understood that he was in William Seward's home state but that the sponsors of the debate came from the anti-Seward wing of the party and therefore favored Salmon Chase. Lincoln could expect few sympathetic supporters in the audience, but having lived for more than two decades in a state and county dominated by Democrats, Lincoln was used to being around people who didn't support him. He stayed out of the fight between Seward and Chase. Instead, he would let them knock each other off in their quest for the nomination. Meanwhile, he would seek to reach the broad middle of the Republican Party as well as Anti-Nebraska Democrats.

A further challenge was not to be overshadowed by the two men who were scheduled to appear before him in the series of lectures scheduled at the Cooper Union Institute that winter. The first was Frank Blair of Missouri, Jackson's longtime friend and a Democratic Party founder who left the party over its embrace of slavery. The former editor of the Democratic Party's favored newspaper, Blair focused his remarks on attacking slavery. The second speaker was Cassius Clay of Kentucky, a cousin of Henry Clay's and an ardent foe of slavery. He attacked slavery just as relentlessly as Blair. Lincoln was on the card because the organizers felt that all three of the speakers—Blair, Clay, and Lincoln—would help Chase by weakening enthusiasm for Seward.

Lincoln had no problem denouncing slavery—he had done that before. But in the Cooper Union address, he felt the need to do something he had not yet done with the diligence it required: deep research on the founding. Following Logan's example as well as his own advice and experiences, he hit the books. Because the material he found was so copious, he made sure he had the written research before him when he spoke. It was only the second time he used a manuscript when giving a major speech.

Lincoln pushed his appearance back to two weeks after his birthday, February 27. He made it later than the organizers had wanted so there would be less time between the event and the Republican national convention scheduled for early that summer. He spent hours in the Illinois State House's library, just across the street from his law office, and, between court appearances, he pored over the history of the Constitution, the Northwest Ordinance, and Jonathan Elliot's multivolume set of the debates on the Constitution in the various state ratifying conventions.

The speech was unique in two ways: its tone and its substance.

Its first section reflected Lincoln's long hours in the law library. Responding to Douglas's claim that the nation's Founders had endorsed popular sovereignty, Lincoln conceded that "our fathers, when they framed the Government under which we live, understood this question just as well, and even better, than we do now."[98] He then demonstrated something he had not done in debates with Douglas but which was enormously effective in this rarified setting: He examined the actions of the signers of the Constitution to establish that "our fathers," about whom Douglas spoke so reverentially, actually supported the power of Congress to regulate slavery in the territories. Systematically going through votes on such measures as the Northwest Ordinance (signed no less than by George Washington, he emphasized), Clay's Missouri Compromise, and the acts that Congress took to organize the Mississippi and Louisiana territories, Lincoln showed that of the thirty-nine men who signed the Constitution, twenty-three had had opportunities to vote on federal authority over slavery in the territories; of them, twenty-one voted to ban slavery from the territories. Turning to the remaining sixteen Founders of the Constitution who never had the chance to participate in the later votes, Lincoln argued that fifteen of them had opposed slavery and left "significant hints" that they would have voted to restrict it from the territories if given the chance to do so.[99] He figured the framers lined up thirty-six to three in favor of the power of Congress to regulate slavery in the territories. He mentioned Douglas by name only five times but pronounced the names of the signers of the Constitution thirty-nine times, George Washington's name eight times, and Thomas Jefferson's name twice.

In the next part of his speech, Lincoln appealed to the South, not unlike the way his mentor Henry Clay had tried to many times on the floor of the Senate. Lincoln hoped to convey to Southerners that *he* was no threat to them. It was Southerners who insisted on straying from the legacy of the framers. Placating the South with half measures like popular sovereignty would abandon the intentions of the framers, Lincoln argued, and it would fail, he predicted, because nothing short of federal activism on behalf of slavery would satisfy Southern demands. If there was a breach coming, it would be the South's fault, not the North's.

Concluding, Lincoln proclaimed the immorality of slavery. He could not entirely ignore the crowd in front of him. So, he felt comfortable saying, "If slavery is right," then "all words, acts, laws, and constitutions against it are themselves wrong, and should be silenced, and swept away. All they ask, we could readily grant, if we thought slavery right."[100] But slavery was not right. Only a platform like the Republican one, based on the idea that slavery was wrong, was morally and politically right. Lincoln concluded by imploring his fellow Republicans not to delude themselves into "groping for some middle ground between the right and wrong," which did not exist, but instead to "have faith that right makes might, and in that faith . . . dare to do our duty as we understand it."[101]

This conclusion sounded less like Clay and more like Lincoln's fiery House Divided Speech, but Lincoln deftly broadened his appeal. He did not emphasize compromise, though his tone was respectful when discussing Southerners, several of whom were long-standing friends of his. Nor did he openly stress Clay's name as he'd done in his debates with Douglas. Douglas was barely in the speech; he didn't need to be. This, after all, was not Illinois, or Clay country. These Republicans were more radical than the

Democrats he lived with. These were Seward and Chase folks, not Lincoln men. Convincing this crowd of his reverence for Clay was unnecessary and unproductive. Clay was there, to be sure, albeit in spirit and Lincoln's arguments, as well as the presence of Clay's cousin. (Abe even chose to stay at the Astor, the same place where Webster and Clay had each spoken.) It was enough that Lincoln knew he was following in the footsteps of his mentors. Lincoln cast the speech in such a way that scholars, to this day, do not agree on whether it was conservative or moderate. The difficulty of pinning it down as one or the other proves that it achieved Lincoln's aim of appealing to both. Yet, in the end, the substance and style were much closer to Clay than to Seward, Chase, or Owen Lovejoy, son of Elijah Lovejoy and a popular abolitionist preacher.

As Harold Holzer explains in his study of the Cooper Union speech and its consequences, Lincoln's delivery was more refined and sophisticated than ever before. Lincoln did not use the same tropes that he had used to reach the voters in Illinois, instead aligning himself and his arguments unmistakably with the framers. As Holzer notes, "Having identified thirty-nine framers whose slavery votes cry out for analysis, [Lincoln] w[ould] repeat the number thirty-nine for emphasis twenty separate times in a parallel burst of repetition for effect."[102] As Holzer notes further, on federal authority to regulate slavery, Lincoln repeated fifteen times the sentence, "Our fathers, when they framed the government under which we live, understood this question just as well, and even better than we do now."[103] Lincoln used the phrase *our fathers* at least five times in the speech and the word *fathers* nine times.[104] Further driving home this message was the technique, used by Clay and Webster, of "alternatively parallel and contradictory double phrasing—the device of antiphony—to neatly set up his audience for his arguments."[105] Antiphony is an old form of singing in which voices alternate, like the recitations in church when the leader of the congregation reads a line followed by the congregation reading another, back and forth, until the end. And so, Lincoln used the phrase *you say* repeatedly to introduce some of the arguments of the Southerners threatening secession but then following each time with his blunt denials, which were sure to resonate with the crowd and those later reading the speech.

When Lincoln finished, the audience erupted in thunderous applause. *New York Times* editor Henry Raymond declared Lincoln a national leader of "preeminent ability" and New York's second choice for the Republican nomination after Seward.[106] Mason Brayman, a Democrat from Springfield, who knew Lincoln from his early days as a lawyer for the Illinois Central Railroad, had called on Lincoln before the speech and agreed to stand in the back of the hall and signal if he could not hear Lincoln's voice. No signal came. Brayman reported that Lincoln's voice, like his rhetoric, filled the room.

The next evening, Lincoln visited the offices of the *New York Tribune* to correct proofs of the speech that would appear in the newspaper the next day. In the weeks that followed, several other newspapers throughout the Northeast and back home reprinted his address. The New York press was the most productive and powerful in the nation, and it churned out favorable news about his Cooper Union address that was read widely throughout the region. Lincoln and his friends distributed copies of the speech as far and wide as they could, while Lincoln began a speaking tour in the Midwest and Northeast. The local *Illinois Journal* produced pamphlets of the speech that it sold in bulk to Republican clubs throughout the country.

VIII

Nothing in Lincoln's life led him to doubt that he had the credentials to become president. Many presidents had been *less* qualified. In his lifetime, he had seen Zachary Taylor, a man with no political experience whatsoever, win his party's nomination and the presidency. Winfield Scott had been the Whig candidate in 1852. He had seen men with considerable political experience—Henry Clay and Lewis Cass—fail repeatedly to win the presidency and losing each time to a candidate with a less impressive record of service to the country. He had seen a man with no meaningful political experience—Franklin Pierce—win the presidency and then stumble so badly in office that he couldn't even win his party's nomination for reelection. He had seen a man with perhaps the most extensive résumé of any politician yet running for the presidency, James Buchanan, fail so miserably as president that he became the second to have no chance even to secure his party's nomination. He remembered his friend and colleague John Quincy Adams, with a résumé as good as Buchanan's, finish his one term without a single legislative accomplishment. Neither of the leaders often considered greatest, Washington and Jackson, had had any executive experience in political office before becoming president. Lincoln did not have their military records, but neither did his likely Democratic opponent. Like Clay, Lincoln had no executive experience, but Douglas could barely claim more, a lackluster stint of less than three months as Illinois's secretary of state.

There were three things a successful candidate needed, and Lincoln had them all. The first was a compelling vision of the Constitution and the future of the country. Vision had trumped experience in nearly every presidential election so far, and when experience seemed to matter (as with John Quincy Adams and Buchanan), it mattered less than the winning candidates' politics, which were simply vision wrapped differently. Lincoln asserted his vision strongly in his debates with Douglas and even more clearly at Cooper Union.

Next in importance was campaign organization. Lincoln's was a patchwork of the networks he had used to disseminate his Cooper Union speech; his many contacts with Republican-friendly newspapers throughout the country; the candidates he'd helped in Illinois, the Midwest, and Northeast; and his close-knit band of supporters in Illinois. While Lincoln was speaking at Cooper Union, his people were already on the ground in Chicago preparing for the upcoming Republican convention. Powerful local newspapers were already singing his praises. The state's largest newspaper, the *Chicago Tribune,* run by his friend Joseph Medill, continued to quote Lincoln's speeches freely and praise his every move, as it had done during his Senate campaign.

The final factor was party unity. Lincoln had been preaching its importance for decades. He had pushed for it in 1844 with Clay, 1848 with Taylor, 1852 with Scott, and 1856 with Frémont. Taylor was the only one of those who had won, but like Harrison, he had died at the beginning of his term. There was no Whig legacy to run on. Taylor's short-lived victory of 1848 was the only high point before the Democratic decline of Pierce and Buchanan. In this election, the winner was likely to be whichever party could hold itself together in addressing the monumental issue of slavery. In his run against Douglas for the Senate, Lincoln had actually gotten more votes than Douglas because the Republican Party organization within the state had performed better than its Democratic counterpart. Districts could swing states, and Republicans held the advantage in organization in almost every region of the country except the South.

The Democratic Party was splintering well before 1860. Douglas's split with Buchanan in 1857 foreshadowed the difficulty that their party faced in the run-up to the 1860 election. If Douglas got the Democratic nomination as expected, it was hardly a sure thing that his party would follow him. It had been hemorrhaging since 1854. But if Lincoln secured the Republican nomination, it was likely that the party would follow.

This brought Lincoln back to his ground game in Chicago. It was no accident the convention would be held in Lincoln's backyard. When the Republican National Committee met in New York on February 22, 1860, Lincoln's friend Norman Judd came as the representative of Illinois. When Seward's and Chase's representatives could not agree on a city, with Seward's pushing for New York City and Chase's pushing for an Ohio city, Judd astutely proposed a neutral city, which he reminded everyone was in a state—Illinois—that Republicans needed to win but had no serious candidate of its own in the mix for the nomination. The committee agreed on Chicago. Judd never mentioned Lincoln but had given him a boost with the convention being held on his turf and not that of any other serious contender.

Earlier in February, newspapers in Springfield and Chicago had endorsed him for president. In New York, Richard McCormick, a member of the Young Men's Republican Union, had generated admirable publicity for Lincoln. Lincoln had won his first election with the wily veteran John Todd Stuart calling the shots. This time, Stuart was not at Lincoln's side; instead, Lincoln turned to the sharpest political veteran available, the Yale-educated judge and former legislator David Davis. With the help of Norman Judd, Joseph Medill, John Palmer, Ward Hill Lamon, William Herndon, and Leonard Swett, Davis had been maneuvering months before the Republican convention to produce a Lincoln victory. For Davis and his team, the Republican convention became just another local convention to orchestrate. Lincoln gave Davis broad instructions on what to do, while Davis handled the day-to-day logistics.

Lincoln was the favorite of the Illinois delegation but of no others, which meant if matters were decided on the first ballot, he would lose. Lincoln and Davis figured the best strategy, just had been the case writ small with Lincoln's Cooper Union speech, was to stay alive as a candidate for as long as possible in the hope that the front-runners—Seward, Chase, and perhaps Bates—knocked each other off. Seward and Chase were well known, but they were well known not as moderates or Clay men but as radical abolitionists. Bates was a weak moderate but had the support of Horace Greeley, the founder and editor of the influential *New York Tribune*. The strategy was for Lincoln's surrogates to get each of the major candidates' camps to consider Lincoln as their second choice. James Polk had entered the 1844 convention in a similar position and come out the winner, albeit after he was proposed a compromise candidate on the eighth ballot.

Despite the odds, Bates mattered because Missouri was a swing state. He had served in the state house and for one term in the U.S. House of Representatives, and he had been a well-regarded Missouri attorney general and a well-known, popular figure in national Whig circles. Bates—and Jackson's friends, the Blair family—had significant sway over whichever way the delegation leaned at the convention.

To get the Missouri delegation to make him their second choice, Lincoln turned to Orville Browning. Browning had come to Illinois by way of Missouri, and he was a longtime friend of Bates, a founder of the Republican Party in Illinois and an old-line Whig who revered Clay. Before the Illinois Republican convention gathered, the two met, and Browning told Lincoln he was going to push for Bates but would back Lincoln as a second choice if Bates faltered. That sounded fine with Lincoln, who was already, unbeknownst to Browning, working through his surrogates to solidify support among Illinois Republican delegates before the convention began. Lincoln's plan worked—Bates's nomination was dead on arrival, and Browning backed Lincoln in Bloomington.

Lincoln asked John Palmer to help Davis in Chicago. Palmer had become a leader in the state's Republican Party after leaving the Democratic Party in disgust over its virulent proslavery orientation. Palmer instructed the Illinois state delegates to use all "honorable" means to secure Lincoln's nomination for president. When the time came to select at-large delegates to the convention from Illinois, Lincoln urged Browning's inclusion. He trusted Browning to support the state convention's decision once Bates collapsed as a candidate. Lincoln had expected Bates to fold early.

Davis, Medill, and Palmer began pushing the Illinois delegates to support Lincoln well before the convention started. With Davis in charge and everyone aware of Lincoln's strategy, Lincoln went to Springfield to await developments. It was no secret that Seward was the front-runner. *Harper's Weekly* published on its cover a large engraving of the eleven leading candidates for the Republican Party's nomination, with Seward as the largest in the center and the others in smaller portraits around the edges. Seward and his mentor Thurlow Weed had been lobbying delegations at least as hard and as long as Lincoln's team. Months before the convention, Seward went from one Republican stronghold to another trying to drum up support for his candidacy.

However, his case did not match the story that Lincoln's friends were spreading throughout the convention to persuade state del-egations to accept Lincoln as a second choice to whomever was their first choice. It was the story of a self-made man, who was born in a log cabin, had no schooling, worked as a farmhand, split rails for a living, and taught himself law. An honest man and a man of the people he was. The nicknames "Old Abe" and "Honest Abe" made the rounds of the convention. Lincoln could not be sure that slogans would win him the presidency, but his aides left nothing to chance, coming up with the memorable image of Lincoln as "The Railsplitter." He had bested Douglas in their debates. It didn't matter that these assertions were not all literally true. Lincoln had learned that what people believed was more important than what actually happened. Myths and stories moved people, and if some exaggeration was part of the game—and it was on all sides—at least it could be applied for noble purposes.

Davis assigned Browning and Swett to lobby state delegations to make Lincoln their second choice, an effective strategy en-suring that once a front-runner stumbled, Lincoln would get his delegates—and Lincoln figured rightly that Seward and Chase each would stumble. On the day before the convention began, Browning wrote in his diary, "By request I went in company with Judge Davis [to] meet and confer with the Maine delegation; and at their solicitation made them a speech. Also called upon the del-egation from New Hampshire. At night we received a message from the Massachusetts delegation, and called upon them at their rooms."[107] Davis and John Palmer, who later would be elected gov-ernor of Illinois, called on the New Jersey delegation. Each del-egation agreed to Lincoln as a second choice. On that same day, Davis and Jesse Dubois wired Lincoln, "We are quiet but moving between heaven & earth. Nothing will beat us but old fogy politi-cians. The heart of the delegates are with us."[108] When Davis was not lobbying state delegations, he met with several old political friends, whom he enlisted to support Lincoln. He persuaded his friends in the Indiana delegation to go with Lincoln, though when they broke his way a rumor began that Davis had promised Caleb Smith, a prominent Indiana lawyer, a Cabinet post. Davis denied it. Lincoln denied it. In 1861, Lincoln selected Smith as his interior secretary.

On the second day of the convention, Browning and Gustave Koerner, a fellow member of the Illinois bar and Lincoln's connection with the growing German American population, were following Francis Blair of Missouri, who visited the Indiana, New Jersey, and Pennsylvania delegations to urge their support for his friend Bates. Browning and Koerner urged each of the delegations to support Lincoln as a second choice. The two met again with the three delegations later in the evening and secured their agreement to favor Lincoln as a second choice if the time came. Although Lincoln telegraphed Davis, "I authorize no bargains and will be bound by none," and attempted, without success, to have a note delivered to Davis declaring, "Make no contracts that bind me," Davis ignored the instructions. Instead, he engaged in negotiations with Simon Cameron of Pennsylvania, one of the weaker contenders for the nomination, that left the impression, at least to Cameron and his supporters, of a deal to eventually deliver his delegation, if needed, to Lincoln in exchange for a Cabinet post.[109]

On May 18, 1860, the balloting began. In keeping with the custom at the time, Judd put Lincoln's name into nomination in a single sentence: "I desire, on behalf of the delegation from Illinois, to put in nomination, as a candidate for President of the United States, Abraham Lincoln, of Illinois."[110]

On the first ballot, Seward led with 173½ votes, while Lincoln followed with 102. Cameron had 50½, Chase had 49, and Bates had 48. It was a surprise to find Seward lacked a majority, but an even bigger surprise that Lincoln was in second place on the first ballot. Lincoln had not only won the unanimous support of the Illinois and Indiana delegations but also unexpected support 7–1 from New Hampshire, where he had spent much of March. Seward received the remaining vote in New Hampshire, while Connecticut gave two of its votes to Lincoln and none to Seward.

On the second ballot, Lincoln showed considerably more momentum than anyone else. Seward gained 11 votes but was well short of the 233 required for the nomination. Lincoln gained 79 because of defections from Rhode Island, New Hampshire, Pennsylvania, and Chase's home state of Ohio, where Lincoln had campaigned hard in the months preceding the convention. After the second ballot, Lincoln was only 3½ votes behind Seward.

The end was clearly in sight. Seward had nowhere to go but down, and the other state delegations were breaking for Lincoln. On the third ballot, more defections from Rhode Island, Pennsylvania, and Maryland went for Lincoln, and he was suddenly only 1½ votes shy of the majority needed for nomination. Ohio, which had elected Chase as both a senator and governor, struck the final blow—it moved four votes over to Lincoln. With that, it was over. Seward's supporters could add as well as anyone else and asked for the nomination to become unanimous. Many Seward delegates cried in shock, while Lincoln's supporters, at Davis's direction, carried out a life-size portrait of the winner onto the stage. The convention chose Hannibal Hamlin, a senator from Maine and a founder of the Republican Party, as Lincoln's running mate.

Nathan Knapp, chairman of the Scott County, Illinois, Republican Party, had been assigned the job of keeping Lincoln informed back in Springfield. At the end of each of the first two ballots, he telegraphed the news to Lincoln. The future president was lounging in a chair at the Springfield telegraph office when Knapp's next telegram came: "We did it. Glory be to God." Lincoln accepted congratulations from all around the crowded room and from the wall of people outside. He was calm. "I knew this would come when I saw the second ballot," he told well-wishers.[111] On breaking free from the crowd, he said, "Well gentlemen there is a little woman at our house who is probably more interested in this dispatch than I am."[112] Koerner, Swett, and Judd were among those telegraphing Lincoln not to come to Chicago. Davis, too, instructed Lincoln, "Don't come here for God's sake. Write no letters and make no promises till you see me."[113] Lincoln did not come, and he made no promises.

Two weeks before the Republican convention, the Democrats had deadlocked and adjourned without naming a nominee. They were more sharply divided than ever before. Eventually, they split into two camps, one favoring the party's eventual nominee, Stephen Douglas, and the other calling itself the Southern Democratic Party, which backed Buchanan's vice president John Breckinridge of Kentucky for president. (The incumbent president, Buchanan, urged Democrats to back his vice president.) Once again, when it came to Lincoln, Douglas was magnanimous. Although James Russell Lowell joined other Eastern newspaper and magazine editors bemoaning the fact that Seward had not won, Douglas told a group of Republicans in Washington that they had made no mistake: "Gentlemen, you have nominated a very able and a very honest man."[114] John Bell, a former House speaker and senator, ran as the candidate for the Constitutional Unionist Party, whose agenda was to appeal to disenchanted Whigs who wished to take no stance on slavery. The Republican Party and several publishers produced hastily assembled campaign biographies of Lincoln, some including the text of the Cooper Union Institute address.

With several Southern states threatening to secede if Lincoln won and the Democratic Party severely split, Lincoln's assignment was simple to understand but difficult to execute: If the Republican Party remained unified as Lincoln urged and he helped them by keeping his own counsel to Taylor to stay silent during the general election (as Lincoln wished Clay had in 1844), the election was his. It was one of the more difficult challenges he ever faced. Surrogates, like Browning, did the talking, as they fanned out to lobby or reassure old Whigs or former Democrats to go with Lincoln. The five months between Lincoln's nomination in May and election day in early November 1860 were the longest stretch in his political life when he made no public appearances and gave no speeches. Lincoln's surrogates, including Browning, who lobbied old Whigs, made his case around the country. But Lincoln stayed silent. In spite of his repeated protestations of being "bored-bored badly" (as Herndon related after Lincoln's death), he followed the advice he had given to Taylor—and party leaders were giving to him—to keep his mouth shut. He did, and the reward was the presidency.

CHAPTER SIX

"HE WAS ENTIRELY IGNORANT
NOT ONLY OF THE DUTIES, BUT OF THE
MANNER OF DOING BUSINESS"
(1860–1861)

In the 1860 election, Abraham Lincoln's lack of executive and congressional experience was both an asset and a liability. On the one hand, it helped him win the presidency. Nearly half a continent away from the disputes ripping Congress apart and several hundred miles from the violence in Kansas, he never had to directly confront, much less vote on, any of the policy proposals bandied back and forth in either place. His lack of a record made him a small target, overshadowed by first-tier candidates Seward and Chase, who took most of the hits. People knew Lincoln by his words, not his actions. In some parts of the country, they had read about him. In the Northeast, many people knew him from his campaigning. (He gave 175 speeches in the run-up to the presidential election.) Newspapers combed his statements for clues, but most journalists concluded he was weak and out of his depth. Indeed, the editors of many newspapers had grave doubts that Lincoln was good at anything else than telling stories and jokes.

Lincoln might have been gratified to know that he didn't have to do much to exceed most people's expectations of him. Unlike Jackson, he came into office with no mandate. Though he had won the election with 180 electoral votes, he had won less than 40 percent of the popular votes, a lower proportion than Jackson had won in 1824. (Lincoln's three opponents together won 123 electoral votes.) With the fragmentation of the Democratic Party, Douglas finished far worse than expected, and Lincoln's closest competitor turned out to be Buchanan's vice president John Crittenden, who had run as the nominee of the Southern Democrat party. Douglas won only one state (Missouri) and received the fewest number of electoral votes of the three candidates running against Lincoln.

Lincoln was the first president to be elected from outside the South since William Henry Harrison's victory two decades before, the first president to come from the West since Jackson (since Tennessee at that time was considered Western frontier), and one-half of the first successful national ticket that did not have a Southerner on it. He was, and still is, the only president who ever argued a case before the U.S. Supreme Court. He was the first man elected president without carrying a single Southern state.

None of these distinctions boded well for Lincoln. Lack of support and lack of experience were hardly a winning combination. He certainly wasn't overconfident. He admitted to his friend Robert Wilson of Pennsylvania "that, when he first commenced doing [his] duties, he was entirely ignorant not only of the duties, but of the manner of doing business" of the presidency.[1]

Where would Lincoln find guidance? He was flooded with advice from everywhere. He listened to much of it but heeded little of it. He declined the proffered services of those hoping to dominate him. He didn't want to make Taylor's mistake of letting Seward and Weed dominate him. Responding to the charge that he would just be Andrew Jackson's puppet, Polk had said, "I intend to be myself the President of the United States." He also said, "I prefer to supervise the whole operations of government myself rather than entrust the public business to subordinates, and this makes my duties great."[2] Lincoln had been there to see how he had done it. Polk was determined to be at the center of his administration. He seldom took others into his confidence and rarely sought the advice of even his closest friends. That same description fit perfectly Lincoln's management style. This was apparent in how Lincoln had secured his party's nomination, by establishing personal bonds with those working for him, emphasizing their loyalty to him and not some greater cause, often tasking more than one person to do a job, while all the while keeping his own counsel. Polk's model was Jackson. Yet Lincoln knew that the intense four years of Polk's presidency had killed him.

Where else, besides the five presidents he had met—Polk, Taylor, and Buchanan while they were president, and Van Buren and Fillmore after each had left office—and the few Illinois men he brought to Washington, would Lincoln turn for guidance and counsel? Where he always did. He looked first to his own experiences and then to the men who had been president before him. Washington was a patrician, both as a general and as president. He rarely consorted with the common man. Adams and his son were both arrogant Harvard graduates. Their arrogance doomed each of them to one term, as it alienated friends and enemies alike. Jefferson, Monroe, and Tyler had all studied at the College of William & Mary; Madison was a graduate of Princeton and had studied abroad; Polk graduated from the University of North Carolina; Pierce, from Bowdoin College in Maine; and Buchanan from Dickinson College, Roger Taney's alma mater. Lincoln lacked the military experience of Washington, Jackson, Harrison, and Taylor, but of these only Andrew Jackson had professed to champion the common man and opposed secession steadfastly. There was much to learn from all of these, both in what to emulate and what not to do. Yet the one figure Lincoln shared most with was Jackson, a self-made man who earned his nickname Old Hickory because he was tough as hardwood and who opposed secession. Lincoln was prepared to align himself with those qualities and that kind of leader.

Once he became president-elect, Lincoln still saw himself as a champion of the common man. In Springfield, he left his office door open so friends and neighbors could drop in to speak with him. He patiently mingled with crowds in the street, not just in Springfield but wherever he went. This was Lincoln's milieu. His philosophy of governance came from Jackson. Jackson had believed his election made him a leader for all Americans, rich and poor, black and white, male and female, free or enslaved. Lincoln believed that to the extent he had authority, it came from the Constitution and "We the People" who had ratified it. Lincoln enjoyed the large crowds as he had in his home state. The people ruled, and he basked in their delegated power. He could joke and tell stories, and he could learn.

Yet he quickly felt the weight of the great responsibilities of his office. In the nearly four months between Lincoln's election as president on November 6, 1860, and his inauguration on March 4, 1861, seven Southern states, beginning with South Carolina on December 20, declared their secession from the Union, and reports spread of South Carolina's intention to capture the two federal forts overlooking Charleston Bay in South Carolina, Sumter and Moultrie, as well as nearby forts in Florida. Browning recalled that, in July 1861, Lincoln "told me that the very first thing placed in his hands," as he first entered his presidential office, was an urgent report from Major Robert Anderson, the ranking officer in charge of Fort Sumter who was worried they were on the verge of being attacked by South Carolina to remove any federal presence. The soldiers of the two Charleston Harbor forts had gathered in Fort Sumter for safety and Major Anderson feared "the impossibility of defending or relieving Sumter" if it were attacked.[3] Anderson's report included a message from Winfield Scott, the Union Army's commanding general, warning the president that there was "no alternative but a surrender."[4] Lincoln told Browning that "of all the trials I have since I came here, none begin to compare with those I had between the inauguration and the fall of Fort Sumter. They were so great that could I have anticipated them, I would not have believed it possible to survive them."[5] With so much chaos around him and considerable intrigue among those angling for appointments, Lincoln looked to the past for guidance on how to be president.

I

Once Lincoln won the presidency, one of his first thoughts was of Andrew Jackson. According to Gideon Welles, a Democrat-turned-

Republican newspaper editor who supported him throughout the 1860 campaign, Lincoln told him that on election night he had dreamed of "what his predecessors had done" when faced with crises—especially Jackson.[67]

Anyone paying attention to the political clashes preceding the Civil War, as Lincoln did, knew that threats of nullification, secession, and invasion of federal territory were not new. In the Hartford Convention of 1814, members of the soon-to-be defunct Federalist Party endorsed resolutions urging secession of the Northern states, among other things, in response to the continuing war with England and the domination of the federal government by a string of presidents from Virginia—four of the first five American presidents were Virginians. Like most everyone else, Lincoln knew that, as soon as the Fugitive Slave Law had been signed into law, the leaders of Northern states urged its nullification. He knew of William Lloyd Garrison's call in 1844 (much repeated later) for Northern states' separation from the Southern states that supported slavery. And he knew that Zachary Taylor and Millard Fillmore had confronted violent threats of treachery against the federal government, Taylor sending federal troops to the border when Texas threatened to invade New Mexico, and Fillmore sending even more troops to dissuade Texas forces from entering federal territory. Lincoln was well versed in the arguments made by Fillmore and Webster on the constitutional obligations of Northern states to comply with the supremacy of federal law. South Carolina's threats to storm two federal forts invited similarly strong responses. Jackson and Taylor had each denounced those threatening disunion as rebels and traitors. Lincoln followed their lead.

As Lincoln sought to determine what steps to take in order to quiet the brewing insurrection, he struggled to have the time to think and to be alone. He was mobbed throughout the day with people seeking jobs and favors and by journalists. The Democratic-leaning *New York Herald* sent Henry Villard to cover Lincoln during the 1860 presidential election and ensuing transition. Villard had covered him in the 1858 Senate campaign. A proud, upstanding German American, Villard was as patrician as he looked. After

Lincoln lost to Douglas in the 1858 race for the Senate, Villard said he grew to like Lincoln but did not respect him, both because of his "inborn weakness" as a candidate and his penchant for telling off-color stories and jokes.[8]

In later years, Villard changed his opinion. He especially delighted recounting the story of how he met Lincoln

> *accidentally about nine o'clock on a hot, sultry night, at a flag railroad station about twenty miles west of Springfield, on my return from a great meeting at Petersburg in Menard County. [Lincoln] had been driven to the station in a buggy and left there alone. I was already there. The train that we intended to take to Springfield was about due. After vainly waiting for half an hour for its arrival, a thunderstorm compelled us to take refuge in an empty freight car standing on a side track, there being no buildings of any sort at the station. We squatted down on the floor of the car and fell to talking on all sorts of subjects. It was then and there he told me that, when he was clerking in a country store, his highest ambition was to be a member of the state legislature.*

Lincoln paused, then confessed, "Since then, of course, I have grown some, but my friends got me into this BUSINESS [the Senate race]. I did not consider myself qualified for the United States Senate, and it took me a long time to persuade myself that I was." With a laugh, he told Villard, "Now to be sure I am convinced that I am good enough for it; but, in spite of it all, I am saying to myself every day, 'It is too big a thing for you; you will never get it. Mary insists, however, that I am going to be Senator and President of the United States, too." Villard wrote that, at this point, Lincoln "followed with a roar of laughter, with his arms around his knees, and shaking all over with mirth at his wife's ambition. 'Just think,' he exclaimed, 'of such a sucker as me President!'" Lincoln's aside—to Villard more of a hedge than an admission of Lincoln's plans—confirmed the journalist's suspicion that Lincoln might be using the Senate race as a springboard for a run for the presidency.

In mid-November 1860, Villard's opinion of Lincoln was still fixed, though it would eventually yield. "I doubt Mr. Lincoln's capacity for the task of bringing light and peace out of the chaos that will surround him,"[9] he reported. He conceded Lincoln was "a man of good heart and good intention" but concluded that "he is not firm. The times demand a Jackson."[10] Many people worried that Lincoln was too frivolous, and Villard agreed, finding Lincoln's "phrases are not ceremoniously set, but pervaded with a humorousness and, at times, with a grotesque joviality that will always please. I think it would be hard to find one who tells better jokes, enjoys them better, and laughs oftener than Abraham Lincoln." Such demeanor might amuse a crowd, but Villard joined the many people who had yet to see any Jackson in him.

Even so, Lincoln won, forcing further assessment. On December 21, 1860, Villard wrote,

> *Mr. Lincoln is known to be an old Henry Clay Whig. He calls the immortal Kentuckian his "beau ideal of a statesman." That his position in reference to the secession issue . . . is the identical one occupied by Mr. Clay in 1850, with regard to the then threatened nullification by South Carolina of the Compromise Measures of that year, will be seen by the following quotations from a letter and speech written and delivered by his prototype during the same period.[11]*

Villard excerpted at length from Clay's final Senate speech, urging his colleagues to endorse the Compromise of 1850. Villard explained at the end of his report, "I have quoted these two passages, for the special reason that Mr. Lincoln has used them within my own hearing, in explanation of his position, to visitors."[12]

Yet as Villard focused on how Clay might influence the priorities of the new president, two days later, on December 23, 1860, he elaborated on his doubts about Lincoln's capacity to rise to the demands of the presidency, suggesting that,

> *although unaccustomed to shape both resolution and execution according to the dictates of [Lincoln's] own clear judgment—to*

measure and pass upon the merits of things with the aid of his
own moral and intellectual standard—the efficacy of this guide,
demonstrated by his success in life, never produced conceit enough
to induce him to overlook altogether the ideas, motives, arguments,
counsels and remedies of others. On the contrary, a coincidence of
his own views with those of the master spirits of his and previous
ages is always greeted by him with great satisfaction and conscious-
ness of increased strength. No one can be more anxious to fortify his
position by precedents. No one rejoices more in the knowledge of re-
flecting the sentiments of the statesman and patriots that illuminate
the pages of the history of his country.[13]

If there were any doubt who these "master spirits" were, Villard
told the world as he recalled Lincoln's steadfast opposition to secession. Lincoln, he said, would not "content himself with supporting his position by democratic authorities" but persistently quoted
Clay at length.[14]

Lincoln often wrote to supporters who shared his reverence for
Clay. Daniel Ullman, a New York Whig, sent Lincoln a bronze to-
ken he had fashioned for the "first citizen of the school of Henry
Clay" to be elected president. He praised Lincoln as "a true disci-
ple of our illustrious friend."[15] Lincoln wrote back "to express the
extreme gratification I feel in possessing so beautiful a memento
of him, whom, during my whole political life, I have loved and
revered as a teacher and leader."[16] When the *Richmond Dispatch*
got wind of the medal and Lincoln's letter praising Clay, its editors
wrote, "His teacher! His leader. Henry Clay the teacher of Mr. Lincoln. What lesson of Henry Clay had he learned? Where does he
follow his leader's footsteps?"[17]

As Lincoln prepared for the presidency, he thought, too, of Zachary Taylor's brief presidency marked by a standoff between him
and Congress over the administration's priorities. At the invitation
of former president Millard Fillmore, he stopped in Buffalo, New
York, for two nights. On the first night, Fillmore made sure people
saw them together so that it could be reported around the country
that they were united. A Buffalo newspaper got the message: "Mr.

Lincoln's ground, most firmly taken, is that he is to be president of the American people and not of the Republican Party." (Unfortunately, Fillmore abandoned that stance and his friend Henry Clay's fierce opposition to secession, when a year later he proclaimed Lincoln, deep into the project of saving the Union, a "tyrant [who] makes my blood boil." In 1864, he voted for McClellan rather than Lincoln, whom he charged with leading the country to "national bankruptcy and military despotism.")[18]

Less than three weeks before his inauguration, Lincoln reassured an audience in Pittsburgh of "the political education" he had received from Taylor that "strongly inclines me against a very free use of" the veto and any other means of usurping congressional authority.[19] "As a rule," Lincoln explained, "I think it better that congress should originate, as well as perfect its measures, without external bias."[20] He was reassuring his Pittsburgh audience and former Whigs elsewhere that, above all else, he remained, in spirit, a faithful Whig, It was the same message he had repeatedly urged Taylor to make during the 1848 presidential campaign.

In his next speech on February 22, 1861, in Philadelphia, Lincoln delivered a passionate expression of his vision of the Constitution. Standing in front of Independence Hall, the president-elect declared,

> *I have never had a feeling politically that did not spring from the sentiments embodied in the Declaration of Independence. I have often pondered over the dangers which were incurred by the men who assembled here, and framed and adopted that Declaration of Independence. I have pondered over the toils that were endured by the officers and soldiers of the army who achieved that Independence. I have often inquired of myself, what great principle or idea it was that kept this Confederacy so long together.*

In substance, these words were another reminder that the Declaration of Independence had, from an early age, made a lasting impression on Lincoln, whose study of the founding and attachment to Clay cemented his belief that it was a founding document that had enduring significance for America. In terms of style, Lincoln's repetitions and use of the first person to gain momentum was straight out of Clay's handbook, but now he was going beyond his mentor in his "shooting low," as he had once encouraged Herndon—speaking without complexity or much detail but using plain and sometimes poetic terms that the crowds listening or reading could understand and remember. (Grappling with the rigor of Euclid's axioms and theorems, Lincoln might have seen their relevance for speaking to the public, to do so plainly, directly, in a straight line, so to speak.)

For Lincoln, the principle at stake, he explained further in Philadelphia, was "liberty, not alone to the people of this country, but, I hope, to the world, for all future time." He asked rhetorically, "Can this country be saved on that basis," and answered his own question, "If it can, I will consider myself one of the happiest men in the world, if I can help to save it. If it cannot be saved without giving up that principle [of the Declaration of Independence], it will be truly awful. But if this country cannot be saved without giving up that principle, I was about to say I would rather be assassinated on this spot than surrender it." He underscored his point at the end: "I have said nothing but what I am willing to live by and, if it be the pleasure of Almighty God, die by."[21]

The closer Lincoln got to the White House, the more he thought about the troubles ahead. Many of those observing and listening to him were surprised that, even at this juncture, he stubbornly insisted the Southern states were merely bluffing. During Frémont's campaign in 1856, Lincoln had proclaimed, "All this talk about dissolution of the Union is humbug, nothing but folly. We do not want to dissolve the Union; you shall not." In 1860, he wrote to a correspondent that he had received "many reassurances [from] the South that in no probable event will there be any formidable effort to break up the Union. The people of the South have too much of good sense, and good temper, to attempt the ruin of the government."[22] Certainly he did not expect a war.

Upon arriving in Washington, Lincoln met with delegates from the Peace Convention, 131 politicians from fourteen free states and seven Southern states. They had come to the capital in early February to forge a compromise to avoid the war and had agreed on a plan that included a proposal to amend the Constitution to prevent the extension of slavery in all new federal territories. When the delegation met with Lincoln to share their plan, his face lit up when he was introduced to a Democratic member of the House named James Clay—Henry Clay's son. Lincoln told him, "Your name is all the endorsement you require. From my boyhood the name of Henry Clay has been an inspiration to me."

While he was dismissing the likelihood of a real battle between secessionist forces and the United States, he was probably still mulling over his Cabinet selections, although he told close aides that he had been pondering the issue since the evening he was elected president. Many years later, he told his private secretaries, John Hay and John Nicolay, "When I finally bade my friends good-night . . . I had substantially created the framework of my Cabinet as it now exists."[23] Nicolay, the former newspaperman, and Hay, the Brown-educated legal apprentice, said in retrospect that in assembling a Cabinet, Lincoln sought "a council of distinctive and diverse, yet able, influential, and representative men, who should be a harmonious group of constitutional advisers and executive lieutenants—not a board of regents holding the great seal in commission and intriguing for the succession."[24] Whig orthodoxy, or what was left of it, held that the Cabinet should be a check on a president, not just an esteemed team of advisers. Whigs expected presidents to follow their Cabinet, but every Whig president before Lincoln—Harrison, Taylor, and Fillmore—had rebelled against that idea once they were in office.

The men Lincoln assembled bore only a faint resemblance to the romantic Whig ideal of a Cabinet, as described by Nicolay and Hay. Its members were neither harmonious in spirit nor particularly loyal to Lincoln, and Lincoln had no intention of deferring to their judgments. He picked prominent men who had considerable experience and reflected some geographical balance, but they were men who had been important in the formation and development of the Republican Party. Three—Seward, Bates, and Chase—had been his rivals for the presidency, and at least one other, Simon Cameron, was anything but a team player. Nonetheless, Lincoln brought them together to facilitate party unity, which he had insisted to Taylor and Crittenden should be the preeminent concern in assembling a Cabinet.

Though Lincoln had told his Springfield friends he expected to return some day, he could not be sure whether that would ever happen. Before leaving Springfield on February 11, 1861, Lincoln stopped to spend a few days with his stepmother. During the break, he visited his father's grave for the first and last time. He never told anyone about what he thought, did, or said there, yet it is not hard to imagine he might have looked down at his father with a mixture of satisfaction and sadness. He could only be proud of how far he had come but must have been sad to remember that his father had never seen greatness in him. It had to be enough that he had proven his father wrong.

II

As plans were being formulated to respond to the impending crises, Lincoln still had to complete his Inaugural Address. In preparation, he consulted only four documents. Besides Jackson's proclamation on South Carolina, he studied Henry Clay's final speech in the Senate, Daniel Webster's 1830 reply to South Carolina senator Robert Hayne's assertion of the state's entitlement to nullify federal laws, and the Constitution, which he quoted or referenced over twenty times in his address. Lincoln considered Webster's speech the single "greatest oration" in American oratory (indeed, Jackson was among those who openly delighted in Webster's speech at the time, which he had "expected" to demolish Hayne's arguments), and Clay's speech eloquently set forth the case against secession as Jackson had done in his proclamation.

For his Inaugural Address, Lincoln solicited direct advice from only a few people. Seward was one. The evening before he received the dispiriting news from Anderson about Charleston, Lincoln had met with Seward. The two men differed in many ways. Lincoln towered over Seward; Seward was mercurial, temperamental, hyperactive, disheveled, but occasionally courtly, while Lincoln was steady, plodding, and unpretentious. Short, with a bulbous nose, Seward was always in motion. They had encountered each other for the first time in 1848 when they were both campaigning for Taylor. From then through the first few months of Lincoln's presidency, Seward did not hide his disdain for Lincoln. He freely shared his harsh criticisms of Lincoln with allies and friends, such as Horace Greeley. Indifferent to decorum, he was even condescending and patronizing in Lincoln's presence.

For much of the transition, Lincoln had let Seward act as a spokesperson for the administration. But as late as the night before the inauguration, Seward was still playing hard to get. If he could not have the throne, he desperately wanted to be the power behind it and was pressing Lincoln to give him the power he craved, including picking the rest of the Cabinet.

Though irritated by the persistent push of Seward and Weed to micromanage his administration, Lincoln needed Seward in his Cabinet. Seward had significant support among abolitionists in the Northeast and would bring lots of votes with him if he joined the Cabinet. As Adams had done with Henry Clay, Lincoln offered his rival the top position in the Cabinet, the post of secretary of state, widely regarded as a stepping-stone to the presidency itself.

Orville Browning was his other sounding board. After Browning had helped to build a bridge between Lincoln and the Bates delegates, he remained a confidant throughout the election and transition. Thomas Hicks, the portrait painter for whom Lincoln sat after winning the Republican nomination for president, wrote that "the one man, in those days, who was always with" Lincoln, "with whom he advised, in whom he confided, with whom he talked over the Constitution of the United States in its relations to slavery, the condition of the South, and the mutterings of slave-owners, whose views accorded with his own, whom he held by the hand as a brother, was Orville H. Browning of Quincy."[25] Hicks continued, "When he and Browning met together, they discussed with thoughtful consideration many events which might occur, among which were the threatening of an unnecessary civil war, the cruelties of which, fortunately, could not be foreseen, in those peaceful days, by his friends and neighbors in the quiet town of Springfield."[26]

As the inauguration approached, Lincoln begged Browning to join the train trip he and his entourage planned to take from Springfield to Washington. Never one to like trains, much less crowded ones, Browning agreed to go as far as Indianapolis. Once there, Lincoln asked Browning back to his room in the Bates House (named for the prominent banker Hervey Bates, no relation to Edward), then the grandest hotel in downtown Indianapolis. Once there, Lincoln retrieved his traveling bag, from which he extracted a draft of his Inaugural Address. He asked if Browning "would not read it over, and frankly tell him my opinion of it."[27] After a quick review, Browning told Lincoln that it seemed "able, well considered, and appropriate."[28] Browning added, "It is, in my judgment, a very admirable document."[29] Lincoln was pleased, but asked Browning to take a closer look but "under promise" that he would speak only to Lincoln about it.[30] Browning agreed "to take it back with me, and read it over more at my leisure."[31] He told Lincoln, "If I see anything in it that I think ought to be changed, I will write to you from home."[32]

As Seward and Browning read over the draft, they unsurprisingly saw the influence of Clay and particularly Jackson. It made eminent sense. Lincoln had, after all, within a few days of the election reviewed Jackson's 1833 proclamation denouncing South Carolina's threat of nullification and secession. As Harold Holzer notes in his study of Lincoln's transition, "It came as no surprise that another visitor to Springfield found Lincoln on November 14th 'reading up anew' on the history of Andrew Jackson's response to the 1832 Nullification Crisis. While he made no effort to conceal 'the uneasiness which the contemplated treason gives him,' Lincoln assured his guest that, like Jackson, he would not 'yield an inch.'"

Nearly three decades before Lincoln's inauguration, Jackson had issued the first presidential statement to reject secession categorically, and it helped to widen the split between him and his vice president, John Calhoun, once and for all. Jackson's proclamation was an important step in a long, intense series of moves in which Calhoun would challenge his commitment to states' rights. They had clashed over appointments as well as when they gave dueling toasts at the end of April 1830. And so it was no surprise when two weeks after Jackson issued his proclamation, Calhoun resigned to protest the president's failure to embrace nullification doctrine, which held that states were entitled, especially when they were a political minority, to block proposals from the more powerful federal government that violated their rights. Some historians believe Jackson's proclamation was largely motivated by his confidence that the issue driving nullification—a rise in tariffs—would not hurt his own plantation and that the threat would in any event eventually vanish. Nevertheless, the proclamation's substance went further to systematically dismantle Calhoun's doctrine. As a result, it had become popular among many Republican leaders, especially those who once had been Jacksonian Democrats.

As his last act as vice president, Calhoun thwarted Jackson's plan to move Van Buren from secretary of state to ambassador to Great Britain, allowing Jackson to keep Van Buren on his team but to have fulfilled his announced aim of reorganizing the Cabinet. When the nomination came to the Senate, Calhoun cast the tie-breaking vote to defeat the nomination. Elated at the outcome, Calhoun said, "It will kill him dead, sir, kill him dead. He will never kick, sir, never kick."[33]

The celebration came too soon. Because Jackson had given Van Buren a recess appointment as the ambassador to Great Britain, Van Buren was in England when he learned the news of his rejection by the Senate. British royalty assured Van Buren that the defeat would make him a martyr. Jackson agreed, "The people will properly resent the insult offered to the Executive, and the injury intended to our foreign relations, in your rejection, by placing you in the chair of the very man whose casting vote rejected you." Jackson was right: After removing Calhoun as vice president, Jackson placed Van Buren on his ticket in the 1832 election.

These events were well known to Lincoln and his growing inner circle, and they were undoubtedly on Seward's mind as he advised Lincoln in the closing days of the transition. Though he had not yet committed to serving as secretary of state, Seward could not keep his hands off the draft. He meticulously scoured it and made over fifty suggestions, almost all of which reflected his concern that the new president not antagonize the South or provoke civil war.[34] Seward's object was conciliation. His suggestions helped Lincoln to soften the tone of the address.

On February 9, shortly before Lincoln and his entourage left for Indianapolis, Browning and Lincoln met privately in Lincoln's room at the Chenery House, a hotel in Springfield, his own house already having been rented out. According to Browning, they "discussed the state of the Country expressing our opinions fully and freely."[35] According to Browning's notes, the president-elect

> agreed entirely with me in believing that no good results would follow the [Peace] convention now in session in Washington, but evil rather, as increased excitement would follow when it broke up without having accomplished anything. He agreed with me no concession by free States short of a surrender of everything worth preserving, and contending for would satisfy the South, and that [Kentucky Senator John Crittenden's] proposed amendment to the Constitution [barring the extension of slavery to any new federal territories] in the form proposed ought not to be made, and he agreed with me that far less evil & bloodshed would result from an effort to maintain the Union and the Constitution, than from disruption and the formation of two confederacies.[36]

That Lincoln took the time to sit with Browning and subsequently adopted his suggestions suggest that he was not merely echoing Browning's ideas to please him.

Back in Quincy, Browning wrote to Lincoln on February 17, 1861, with his suggestions on the draft.[37] Browning agreed with

Lincoln on the arguments against secession and proposed that Lincoln's first move—to send supplies or arms to Sumter—would likely induce South Carolina to attack the fort, "and then the government will stand justified before the entire country, in repelling that invasion, and retaking the forts."[38] He advised, "Without an aggressive act by the federal government, the South would appear to be in an unjustified position."[39] Lincoln agreed and therefore dropped a clause from the draft in which he had threatened to lead the federal government into reclaiming seized federal property in the South. (Lincoln's private secretaries later described Browning's suggestion as "the most vital change in the document.")[40] With Browning's help, Lincoln had his commitments set forth more clearly and also had a plan for addressing the immediate threats to disunion stirring in South Carolina almost a month before his inauguration—one nearly identical to the plan that he eventually followed.

Lincoln's Inaugural Address was only the second presidential declaration formally opposing secession. On this occasion, as had been the case for Jackson, the most direct threat to the Union came from South Carolina. The inaugural crowd was substantial, so consumed were the citizens in and around the District of Columbia with worry about the country's future. As Lincoln had prepared to take his oath of office, dozens of newspapers in the North, Midwest, and West urged Lincoln to emulate Jackson. Lincoln made it clear he had gotten the message. His speech was a unique blend of Jackson, Clay, and Webster, with vivid imagery and language inspired by decades of reading Shakespeare and other poetry. Lincoln had adapted Jackson's arguments and even some of its wording to the current crisis facing the nation. Jackson had declared that the "most important" of the Constitution's "objects" was "'to form a more perfect Union.'"[41] Lincoln said, "One of the declared objects for ordaining and establishing the Constitution, was 'to form a more perfect Union.'"[42]

Pierce and Buchanan had blamed the impending hostilities on Northern abolitionists. Like Clay and Jackson before him, Lincoln blamed them on Southern secessionists, agreeing with Jackson that nullification and secession undermined the all-important object of maintaining the Union. In Jackson's words, "I consider, then, the power to annul a law of the United States, assumed by one State, incompatible with the existence of the Union, contradicted expressly by the letter of the Constitution, unauthorized by its spirit, inconsistent with every principle on which it was founded, and destructive of the great object for which it was formed."[43] Lincoln echoed him: "But if destruction of the Union, by one, or by a part only, of the States, be lawfully possible, the Union is less perfect than before the Constitution, having lost the vital element of perpetuity."[44]

Because the objective of the Constitution was to "form a more perfect Union," Jackson had suggested that nullification was treason.[45] "To say that any State may at pleasure secede from the Union, is to say that the United States is not a nation."[46] Lincoln went further, arguing, as Webster had in his widely known debate with Hayne, that secession, like nullification, promised "anarchy."[47] Like Jackson and Webster, Lincoln refuted the right of a political minority to refuse to abide by a majority's will, the right that Calhoun and Hayne had insisted made secession legitimate. Lincoln said, "If a minority . . . will secede rather than acquiesce, they make a precedent which, in turn, will divide and ruin them; for a minority of their own will secede from them, whenever a majority refuses to be controlled by such minority."[48] Lincoln then asked rhetorically, "Why may not any portion of a new confederacy, a year or two hence, arbitrarily secede again. [All] who cherish disunion sentiments, are now being educated to the exact temper of doing this."[49] Disunion was a word that was common to Jackson, Clay, and Webster; they had used it in each of their famous declarations opposing nullification. Lincoln's use of the same term linked his message to theirs.

Jackson had gone further to refute the idea that the sovereignty of states was absolute. With some irony, he listed many of the same constitutional provisions that John Marshall had used in some of his most famous cases to support the basic idea that the Constitution itself and any federal laws consistent with it were the supreme law of the land. One plain inference from this foundational concept was that states were not preserved certain rights under the Constitution, but rather that states could not impede lawful federal action.

Next, Lincoln again echoed Jackson in emphasizing that the Constitution derives its authority not from the states but from the people of the United States, who were the country's principal sovereign. Jackson had declared,

> The people of the United States formed the Constitution, acting through the State legislatures, in making the compact, to meet and discuss its provisions, and acting in separate conventions when they ratified those provisions; but the terms used in its construction show it to be a government in which the people of all the States collectively are represented. We are ONE PEOPLE in the choice of the President and the Vice President.[50]

Describing the Constitution as a "contract" that could not be nullified by a single party, Lincoln agreed with Jackson that "the Chief Magistrate derives all his authority from the people."[51]

Jackson had emphasized that his "oath" and presidential duties required him to stand firmly against nullification or any other effort that threatened to undermine the Union and the Constitution, declaring that it "is the intent of [the Constitution] to PROCLAIM [that] the duty imposed on me by the Constitution 'to take care that the laws be faithfully executed,' shall be performed to the extent of the powers already vested in me by law, or of such others as the wisdom of Congress shall devise and Entrust to me for that purpose."[52] Near the end of his proclamation, Jackson reiterated the point but with greater clarity and bluntness:

> I rely with equal confidence on your undivided support in my determination to execute the laws—to preserve the Union by all constitutional means—to arrest, if possible, by moderate but firm measures, the necessity of recourse to force, and if it be the will of Heaven that the recurrence of the primeval curse on man for the shedding of a

*brother's blood should fall upon our land, that it not be called down
by any offensive act on the part of the United States.*[53]

With greater brevity, now President Lincoln declared in a steady
voice, "I therefore consider that, in the view of the Constitution
and the laws, the Union is unbroken; and, to the extent of my ability, I shall take care, as the Constitution itself expressly enjoins
upon me, that the laws of the Union be faithfully executed in all
the States."[54] Drawing on Jackson's widely accepted view of the
president as an agent of the people, Lincoln continued, "Doing this
I deem to be only a simple duty on my part; and I shall perform it,
so far as practicable, unless my rightful masters, the American people, shall withhold the requisite means, or, in some authoritative
manner, direct the contrary."[55]

Jackson had ended his proclamation by declaring that whether
conflict would result from the nullification effort was up to South
Carolina. "There is yet time," he pleaded, "to show that the descendants" of the great leaders from South Carolina that had joined the
American Revolution, "will not abandon that Union, to support
which so many of them fought and bled and died. I adjure you . . .
to retrace your steps."[56]

In a similar vein, Lincoln concluded thus: "Fellow-citizens! the
momentous case is before you. On your undivided support of your
Government depends the decision of the great question it involves,
whether your sacred Union will be preserved, and the blessing it
secures to us as one people shall be perpetuated."[57] Lincoln again
reminded Americans that whether there would be bloodshed was
up to those pressing for secession. "In your hands, my dissatisfied
fellow countrymen," he told the people of the South, "and not in
mine, is the momentous issue of civil war. The government will
not assail you. You can have no conflict, without being yourselves
the aggressors."[58]

In his final Senate oration Clay had appealed "to all the South"
and for the country "to elevate ourselves to the dignity of pure and
disinterested patriots."[59] Clay called upon both sides to forget the
"bitter words, bitter thoughts [and] unpleasant feelings" in their

debate over the great compromise.[60] "Let us go," he admonished them, "to the altar of our country and swear, as the oath was taken of old, that we will stand by her; we will support her; that we will uphold her Constitution; that we will preserve her Union." Now Lincoln twice invoked past patriots as reminders of the sacrifices made on behalf of the Union by asking, "To those, however, who really love the Union may I not speak?"[61]

Having immersed himself in the records of the founding, Lincoln mentioned "precedent" three times in asking all the key players in the national drama to think hard about the consequences of their actions. Lincoln asked a series of questions, urging Clay-like caution: "Why should there not be a patient confidence in the ultimate justice of the people? Is there any better, or equal hope, in the world? In our present differences, is either party without faith of being in the right?"[62]

In his character, acting abruptly was less an option for Lincoln than for either Jackson (who used his mercurial temper to intimidate people) or Clay (whose eagerness to please sank his chances in the 1844 presidential election). Lincoln said, "If it were admitted that you who are dissatisfied, hold the right side in the dispute, there still is no good single reason for precipitate action."[63] Instead, he urged, in an appeal reminiscent of Clay: "Intelligence, patriotism, Christianity, and a firm reliance on Him, who has not yet forsaken this favored land, are still competent to adjust, in the best way, all our present difficulty."[64] Unlike Clay, Lincoln did not use the word *compromise* at the beginning of his great speech, but he held open its prospects by devoting eight of the first nine paragraphs of his address to reiterating his determination not to force the end of the institution of slavery. No one could miss his point—indeed, that *was* his point. Lincoln would not make Polk's mistake of lying about who fired the shot that started a war. Instead, Lincoln let the world know that it was entirely up to the Southern states to decide whether or not there would be a conflict.

Clay famously declared that the compromise he proposed "is the re-union of this Union. I believe it is the dove of peace, which, taking its serial flight from the dome of the Capitol, carries the glad tidings of assured peace and restored harmony to all the remotest extremities of this distracted land."[65] Lincoln's more famous conclusion dropped Clay's well-worn use of the dove of peace as well as the word *harmony*, though harmony was the theme of his address. Browning and Seward had worked on his message, but they could not match Lincoln in the precision and elegance of his language. He concluded:

> *We are not enemies, but friends. We must not be enemies. Though passion may have strained, it must not break our bonds of affection. The mystic chords of memory, stretching from every battle-field, and patriot grave, to every living heart and hearthstone, all over this broad land, will yet swell the chorus of the Union, when again touched, as surely they will be, by the better angels of our nature.*[66]

III

Of course, an Inaugural Address is just one thing every president has to do. A more fundamental task was to figure out how to act as the president. The only chances Lincoln had to observe a president in action were when he watched Polk for two years and the day of Taylor's inauguration, when he briefly saw both him and Taylor together. Lincoln had the sophistication and intelligence to find some things he could learn from Polk, particularly his hard work ethic, announcing his goals clearly, sparingly sharing the strategies on how to achieve those goals, and monitoring his subordinates to ensure they were doing what he wanted done. Having condemned Polk for his deceptions and watched from afar as the corruption of Taylor's Cabinet nearly brought down his administration, Lincoln was determined to keep faith with the American people by being a model of integrity. The country had had to endure the divisive, mean-spirited rhetoric of all the Democratic presidents in Lincoln's lifetime—Jackson, Polk, Pierce, Buchanan. Lincoln's job was to bring people together, not turn them against each other. That called for a tone of moderation.

Perhaps most important, Lincoln understood that, as president, he had to be a model for all Americans, not just for the present generation, but also for those who followed. When he was repeatedly being admonished to be like Jackson, he took that to mean that he had to find a way to be himself but limit his propensity for compromise, not relenting on his determination to keep the Union intact, rising to the occasion, defending the Constitution, and being responsible and attentive to all Americans, not just his friends and fellow Republicans. Lincoln had to find a way to be Lincoln but act like Jackson.

Finding his way took time and effort. For many observers, the election had made Lincoln humbler and more serious. The time was over for his biting wit, ridicule, off-color jokes, saucy stories, and partisan sniping. "Even before his inauguration," it was reported, "Abe is becoming more grave. He doesn't construct as many jokes as he did." His first crucial speeches—his Inaugural Address and July message opening Congress's special session on the war—"were marked by an earnest appeal to patriotism and a sober explanation of why the rebellion had to be put down; only some quaint expressions and an occasional touch of irony hinted at the author's underlying sense of humor."[67] Lincoln stuck with the same strategies that had gotten him this far, particularly at the convention—listening carefully and patiently to all who sought his counsel or were giving theirs to him, treating everyone with respect, being honest rather than crafty as Polk and Jackson had often been, gathering as much data as he could before making decisions, taking no single person as a confidant but instead tasking several of them with the same mission to ensure the job got done, and standing firm, when he had to, like Jackson and Clay in defending the Union.

If Lincoln failed, his mistakes would become lessons to avoid for his successors, assuming there would be any. If he succeeded, his achievements would be sung for the ages. Either way, history was the judge—a theme he repeatedly emphasized throughout his life. His friend Joshua Speed recalled Lincoln's letter, written in the depths of his despair in 1841, "that he had done nothing to make any human being remember that he had lived—and that to connect his name with the events transpiring in his day & generation and so impress himself upon them as to link his name with something that would redound to the interest of his fellow man what he desired to live for."[68] In 1858, Lincoln had observed,

> In the first place, let us see what influence [Douglas] is exerting on public opinion. In this and like communities, public sentiment is everything. With public sentiment, nothing can fail; without it nothing can succeed. Consequently, he who molds public sentiment goes deeper than he who enacts statutes or pronounces decisions. He makes statutes and decisions possible or impossible to be executed.[69]

In his narrative, he was the man at the center of the storm, the man whose charge was to lead the country out of harm's way or die trying. Long after he was gone, people would be reading his story, as he had read and reread Washington's. In his story, Lincoln would be what Clay had helped him to be—the ultimate manifestation of the self-made man, who had risen from "humble" beginnings to the highest office in the land. In this story, Lincoln was the hero, even if it killed him. The most important thing was how he would be remembered, Lincoln often said. Later, in the thick of the war in 1862, he told Congress, "In times like the present men should utter nothing for which they would not willingly be responsible through time and in eternity."[70]

Much of Lincoln's days were structured, which irritated him when he felt too constrained but pleased him when it gave him something worthwhile to do. With the Inaugural Address done, the next business on his agenda was to meet with his Cabinet. (In those days, the White House was open to the public and, like the presidents preceding him, he had to thread his way through people lobbying for appointments whenever he ventured into public areas.) After many twists and turns, he had settled on the seven men who were on his list all along, reshuffling them until he finally found the combination that suited his desires and their ambitions. Finalizing the Cabinet was Lincoln's strongest demonstration of, as then New York senator William Marcy memorably put it in 1828, "the Jackson 'doctrine' that to the victors belong the spoils[,] universally the creed of all politicians."

A long-standing tradition in American politics held that the "most prominent" remaining member of the victorious party should be offered the State Department. In 1824, Adams offered that post to Henry Clay, just as Jefferson had appointed his preferred successor, James Madison, in 1808 and Madison in turn had appointed his onetime rival James Monroe to it in 1816. Everyone, including Lincoln, knew that Seward was the logical choice, and though bitter after the election, Seward grudgingly agreed to exchange letters with Lincoln. Knowing Hannibal Hamlin, his vice president, had been good friends with Seward in the Senate, Lincoln asked him to hand Seward a letter. It read, "With your permission, I shall, at the proper time, nominate you to the Senate, for confirmation, as Secretary of State for the United States."[71] Lincoln later told Weed, men "[like] a compliment."[72] But, Weed told Lincoln he thought while Seward had earned the post, he would decline it, as Seward did in response to the letter given to him by Hamlin. Weed reminded Lincoln that when William Henry Harrison had been elected president in 1840, Harrison had traveled to Clay's home for advice. Lincoln might have known the truth, which was quite different—Harrison tried mightily to avoid Clay during the transition, because he did not want to be cornered into giving Clay power over his administration. When Harrison traveled to Kentucky to speak with friendly crowds and supporters, Clay was already lying in wait for him. The conversation did not go well. Clay stormed out when Harrison insisted that he, not Clay, was the president. Weed urged Lincoln to do the same, and travel to Seward's home in Auburn, New York. Gideon Welles said, "Mr. Lincoln declined to imitate Harrison."[73]

Instead, Lincoln kept up his correspondence with Seward, and slowly, letter by letter, coaxed him into a political friendship they both began to enjoy. Seward warmed up when Lincoln sent a personal note asking him for his help in selecting the rest of the Cabinet. Unhelpfully, he replied with an ultimatum for taking the job—denying Chase, Blair, and Welles anything in the Cabinet. Having once been Democrats, Seward distrusted them all. Lincoln ignored the demand, telling Nicolay he could not "afford to let Seward to take the first trick."[74] After the inaugural ceremonies on March 6, 1861, Lincoln again approached Seward, again with a compliment, that he needed him as secretary of state. The personal touch made the difference, and Seward agreed. Seward could not sit on the sidelines with the fate of the country at stake, and Lincoln did not want him there beyond his control.

Lincoln planned to fill his Cabinet partly with men from states he needed to win again. Welles, from New England, fit the bill. Having once been a close ally of Martin Van Buren, he became a Republican, opposed to slavery and a supporter of Lincoln throughout the presidential election. Welles came with considerable credibility as a reasonable man with good judgment and experience, as a former newspaper reporter, Connecticut comptroller, and Jacksonian Democrat, who left the party to protest the Kansas-Nebraska Act. Lincoln called him Father Neptune because he was big, burly, and had the longest beard Lincoln had ever seen and thus reminded him of the King of the Sea. His experience as chief of the Bureau of Provisions and Clothing for the Navy under Polk made him a logical choice for Navy Secretary. Lincoln loved having Father Neptune nearby; Welles enjoyed Lincoln's stories more than anyone else in the Cabinet.

Coming from Ohio with a long record of opposing slavery, he seemed an inevitable choice, but Lincoln did not want him: a large man with an oversize ego, Chase had his followers, but most people found him overbearing. Yet Lincoln found Chase irresistible because Chase no more wanted Seward in the Cabinet than Seward wanted him. This made for a perfect match, in Lincoln's judgment, as they would either balance or cancel each other out. Chase had just won a seat in the Senate and was reluctant to give it up. Again, it was a matter of coaxing. It became harder because Simon Cameron was telling newspapers Lincoln had offered him the post of secretary of the Treasury. Eventually, Lincoln convinced Chase to take the Treasury by presenting it as a chance to keep an eye on Seward.

Slight, bespectacled, and with a beard that rivaled Welles's, Edward Bates appealed to Lincoln for many reasons. He had been urged upon Lincoln by many friends in the Republican Party, especially Browning and Horace Greeley, who served briefly in the House of Representatives and was the powerful publisher of the *New York Tribune* (the most widely circulated newspaper in the United States at that time). Bates had been a Whig, like Lincoln, and had been offered but turned down Fillmore's invitation to be his secretary of war. Since Lincoln wanted a Republican leader from the West in his Cabinet, Missouri's Bates was perfect. Lincoln needed Missouri again in his corner. Bates had been Missouri attorney general and had a distinguished career in the Missouri bar; he seemed a perfect fit as U.S. attorney general.

There were three posts left to fill. One was the Department of the Interior. With few clamoring for it, Lincoln thought of Caleb Smith. The two men had served together in the House, and Smith came from Indiana, another state he wanted to keep in his column. Lincoln, however, seemed to be one of the few men who thought Smith was up to the job—indeed, he hesitated because he agreed with Villard that Smith was not just dumb, but "worse than mediocrity."[75] He could not, however, ignore the debt he felt to him, because Indiana had come to his aid at the convention when he most needed it and Smith had been the man to make that happen. He needed a Midwesterner in the Cabinet. Smith was the man.

Nor could Lincoln ignore Simon Cameron's persistence in demanding a Cabinet post. Cameron felt entitled to the Treasury and insisted on reminding Lincoln at every opportunity that the post should be his, forcing Lincoln to tell him, "Since seeing you things have developed that make it impossible for me to take you into the Cabinet."[76] Ongoing rumors of his corruption made Lincoln less enthusiastic, but the constant pressure he felt from Pennsylvania because Cameron had campaigned around the state showing everyone Lincoln's December 31 letter offering him a post (while concealing the January 3 letter rescinding it) shamed him into offering Cameron a Cabinet position. Mindful that he should avoid writing letters that could came back to haunt him, Lincoln grudgingly appointed the Pennsylvanian secretary of war.

This left the position of postmaster general, perhaps the least prestigious Cabinet office, yet it was essential for ensuring communications with the army if war came. Lincoln chose Montgomery Blair, a member of the influential Blair family of Missouri. There was much to be said for Blair's inclusion. He had been well respected as a lawyer, including as a counsel for Dred Scott. He had served in multiple offices before, including as a judge of the Court of Common Pleas, U.S. solicitor in the Court of Claims, and U.S. district attorney. Blair knew his way around government. The problem was that no one but Lincoln liked Montgomery Blair. A graduate of West Point, Blair wanted to be war secretary, but he was a notorious malcontent and contrarian, who, as the journalist Noah Brooks once wrote, "was a relentless mischief-maker, . . . and he was apparently never so happy as when he was in hot water or making it hot for others."[77] He quickly alienated nearly everyone he worked with in the new administration.

It was no accident that more than half of Lincoln's Cabinet had been Jacksonian Democrats. Though neither he nor the Blairs respected Franklin Pierce (much less agreed with him on anything), his was the only Cabinet yet in American history to have stayed intact for a president's entire term. Its endurance lent the weak-willed Pierce a semblance of stability. Montgomery Blair's brother, Francis Preston Blair Jr., recalled that Buchanan had "put in his cabinet his enemies—men who felt his nomination a blow to their ambitions."[78] He remembered that Buchanan also "named former Democratic presidential candidate Lewis Cass secretary of state, and Fillmore's [Cabinet] had such luminaries as Daniel Webster, Thomas Corwin, and John Crittenden"[79]—the result hardly harmonious. Lincoln took a page from the experiences of both presidents. He had met Fillmore even before he became president in 1850 and met Buchanan at his own 1861 inauguration, making a total of five presidents he had met before he took the oath of office.[80] He assembled a Cabinet of political leaders from throughout the nation and the political spectrum—with the obvious exception of extremist Democrats like Jefferson Davis, who had been sworn into the presidency of the Confederacy two weeks before Lincoln's inauguration.

The composition of Lincoln's Cabinet should have left no doubt about his determination to be inclusive and his confidence in managing a group that included men who looked down on him. (When told that Chase thought he was bigger than Lincoln, Lincoln said, "Well, do you know of any other men who think they are bigger than I am? Because I want to put them all in my cabinet.") It also showed his intent to follow Jackson and his strong stance against secession. To remove any lingering doubt, one of Lincoln's first decisions upon entering the presidential office was to choose a portrait to hang over the mantelpiece. He asked for the official portrait of Andrew Jackson to be placed there. For the rest of Lincoln's presidency, Jackson looked down upon the long table where the Cabinet met every Tuesday and Friday. The choice of Jackson was obvious; it underscored Lincoln's recognition of Jackson's impassioned and effective commitment to preserving the Union. Lincoln used the portrait to great effect throughout his presidency.

Lincoln hung no portraits of Henry Clay. He didn't need any. He walked, talked, and thought about Clay nearly all the time; he had told Clay's son as much, and nearly anyone else who listened, as he quoted Clay at length. If Lincoln needed any further reminder of his mentor, he had his collected speeches nearby on his desk, alongside his beloved Shakespeare, available whenever he needed comfort or inspiration from either.

As people looked to the White House, they saw something never seen before—a president who was committed to following Jackson and Clay. The question they all had was, could he pull it off?

IV

Two days after Lincoln's inauguration, the Senate confirmed all seven members of his Cabinet, as well as John Nicolay's nomination as Lincoln's principal secretary. As had been done in prior administrations, the Cabinet met at a long rectangular hard walnut table in the president's office. Lincoln's third secretary, William Stoddard, described what visitors saw when they entered his office: "Folios of maps leaned against the walls or hid behind the sofas. Volumes of military history and literature came and went from various libraries and had their days of lying around the room or on the President's table."[81] The Jackson portrait hung just to Lincoln's left whenever he sat at the head of the Cabinet table. On the same wall hung a photograph of John Bright, a staunch supporter of the United States in Parliament since he entered in 1843 and a steadfast opponent of slavery. Lincoln said of Bright, "I believe he is the only British statesman, who has been unfaltering in his confidence in our success." (His admiration for Bright was evident when, after his assassination, his wallet was found to contain a clipping of a letter Bright sent to Horace Greeley about Lincoln's reelection, praising it for showing that "Republican institutions, with an instructed and patriotic people, can bear a nation safely and steadily through the most desperate perils.")

Lincoln called the Cabinet into his office for their first meeting on March 6. He did not mention Fort Sumter. On March 9, he brought the Cabinet back together to share new information he had just received on the growing threat in South Carolina. After a vigorous discussion, every Cabinet member except Montgomery Blair urged Lincoln to abandon the fort.[82]

Blair was unhappy, a circumstance that came as no surprise to anyone who knew him. Lincoln had long counted among his friends Blair's father, Francis Sr., the stern head of a political dynasty. In spite of their long attachment to the Democratic party, the Blairs had fled the party in opposition to slavery and the Kansas-

Nebraska Act. Buchanan hired him to serve as the government's top lawyer for the Court of Claims but then fired him because of his strident opposition to the administration's proslavery positions. Though he opposed slavery, Blair was not sufficiently extreme in his support of the rights of African Americans to appease Radical Republicans, nor was he as conservative as many other Republicans who were less absolutist in opposing slavery and more eager to avoid war. As a result, Blair ended up as postmaster general, not in the center of power but near it. Noah Brooks reported, "Blair, though a good Postmaster General, was the meanest man in the whole government."[83]

True to form, Blair did not hesitate to take advantage of Lincoln's trust. After the March 9 Cabinet meeting in which he found himself virtually alone on the question of how to handle Sumter, he threatened to resign. As Navy Secretary Welles related, Blair was "determined not to continue in the Cabinet if no attempt were made to relieve Fort Sumter."[84] Welles was as close to a natural ally to Blair as there could be. Like Blair, he had been a Jacksonian Democrat who had left the party to oppose slavery and had enthusiastically supported Lincoln during the 1860 election. Both men distrusted Seward: In the 1860 convention, Welles, who'd led the Connecticut delegation, had been unsettled by Seward's continuing attempts to undermine Lincoln throughout the convention, even after Lincoln had secured the nomination. Blair agreed with Welles that Seward was more interested in promoting his own career than in helping Lincoln succeed or protecting the Union. Now, with the Cabinet favoring appeasement and opposing any effort to salvage the fort, Blair told Welles he was disgusted and was considering resigning.

Blair's father, Francis, from whom Montgomery undoubtedly got his stubbornness, was apoplectic. On March 11, Francis Blair barged past Lincoln's secretaries to speak with Lincoln. He was determined that Lincoln not accept Montgomery's resignation but to resolutely stand by Fort Sumter. Lincoln knew Francis well enough to understand why he was agitated, and he anticipated what was coming. Everyone knew that the old man revered Jackson; Francis had been not only one of his earliest supporters but also a close adviser to President Jackson. After leaving the Democratic Party in 1854, Francis became one of the first prominent figures to join the founding of the Republican Party. In the 1860 Republican convention, the elder Blair initially supported his fellow Missourian Bates but quickly threw his support behind Lincoln when it became clear Bates had no chance. He was also, like Clay and Jackson, a strong advocate of gradual emancipation as a solution to the problem of slavery.

Now, with Jackson peering down from his portrait on Lincoln and Blair, and with Gideon Welles taking notes, the elder Blair "entered his protest against the non-action, which he denounced as the offspring of intrigue."[85] Francis told the president bluntly that doing nothing to save Fort Sumter was "virtually a surrender of the union."[86] Not mincing words, he told Lincoln, "It would be treason to surrender Sumter, sir. . . . If you abandon Sumter, you will be impeached!"[87] Welles observed that Blair's "earnestness and indignation aroused and electrified the President; and when, in his zeal, Blair warned that the abandonment of Sumter would be justly considered by the people, by the world, by history, as treason to the country, he touched a chord that responded to his invocation."[88] As Welles recalled, "The President decided from that moment that an attempt should be made to convey supplies to Major Anderson, and that he would reinforce Sumter."[89] It was the same basic plan that Browning had proposed to Lincoln in February before the president-elect left Illinois for his inauguration in Washington.

A letter Francis wrote to his son Montgomery the next day, March 12, confirms that Jackson was on his mind when he urged Lincoln to be firm. Though expressing misgivings about having spoken so bluntly to the president, Francis mentioned Jackson twice. First, he told Montgomery that the current situation demanded an "exposition" from the president "even more than the one faced by Genl Jackson" in 1832.[90] He also stressed that "there never was an occasion when an eloquent appeal by the President to the people like that of Genl Jackson in the crisis of 1832, could be of more use."

Lincoln agreed. On March 13, he met with Montgomery and his brother-in-law Gustavus Fox, a former Navy lieutenant. Fox had tried but failed to persuade President Buchanan to let him lead a reconnaissance expedition to learn firsthand the best ways to resupply Fort Sumter. Fox asked for permission to do this now. Lincoln said he would consider it.

Two days later, on March 15, the president requested each Cabinet officer to respond in writing to the question of whether it was "wise to attempt" to deliver provisions to Fort Sumter.[91] Blair was the only Cabinet member to unequivocally answer yes.[92] Seward and Chase were not alone in worrying Lincoln had "no conception of his situation."[93]

Lincoln was determined not to authorize any "hasty action" but instead wanted, as Welles noted, "time for the Administration to get in working order and its policy to be understood."[94] Lincoln talked further with Fox, then sent him to Charleston to get a look firsthand at Fort Sumter and the environs, get a sense of its vulnerability to attack, and assess the most feasible way to resupply it. Because Seward had insisted that the people of South Carolina might not want war, Lincoln asked Stephen Hurlbut, an old friend and fellow lawyer from Illinois, and Ward Hill Lamon, a former law partner who opposed abolition, to travel to Charleston and assess public opinion as best they could.[95] Lincoln understood the utility of spies, as George Washington had relied on Native Americans for intelligence during the French and Indian War and put together an underground spy network to track the British forces during the Revolutionary War. Winfield Scott had used a band of Mexican outlaws and army engineers to collect intelligence on the enemy's movements during the Mexican War, and Lincoln himself had served for twenty days with a special company of spies and scouts doing reconnaissance during the Black Hawk War.

Just as Lincoln's agents left to gather the intelligence he needed to firm up his plans, Lincoln heard again from Francis Blair. The senior Blair could not refrain from pushing Lincoln again. On March 18, he wrote the president to reiterate his demands that Lincoln should stand firmly by Fort Sumter, and he warned Lincoln that Seward was a "thoroughly dangerous counselor."[96]

Lincoln barely had time to digest Blair's opinions. He received more compelling news from both Fox and Hurlbut. Fox reported the logistics required to reinforce Sumter, while Hurlbut shared the disquieting news that the South Carolinians whom he had seen and spoken with "had no attachment to the Union."[97]

As the time for action grew short, Lincoln had to work with what he had. After a state dinner on March 28, he asked his Cabinet to remain so that he could update them on the Sumter situation. He shared a letter he had received from General Scott suggesting that it would be necessary to abandon Fort Sumter as well as Fort Pickens on the Florida coast in order to "soothe and give confidence to the eight remaining slave-holding States, and render their cordial adherence to the Union perpetual."[98] Montgomery Blair "smelled a rat." He erupted, denouncing Scott for "playing politician" rather than acting as a general.[99] Everyone present understood Blair's reference was really directed at the secretary of state.[100] By the end of the meeting, Seward alone stood by the general, while the rest of the Cabinet, much to Blair's surprise, agreed with him.[101]

On March 30, Lincoln reassembled the Cabinet to hear his plan to shore up the fort. With his mind made up, Lincoln marched back and forth at the front of the room as if he were addressing a jury, musing aloud about the arguments for and against his authorizing Fox to lead a clandestine expedition to bring supplies to the fort. The presentation worked. Over the objections of Seward and Interior Secretary Caleb Smith, who'd chaired Indiana's delegation at the Republican convention, the Cabinet approved the plan, though some members were concerned about whether Lincoln was up to the job ahead.

V

The execution of the plan was less than perfect. Lincoln bypassed Simon Cameron, the aging war secretary, who had missed most of the important meetings of the Cabinet and seemed clueless when it came to talking substance or strategy. Instead, Lincoln turned to Seward, Welles, and Blair, all men of action. The problem was that Seward and Welles disliked each other, while no one much liked talking with Blair. Lincoln still did not trust Seward, but he insisted on being involved, and Lincoln saw no problem with allowing him a say.

Seward was convinced Sumter was a lost cause. At the March 30 Cabinet meeting, he had proposed as an alternative to Fox's expedition that a separate one, led by Captain Montgomery Meigs, the army engineer in charge of the construction of the Capitol, should be sent to reinforce Fort Pickens as a base in Florida. Seward followed up the meeting with a memorandum pressing Lincoln to abandon the Fox expedition in favor of the Pickens expedition.[102]

Lincoln stuck by his commitment to Fox's resupply effort. On his own volition, Seward reached out to the official commissioners that the Confederate States of America (the name adopted by the eleven secessionist states) had sent to Washington, in order to determine if any peaceful settlement was possible. Nothing came of the scheme, except for distancing Seward even further from the Navy venture Welles was organizing.

On April 1, Lincoln directed Fox to lead an expedition down to Charleston to deliver supplies to Fort Sumter.[103] Unfortunately, Lincoln did not realize that he had already ordered the ship he was intending to be sent with Fox down to Florida—the *Powhatan*, the most powerful in the Navy. Shortly after the March 30 Cabinet meeting, Seward had brought a large stack of papers for Lincoln to sign, but Lincoln was busy and signed them without carefully looking. One authorized the *Powhatan* down to Florida.

When Welles discovered on April 1 that Seward had tricked

Lincoln, he hauled Seward to the White House. It was midnight, but the president had not yet gone to bed. Welles demanded Seward explain himself to Lincoln. Seward reminded the president of his plan to send reinforcements to Fort Pickens and of the fact that the president had signed the paper authorizing them. Welles recalled Lincoln "took upon himself the whole blame, said it was carelessness, heedlessness on his part" and that "he ought to have been more careful and attentive."[104] Then, with both Seward and Welles beside him, Lincoln directed that the *Powhatan* be redirected so that it could support Fox's expedition.[105]

Seward kept hedging his bets. He telegraphed Lieutenant David Porter, who was in command of the *Powhatan,* to change course from sailing to help Fort Pickens in Florida and instead go to Charleston to support Fox and Fort Sumter. But he signed the telegraph "Seward," and Porter declined to follow the direction, since an order from the secretary of state could not countermand the original order, which had been signed by the president. As a result, the *Powhatan* remained on its path to Fort Pickens. This left Fox's Sumter expedition so seriously weakened that Fox's wife, Virginia, the daughter of Levi Woodbury, a former Navy secretary and Supreme Court justice, later described Seward's actions as "cruel treachery."[106]

On April 6, with Fox hoping in vain that his expedition could have been kept secret, President Lincoln agreed to follow Browning and Seward's counsel to send a messenger from the State Department to inform the governor of South Carolina of Lincoln's intention to send supplies, but not arms and ammunition, to Fort Sumter. Lincoln had no illusions about the response. His spies had informed him about the local population's and government's hostility toward the Union. Still fresh in his mind was Browning's prediction, made a month before his inauguration, that South Carolina would attack any effort to resupply the fort. Other advisers agreed that such an attack was highly likely under the circumstances.

On April 12, the governor of South Carolina did just as Lincoln and Browning had predicted and Seward feared. With Fox and his two hundred reinforcements watching helplessly, South Carolina began bombarding Fort Sumter with heated cannonballs and Fort Moultrie with shots from forty-three guns and mortars. Thirty-six hours later, Major Anderson and his garrison at Sumter surrendered.

The bombardment of Fort Sumter signified the beginning of the Civil War, though many people hoped reconciliation was still possible. Over the next few weeks, newspapers and politicians from both parties, including Seward, pressed Lincoln not to engage Southern forces. But Lincoln knew the die had been cast. When a delegation from Maryland, including the governor and the mayor of Baltimore, urged him to avoid war, he pointed to the portrait of Jackson and praised the former president as an exemplar of the firmness he now needed to emulate. Lincoln vowed to emulate Jackson's "manliness" in doing whatever was necessary to protect the Union and the fort.[107]

On April 22, Lincoln responded to the Maryland delegation's letter, pointing out that they were urging him to "ask for peace on any terms, and yet you have no condemnation for those who are making war on us."[108] He told them, "You would have me break my oath and surrender the Government without a blow. There's no Washington in that—no Jackson in that—no manhood nor honor in that."[109] Now that war was imminent, Jackson was Lincoln's north star, not Clay.

South Carolina's attack rallied both sides to their respective causes. On April 15, Lincoln had implemented a draft for seventy-five thousand recruits and called for a special session of Congress to convene on July 4 to discuss the impending war.[110] While support for Lincoln and the Union was never stronger throughout the North, each of the four Southern states that had not yet seceded promptly did so—North Carolina, Virginia, Arkansas, and Tennessee. They joined the Confederacy, which moved its capital to Richmond. Meanwhile, Lincoln communicated with governors throughout the North and met with state delegations, as well as on April 14, for several hours, with Stephen Douglas, who was eager to help the president put down the rebellion of the secessionist states.

Lincoln read Douglas the proclamation calling for conscripting seventy-five thousand troops. Douglas said, "Mr. President, I cordially concur in every word of that document, except instead of a call for seventy-five thousand men I would make it two hundred thousand. You do not know the dishonest purposes of those men [the rebels] as I do."[111] He then showed Lincoln "the strategic points which" needed to be "strengthened for the coming contest."[112]

VI

Before the special session of Congress began on July 4, 1861, Lincoln made one of the most controversial decisions of his presidency. On April 27, he suspended the writ of habeas corpus to give military authorities the power to jail anyone without due process whom they deemed to be a traitor or who was stirring rebellion between Washington and Philadelphia. The decision provoked a confrontation between Lincoln and Jackson's old friend, Roger Taney, the chief justice who had sworn Lincoln into office. Ironically, here too, Lincoln's model was Jackson.

Maryland was the problem. It was split over whether to secede or to help the Union, particularly whether to assist, even indirectly, with fortifying the capital. At the April 15 meeting with the delegation from Baltimore, President Lincoln did more than refuse to agree to their pleas that he prohibit his troops from moving anywhere through Maryland.[113] With Welles taking notes, Lincoln explained further, "Our men are not moles, and can't dig under the earth; they are not birds, and can't fly through the air. . . . Go home and tell your people that if they will not attack us, we will not attack them; but if they do attack us, we will return it, and that severely."[114]

The situation quickly worsened, as Marylanders destroyed railroad bridges and cut telegraph lines linking Maryland to the

North. On April 25, reinforcements finally arrived in Washington, but Maryland remained a hotbed of Confederate sympathizers, who impeded federal troops and encouraged interference with their operations.

Unrestricted by habeas corpus, federal authorities, led by General George Cadwallader, promptly imprisoned a man named John Merryman for recruiting, leading, and training a drill company in Maryland in service of the Confederacy. Lincoln had yet to ask Congress to declare war but instead to treat those joining or helping the rebellion as traitors, the same way Taylor and Fillmore had regarded forces rebelling against federal authority.

Imprisoned in Fort McHenry in Baltimore, Merryman directly appealed to Chief Justice Roger Taney for a writ of habeas corpus. (Because Taney also sat as a U.S. Circuit Judge in Maryland, the petition came directly to him.) The writ would have required Merryman's jailer to come before Taney to explain Merryman's confinement. But when the chief justice ordered the writ to be delivered to General Cadwallader for an answer, the general ignored it. Incensed by Cadwallader's insolence, Taney granted the writ and issued an opinion explaining his reasoning and denouncing Lincoln's actions as unconstitutional. Taney stated that only Congress had the power to suspend the writ and rejected Lincoln's argument that he had the authority to suspend habeas corpus while Congress was in recess. Taney did not directly order Lincoln or anyone in his administration to release Merryman, making it easier for Lincoln to ignore Taney's opinion. Besides having questioned the legitimacy of Taney's *Dred Scott* decision, he was now open to the charge of flouting the Constitution and Taney's authority.

Yet the precedent for suspending habeas corpus and ignoring Taney's decision came from Andrew Jackson. After victories over the British in Mobile, Alabama, Major General Jackson directed his forces to head off the British army before it could take New Orleans. Arriving before the British, Jackson declared martial law on December 14, 1814. Over the next few months, he imposed a curfew, censored a newspaper, came close to executing two deserters, arrested a hundred soldiers for mutiny and desertion, banished Frenchmen newly naturalized as American citizens, ignored the Louisiana governor's order to stand down, and jailed a congressman, a federal judge, and the federal district attorney. When he was confronted with a writ of habeas corpus, he ignored it. Even though the Supreme Court had declared not long before that only Congress had the authority to suspend the writ of habeas corpus, Jackson decided, on his own initiative, to suspend it.

When news finally reached Jackson that a peace treaty had been signed to end the hostilities, he relented and grudgingly lifted his order of martial law. After he was released, John Dick, the federal district attorney, demanded that Jackson be brought before the federal judge, Dominick Hall, to explain himself. When Jackson appeared before Judge Hall, he refused to answer any of his questions. Judge Hall found Jackson in contempt of court and fined him $1,000.

It was not in Jackson's nature to forget any slight—in this case, the fine. Nor did he forget how Henry Clay had opposed any efforts in Congress to erase the fine. Jackson never gave up trying to have the fine wiped from his record. After leaving the presidency, he got Polk's help to expunge the fine once and for all. Shortly before he died, he asked Congress to reimburse the fine. On January 8, 1844, Congress, on the twenty-ninth anniversary of the Battle of New Orleans, agreed.

There was no mention of Jackson's declaration of martial law in George Prentice's 1831 biography of Clay, for Clay was out of the country at the time as a member of the presidential commission charged with negotiating the Treaty of Ghent, which ended the War of 1812. But Lincoln must have known about Congress's indemnifying the fine, since he was eyeing a run for the House as early as 1844 and discussion of the reimbursement was one of the most heated debates of the time.

There was also the 1832 Supreme Court opinion, written by Chief Justice John Marshall, that invalidated a Georgia criminal statute that prohibited non–Native Americans from being present on Native American lands without a license from the state of

Georgia. Marshall explained that the statute was unconstitutional because only the federal government had the authority to interact with Native American tribes. Jackson is said to have responded, "John Marshall has made the decision, now let him enforce it."[115] Although the comment is probably apocryphal, both Jackson and the State of Georgia ignored the decision.

Marshall had not addressed any order directly to either Jackson or the State of Georgia, even though the State of Georgia was holding three missionaries in its prison for having violated the state statute. Rather than abide by the decision, Georgia authorities pressed the federal government to remove the Cherokees from the land that the state was trying to regulate on its own terms. If Jackson did not enforce the Court's decision, none of the missionaries would be released. Though the missionaries were released a year later, Jackson did nothing in the interim. Having lived among die-hard Democrats for decades, Lincoln likely often heard praise for Jackson's defiance of the Court's order in 1832. Lincoln was even more familiar with Jackson's veto of the national bank, which rejected any obligation on the president's part to follow the Supreme Court's earlier decision upholding the national bank's constitutionality.

By the time Lincoln was president, there was no question he knew of Jackson's actions and approved of them. In an address to Congress on July 4, 1861, and in his first Annual Message delivered at the end of the year, he asked the same rhetorical question, "Are all the laws, but one, to go unexecuted, and the government itself to go to pieces lest that one be violated?"[116] He answered the question the same way in both, by citing the only precedent he thought was relevant—the 1844 refund demonstrating Congress's approval of Jackson's declaration of martial law, including his suspension of habeas corpus.

Throughout the remainder of 1861, Congress debated but never reached consensus on the conditions required for the suspension of habeas corpus, and Lincoln felt compelled further to suspend the writ on the Florida coast and in the area between New York and Philadelphia. In the meantime, Henry May, who had been elected as a Democratic representative to the House from Maryland in the 1850s, returned to the House in 1861 as a member of the newly formed Unionist Party, which was made up of former Whigs who wanted to stop the movement toward secession over the issue of slavery.

After the special session of Congress that Lincoln had called, May was taken into custody, without charges or recourse to habeas, on suspicion of treason. His crime was strongly objecting to Lincoln's war policies. Eventually, May was released, and in December 1861, he returned to his seat in the House, where he sponsored a bill that would have made it impossible for someone charged with a federal offense to be incarcerated pending trial and conviction. In 1863, the Senate approved a law incorporating May's bill, which became known as the 1863 Habeas Corpus Suspension Act. President Lincoln signed the act into law, which effectively ratified his suspension of habeas corpus. As Jackson had done, Lincoln had found a way for Congress to vindicate his actions.

VII

Stephen Douglas had done everything he could to fight secession and the prospect of war. While Lincoln remained silent in public during the 1861 presidential campaign, Douglas did not. Knowing he would lose the general election, Douglas did what he could do to preserve the Union, campaigning vigorously, particularly in the South, denouncing secession, and urging reconciliation and compromise everywhere he went. (He was spending the night in Mobile, Alabama, when he received the news that he had won only a single state in the election, while other Democratic candidates had won fourteen, and Lincoln had won with eighteen states and a majority in the Electoral College.) Shortly after the election, Douglas met with Lincoln and pledged his support to his success and preservation of the Union. On Inauguration Day, he dramatically stepped forward to hold Lincoln's hat and cane while Lincoln read his Inaugural Address. With Lincoln's knowledge and gratitude, Douglas traveled widely throughout the spring and early summer of 1861 to rally support among conservatives for maintaining the Union, but on the Southern portion of his trip he contracted typhoid fever, and on June 3, 1861, Douglas died in the arms of his wife. Upon hearing the news, Lincoln told those around him that he and Douglas "are about the best friends in the world" and then, in a rare display of emotion, burst into tears.[117] The two men had known each other—and battled each other—for three decades. The only public statement from the administration came from Simon Cameron, who had known Douglas for years as a colleague in the Senate. In a rare moment of leadership of the War Department, Cameron issued a circular to be distributed throughout the Union Army announcing "the death of a great statesman, [a] man who had nobly discarded party for his country."[118] The Little Giant was forty-eight years old.

The vacancy in the Senate opened up an opportunity that Lincoln quickly seized. With the Illinois legislature in recess, the state's Republican governor, Richard Yates, in consultation with Lincoln, made the appointment of Orville Browning on June 12, 1861, to take Douglas's seat. In early July, Lincoln's spirits visibly lifted when Browning arrived. Senator Trumbull presented Browning's credentials to the Senate, and in his first act as a senator, Browning joined his new colleagues in eulogizing Douglas. He emphasized the fact that Douglas had "placed patriotism above partisanship."[119]

In characteristic fashion, Lincoln unburdened himself to Browning. Browning did not hesitate to speak his mind, though the two did not always agree. Well before Browning arrived in person in July, he had written to the president, on March 26, saying, "You should not permit your time to be consumed, and your energies exhausted by personal applications for office."[120] Lincoln demurred: "I must see them."[121] Yet Lincoln was happy to see Browning, upon his return to Washington, sharing the news that "The plan succeeded." According to Browning, Lincoln explained,

"They attacked Sumter—it fell and thus, did more service than it otherwise could."[122]

Upon Fox's return from South Carolina, Lincoln appointed him an assistant secretary of the navy and consoled him, "You and I both anticipated that the cause of the country would be advanced by making the attempt to provision Fort Sumter, even if it should fail; and it is no small consolation now to feel that our anticipation is justified by the result."[123] During the special war session, Lincoln told Congress the same thing: "No choice was left but to call out the war power of the Government; and so to resist force, employed for its destruction, by force, for its preservation."[124] Perhaps Lincoln was trying to make the best of a bad situation, to control the narrative as best he could, or to show that he had not followed Polk's haste in making war. In any event, both the fact that South had fired the first shot and the perception of the Union's needing to use force to defend itself against the South's aggression broadened Lincoln's public support in the critical early days of the Civil War.

Nicolay recalled that Browning and Lincoln conversed daily in the White House and frequently rode and dined together, sometimes in the company of Lincoln's wife and family. Browning was more than a friend—he knew what Lincoln needed to become his best. Over the next year and a half until the end of Browning's Senate term in January 1863, no senator visited the White House more than he did. He became Lincoln's "eyes and ears" and leading spokesman in the Senate.[125] It was good to have someone to confide in, especially as Lincoln could not have imagined the challenges that were about to beset his family and the growing conflicts that he had to address with the Cabinet, Supreme Court, Republican Party, and Congress as well as on the bloody battlefields in the South.

CHAPTER SEVEN

COMMANDER IN CHIEF
(1861–1864)

Of the nation's first sixteen presidents, Abraham Lincoln had nearly the least military experience. Only two—John Quincy Adams and Martin Van Buren—had less: each had none. Lincoln's brief experience fighting mosquitoes in the Black Hawk War could hardly match the experience and know-how of the legendary generals Washington, Jackson, and Taylor. Aside from the presidents who, in office had directed or prior to taking office, ordered the slaughter of Native Americans—Washington, Jackson, Harrison, and Taylor, among them—James Madison was the only president before Lincoln to serve as commander in chief in a war on American soil, but his fleeing the White House in 1814 to escape the invading British soldiers, who torched the place in retaliation for the U.S. invasion of Ontario two years before, hardly set the example of the kind of commander Lincoln needed to be.

Lincoln had the complicated example of Polk's management—or as he saw it, the mismanagement—of the Mexican War. He had criticized Polk for his lies in starting the war, his poor relations with Congress during the war, and especially his refusal to share information about the war with Congress, based on "the important principle, always heretofore held sacred by my predecessors," to decline congressional requests for internal executive branch documents.[1] Polk cited Washington as a precedent for his defiance, but John Quincy Adams, with Lincoln sitting nearby, had thundered on the House floor, "Although the very memory of Washington, by everybody in this country, at this time (and by none more than myself), is reverenced next to worship—the President was wrong in that particular instance, and went too far to deny the power of the House; and as to his reasons, I never thought they were sufficient in that case." The case involved the Jay Treaty (forged in 1795 to avert further war with England, settle debts, and provide a framework for peaceful relations), and Adams noted that friend and foe alike in Congress opposed Washington's refusal to release documents.[2]

In Congress, Lincoln never seriously objected to Polk's vigorous use of his war powers once the conflict had begun, even though Polk had battled with his two Whig generals, Taylor and Scott. Moreover, Democrats were at the top of Lincoln's list when appointing generals and other officers at the start of the war, among them John McClernand, who had served with Lincoln in Congress and been an outspoken critic of the Wilmot Proviso; Benjamin Butler, who had supported Jefferson Davis for the Democratic nomination for president in 1860; and John Dix, who had served as Buchanan's secretary of the Treasury. As president, "Lincoln never accused Democratic generals of sabotaging the war effort. Polk rarely mentioned Taylor and Scott without making such an accusation."[3] Though some Democrats were disasters in the field, Lincoln's appointments pleased their constituents.

The war was not the only thing Lincoln confronted in these tense years, just the most important. Not only were he and his army fighting to save the Union, but he and Congress were also refashioning America, just as Clay had envisioned it. In signing legislation authorizing two companies to build a transcontinental railroad to link East to West, Lincoln was effectuating a central component of Clay's American System, reassuring former Whigs and others in the mainstream that Clay's dream was still alive. He reshaped the Supreme Court, as only George Washington and Andrew Jackson had done before him. In repeatedly clarifying the objectives of the war, Lincoln did the opposite of what Polk had done in obscuring the reasons for the Mexican War. Lincoln revised the objectives several times, finally settling on the abolition of slavery as instrumental to maintaining the Union.

I

Shortly after the war began, Lincoln told his personal secretary John Hay that "the central idea pervading this struggle is the necessity that is upon us, of proving that popular government is not an absurdity. We must settle this question now, whether in a free government the minority have the right to break up the government whenever they choose."[4] Secession "is the essence of anarchy," he echoed Jackson and Clay on another occasion, "for if one state may secede, then others could claim the same entitlement until no government and no nation were left."[5] In his war message to Congress in July 1861 as well as his Annual Message delivered at the end of that same year, Lincoln made clear that the objective of the war was no less than to preserve the way of life of the United States. "This is essentially a people's contest. On the side of the Union it is a struggle for maintaining in the world that form and substance of government whose leading object is to elevate the condition of men to lift artificial weights from all shoulders; to clear the paths of laudable pursuit for all; to afford all an unfettered start, and a fair chance in the race of life."[6]

The way of life that Lincoln declared the Union Army was protecting was nearly identical to the political and economic vision underlying his primary mentor's conception of the American ideal. Lincoln said, "This just and generous, and prosperous system . . . opens the way for all—gives hope to all, and energy, and progress, and improvement of condition to all."[7] The freedom to become a "self-made man" was now the fundamental ideal that Lincoln believed the war was being fought to protect.[8] The foundation for linking the purpose of the war to eradicating bondage was thus set.

However, Lincoln encountered two immediate problems as commander in chief. First was his lack of any experience and knowledge of war compared with the fanatical leader on the other side. Jefferson Davis was a graduate of West Point and had distinguished himself as a colonel during the Mexican War. Only self-education could fill the absence of anything in his background to match that. Throughout the transition and his presidency, Lincoln tackled the study of military strategy as thoroughly as he had taught himself grammar, the law, geometry, and land surveying. "I am never easy now," he once explained, "when I am handling a thought, till I have bounded it north and bounded it south and bounded it east and bounded it west."[9] Herndon had witnessed firsthand that Lincoln "not only went to the root of a question, but dug up the root, and separated and analyzed every fiber of it."[10] John Hay, too, saw how Lincoln "gave himself, night and day, to the study of the military situation." Carl von Clausewitz, a Prussian general and military theorist, published posthumously his masterwork, *On War*, in 1832, the same year Lincoln was entering the state legislature. The leading treatise in the field, it defined war as "the continuation of politics by other means." Lincoln agreed. He was witness to the breakdown in American politics that brought the contending sides to war. He "pored over the reports from the various departments and districts of the field of war. He held long conferences with esteemed generals and admirals, and astonished them by the extent of his special knowledge and the keen intelligence of his questions."[11]

Lincoln familiarized himself, too, with the relevant precedents as to the basic chain of command set forth in the Constitution; commanding generals reported to the secretary of war, who in turn reported to the president. Ironically, this principle of civilian control of the military had been cemented most clearly and recently by Jefferson Davis when he served as Pierce's secretary of war after he had had trouble getting the army's commanding general, Winfield Scott, to report to him rather than directly to the president. Pierce came down on the side of Davis and the idea of civilian control of the military, ordering Scott to report to Davis, who in turn would report to him. Unhappily, Scott obliged.

As war secretary, Jefferson Davis had overseen the improvement of American weaponry and the professionalization of the army. Because of him, the Union Army was in better shape in 1861 than it had ever been before, with more advanced training

and arms, as well as new standards for promotion that were designed to ensure that the best officers moved up the ranks. Lincoln was also familiar with presidents reprimanding or removing
incompetent or disloyal generals, as Polk claimed to have done
with Taylor, who had defied his orders, and as Monroe had done
with Jackson during the Seminole War for going well beyond his
instructions.

As Lincoln explained to Nicolay, Simon Cameron had been of
no help in the struggle threatening the Union. He was, Lincoln
said, "utterly ignorant and regardless of the course of things . . .
Selfish and openly discourteous to the President. Obnoxious to the
Country. Incapable either of organizing details or conceiving and
advising general plans."[12] Because Cameron was inept and often
absent and unreachable, Lincoln requested Scott on April 1, 1861,
to "make short, comprehensive daily reports to me of what occurs
in his Department, including movements by himself, and under
his orders, and the receipt of intelligence."[13] Getting the facts was
essential. Lincoln would visit battlefields at least a dozen times over
the course of his presidency, lifting men's spirits when he could and
assessing the progress of war, as well as the men he had charged to
end it. Lincoln respected the opinions of experts, the experienced
military personnel in the field. Scott was fussy, as everyone said,
but Lincoln did not care about his demeanor, and trusted his opinion more than that of anyone else around him. Nothing was more
important than winning the war, so Lincoln put aside his ego to
find and listen to the generals who could end it as soon as possible.

Scott's place in the firmament did not last long, however. It soon
became clear that advanced age, poor health, lack of energy, and
the inability to mediate disputes about scenarios and plans among
his generals made it impossible for Scott to run the army compe-
tently, and he submitted his resignation letter to Lincoln. At first,
Lincoln did not accept it. He was unsure who would be a suitable
replacement. Scott urged Lincoln to name his chief of staff, Henry
Halleck, as his replacement. Nicknamed Old Brains because of his
high forehead and supposedly high intellect, Halleck had returned
to the army only a couple of months before, after having served for

many years as an expert on mining law in California. The other possible choice was General George McClellan, who was pushing hard for the job. After the Union forces led by Brigadier General Irvin McDowell, who reported to Scott, had been routed in the First Battle of Bull Run, in Virginia on July 21, 1861, Lincoln summoned McClellan from western Virginia, where his forces had been more successful than Scott's men had been. On July 26, the Department of the Shenandoah (under Major General Nathanial Banks) was merged with McClellan's Division of the Potomac (which included the Department of Northeast Virginia, led by McDowell, and the Department of Washington, under Brigadier General Joseph Mansfield). The merged forces became known as the Army of the Potomac, the Union's principal army in the eastern theater of the war. However, McClellan almost immediately began clashing with Scott and Halleck over nearly everything, from tactics and strategy to how much autonomy he had. Aware that Scott was ailing, McClellan met with senators to lobby for Scott's position and to force the old general out. On October 18, 1861, Lincoln and his Cabinet accepted Scott's resignation, which he had resubmitted, and on November 1, Lincoln named McClellan as his replacement. On turning the entire command over to McClellan, the president confided to him his concerns that "this vast increase of responsibility . . . will entail a vast labor upon you."[14] McClellan assured him, "I can do it all."[15]

II

At thirty-four, dashing George McClellan was the youngest man ever placed in command of the U.S. armed forces. Though his appointment raised great hopes for a swift Union victory, it took only four months for him to be a greater disappointment than Scott. He had graduated second in his class at West Point but was egotistical and duplicitous. As Lincoln's biographer Michael Burlingame suggests, "Compounding his paranoia was a streak of narcissism, predisposing him to envy, arrogance, grandiosity, vanity, and hypersensitivity to criticism."[16] An unabashed Democrat, McClellan was a protégé of Jefferson Davis, but Lincoln figured this might be an asset for McClellan in anticipating the enemy's moves. Lincoln was wrong. Except for Davis, McClellan had a record of holding every other one of his superiors in contempt, especially Lincoln. McClellan told his wife that Lincoln was his "inferior" and "nothing more than a well-meaning baboon."[17] When in Lincoln's presence, he could barely look at him, much less speak with him.

McClellan's downfall was more than a story of his own undoing. It was the story of Lincoln's mastering one of the most important but most underestimated powers of the presidency—the power to remove, without any other branch's approval, badly performing, disloyal, or incompetent executive branch officials. In this case, Lincoln had plenty.

III

Of the six presidents preceding Andrew Jackson, only one—Thomas Jefferson—had been confident that the Constitution gave the president the authority to remove Cabinet and other officers whenever he saw fit, regardless of whether the Senate had confirmed them. Proclaiming himself the heir to Jefferson, Jackson had taken this practice to a new level. He called it the principle of rotation, which merely meant that a president could dismiss officials and replace them with his friends and allies as he pleased.

Whig presidential candidates campaigned hard against the principle of rotation. They thought it was just a cover for the spoils system and that it encouraged corruption and undercut the professionalism and expertise that they hoped would distinguish the federal workforce. Nevertheless, when Whig presidents got into office, they followed Jackson's model anyway. Subsequently, Tyler and Fillmore, the latter perhaps the most faithful Whig president of all, removed their Cabinets when they didn't obey. Zachary Taylor removed nearly two-thirds of his predecessors' political appointees during his first year in office and was on the verge of replacing his entire Cabinet before he died.

Once he became president, Lincoln did Taylor one better and orchestrated the largest turnover in office of any president up until that time. He was convinced that his power to remove men not performing as he liked was his most important weapon for winning the war. He not only rotated Buchanan's entire Cabinet out of office, but also removed 1,457 men from the 1,639 offices to which he was entitled to make nominations. Like Jackson, who had introduced the spoils system to American politics, Lincoln understood, as David Herbert Donald observed, that "patronage is one sure way of binding local political bosses to the person and principles of the President, and for this reason [Lincoln] used and approved the spoils system . . . Lincoln's entire administration was characterized by astute handling of patronage."[18] Lincoln proudly declared that his administration "distributed to [its] party friends as nearly all the civil patronage as any administration ever did."[19] Yet, removal was easier for Democrats who believed that the Cabinet was supposed to serve the president rather than for the Clay Whigs, who believed that the president served the Cabinet. Many of the former Whigs in Lincoln's Cabinet—like Seward and Chase—would have preferred that Lincoln do no tinkering with the Cabinet but instead defer to them on whether or not to dismiss any of their underlings.

When it was Lincoln's turn to decide whether or not he had the unilateral authority to remove a Cabinet officer, he deftly tried to follow the Jackson model but paid lip service to the Whig orthodoxy of seeking congressional acquiescence, if not approval. Whigs, particularly Henry Clay, had made this a central tenet of their party in response to what they perceived as Jackson's arrogation of congressional authority through his overabundant use of the veto and determination to impose his will on the entire executive branch, beginning with the Cabinet. If presidents allowed their Cabinets to give them direction on domestic issues, their function would become more confined to carrying out the will of either the Cabinet or Congress. Either way, the president would be contained.

Harrison was president only for thirty-one days, but from the first day of his administration, Harrison bristled at suggestions from his Cabinet, including Secretary of State Daniel Webster, that decisions should be made by majority rule, with each Cabinet member having a single vote and with the president having only a tie-breaking vote if the Cabinet was deadlocked. Harrison opposed the idea, and he kept his temper in check until the day when Webster told him that the Cabinet had rejected his preferred candidate John Chambers for the position of governor of Iowa and instead appointed someone else more to their liking. After a few seconds of awkward silence, Harrison motioned for a piece of paper on which he wrote a few words. He asked Webster to read the message to the Cabinet; the message was succinct: "William Henry Harrison, President of the United States." Harrison then rose to his feet and angrily told the Cabinet, "—And William Henry Harrison, President of the United States, tells you, gentlemen, that . . . John Chambers shall be Governor of Iowa."[20]

In early January 1862, Lincoln did not formally seek his Cabinet's approval to dismiss Cameron. In this case, several Cabinet members—Seward, Welles, and Chase—had been encouraging Lincoln for some time to remove him, making this a decision unlikely to backfire. Besides concerns about inadequacy, corruption, and mismanagement of the department's finances (the War Department was commonly described as "the lunatic asylum," with generals running things as they saw fit), Lincoln ordered Cameron to withdraw a declaration that he had made in December 1861 announcing, in an effort to ingratiate himself with Radical Republicans, the emancipation of all rebel-owned slaves. Congressional leaders were aghast that Cameron had done this on his own volition, so when the time came to replace him, Lincoln had the tacit approval of Congress. Lincoln cushioned the dismissal with an offer to appoint Cameron U.S. minister to Russia.

Lincoln's choice of Edwin Stanton to replace Cameron surprised nearly everyone. Besides insulting Lincoln when they first met in 1855, Stanton had been a loyal Democrat who had served as Buchanan's attorney general and a confidant of McClellan. (McClellan's reference to Lincoln as a "baboon"—or "gorilla," as sometimes quoted—likely was borrowed from Stanton.) However, Lincoln needed competence, decisiveness, intelligence, and energy at the helm of the War Department, not a friend. The appointment would be a helpful bridge to Democrats who wanted a voice in the administration, and Stanton, renowned for his integrity and relentless commitment to excellence and organization, would bring to the War Department sorely needed administrative leadership. Indeed, Lincoln knew Stanton had tried during the last months of the Buchanan administration to do what his boss refused to do: find a way to help the federal forts under siege in South Carolina and Florida. That effort, though unsuccessful, strengthened his suitability for the appointment.

Stanton enjoyed considerable support with influential leaders in both parties. Both Seward and Chase favored his appointment. Even Cameron is said to have approved of, or at least taken credit for, Stanton's replacing him. The Senate confirmed Stanton on January 15, 1862, eight days after Cameron's removal.

A few months later, Cameron's nomination as minister to Russia was delayed while a congressional committee considered censuring him for financial mismanagement in the War Department. Once Lincoln assured committee members that Cameron was not responsible for the irregular procurement practices of his department thus far in the war, the committee relented, and Cameron was confirmed.

While Cameron lasted less than a year in his new position, Stanton did all that Lincoln wanted and more. Over the next few years, he brought order, high standards, and efficiency to the War Department. He continued in the position until after Lincoln's death, when Andrew Johnson fired him. His dismissal became a basis for Johnson's impeachment, because Congress, after the assassination, had, based on its distrust of Johnson, modified its

Tenure in Office law to require Senate approval as a condition for removal of a Cabinet officer.

Rotation in office was not the only Jacksonian principle that Lincoln followed as president. He met with his Cabinet only when he felt the need. Even then, he used it primarily as a sounding board. He never expected the Cabinet to be harmonious or loyal, but he did expect it to be helpful. Thus he was following the predominant models of presidential-Cabinet relations. (The composition of Pierce's Cabinet had remained steady, although it sometimes tried to impose its will on the president.) Jackson and Polk, too, had used their Cabinets primarily as sounding boards and to rally support for and help in implementing the president's policies.

One dramatic episode illustrating this help arose in December 1861, when two Confederate envoys, James Mason and John Slidell (the latter of whom Polk had previously used to try to settle the tensions with Mexico before the conflict) were seized from the British passenger ship *Trent* by Union officers. Fears of a large-scale conflict with Britain had already prevented the sale of bonds in Britain to finance the war against the Confederacy. Lincoln consulted his Cabinet, as well as Browning, who wrote a memorandum for Lincoln on the points of international law involved in the removal of Mason and Slidell from the *Trent*. Browning initially favored using force if Britain "were determined to force a war upon us," but he and Lincoln eventually "agreed that the question was easily susceptible of a peaceful solution if England was at all disposed to act justly."[21] Browning urged a policy of conciliation—in order to ensure that the Union was fighting just one war at a time—which Lincoln followed in settling the matter by letting the two envoys go.

Lincoln handled the Cabinet much as he had dealt with temperamental foes in legislatures, courtrooms, and conventions. Perhaps illustrating the truth of John Todd Stuart's insight that Lincoln's wrestling match with Armstrong was a turning point in his life, Lincoln surprised opponents by using their own arguments and actions against them. He followed the same pattern in deciding to remove McClellan as the general in chief.

In his four-month tenure, McClellan strained Lincoln's patience to the breaking point. Less than two weeks after he was appointed supreme commander, Lincoln, Seward, and Hay visited his home on the evening of November 13, 1861, to check on the progress of the war. Told McClellan was out, the trio waited for his return. After an hour, McClellan returned through a different entrance. Notified by a servant that Lincoln and two others were waiting for him, McClellan made no comment and went straight to his room. After another half hour of waiting, Lincoln inquired again about McClellan's availability and was told that he had already retired for the evening. Hay was outraged and begged Lincoln to do something about such insolence, but Lincoln responded that it was "better at this time not to be making points of etiquette and personal dignity."[22] Lincoln could put up with anything if it helped to end the war as soon as possible. Although McClellan raised morale, the troops under his command lay fallow and inactive. Lincoln understood that victory meant destruction of the enemy and that such destruction required engagement and bloodshed, which McClellan appeared to want to avoid as much as possible.

McClellan's constant requests for more men and resources with no apparent plan for using them was testing everyone's patience. On January 10, 1862, Lincoln called a meeting of top generals and directed them to formulate a plan of attack. Claiming illness, McClellan refused to attend. Lincoln told the council, "If General McClellan did not want to use the army, [I] would like to borrow it."[23] When word reached McClellan that Lincoln was moving ahead with plans without him, he came to Washington and met with Lincoln and the other generals on January 12. Reluctantly, McClellan revealed—for the first time to Lincoln—his plan of attack. It entailed transporting the Army of the Potomac by ships to Urbanna, Virginia, on the Rappahannock River, for the purpose of outflanking the Confederate forces near Washington. From there, McClellan explained, the army would proceed to capture Richmond. Even when pressed, McClellan refused to give any further details to either Lincoln or his newly appointed secretary of war, Edwin Stanton.

Though pleased that McClellan had a plan, both Lincoln and Stanton were dubious. On January 27, 1862, Lincoln issued General Order No. 1, which specified that the "Land and Naval forces" should move "against the insurgent forces" on or before February 22.[24] Four days later, Lincoln issued a supplemental order directing the Army of the Potomac to move against the railroad supplying the Southern forces gathering at Manassas, Virginia, south of the national capital, on or before the same date. McClellan replied with a twenty-two-page letter objecting in detail to the president's plan and defending his own. By early March, McClellan and his superiors were at a standstill, and no engagement had yet occurred. Frustrated, Lincoln told a congressman, "If General Washington, or Napoleon, or General Jackson were in command on the Potomac they would be obliged to move or resign the position."[25]

Lincoln was hardly the only one whose patience had run out. Often during his visits to the White House, Browning scanned the battle maps lying around while Lincoln reviewed news from the front. They frequently talked about Lincoln's difficulty in finding the right general to lead Union forces and particularly about McClellan. Browning was present when Lincoln was visited by the members of the Joint Congressional Committee on the Conduct of the War, formed in December 1861, to tell Lincoln to push McClellan harder or fire him. After tepidly defending McClellan, Lincoln agreed. McClellan's friend and ally Edwin Stanton agreed, too.

McClellan had been overjoyed by the news of Stanton's appointment, which he had hailed as "a most unexpected piece of good fortune."[26] After just a few days in office, however, Stanton had a remarkable turnaround after seeing for himself how McClellan had mismanaged the situation. At the time, he wrote the president, "As soon as I can get the machinery of office going, the rats cleared out, and the rat holes stopped, we shall move. This army has got to fight or run away."[27] He added, "[The] champagne and oysters on the Potomac must be stopped."[28] On March 11, Lincoln met with his Cabinet, which agreed to end McClellan's short tenure as the commanding general of the Union forces. Lincoln told McClellan his dismissal was necessary so as to devote attention to leading the Army of the Potomac against Lee's operations in Virginia.

Despite McClellan's mixed results, Lincoln named McClellan on September 12, 1862, to command "the fortifications of Washington, and all the troops for the defense of the capital."[29] A majority of the Cabinet sharply disagreed, declaring "our deliberate opinion that, at this time, it is not safe to entrust Major General McClellan the command of any of the armies of the United States."[30] Lincoln, backed by Browning and Stanton, felt that no one could do the job better than McClellan. The final clash between McClellan's forces and Lee's occurred at the Battle of Antietam in September 1862. The fight was a draw, after which Lee withdrew to the South.

Shortly after visiting an openly disrespectful McClellan on the battlefield in October, Lincoln had had enough. He ordered Stanton to remove McClellan from command entirely. Upon receiving the message of dismissal from Stanton, McClellan swore to his wife that Lincoln and Stanton "have made a grave mistake."[31] When the old political warrior from Missouri Frank Blair visited Lincoln on November 6, 1862, to protest McClellan's removal from general command of the Union's forces, Lincoln told Blair, "I said I would remove him if he let Lee's army get away from him, and I must do so. He has got the 'slows,' Mr. Blair."[32] Just as Taylor had used his dismissal as a platform to run for president, McClellan did the same. Once he was out from under Lincoln's command, he began assembling his own run for the presidency. He would be Taylor to Lincoln's Polk.

Lincoln struggled to maintain a good working relationship with members of Congress, many of whom fervently believed that they, not Lincoln, knew best how to win the war. The conflicts came to a head near the end of 1861.

In two long caucus meetings on December 16 and 17, Republican senators voted to press for a reorganization of Lincoln's Cabinet to secure "unity of purpose and action."[33] They were outraged over the outcome of the Battle of Fredericksburg, fought December 11–15, 1861, during which the Army of the Potomac incurred casualties three times as heavy as those incurred by Lee's forces. The senators blamed Seward for the debacle. This conveniently dovetailed with Treasury Secretary Chase's eagerness to get rid of Seward, who, Chase kept telling them, wielded too much influence over Lincoln, just as had he done over Taylor.

When he was a member of the House, Lincoln had urged transparency and candor upon the White House. But he would not allow himself, any more than Polk ever did, to be subservient to the House or Senate or a small band of senators, even if from his own party. On the evening of December 16, a messenger, accompanied by Senator Preston King of New York, brought to him a curt letter of resignation from Seward. Seward's son, Frederick, included his resignation as an assistant secretary of state. Lincoln rushed to Seward's house. Seward and his son were packing for their return to New York. Seward was adamant that Lincoln accept his letter of resignation in order to ease relations within the Cabinet and between the president and Congress. Lincoln strongly disagreed and urged Seward to stop packing. He asked Seward to keep the matter confidential until he had a chance to address the charges of discord in the Cabinet. Seward reluctantly agreed.

On the afternoon before the evening of his scheduled visit with the Senate delegation on December 18, Lincoln met with Browning, who reported what had happened during the Senate caucus meetings on the two days prior. Browning explained that he had defended Lincoln and Seward during the meetings, and that had Lincoln "caved in" and accepted Seward's resignation, he would have risked losing control over his administration.[34] Browning encouraged Lincoln to consider reorganizing his Cabinet. Lincoln listened, but regardless of the merits, the brewing insurrection within the members of his own party in the Senate infuriated him. He nearly shouted at Browning, "What do these men want?"[35] Lincoln then answered his own question. "They wish to get rid of me, and I am sometimes half disposed to gratify them. . . . Since I heard last night of the proceedings of the caucus I have been more distressed than by any event of my life."[36] Lincoln confided, "We are now on the brink of destruction. It appears to me that the Almighty is against us, and I can hardly see a ray of hope."[37]

When the senators arrived at the White House that evening, Lincoln had devised a plan. He kept the news of Seward's letter to himself. Once inside with the caucus, Lincoln listened patiently to the senators' complaints "attributing to Mr. S[eward] a lukewarmness in the conduct of the war, and seeming to consider him the real cause of our failures."[38] Benjamin Wade of Ohio blamed Lincoln for entrusting the conduct of the war to "men who had no sympathy with it or with the cause."[39] Wade further blamed Republican defeats in the recent midterm elections on the fact that the president had placed the direction of military affairs "in the hands of bitter and malignant Democrats."[40] William Fessenden of Maine added "that the Cabinet were not consulted as a council—in fact, that many important measures were decided upon not only without consultation, but without the knowledge of its members."[41] Fessenden denounced Seward for undue influence over the war's management and McClellan for being "pro-slavery," "sympath[izing] strongly with the Southern feeling," and unfairly blaming the administration for its failing to support the army.[42]

At this point, Lincoln interrupted. After years of experience in trying cases and in debating formidable foes, Lincoln had no intention of letting the opposition pull off a filibuster with no rebuttal; he had never allowed that to happen in court, and he would not allow it here. Producing a large stack of papers, he slowly read for more than half an hour the letters that he had written to McClellan to demonstrate his long-standing commitment to helping him and the war effort. His recitation caught the senators by surprise; they had no ready response. Without committing himself, the president invited the senators back the next evening, and they agreed.

The first thing the next morning, Lincoln assembled his Cabinet with the exception of Seward. He informed them of Seward's resignation and the visit from the group of nine senators representing the Republican caucus. "While they believed in the President's honesty," he told them, "they seemed to think that when he had in him any good purposes Mr. S[eward] contrived to suck them out of him unperceived."[43] Lincoln asked the Cabinet to return that evening "to have a free talk."[44]

When everyone arrived at seven thirty that evening, both the senators and Cabinet members, sans Seward, were surprised; neither group had had any idea that the other was coming. With senators and Cabinet members sitting uncomfortably across the table from each other, Lincoln delivered a long statement, commenting "with some mild severity" on the resolutions presented the evening before by the senators and explaining that whenever possible he consulted the Cabinet about important decisions but that he alone made the decisions, especially on matters of military strategy and command.[45] He said that members of his Cabinet sometimes disagreed but all supported a policy once it was decided, that he was "not aware of any divisions or want of unity," and that Seward was a valuable member of his administration.[46] Then Lincoln turned to the Cabinet members and asked them "whether there had been any want of unity or of sufficient consultation."[47]

Lincoln did not have to say what everyone present already understood, that he had just put Chase on the spot. Lincoln was aware that Chase had been the one who told the senators that Seward was the main source of all the problems in the Cabinet. Lincoln understood that if Chase now agreed with Lincoln, he would lose face with the senators who were present, but if Chase disagreed openly with the president, he would then lose the president's confidence. With all eyes on him, Chase took a moment to compose himself. He began defensively by saying "that he should not have come here had he known that he was to be arraigned before a committee of the Senate."[48] With everyone waiting for more, Chase grudgingly agreed "that questions of importance had generally been considered by the Cabinet, though perhaps not so fully as might have been desired" and that there was no want of unity in the Cabinet.[49] The meeting went on until one in the morning, but no one left thinking there would be any change in the Cabinet.

Much embarrassed, Chase came to the White House the next day to submit his resignation. "I brought it with me," said Chase.[50]

"Let me have it," Lincoln said, as he took the letter from Chase.[51] "This . . . cuts the Gordian knot," he said. "I can dispose of this subject now."[52] When Stanton, who had asked to be present, offered his own resignation letter to allay fears that senators were most concerned about the lack of progress in the war, Lincoln swiftly declined and ordered him to "go to your Department. I don't want yours."[53] He placed both in his desk.

In recounting the developments later to Senator Ira Harris of New York, Lincoln shared an anecdote about the time when he was a boy and had learned how to carry pumpkins while riding horseback. "I can ride on now. I've got a pumpkin in each end of my bag," he told the senator.[54] Lincoln had letters of resignation from his two most ambitious and meddling Cabinet secretaries— Seward and Chase—in hand, but he had no present intent to cash in on either. Later, he told Browning that he felt that he had shown that "he was master" of his administration and the senators "should not" have attempted to seize control of his Cabinet.[55]

A year after the Cabinet crisis of December 1862, Lincoln told John Hay, "I do not see how it could have been done better. I am sure it was right. If I had yielded to that storm and dismissed Seward the thing would all have slumped over one way and we should have been left with a scanty handful of supporters. When Chase sent in his resignation I saw that the game was in our hands and I put it through."[56] In the intervening months, before Lincoln made that comment to Hay, he and his Cabinet had addressed an even larger challenge in 1863—deciding whether the objective of the war was to maintain the Union, abolish slavery, or both.

IV

Settling on the objective of the war proved nearly as vexing for Lincoln as figuring out how to end the conflict. In his Inaugural Address, Lincoln had declared that the preservation of the Union was the war's objective—that and nothing more. He later explained that preserving the Union meant guaranteeing all Americans the freedom to become self-made men, on whatever terms they wished.

Lincoln appreciated both the legal and political problems with that objective. Lincoln was unsure whether the North could remain unified if the Union's fate turned on abolishing slavery. As a constitutional matter, it was unclear after the *Dred Scott* decision how far the federal government could go in regulating slavery. Was it barred from doing anything? Could it abolish slavery in the states, or at least the District of Columbia? Could it take intermediate steps, such as abolishing the slave trade in the District of Columbia or perhaps arrange funding to buy slaves and send them to Africa? Or was it required to allow slavery to spread without interference?

As Lincoln's presidency progressed, Radical Republicans and the members of the congressional Joint Committee on the Conduct of the War argued that the preservation of the Union and the abolition of slavery were intertwined. This raised other important but more technical questions: Did the president have inherent authority over the spread of slavery or status of those deemed slaves in the South, and to what extent did the president require congressional support or authorization to take any action, even as commander in chief, to interfere with slavery? As president, Lincoln worked through these questions step by step, and oftentimes with congressional approval or acquiescence, on a path that led him to issue one of the most famous executive actions in American history. In retrospect, the journey was not surprising. Through it all, Lincoln kept faith with the ideals he'd professed for decades as a Clay Whig.

The first step did not require Lincoln's participation at all. In fact, it was taken in the opposite direction of emancipation. In March 1861, Lincoln had insisted in his First Inaugural Address that the war's objective was to maintain the Union and pledged not to interfere with the institution wherever it existed. But by July, Confederates routed Union forces in the First Battle of Bull Run.

On July 25, 1861, all but a handful of senators voted in favor of a resolution sponsored by Representative John Crittenden of Kentucky (he entered the House after declining a third-party presidential nomination in 1860) and Senator Andrew Johnson of Tennessee, the only senator from a seceded state who remained loyal to the United States and remained in Congress after the Civil War began. The resolution affirmed that the war was being fought not for the purpose of "overthrowing or interfering with the rights or established institutions of those States," but only "to defend and maintain the supremacy of the Constitution and to preserve the Union."[57]

The second step toward emancipation occurred a few weeks later. On August 6, Congress passed the First Confiscation Act. The law authorized the federal government to seize the property of all those participating directly in rebellion. The law purposefully avoided specifying the permanent future status of confiscated slaves, but few expected that they would be returned to slavery. Without comment, Lincoln signed the bill into law. Privately, he told Browning, who had voted for it, that "the government neither should, nor would send back to bondage such as came to our armies."[58] Lincoln's position might have reflected the fact that as a former Whig he was prepared to approve laws that were not clearly unconstitutional and that this law, in any event, was consistent with the long-standing international law of war, which authorized the seizure of any property, including slave property. Also, the confiscation of slaves was a move long considered and contemplated among Whigs like Clay, for years, though they had envisioned the possibility of compensating slaveholders. With war, such financial niceties were no longer on the table.

The next step toward emancipation occurred shortly after Lincoln had signed the First Confiscation Act. Lincoln had assigned John Frémont, as head of the Department of the West, to clear Missouri of secessionists. On August 30, 1861, Frémont issued a proclamation in which he implemented martial law in the state of Missouri and ordered the confiscation of property, including slaves, of those who were resisting the Union. The reverberations of his proclamation were felt all the way back to Washington, where Lincoln countermanded Frémont's declaration on September 11,

1861. Lincoln had many problems with Frémont's proclamation. One was his conviction that the action breached the chain of command; Lincoln believed any such order should have become from the president, not a general, assuming that the president even had the power to do so. Lincoln ordered Frémont to revise his proclamation to conform to the Confiscation Act.

As soon as he learned of the trouble, Browning wrote to Lincoln on September 17, expressing his hope that the rumors he was hearing that the Cabinet had disapproved the proclamation were unfounded. He went further, in brash terms, to say that all truly loyal citizens favored the Frémont proclamation and that rescinding it would be demoralizing to many pro-Union Americans. He pointed out that there was no statute providing for the court-martial of enemies caught behind one's own lines, but everyone, he argued, agreed that such treatment of spies and traitors was perfectly legal. Why should those who rejected the Constitution expect to enjoy its protection? He said Frémont should receive unqualified backing from the administration, and he hoped the rumors that Lincoln planned to replace him were untrue. He went further to say, "I do think measures are sometimes shaped too much with a view to satisfy men of doubtful loyalty, instead of true friends of the Country. There has been too much tenderness towards traitors and rebels. We must strike them terrible blows, and strike them hard and quick, or the government will go hopelessly to pieces."[59]

Browning's tone stunned Lincoln. In a strongly worded letter on September 22, Lincoln outlined his national strategy. It was one of the longest letters he ever wrote in defense of his policies. Lincoln responded that Frémont's proclamation was "purely political and not within the range of military law or necessity."[60] He said that a general might, on grounds of military necessity, seize property from the enemy, including slaves, but "when the need is past, it is not for him to fix their permanent future condition."[61] He added, "You speak of it as being the only means of saving the government. . . . Can it be pretended that it is any longer the government of the U.S.—any government of Constitution and laws,—wherein a General, or a President, may make permanent rules of property by proclamation?"[62] It was Congress's job to make such rules, Lincoln reminded his fellow former Whig. He recalled that Congress had actually passed the Confiscation Law in the previous session before Frémont issued his proclamation and that Browning had voted for the law. To be consistent, Browning should give up his "restlessness for new positions, and back me manfully on the grounds upon which you and other kind friends gave me the election, and have approved in my public documents."[63] In other words, sometimes Lincoln just needed Browning to be a friend, not a mentor—or worse, a nag.

Another reason for the order countermanding Frémont's proclamations, Lincoln wrote, was the need to keep the border states in the Union. He told Browning there was a great deal of credible evidence that Kentucky would have gone over to the Confederacy if Frémont's proclamation had stood. "I think to lose Kentucky is nearly the same as to lose the whole game. Kentucky gone, we can not hold Missouri, nor, as I think, Maryland. These all against us, and the job on our hands is too large for us. We would as well consent to separation at once, including the surrender of this capitol [*sic*]."[64] Yet Lincoln emphasized that he did not issue his order to Frémont simply because of his concerns about Kentucky, for Kentucky had not yet taken a position. Lincoln assured Browning that he had no thought of removing Frémont because of what he had done and that he hoped it would not be necessary to remove him for any other reason.

Self-awareness was not one of Browning's strengths. He did not relent. On September 30, he responded with a long statement about the nature of war and its relationship to Frémont's proclamations. He believed that the law of nations furnished sufficient authority to use every advantage to weaken the enemy. He cited authority showing that a government waging war against a public enemy had a preexisting right to use the enemy's property to secure the ends of war. The people of Kentucky, Browning said, would not have opposed confiscation of horses to aid the federal troops; therefore, they should not oppose the confiscation of slaves when the exigencies of war and the preservation of the Union required it. He disagreed with Lincoln that the matter fell within the sphere of Congress's authority and therefore he felt no need to reconcile his arguments now with those he had had when Congress enacted the Confiscation Act. He did not take this situation as a pretext for breaking with the administration, and he assured Lincoln that he would continue to support him without wavering from his zeal for the welfare of the Union. He told Lincoln that he tried to share his suggestions in a friendly and helpful spirit.

Lincoln did not respond, instead leaving the matter where he thought it then belonged: Congress. Later, in October, when a congressional committee investigated Frémont's activities, Browning was invited to attend, but he declined. When he learned the committee had uncovered substantial corruption in Frémont's headquarters, he made clear his belief that it was not Frémont's fault but the fault of scoundrels whom Frémont naïvely allowed to be a part of his operations.

The next moves toward emancipation came largely from Congress. Each were critical steps in reshaping the objective of the war. In December 1861, as more escaped slaves joined Union forces as they pushed more deeply into the South, a solid Republican vote in the House passed a new resolution overriding the Crittenden-Johnson one that had disavowed any antislavery purpose for the war. In his end-of-the-year message to Congress, Lincoln felt the need to address a question that kept coming back to him—and indeed had been a theme in Browning's letters. This was the question of what initiative, if any, the president should take in helping to abolish slavery. The Whig in Lincoln called for deferring entirely to Congress, but as president, he appreciated that doing so was not a well-thought-out constitutional strategy.

Instead, Lincoln said, "In considering the policy to be adopted for suppressing the insurrection, I have been anxious that the inevitable conflict for this purpose shall not degenerate into a violent and remorseless revolutionary struggle."[65] This statement might have simply reflected Lincoln's judgment on the awfulness of war. It could also have been a subtle reference to a hope that the conflict would entail only a minimal transformation of the South and no serious damage to the Southern economy or quality of life. He also rejected the idea that "the Presidency conferred upon me an unrestricted right to act officially upon this judgment and feeling"[66] that slavery was immoral. However, as Civil War historian James McPherson notes, "Another passage in the same message—little noticed at the time—pushed that minimum beyond what it had been when he signed the Confiscation Act the previous August. He referred to the contrabands affected by that law as 'thus liberated'— that is, free people who could not be returned to slavery."[67] Lincoln had effectively adapted Clay's and Jackson's long-standing project of gradual emancipation to the circumstances at hand.

In March 1862, Lincoln and Congress took two further steps closer to demanding an end to slavery altogether. Though no one had any idea how much longer the war might last, Lincoln had begun to see that Clay's dream of gradual emancipation was within the federal government's grasp. On March 6, Lincoln sent a special message to Congress recommending passage of a joint resolution offering financial assistance to any state "which may adopt gradual abolishment of slavery."[68] Congress passed the resolution, with Republicans unanimously in favor and almost all Democrats opposed. Then, a week later and a mere two days after Lincoln sacked McClellan, on March 13, 1862, Congress gave the Union Army the right to take any and all personal property from rebellious persons, including slaves. It declared that captured slaves would not be returned to their owners, and it prohibited army officers, under pain of court-martial, from returning escaped slaves to their masters. Lincoln signed the bill.

On April 16, 1862, Lincoln signed yet another law, this time a bill that abolished slavery in the District of Columbia. He undoubtedly recalled, as did many of those who had supported him, that an identical law had been part of Clay's Compromise of 1850. The act was also a repudiation of the Supreme Court's decision in *Dred Scott,* which had ruled the Missouri Compromise unconstitutional because it violated the right of slave-owners to their so-called property.

By May, the Union appeared to have the momentum in the war.

It had scored a series of victories everywhere but Virginia. Building on that momentum, Congress, on June 19, 1862, prohibited slavery in all current and future territories, though not in any current or future states. Again, without comment, Lincoln quickly signed the bill. Once Congress had decided to ignore the *Dred Scott* ruling, Lincoln obviously had no problem in going along.

On July 16, 1862, Congress took another significant move toward emancipation when it passed the Confiscation Act of 1862, which made court proceedings available to slaves freed from owners who had engaged in the rebellion. The next day, Lincoln took the extraordinary step of preparing a veto message, the first of his presidency. He objected to the forfeiture of property beyond the life of the person convicted of treason. He suggested that this was tantamount to "corruption of blood" or visiting the sins of the father on his descendants.[69] Lincoln found fault in the law's use of in rem proceedings in the courts, which would authorize forfeiture based on status as a slaveholder but not necessarily on evidence of treason. He thought that the defendants in such proceedings required more time to prepare their defenses than the act allowed. In response to the prospect of a veto, Senate leaders hurriedly drafted a resolution to bar the punishment exacted by the law to "work a forfeiture of the real estate of the offender beyond his natural life."[70] They did not have time to fix any other parts of the act. Lincoln signed the law. His sensibilities as a Whig kept him from interfering too much in the legislative process and to enforce the policy enacted by Congress even if it was not perfect and he did not completely agree.

In late July, he convened his Cabinet to announce his intention to issue an emancipation proclamation. He likely based his reasoning on a pamphlet published by a lawyer he had appointed to the Interior Department, which argued that the laws of war "give the President full belligerent rights" as commander in chief to seize all enemy property, including slaves, being used to wage war against the United States.[71] Blair opposed going all the way, while Seward counseled Lincoln to postpone doing it "until you can give it to the country supported by military success."[72] Seward's advice "struck me with very great force," Lincoln admitted later.[73] He pocketed the proclamation until a more propitious moment.

Lincoln continued to correspond over the next few months with Browning, who was campaigning for reelection in Illinois. Earlier that year, in February, Browning had spent hours with the Lincolns after the death of his eleven-year-old son, William. Mary Todd was inconsolable, while Browning kept a close watch on Lincoln, who he knew was prone to bouts of melancholy. Come fall, he vigilantly did what he could to keep Lincoln's spirits up as the war dragged on. Browning reassured Lincoln, "The skies do not appear to be very dark to me. . . . Be of good cheer—hold yourself up to the work with a pure mind, and an eye singled to your country's good, and all things will yet be well."[74] Though Lincoln heard otherwise from other sources, Browning further assured him that "the hearts of the people were never warmer for you than they are today."[75]

In the summer of 1862, the pressure on Lincoln to take a strong stand against slavery grew. Both Browning and Lincoln's old friend Joshua Speed of Kentucky counseled him further on the propriety of issuing an emancipation proclamation. Speed had previously advised Lincoln on how to keep the border state of Kentucky in line, having urged him the previous year to overrule Frémont's proclamation. But now Lincoln wrote to Speed, "I believe that in this measure . . . my fondest hopes will be realized."[76]

On September 22, 1862, a few days after the Battle of Antietam and one year to the day after Lincoln had written to Browning that he doubted a general or president had the authority to issue an emancipation proclamation, Lincoln did just that, declaring slaves in rebellious states "forever free" as of January 1, 1863, unless those states returned to the Union within one hundred days.[77]

When he heard the news, Browning, perfecting his contrariness, was skeptical. Upon his return to Washington in November, he promptly had an extended conversation with Lincoln. In the intervening year, the two men exchanged positions, Browning now explaining his objections and Lincoln defending what he had once criticized Frémont for doing. Browning believed that Lincoln's planned proclamation had had a disastrous effect on the Republicans during the 1862 midterm elections and that withdrawing or altering it would bolster the war effort. When Lincoln showed no interest in changing his mind, Browning met with Seward, who had been persuaded by Lincoln that the proclamation made sense because of the signal it sent other countries. Seward told Browning that the proclamation showed other countries the true purpose of the war—the United States' commitment to abolishing slavery. Browning could do nothing to stop the proclamation from going into effect, as planned, on January 1, 1863.

One month before the deadline, on December 1, 1862, Lincoln delivered his Annual Message to Congress. He devoted most of it to the recommendation of a constitutional amendment to offer federal compensation to states that abolished slavery before 1900. The proposal confused many of his fellow Republicans in Congress, but Lincoln's proclamation was aimed at freeing slaves in the eleven states in rebellion and compensation for others for freeing slaves. Yet, in his message, just a month before the effective date of the Emancipation Proclamation, he continued to refine his articulation of the war's purpose and admonished Congress, "The dogmas of the quiet past, are inadequate to the stormy present."[78]

Lincoln warned all that the issue was not only about legality but legacy. "In times like the present men should utter nothing for which they would not willingly be responsible through time and in eternity," admonishing his audience that

> we can not escape history. We of this Congress and this Administration will be remembered in spite of ourselves. No personal significance or insignificance can spare one or another of us. The fiery trial through which we will pass will light us down in honor or dishonor to the latest generation. We say we are for the Union. The world will not forget that we say this. We know how to save the Union. The world knows we do know how to save it. We, even we here, hold the power and bear the responsibility. In giving freedom to the slave

we assure freedom to the free—honorable alike in what we give and what we preserve. We shall nobly save or meanly lose the last best hope of earth. Other means may succeed; this could not fail. The way is plain, peaceful, generous, just—a way which if followed the world will forever applaud and God must forever bless.[79]

The repetitive contrasts—freedom and bondage, remembering and forgetting, the individual and the nation, achieving eternal praise or admonishment—were more than echoes of Shakespeare and Burns. Lincoln was doing more than using the rhetorical techniques of the great poets. He was adapting them to the present circumstances by using the plain language of Americans to profound effect. His speech was all the more powerful because he was sharing with the world his own mindset, the urgency of contemplating each day, each step, in light of how history would judge him and judge them all.

Slightly more than two weeks later, on December 17, 1862, General Ulysses Grant, then leading Union forces in the vast Department of the Tennessee, surprised nearly everyone when he issued General Orders No. 11. When Grant caught wind that peddlers were cheating army officers under his command (and Jewish cotton traders might have been doing the same to his father), he ordered that "Jews, as a class, violating every regulation of trade established by the Treasury Department, and also Department [of War] orders, are hereby expelled from the Department."[80] Grant directed all Post Commanders within twenty-four hours of receipt of his order "to see that all of this class of people are furnished with passes and required to leave, and anyone after such notification, will be arrested and held in confinement until an opportunity occurs of sending them out as prisoners unless furnished with permits from these headquarters."[81]

While anti-Semitism was common in that era, a government command based on it was not. Henry Halleck, who was then the general in chief for all the Union forces, had concerns about Grant even before the order. A West Point graduate and veteran of the Mexican War, Grant had resigned from the army in 1854 because he saw little future in it and "the vice of intemperance had not a little to do with my decision to resign."[82] Elihu Washburne, an Illinois congressman and long-standing friend of Lincoln's, had found a place for Grant to return to the army shortly after the outbreak of the Civil War, first as a captain, then as a colonel, and eventually as a brigadier general on the western front. In less than two years, Grant had steadily risen in rank because the armies he led delivered much more often than not, including as recently as October 3–4, 1862, when troops from the Army of the Mississippi had repelled Confederate forces in Corinth, Mississippi.

The timing of Grant's General Orders No. 11 was awkward, both for him and the Jews who were its subject. It overshadowed the Union victory just a little more than a week before at Vicksburg, the last Southern stronghold on the Mississippi. At the same time, the Treasury Department desperately wanted to restore business within occupied areas to win back the inhabitants' loyalty, while the War Department worried that Southern profits from the cotton trade could be used to help the Confederate troops. The inflammatory directive barred Jews from residing or doing any business within the area under Grant's command. Grant's adjutant, Colonel John Rawlins, urged Grant not to promulgate the order, but Grant responded, "They can countermand this from Washington if they like."[83]

In fact, General Orders No. 11 was the most sweeping anti-Semitic governmental action ever undertaken in American history, but less than seventy-two hours after Grant issued it, implementation was delayed because several thousand troops led by Major General Earl Van Dorn attacked his forces at Holly Springs and General Nathan Bedford Forrest's cavalry attacked Grant's troops from the opposite direction, destroying fifty miles of railroad and telegraph lines. Communications to and from Grant's headquarters were disrupted for weeks because of the attacks, and therefore news of the order spread slowly, if at all. Once Grant and his officers got around to enforcing the order, in Paducah, Kentucky, on December 17, 1862, Jewish merchants and residents who were being expelled sent a telegram to Washington protesting their expulsion. In all likelihood, Lincoln never saw Grant's telegram until after January 1, if he ever saw it.

On the afternoon of New Year's Day, Lincoln attended a reception at which he shook hands for more than three hours. Afterward, he invited several members of his Cabinet back to his office to watch him sign the ground-breaking Emancipation Proclamation. When he first tried, his hand trembled so badly that he set the pen down, because "all who examine the document hereafter will say, 'He hesitated.'"[84] Lincoln was determined not to have that happen. To those gathered, he said, "I never in my life felt more certain that I was doing right than I do in signing this paper."[85] He added, "If my name ever goes into history, it will be for this act, and my whole soul is in it."[86] He tried again, but his hand still trembled. "The South had fair warning," he said as he looked at those assembled, "that if they did not return to their duty, I should strike at this pillar of their strength. The promise must now be kept, and I should never recall one word."[87] He then signed the proclamation without a tremor. "That will do," he said.[88] With the stroke of the pen, Lincoln had taken the biggest step ever taken to advance what he believed Jefferson and Clay had set in motion.

In spite of the historical magnitude of what Lincoln had done, the press was much more focused on reporting the effects of Grant's General Orders No. 11. Telegrams flooded the White House in protest, and two days after Lincoln signed the Emancipation Proclamation, he supposedly had a meeting on January 3, 1863, with Cesar Kaskel, a merchant from Paducah, Kentucky, and Congressman John Gurley of Ohio. In their presence, he is said to have immediately agreed to reverse Grant's order. On that day, Halleck telegraphed Grant that "[a] paper purporting to be General Orders No. 11, issued by you December 17, has been presented here. By its terms, it expels all Jews from your department. If such an order has been issued, it be immediately revoked."[89] On January 7, Grant's headquarters answered, "By direction of the General-in-Chief of the Army at Washington, the General Order from the Head Quarters expelling Jews from this Department is hereby revoked."[90] As he had done with Frémont and Cameron, Lincoln vigilantly enforced the chain of command. When outraged Jewish leaders met with Lincoln that same day, he reassured them that "to condemn a class is, to say the least, to wrong the good with the bad. I do not like to hear a class or nationality condemned on account of a few sinners."[91] On January 21, Halleck transmitted to Grant Lincoln's reaction to his order: "The President has no objection to your expelling traders & Jew peddlars, which I suppose was the object of your order, but as it in terms Proscribed an entire religious class, some of whom are fighting in our ranks, the President deemed it necessary to revoke it."[92]

Luckily for Grant, Republican Elihu Washburne, his longtime supporter, was still a member of the House and still on Grant's side. "Your order touching the Jews has kicked up quite a dust among the Israelites," he wrote Grant.[93] "They came here in crowds and gave an entirely false construction to the order."[94] Extolling Grant as "one of our best generals," Washburne successfully got a House censure motion tabled by a narrow margin of 56–53.[95] In the Senate, Republicans, sticking by the president and war effort, defeated a similar motion to censure Grant 30–7.

While Lincoln did not share, at least in writing, any further thoughts about the connection between the proclamation and his reversal of Grant's order, some things were clear. President Lincoln never spoke of it again after the censure effort died down, while Grant did only to express deep remorse over his order. We also know that in the frantic period from mid-December 1862 through the first few days of January 1863, Lincoln was deeply immersed in thinking about the legal and political ramifications of the ideal of equality as expressed in the Declaration of Independence and protected by the Constitution. We know, as well, that the actions Lincoln took during the winter of 1862 reconfigured the objective of the war. It was now the army's task, with about seven thousand Jews and a growing number of African Americans in its ranks (eventually reaching more than 170,000), to finish the job of suppressing the rebellion against the ideal of equality that Clay had long extolled and Lincoln had been enforcing, culminating in the Emancipation Proclamation and revocation of Grant's anti-Semitic order.

V

It was hard for Lincoln to escape the gloom of war, but he tried. Having entered the presidency with acute awareness of the stakes involved in the days, weeks, and months ahead, Lincoln took time, when he could pull himself away, to do things that had always helped to keep him steady and buoyant.

Two episodes illustrate how he used humor to lighten spirits. As his Cabinet members walked into his office for the meeting at which he first sprang the news of his planned emancipation proclamation, Stanton recalled that they found the President

> reading a book of some kind, which seemed to amuse him. It was a little book. He finally turned to us and said: "Gentlemen, did you ever read anything by Artemus Ward? Let me read you a chapter that is very funny." Not a member of the cabinet smiled; as for myself, I was angry, and looked to see what the President meant. It seemed like buffoonery to me. He, however, concluded to read a chapter from Artemus Ward, which he did with great deliberation, and, having finished, laughed heartily, without a member of the Cabinet joining in the laughter. "Well," he said, "let's have another chapter," and he read another chapter, to our great astonishment. I was considering whether I should rise and leave the meeting abruptly, when he threw his book, heaved a sigh, and said: "Gentlemen, why don't you laugh? With the fearful strain that is upon me, day and night, if I did not laugh I should die, and you need this medicine as much as I do."[96]

Later that year, on July 24, Martin Van Buren passed away. Lincoln had said nothing when Jackson and Polk had died, but this was different. Lincoln was now president and thus felt obliged to express gratitude for another president's distinguished career, especially one who, like Van Buren, had defended the Union to his last breath. More important, Lincoln had met Van Buren—indeed, he was the first president Lincoln met. A little more than a year after leaving office, Van Buren planned to visit Democrats in Springfield on June 14, 1842, but he got stuck in Rochester, Illinois. When "the leading Democrats" in Springfield learned he was delayed there, they "hurried out to meet the distinguished visitor."[97] As Herndon wrote years later about the meeting, "Knowing accommodations at Rochester were not intended for, or suited to the entertainment of an ex-President, they took with them refreshments in quantity and variety, to make up for all the deficiencies." They also brought with them their state representative, Abraham Lincoln, "whose wit was as ready as his store of anecdotes was exhaustless." Lincoln, then in his last term in the Illinois legislature, dressed in his haphazard way, towered over the short Van Buren, dressed as dandily as ever. Throughout the evening, Lincoln had "a constant supply (of stories), one following another in rapid succession, each more irresistible than its predecessor." Van Buren had his own anecdotes about politics in New York when he was a young man and his early interactions with the likes of Alexander Hamilton and Aaron Burr. The laughter lasted late into the evening, when Van Buren excused himself "because his sides were sore from laughing."[98] Later, he said he had never "spent so agreeable a night in my life."[99]

Lincoln did not forget that evening either. Nor did he forget that, in 1860, Van Buren had cast aside party loyalty and voted for him as president, in the hope that the election could avert civil war. It did not, but Van Buren kept looking for ways to help keep the Union intact until he fell ill for the last time. "[Out] of tribute to their friendship and respect to a former president," particularly one who stood by the Union, Lincoln "ordered a special military salute in Van Buren's honor."[100] As Lincoln had told young lawyers many years before in Springfield, a foe can become a friend. Indeed, they could come from the unlikeliest places, even among those closest to Jackson, Henry Clay's greatest foe.

VI

Democratic appointees had dominated the Supreme Court for nearly all of Lincoln's professional life. Jackson had made six appointments to the nine-member Court, while the three Whig presidents—Harrison, Taylor, and Fillmore—together had managed to make only one. Adding insult to injury, Fillmore's appointee, Benjamin Curtis, left the Court to protest *Dred Scott* and had his seat filled by Buchanan.

No president other than George Washington had as many vacancies to fill in as short a time as Lincoln did: Washington appointed ten justices (including one recess appointment), all of whom were strongly committed to the Constitution and the Federalist vision of a strong national government. Jackson's five appointees transformed the Court to become more protective of private property and state autonomy from federal dominance, but their installments had stretched out over a much longer period than it took Lincoln. Within fifty-two days of taking the oath of office as president, Lincoln had three vacancies on the Court to fill, and he got a fourth in his second year in office. Lincoln had even come into office with a vacancy to fill; one seat had been open since Justice Peter Daniel died nearly one year to the day before Lincoln's inauguration, and the Senate had not allowed Buchanan to fill it. A second opened when Justice John McLean died during Lincoln's first month in office; and the third seat became vacant less than a month after McLean died, when Justice John Campbell, appointed by Pierce, left the Court to return to his home state of Alabama to join the Confederacy. With solid Republican majorities in both the House and Senate, Congress took the unprecedented step in 1862 of adding a seat to the Court to enable Lincoln to increase his influence.

Lincoln did not, however, move quickly to make the appointments. Facing several court actions against the war, Lincoln sought justices who strongly supported the war effort and therefore would be disposed to uphold the constitutionality of what he had done to save the Union. Lincoln followed Congress's preferences in filling two of the seats because of his long-standing belief as a Whig in deferring to that body and because he knew the Senate was likely to use the same criteria as he in filling the seats. For the other two, he did what Jackson had done: he used the appointments to reward political allies and fortify his base.

Initially, Lincoln focused on filling McClean's seat, perhaps because it was the easiest. At that time, Congress had divided the federal courts system into several circuits, and it configured the Supreme Court so that its seats were aligned with those circuits. Supreme Court seats therefore had geographical requirements, and because McClean came from Ohio, Lincoln looked to Ohio for his replacement. Lincoln was happy to do this, because he owed Ohio Republicans for their vital third-ballot support at the Republican national convention in 1860. The Ohio congressional delegation was already lobbying Lincoln hard to appoint Ohio lawyer Noah Swayne. Indeed, before he died, McClean had recommended that Lincoln appoint Swayne to replace him. Lincoln was impressed with Swayne as an abolitionist; he had freed his slaves and moved from Virginia to Ohio in protest over Virginia's strong support for slavery. Swayne's Virginia ancestry probably would have appeal to the border states, as would the fact that Jackson had appointed him to serve as the U.S. attorney in Ohio. Lincoln also liked the fact that Swayne had served in both chambers of the Ohio legislature. Three days after Lincoln nominated Swayne, the Senate confirmed him by the overwhelming vote of 38–1.

Lincoln turned his attention next to the seat that had been vacated due to Peter Daniel's death. Daniel came from Virginia, which Lincoln felt no need to appease, especially with a seat on the Supreme Court. Instead, he deferred almost completely to Congress. Indeed, the lobbying done by members of Congress and Western political leaders to fill the seat was unprecedented. Western governors, Iowa's attorney general, and the entire Iowa Supreme Court all favored Iowa's most distinguished lawyer, Samuel Freeman Miller. Moreover, 129 of 140 House members and all but 4 senators petitioned Lincoln to appoint Miller. No one from Iowa or born west of the Appalachian Mountains had ever been appointed before the Court, and Miller's credentials were impeccable—a native of Kentucky, he had studied medicine at Transylvania University in Lexington, which Lincoln knew well as the alma mater of his father-in law. Miller had been a physician for a dozen years before he earned his law degree. He'd left Kentucky for Iowa in protest over slavery and been one of the first and most prominent Republicans there, and he had done everything a lawyer could do in his community, state, and region in a distinguished practice. Within thirty minutes of Miller's nomination to the Court, the Senate unanimously confirmed him.

This left the third Supreme Court vacancy to fill. Lincoln felt no more need to appease the South in filling Campbell's vacated seat than he had in filling Daniel's. Free to do as he pleased, he very quickly narrowed his choice down to two people, his old friend and state judge David Davis and Orville Browning. Both had been precluded from consideration for the initial vacancy for circuit reasons and for the second after Lincoln decided it should go to someone from the far Western states. Both Davis and Browning wanted the seat desperately, and each lined up considerable support to strongly lobby Lincoln. On April 9, 1862, Browning had written sheepishly asking for the appointment, but his wife wrote soon thereafter to press his case harder. Lincoln understood Browning's confirmation might have been easier than Davis's because other senators tended to support one of their own when nominated to the Cabinet or other offices. But Lincoln did not relish losing Browning to the Court. He also appreciated that Davis's constitutional views were more in line with his own than Browning's were. Lincoln wanted to please them both, and at one point he considered appointing Davis to the Cabinet and Browning to the Court. It was a difficult choice, as reflected in the fact that Lincoln left the seat vacant for more than a year as he decided what to do.

After Lincoln's death, Herndon shared a note that he said Lincoln had written during the year when he considering whom to appoint to take Campbell's seat on the Court, confessing, "I do not know what I may do when the time comes, but there has never been a day when if I had to act I should not have appointed Browning."[101] So why did Lincoln not choose Browning for the Court? Herndon suggests that there was a crucial turn of events when Lincoln's friend Leonard Swett met with Lincoln in August 1861 to discuss the appointment. Swett had pushed Lincoln in writing to make the appointment, but he supposedly told Lincoln that "he could kill 'two birds with one stone' by appointing Davis."[102] Believing Lincoln owed him and other supporters in Illinois a favor for their support, Swett explained that he "would accept [the appointment of Davis] as one-half for me and one-half for the Judge; and that thereafter: If I or any of my friends ever troubled him, [Lincoln] could draw [Swett's] letter as" proof he made the appointment to pay Swett back for his support.[103] Swett said Lincoln nodded in agreement and responded, after some thought, "If you mean that among friends as [the letter given to him by Swett] reads I will take it and make the appointment."[104] Swett later said that the meeting was the decisive moment sealing Davis's appointment.

The fact that at least a year went by after the meeting before Lincoln actually made the appointment weakens Swett's claim. Browning enjoyed strong support in the Senate, and he had other prominent political leaders backing him, including Attorney General Edward Bates. In March 1862, Noah Swayne told Bates of a rumor going around that Caleb Smith, the secretary of the interior, might get the open seat, but Bates said he did not believe that it would interfere with Browning's being nominated to the Court. Later that same day, Bates wrote in his diary, "Nobody [I] think objects to Browning—He is a proper man."[105] Nevertheless, throughout this same time, Davis's friends were flooding Lincoln with letters hailing him, Lincoln's former partner Stephen Logan among them. John Todd Stuart wrote to Lincoln that the appointment would be especially "pleasing to the circle of your old personal friends."[106] As it was, the numbers of supporters pushing for Davis exceeded those pushing for Browning. In the longest letter Lincoln ever received on the question of which person to choose, a Bloomington, Illinois, Republican told Lincoln that the public favored Davis, but beyond that, fairness demanded that Lincoln appoint Davis because of the large political debt Lincoln owed him, and because the public would question Lincoln's generosity and benevolence if he did not appoint him. Davis had obviously done more to get Lincoln elected than Browning, and he had made it crystal clear that nothing but appointment to the Supreme Court would satisfy him. Lincoln also knew, as Stuart and Joseph Medill had stressed to him, that as someone who had been a highly respected judge, Davis had a temperament better suited for appointment to the Court. Lincoln did not need reminding that Browning was mercurial.

Davis was not perfect. He was a hard-core partisan who complained Lincoln did not listen to him enough. This time, however, Lincoln listened. On December 8, 1862, he nominated Davis to the Supreme Court. Later that day, the Senate confirmed him.

Losing the nomination was hard for Browning, and the month got more difficult for him. He had lost his Senate seat when Democrats, in control of the Illinois state legislature, chose to replace him with William Richardson, a former House member, longtime friend of Lincoln and Browning, and campaign manager for Douglas during the 1856 and 1860 Democratic presidential nominating conventions. As Browning looked back at the past few months, he confided in his diary, "The counsels of myself and those who sympathize with me are no longer heeded. I am despondent, and have but little hope left for the Republic."[107]

All three of Lincoln's first three appointments to the Court subsequently supported his administration when challenges to his actions or policies came before it. In one of the first and most important, known as the *Prize Cases* because the fate of prizes of war was at issue, the question was whether Lincoln as president had the authority to order the seizure of vessels bound to or from Confederate ports prior to July 13, 1861. On July 13, Congress declared a state of insurrection, but Lincoln had ordered the blockade before then, in April. On March 10, 1863, the Supreme Court, by the narrow margin of 5–4, announced its decision agreeing with Lincoln. It noted, "As a civil war is never publicly proclaimed [as a formal matter] against insurgents, its actual ex istence is a fact in our domestic history that the court is bound to notice and to know."[108] Given the circumstances, the Court reasoned that the president was "bound to meet [the war] in the shape it presented itself, without waiting for Congress to baptize it with a name."[109] The four dissenting justices included Chief Justice Taney. All three of Lincoln's appointees joined with two Democratic appointees to form the five-member majority. Their decision ultimately provided the legal foundation for Lincoln's use of emergency powers to combat the seven Southern states' rebellion against the United States. Historian Mark Neely described the case as "the most important Supreme Court decision of the Civil War."[110]

On the same day that the Court decided the *Prize Cases,* the Senate unanimously confirmed Lincoln's fourth nominee for the Court, Stephen Field of California. Browning was not a candidate for the fourth seat, since Congress had created it solely for a new circuit, which included the states of California, Oregon, and later Nevada. Field was an obvious choice, since he had served with distinction as both an associate justice and chief justice of the California Supreme Court, graduated first in his class at Williams College, and was a Democrat who had been a leader in keeping California within the Union. His brother, David Dudley Field, was a prominent advocate for legal reform and abolition. He had helped Lincoln win the presidential nomination in 1860 but became one of the president's sharpest critics among Radical Republicans, who thought he moved too slowly and timidly in eradicating slavery. The nomination did not silence Dudley Field, but it did reward his brother, who was a fierce defender of the Union and had strong political support, including from California's governor, Leland Stanford.

The fact that Field's appointment was the first in history in which a president had crossed major party lines was no accident. With his chances for reelection the next year already looking bleak, Lincoln had to attract some Democratic support to have any chance at all.

VII

The war dragged on. Both the North and South were desperately looking for ways to expand the numbers of their troops. With only limited success, the Confederacy kept trying to expand the requirements for service in the military but met with resistance, sometimes violent. Lincoln had signed a series of laws, including as recently as March 3, 1863, to register all males between twenty and forty-five, including aliens with the intention of becoming citizens, by April 1. Lincoln had once opposed Douglas's and the Democrats' efforts in Illinois to count aliens as residents, but of the 168,649 people the draft reached, nearly two-thirds were substitutes and around seventy-five thousand were actually pressed into service. These numbers barely told the story. Over the course of the war, nearly 2,000,000 troops fought for the Union as compared with 750,000 for the Southern Confederacy.

Each conflict seemed more momentous than the ones before. This was especially true when, on July 1–3, 1863, the Union Army of the Potomac and Robert E. Lee's Army of Northern Virginia clashed at Gettysburg in one of the most decisive battles of the war. Many believed that the fate of the Civil War was at stake.

Such a clash had been a long time coming, and each side had steadily amassed the forces to annihilate the other. Lee had rarely been beaten and never caught and had thus become the bane of the Union's existence. Having defeated Union forces at the Battle of Chancellorsville in Virginia, Lee turned his army northward toward Pennsylvania, only the second time after Antietam that Lee brought his forces north. He aimed to bring the war into the Union's own territory and once and for all break the will of stubborn Northern politicians who had been pressing for continued engagement with the South. Lee would bring with him nearly seventy-five thousand troops.

Aware that Lee's forces were heading North for what might be a decisive confrontation with the Union, just three days before one of the most famous battles of the Civil War, Lincoln decided to replace the Army of the Potomac's commanding general, Joseph Hooker, who had been reluctant to reengage with Lee's forces after his defeat at Chancellorsville. Lincoln's replacement was General George Meade. A career army officer, Meade had graduated from West Point and distinguished himself in the Second Seminole War and the Mexican War. Meade had been a temporary commander at the Battle of Antietam in September and was one of the few commanders who were not disgraced by the South's slaughter of Union troops at the Battle of Fredericksburg in mid-December 1862.

The two great armies clashed near the small Pennsylvania town of Gettysburg, where they fought for nearly three days in a battle won by the Union but that produced more than fifty thousand casualties, the largest number of any battle in the entire Civil War. So many men died on both sides that, in the aftermath, both Lee and Meade tried in vain to submit their resignations to their respective leaders, Lee because the fighting had ended so badly (and, to many, inexplicably) and Meade because of the catastrophic losses at Gettysburg compounded by his failure to prevent Lee and his army from escaping across the Potomac and retreating back into Virginia. When Meade told Lincoln that Lee and his men had fooled his entire Army of the Potomac by leaving campfires lit to give the appearance that the Confederate troops were still encamped and not escaping stealthily at night, Lincoln exploded in anger, "We had them within our grasp. We had to only stretch our hands and they were ours."[111] On July 14, he drafted a letter he never sent to Meade explaining his "deep distress" over Meade's failure to have his men pursue Lee's army and crush them once and for all.[112]

On the evening of November 18, 1863, more than four months after the battle, Lincoln visited Gettysburg for the first time. He arrived as one of a handful of speakers to dedicate the battlefield to honor fallen Union soldiers of the conflict. He came knowing that, in spite of some notable Union victories that year, no end to the war was in sight. Still, after so many bloody battles, the carnage at Gettysburg was unprecedented. His speech was planned as the shortest and billed in the program merely as "Dedicatory Remarks."[113] The featured speaker was Senator Edward Everett of

Massachusetts, who was scheduled to deliver the only "oration" for the program.[114] Everett was a close ally and protégé of Daniel Webster, and widely considered to be nearly Webster's equal at great oratory. In 1860, conservative ex-Whigs placed him on the ticket of the Constitutional Union Party as a vice presidential candidate alongside its presidential candidate John Bell, but in winning thirty-nine electoral votes they mostly ensured Lincoln's victory and Douglas's loss. Everett was among the many people Lincoln welcomed the chance to work with to save the Union, in spite of past political differences.

At Gettysburg, Everett spoke, as people often did at such ceremonies, for more than two hours. In contrast, Lincoln's "few remarks," as he called them, lasted for three minutes. There is no consensus on precisely every word Lincoln said. At least five different versions of the text written in Lincoln's hand can be found, and Lincoln might have deviated from the written text when he spoke. Even the four stenographers working the event did not report the same words.

The first notable thing about Lincoln's speech is what it was not. Classical funeral orations, like those he delivered for Clay and Taylor or like what Everett delivered at the Gettysburg ceremony on November 19, were of epic duration. In contrast, Lincoln spoke only 271 or 272 words (scholars agree on that range). Historical accuracy was one of the aims of those longer orations, as were marking the significance and achievements of the person(s) who had died. Everett did all of that and more, mentioning the names of many of the fallen, incanting them like the tolls of a bell. Lincoln, on the other hand, never mentioned slavery or the names of any soldiers who died there.

Lincoln's deliberate concision reflected the maturation of his rhetorical development. Clay's most famous speeches were lengthy, and the vast majority of Lincoln's, ranging from the Lyceum Address to each of his debates with Douglas, also had been protracted. Long, complex sentences were common in Clay's speeches and many of Lincoln's earlier ones. It is not because their thoughts were unclear or meandering. They were made this way, as exemplified in the last sentence of the Gettysburg Address, because they were to be spoken slowly and to be heard. The delivery was the important thing. However, as president, Lincoln had come to believe that the public had no patience for long speeches. More important, they would remember nothing from them.

From his decades of studying the orations of his predecessors, Lincoln had come to appreciate the adage, often attributed to the French intellectual Blaise Pascal, "If I had more time, I would have written a shorter letter." Just a few weeks before his address in Gettysburg, Lincoln had referred to the character Polonius in *Hamlet,* the same Polonius who had admonished his son, Laertes, "Brevity is the soul of wit" just before Laertes left for school.[115]

Brevity was a virtue, particularly for presidents—it could be easily grasped, recorded, and disseminated. In his eulogy for Clay, Lincoln had praised Clay's "impassioned tone," but for Lincoln that tone required plainness of language. Lincoln understood that both Clay and Webster each had achieved their unique kind of eloquence, but neither was plain nor concise in his rhetoric. A marriage of condensation and majesty was harder to achieve than prolixity but more memorable, and worthy of the grandeur of both the office and the message. As president, Lincoln no longer spoke as a partisan. As president, he was obliged to act in the best interests of all Americans and the Constitution. He expected people would be reading and reciting his remarks aloud, as he had done himself for other speeches for decades.

Everett came to Pennsylvania to do what was expected in commemorating battlefields; this was not his first time to do so. But honoring the battle was secondary to Lincoln. He had his eyes on the bigger picture. What had happened at Gettysburg was monumental, but it was only part of the larger Civil War, which remained unsettled.

Politics were not entirely absent from his remarks, but they were, Lincoln believed, of a greater strategic nature that went beyond party. Pennsylvania's governor, Andrew Curtin, was facing a difficult reelection campaign, and Lincoln's own reelection was less than a year away. From where (and when) he stood in Gettysburg, his prospects looked no better.

The questions he had not yet answered to the public's satisfaction were, What were these soldiers dying for? and, Why reelect the president?

The answer came in the opening line of his remarks, "Four score and seven years ago our fathers brought forth, on this continent, a new nation, conceived in Liberty, and dedicated to the principle that all men are created equal."[116] This was why they had gathered, this was why they had fought, and this was why the Union needed to win, an imperative that Lincoln affirmed in his next sentence: "Now we are engaged in a great civil war, testing whether that nation, or any nation so conceived and so dedicated, can long endure."[117] Later, many newspapers expressed outrage that Lincoln had redefined the purpose of the war to include the securement of not just liberty but equality, but for Lincoln this objective reflected the inextricable connection between the Constitution and the Declaration of Independence, a synthesis that Clay had spent his adult life advocating and Lincoln his life learning. Lincoln was not oblivious to the fact that the founding document of the nation was the Constitution, not the Declaration, but he understood the Constitution as built on the foundation of the Declaration. Lincoln had also come to understand, through his own painful struggles and those of the nation, that his link was not widely appreciated in the United States. With newspapers taking down every word he spoke, this was his moment to commemorate this "new birth of freedom" to the American people.[118]

Webster had built a concept of constitutional union that was precisely what Lincoln saw himself, his administration, and the Union Army defending. Lincoln still recited to himself lines from Webster's extraordinary response to Hayne's promotion of the dangerous doctrine of nullification, and his argument that Americans had come together as one people long before the Constitution was drafted and ratified. "It is," Webster had declared in his reply, as he stared at Calhoun as presiding officer of the Senate, "the people's Constitution, the people's government, made for the people, made by the people, and answerable to the people."[119] (Lincoln was fond of this phrasing. In the 1850s, he had filed a copy of an address from a speech by abolitionist Theodore Parker, in which Parker defined democracy as "Direct Self-government, over all the people, for all the people, by all the people.") Rejecting Hayne's notion that all federal power came from the states, Webster declared, "We are here to administer a Constitution emanating immediately from the people, and trusted by them to our administration. It is not the creature of State governments."[120]

Lincoln had adopted the same understanding of democracy, using similar words, in his First Inaugural Address. Tracking the same argument that Webster repeatedly had made, Lincoln explained, in his First Inaugural, that it was the people, not the states, who existed before the Constitution, and that the people, not the states, were the source of authority for the Constitution itself. If that were not the case, Lincoln explained, "The United States [would] be not a government proper, but an association of States in the nature of a contract merely."[121] He further declared, "Descending from these great principles, we find the proposition that, in legal contemplation, the Union is perpetual, confirmed by the history itself."[122] Lincoln then traced, as Clay and Webster each had done, the lineage of the Constitution back to its original source, the Declaration of Independence. He had no intention of delivering the same history lesson again in his brief Gettysburg remarks. Instead, he asked the thousands gathered there (and the thousands more who would read the remarks) to "resolve that the dead shall not have died in vain" and "that the nation shall, under God, have a new birth of freedom, and that government of the people, by the people, and for the people, shall not perish from the earth."[123] Here was Webster's great articulation of American democracy reformulated into simpler, more easily remembered words. Complexity of language remained, but to create rhythmic momentum, as, for example, Lincoln's contrasting "those who here gave their lives" with the "people," whose system of government "shall not perish from the earth." Lincoln juxtaposed references to the past and the present,

the dead and the living at Gettysburg, and the "new birth of freedom" against the Founding Fathers' bringing forth "the great task
remaining."[124] Lincoln concluded his remarks with an eighty-two-
word sentence in which devotion to a worthy cause is forcefully
driven home:

> It is rather for us to be here dedicated to the great task remaining
> before us—that from these honored dead we take increased devotion
> to that cause for which they gave the last full measure of devotion—
> that we here highly resolve that these dead shall not have died
> in vain—that this nation, under God, shall have a new birth of
> freedom—and that government of the people, by the people, for the
> people, shall not perish from the earth.

Edward Everett's most famous student, Ralph Waldo Emerson,
immediately recognized (as did Everett) the grandeur of Lincoln's
sparse remarks: "His brief speech at Gettysburg will not easily be
surpassed by words on any recorded occasion."[125] Emerson's assessment was in stark contrast to how he had judged Daniel Webster's
speech defending the Compromise of 1850 and its noxious fugitive slave provision for the sake of maintaining the Union. "Let
Mr. Webster for decency's sake," Emerson had declaimed, "shut
his lips once and forever on this word [liberty]. The word liberty in
the mouth of Mr. Webster sounds like the word love in the mouth
of a courtesan."[126] With less grandiosity than Webster, Lincoln declared, "The world will little note, nor long remember, what we
say here," though of course it did because of his eloquence that
day.[127] Lincoln stood where Clay and Webster had dreamed of
standing, and had the confidence, born from years of speaking to
ordinary citizens, to take what those two great orators had done
and do it better. Lincoln had taken the additional step, urged for
decades by Clay and Webster, to equate liberty and union. Here
was a renewed understanding of its foundation in the fulfillment
of the promises made in the Declaration of Independence. Lincoln
understood that Clay and Webster each had achieved their unique
kind of eloquence, but neither spoke to the common folks that

Lincoln had always aimed to reach. Jackson and Taylor were each brief in most of their orders and proclamations, but neither was eloquent. Lincoln aspired to be both concise and eloquent.

Lincoln was not the kind of man who left things to chance. He polished his sparse remarks as if they were fine diamonds. Rather than having written them on an envelope at the last moment, he was seen working on them, off and on, for days, and he had seen Everett's lengthy oration the evening before the day of the dedication. Days before the event, Lincoln asked aides to review schematics of the area. They did the evening before his remarks and reported to him the size of the space and how the speech would carry.

Up until the late 1850s, Lincoln mostly relied on his handwritten notes, not a manuscript, when making a speech, though he used manuscripts for special occasions—the House Divided and Cooper Union speeches as a candidate for office, and as president the First Inaugural and now the Gettysburg Address. He continued to rework his draft as late as the evening before. He did not work alone. According to the daughter of William Slade, an African American who had long been Lincoln's servant and traveled with him,

> the president locked himself in his [hotel] room with only Slade present. He then began carefully to weigh every thought and carve every word in the address which has become so famous. After writing a sentence or so he would pause, and read the piece to Slade. He would then say, "William, how does that sound?" Slade, who by this time was quite a critic, would express his opinion. This went on until all was completed and he then sent for his secretary and others to hear it. Having received the praise and criticism of his messenger Lincoln felt that even the most ordinary person would understand his speech.

This account resonates with Lincoln's own account of how he wrote. As he told a law student in the 1840s, "I write by ear. When I have got my thoughts on paper, I read it aloud, and if it sounds all right I just let it pass."

The next day after Lincoln delivered the speech, John Hay

confirmed in his diary how "the President, in a fine, free, way, with more grace than is his wont, said his half dozen words of consecration."[128] While virtually every contemporary report on the event focused primarily on Everett's address, Everett well understood the significance of what Lincoln had said in his three minutes. The day after the event, Everett wrote Lincoln a short note: "I should be glad, if I could flatter myself that I came as near the central idea of the occasion in two hours, as you did in two minutes."[129] Everett's praise was not mere puffery. He had helped to write some of Webster's finest speeches and had a distinguished career in his own right—member of the House of Representatives, governor of Massachusetts, and president and professor of Greek Literature at Harvard before becoming secretary of state and senator. No one had better claim to being the leading expert on American oratory than Edward Everett.

Lincoln's remarks at Gettysburg became known as an "address" because their level of eloquence was much higher and commanding than that of other presidential remarks. As compared with their all too frequent off-the-cuff, forgettable remarks, Lincoln's were aimed at something different. They reflect the continuing influence of the theater, Shakespeare, classical tropes, and the Bible on his rhetoric. The influence of each of these may be found at length in the voluminous literature on Lincoln's remarks. Clay was best remembered for his theatrics, the most distinctive part of his speeches. The words on the page often seem flat. But Clay was a man on fire when he spoke, and it was that spectacle that many of his colleagues in Congress considered to be what distinguished his oratory.

Lincoln did something no president had done—not Washington, not Jefferson, not Jackson. He had spoken in the rhythm of America's greatest poetry. Lincoln captured in the brevity of his rhythmic verse the solemnity of the recommitment of the nation and its people to the "unfinished work" of the war, which was to ensure that the Constitution guaranteed liberty and equality to all citizens.[130]

As Shakespeare's Henry IV rallied his "band of brothers" to his cause, Lincoln hoped to do the same for his. Certainly Lincoln's words could rally the people to fight for a worthy cause, but the fighting still had to be done. Less than a week after Lincoln's remarks at Gettysburg, the Union scored another significant victory. On November 23–25, the Union Army, under the command of Major General Ulysses Grant, broke the Confederate siege of Chattanooga, ultimately forcing the Confederate Army, under the command of General Braxton Bragg, to retreat back into Georgia. The defeat was so severe that Jefferson Davis recalled Bragg to Richmond. After a draw one week later at Mine Run Creek, Confederate forces under the command of General James Longstreet, a veteran of the Mexican War and Gettysburg, lay siege to Knoxville, where Union forces successfully rebuffed their attack. The rebels were losing more than they were winning, but the final defeats were yet to come as Lincoln let his army do the talking.

VIII

The war dominated the shifting political landscape. The longer it lasted, the more trouble Republicans were facing at the polls, particularly in the border states. The shifts were apparent even in Illinois, where Republicans had never dominated. One of the casualties was Orville Browning. In early 1863, he left the Senate, only to return to Washington as a partner in a small law firm. He would be of less use to Lincoln as an outsider who was becoming increasingly pessimistic about the progress of the war and Lincoln's chances for reelection. The two interacted often, but Browning never felt that Lincoln sought his counsel as much as he once had, perhaps because Lincoln likely figured that Browning could not offer the inside information he once had and was not supportive of his reelection or policies.

In another sign of the shifting political landscape, John Todd Stuart was returning to Washington, as the representative for the eighth district of Illinois, though this time no longer as a Constitutional Unionist but as a Democrat. He had won the seat in a close contest against Leonard Swett, his and the president's old friend. Lincoln backed Swett but did not campaign back home out of respect for Stuart. Stuart won.

The shifting political landscape, exemplified in the exodus of Browning and the return of Stuart, underscored several problems Lincoln was facing at the end of his last full year in office before the presidential election. The first was that Lincoln was more isolated and alone. In spite of their differences, Browning and Lincoln always could speak honestly with each other, though Lincoln had become increasingly less likely to hear Browning's advice. Lincoln and Stuart still enjoyed a cordial relationship, undoubtedly a testament to how each managed to keep the vicious politics of the time from becoming overly personal to either of them. Stuart knew as well as Lincoln did that Browning provided better and stronger emotional support than he could. Browning provided better insight into substantive matters, too. Stuart simply was not the deep, pondering thinker that Browning was, nor was he the strong party man that either Browning or Lincoln was. (Browning was a Whig for decades and a Republican until 1869; Stuart had switched parties more than once and was returning as a Democrat.) Though Stuart remained friendly with Lincoln and informed him of House activities, he was no longer someone on whom Lincoln could count for support.

Of even greater import, Lincoln could not escape the ever increasing toll of the protracted war. In 1863, the Union had scored major victories at Gettysburg and Vicksburg, but they were achieved at an awful cost in lives and did not seem to have brought the war any closer to an end. None of Lincoln's generals had succeeded yet in doing what he kept insisting be done—fulfill the objective that Scott had identified at the outset of the war: crushing the enemy to death. Lee had lost multitudes of men, including some of his ablest generals (Stonewall Jackson had died of pneumonia eight days after being shot at the Battle of Chancellorsville), but others were out there, including Lee, as elusive and dangerous as ever. The Union still had superior resources, including far greater manpower, but Lincoln stayed up late into the night, wracked with insomnia, worrying about how his army's advantages were being squandered.

Lincoln worried, too, about what he should do if the war ever ended. Even before the Union victories of 1863, he and his allies were trying to look ahead. In early January 1863, ground was broken in Sacramento to begin construction on the transcontinental railroad approved the prior year by Congress. More than a few, including Lincoln, thought that the Union could develop a policy on reunion sufficiently appealing to the war-weary Southerners that it might erode their continued will to fight. Lincoln, after all, had never been a prosecutor or long-serving judge. He was a deal-maker, having learned the art from Stuart and through decades of negotiations in courtrooms, conventions, and legislatures. On December 8, 1863, he delivered his last Annual Message to Congress before the beginning of the presidential election year, a message that was pervaded by a surprisingly strong sense of optimism for the future. He acknowledged that the Emancipation Proclamation, which began the year on a forceful note, had been "followed by dark and doubtful days."[131] Yet Lincoln's confidence had not been shaken. Now, near year's end, "the crisis which threatened to divide the friends of the Union is past."[132] He reassured Congress and the nation that the African American troops who were joining the army were "as good soldiers as any" and had helped convert many opponents to supporters of emancipation.[133] (There was precedent: African American soldiers served under Washington during the war of independence and served under Jackson at the Battle of New Orleans.) Referring to developments in Maryland and Missouri, which were both exempt from his Emancipation Proclamation, Lincoln said that neither of those states "three years ago would tolerate any restraint upon the extension of slavery into new territories," but they "only dispute now as to the best mode of removing it within their own limits."[134]

Lincoln had attached to his Annual Message a document entitled Proclamation of Amnesty and Reconstruction.[135] He explained

that, under his constitutional authority to grant pardons for of-
fences against the United States, he was offering "full pardon" and
restoration of property "except as to slaves" to former participants
in the rebellion who would swear an oath of allegiance to the
United States and to all laws and proclamations concerning emancipation.[136] When the number of voters taking the oath in any state
equaled 10 percent of the number of people who had voted in 1860,
this contingent could reestablish a state government to which Lincoln promised executive recognition.

While the Republican majority in the House had narrowed as
a result of the most recent midterm elections, the party had expanded its margin of control in the Senate. This was not all good
news for Lincoln. As 1863 gave way to 1864, Lincoln faced a Congress in disarray, with Republicans sharply split into radical and
conservative camps. Radicals wanted to be tougher on the rebels,
while conservatives urged Lincoln to be more solicitous of the
South than he had been thus far. He defended his amnesty plan as
a wartime measure to weaken Southern resistance. A "tangible nu-
cleus" of loyal citizens was all that was needed to spark a state's re-
entry into the Union. In March 1864, he continued to insist that he
had made his proposal "to suppress the insurrection and to restore
the authority of the United States,"[137] but the plan went nowhere.

As the legislative session of 1863–1864 was drawing to a close,
there was little good news for Stuart to report to Lincoln. Congress seemed paralyzed until Radical Republicans mustered sufficient support in early July for both chambers in Congress to
approve an alternative to the scheme Lincoln was proposing.

The alternative had been put together by Representative Henry
Winter Davis and Senator Benjamin Wade. Davis called their proposal "the only practical measure of emancipation proposed in
this Congress."[138] It required, as a first step in the reorganization
and readmission of any Southern state into the Union, that it commit to completely abolishing slavery. The bill specified further
that 50 percent, rather than the 10 percent Lincoln suggested, of
the 1860 voters must participate in elections to reorganize their
respective state governments. In addition, the bill required that

the electors in any constitutional conventions in any of the states that attempted to secede take a different oath than the one Lincoln had proposed, which had merely entailed swearing future fealty to the Union. Instead, the Wade-Davis bill required them to take an "iron-clad" oath swearing that they had never voluntarily borne arms against the United States or aided the rebellion. Those taking the oath would be blaming the state's leaders for the rebellion.

The bill posed a dilemma for Lincoln. Its substance was not just more extreme than anything he had previously supported, but the bill also would have forced him into aligning himself and his administration with the Radical Republicans, a realignment that chafed Lincoln's moderate impulses and would almost certainly doom his chances for reelection, which depended on maintaining support from his base: Democrats who supported the Union and moderate Republicans.

A faithful Whig was supposed to follow the lead of Congress. With his December message, Lincoln was reversing that arrangement and, in doing so, violating again a central tenet of Clay's conception of the presidency. For much of 1863, Lincoln had avoided that dilemma. Congress had ultimately been inert, and he had already exploited a defect in the Whig orthodoxy, which never spoke to executive power in wartime. Lincoln was convinced that as commander in chief in the midst of the war he could take measures like the Emancipation Proclamation, aimed to press the war to its end. Come the middle of 1864, he had no choice but to confront the dilemma of whether to revert to the Whig philosophy of deferring to Congress or help his own reelection. It was not a hard choice. He chose the presidency and his political future over fealty to Congress or one faction within his party. He chose to let the Wade-Davis bill die through a pocket veto, a rarely used means of killing a bill passed at the end of a congressional session by simply not signing it. Any further pretense that Lincoln was a Clay Whig was discarded. Lincoln had surpassed his mentor in both word and deed.

CHAPTER EIGHT

FINAL ACT
(1864-1865)

In 1860, Abraham Lincoln was the third-youngest man ever elected president. When he won reelection four years later, he became the youngest president to be reelected. He was the fourth-youngest person to have won two successive presidential terms until the only other president from Illinois, Barack Obama, was reelected nearly 150 years later.

Entering what most people expected would be his final full year as president in 1864, Lincoln was fifty-five. It was thirty-two years since Lincoln had cast his first vote in a presidential election when Henry Clay, then fifty-five, lost his first presidential race to Andrew Jackson. At fifty-five, Jackson had suffered a physical breakdown. With two bullets lodged in his body, he was completely exhausted from years of intensive military campaigning. He was coughing up blood, and his body shook uncontrollably. After several months of rest, he began to recover. Two years later, he mounted his first serious run for the presidency, in 1824. At fifty-five, Zachary Taylor was still in the army, working his way to becoming a colonel in the Black Hawk War in 1832.

Now Lincoln squarely faced not just the question whether he would be reelected or not, but how he would be remembered. If the Union won the war, he could be sure to be remembered as one of America's great presidents. If the Union did not, he would likely be its last.

Throughout the first seven months of 1864, Lincoln, like most others, expected his term to end with the election of McClellan as president. He was preparing to lose, and he would have been hard-pressed to identify his accomplishments—not the closure of the war, not the establishment of the Republican Party, and neither the Thirteenth Amendment nor the formal abolition of slavery. His rhetorical flourishes might have died with him, considered an oddly poetic interlude in the Union's final years.

Perhaps his legacy would have been nothing more than that of all the other one-term presidents in the nineteenth century. Americans like a winner. They rarely fete the loser. If Lincoln failed to be reelected, he would likely have been remembered, if at all, for mishandling the war, placing the once heavy-drinking Grant (whom Mary Todd called a "butcher"[1]) in charge of the Union Army, and handing over to his successor a federal government depleted of precious resources and lives squandered on behalf of an impossible dream. Slavery would have endured and almost certainly expanded within and beyond the United States, subjugating entire new classes of people to bondage, bigotry, and avarice. Lost would have been Lincoln and Clay's dream of sealing the connection between the Declaration of Independence and the Constitution. Had Lincoln failed to be reelected, his idolization of Clay and Taylor would have mattered little; to the extent he had any right to be viewed as their heir, he would have been a failed one, no more successful than either of them had been in averting civil war and saving the Union. Lincoln and the Republican Party would not be seen as the architects of "a new birth of freedom"[2] but as the precipitating causes of the greatest destruction ever brought against whatever was left of the Union.

In 1864, Orville Browning was no apologist for Lincoln. He shared with his friend Edward Cowan his opinion of Lincoln as president: "I faithfully tried to uphold him, and make him respectable; tho' I have never been able to persuade myself that he was big enough for his position. Still, I thought he might get through, as many a boy in college, without disgrace, and without knowledge; I fear he is a failure."[3] Browning was far from alone in that harsh assessment.

It is tempting to think of Lincoln's final acts as preordained. As the presidential election of 1864 approached, he increasingly spoke of fate, divine will, and his belief that events were controlling him, not the other way around. This kind of talk might simply have been his way of hedging his bets or adopting Clay's strategy of projecting humility. At the same time, Lincoln did not question success. He took it in stride, just as Clay, Jackson, and Taylor had each done. However, through the summer of 1864, nothing happening in the war indicated Lincoln would repeat Jackson's feat of reelection.

Still, even if greater forces shaped events, Lincoln never waited passively for events to break his way. As often as Lincoln spoke of forces beyond his control, he stubbornly thought of himself as a "self-made man" and wondered aloud how future generations would judge his presidency. No one knows what Lincoln thought late at night when he sat alone in his office with the portrait of Jackson hanging overhead, but it seems possible that he, as well as loyal friends like the Blairs, would have recalled the simple fact that Jackson had not gotten as far as he had without doing the hard work. Neither Jackson, nor Clay, nor Taylor left anything to chance.

For most of the preceding three years, Lincoln had put into place an organization that would help him win reelection, but like Jackson and Clay, he renamed his party to serve his purposes. But some things had not changed. Browning and Stuart both continued to visit, albeit not as frequently, and the Blairs, particularly Jackson's old friend Frank Blair, peppered Lincoln with advice. The Jackson portrait never moved.

A remarkable feat in Lincoln's final year in office was congressional approval of the joint resolution to submit the Thirteenth Amendment to the states for ratification. Though not formally required for the amendment process in the Constitution, Lincoln signed a copy of the Thirteenth Amendment to emphasize his approval and the responsibility he felt. If things turned around for Lincoln and the country during the last year of his presidency, it is because Lincoln, the people in his administration and in the army, and the voters who stood by them all helped to turn them around.

Lincoln's reelection brought him unprecedented relief and a new boost of confidence. For the first time, he consulted almost no one on his major speeches, including his last. Long attentive to the lessons his mentors had set for him, now he sometimes ignored them. Had he paid closer attention, he might have lived longer.

I

By March 1864, Lincoln had had enough. No matter how much experience his commanding generals had, they were not hastening the war's end. Even though it was an election year, he again had to make a change at the top. Voters needed to know that he was not passively waiting for fate to turn his way, in spite of his remark that his "policy was to have no policy."[4] This comment did not mean Lincoln was clueless but rather, like Taylor, determined to be flexible and not going to commit himself to say or do anything more than he needed to. He was not going to telegraph his strategy to the enemy, and he was determined not to share his final plans with the Cabinet or members of Congress until ready.

Henry Halleck had been the general in chief since 1862, but Lincoln—and many Republicans in Congress—had wanted Halleck out for some time. Lincoln told John Hay that after McClellan's failure Halleck had requested that he "be given full power and responsibility to run the Union army on that basis till [Major General John] Pope's defeat [at the second Battle of Bull Run August 28–30, 1862]; but ever since that event, [Halleck] had shrunk from the responsibility whenever it was possible."[5] In the interim, one name for Halleck's replacement repeatedly came to the attention of the President. It was certainly not Meade, whom Lincoln never forgave for not chasing Lee's army when it was in retreat. It was the commanding general of the Army of Mississippi, Ulysses Grant. Grant had graduated from West Point but left the army when it appeared he could rise no higher than second lieutenant after the Mexican War. He tried his hand at business but had no better luck there. When the war broke out, he persuaded his congressman, Eli Washburne, to find a place for him in the army, and Washburne did. Grant had been working his way up since then, steadily rising in the ranks because of a string of victories and his stubbornness to keep at it until the enemy relented or was crushed.

Before making any final decision, Lincoln reached out to Washburne for confirmation that Grant was up to the task. "All I know of Grant," Lincoln told Washburne, "I have got from you. I have never seen him. Who else besides you knows anything about Grant?"[6] In particular, Lincoln wanted a sense of his personal ambitions, particularly whether he was inclined to mount a presidential run.

Washburne told the President that he should talk to J. Russell Jones, the U.S. Marshal for Chicago, who was from Grant's hometown, Galena, Illinois, and corresponded regularly with Grant. Jones wrote Grant and asked him whether he had interest in running for the presidency, as many members of Congress were hoping. Grant answered directly, "I already have a pretty big job on my hands, and my only ambition is to see this rebellion suppressed. Nothing could induce me to think of being a presidential candidate, particularly so long as there is a possibility of having Mr. Lincoln re-elected."[7] When Jones visited Lincoln in February 1864, Lincoln asked him whether Grant wanted to be president. Jones showed him Grant's letter. "My son," Lincoln responded, "you will never know how gratifying that is to me."[8]

Assured that Grant's focus would be on winning the war and not his political fortunes, Lincoln lent his support to the bill circulating in Congress to revive the rank of lieutenant general. It was a rank that no American commander other than George Washington ever had. The measure passed the House (117–19) on February 1, 1864 and the Senate (31–6) on February 26, and Lincoln signed it into law on February 29, 1864. Halleck then wrote to Grant to inform him that Lincoln had signed his commission as lieutenant general and to "report in person to the War Department as soon as practicable."[9]

Grant immediately headed east from his headquarters in Nashville, and his arrival in Washington on March 8, 1864, was characteristic of the man, turning up with his son but with no fanfare, fancy uniform, or welcoming committee. Once he signed into his hotel, the word spread so quickly that by the time he returned to his room from dinner an invitation to the White House was waiting for him. Grant immediately ventured back out still wearing the rumpled clothes that he had traveled in. He was quickly rushed into the East Room, where a reception was taking place. The room fell silent when he arrived, as all eyes turned toward him. Lincoln feigned surprise, exclaiming, "Why, here is General Grant! Well, this is a great pleasure, I assure you."[10] Grant blushed as the esteemed guests, including Seward and the First Lady, greeted him warmly. He followed Seward's suggestion to stand on a sofa to acknowledge the applause. "For once at least," a newspaper reporter wrote, "the President of the United States was not the chief figure of the picture. The little, scared-looking man who stood on the crimson-covered sofa was the idol of the hour."[11]

After the ceremony, Lincoln took Grant upstairs for a private meeting. Lincoln explained, with some humility, that he had not been a soldier and had no special expertise in military affairs. He told Grant of his impatience with the procrastination of previous commanders and the pressure from Congress that had forced him into issuing direct orders to them, as he had done with both McClellan and Halleck. As Grant recalled, Lincoln said,

> He did not know but they were all wrong, and did know that some
> of them were. All he wanted or had ever wanted was someone who
> would take the responsibility and act, and call on him for all of the
> assistance needed, pledging himself to use all the power of the gov-
> ernment in rendering such assistance. Assuring him that I would do
> the best I could with the means at hand, and avoid annoying him or
> the War Department, our first interview ended.[12]

The next day, Lincoln held a small ceremony for Grant to meet the Cabinet. He met Lincoln again two weeks later, after he had had a chance to visit his generals in the field and assess their readiness to do what Lincoln wanted—take the war to the enemy and never cease hounding them until the war was done.

Grant's ambition was to emulate Zachary Taylor. No one admired Taylor more than Ulysses Grant. Nearing the end of his life in 1883, he confided in his memoirs, "There was no man living who I admired and respected more highly" than Zachary Taylor.[13] During the Mexican War, Grant served directly under Taylor and ever since modeled himself on the future president. Jean Edward Smith, notable biographer of Grant's, wrote, "What few recognized was that Grant's attitude had been nurtured fifteen years earlier in Mexico watching the way Zachary Taylor operated."

Similarly, Grant's biographer Ron Chernow observed, "In describing Taylor, Grant provided a perfect description of his own economical writing style: 'Taylor was not a conversationalist, but on paper he could put his meaning so plainly that there could be no mistaking it. He knew how to express what he wanted to say in the fewest well-chosen words.'"[14] Like Taylor, Grant was not disposed to making fancy, high-sounding pronouncements; both men were direct, succinct, to the point. "He is a copious worker and fighter," Lincoln said, "but a very meager writer, or telegrapher."[15] In 1850, he had noted that "General Taylor's battles were not distinguished for military maneuvers; but in all, he seems rather to have conquered by a sober and steady judgment, coupled with a dogged incapacity to understand that defeat was possible. His rarest military trait, was a combination of negatives—absence of excitement and absence of fear. He could not be flurried, and he could not be scared."[16] If there was a difference between Grant and Taylor, it was that Grant, for many years, loved having a drink or several. That never seemed to bother Lincoln, who made his confidence well known, saying Grant "doesn't worry and bother me. He isn't shrieking for reinforcements all the time. He takes what troops we can safely give him . . . and does the best he can with what he has got."[17] In 1863, there arose a story, probably apocryphal, that when commanders asked Lincoln to remove Grant because of his excessive drinking, Lincoln said that "if anyone could find out what brand of whiskey Grant drank, he would send a barrel of it to all the other commanders."[18]

In addition to how he framed his orders, Grant admired Taylor's style, because he didn't trouble

> the administration much with his demands, but was inclined to do the best he could with the means given him. If he had thought that he was sent to perform an impossibility, he would probably have informed the authorities and left them to determine what should be done. If the judgment was against him he would have gone on and done the best he could . . . without parading his grievance before the public.[19]

Grant also admired Taylor's understanding of the role of the soldier; Taylor, he said, "considered the administration accountable for the war, and felt no responsibility resting on himself other than the faithful performance of his duties."[20] He even donned a linen duster and a battered civilian hat, like those that Taylor liked to wear.

George Meade, who had served with Grant under Taylor, observed that Grant "puts me in mind of old Taylor, and sometimes I fancy he models himself on old Zac."[21] Perhaps most important, Grant had witnessed firsthand how Taylor carried the fight to the enemy, precisely what Lincoln wanted and what he intended to do. Grant's sense of duty was evident in his unquestioning acceptance of Lincoln's policies on emancipation and the recruitment of Negro troops. Unlike McClellan and Buell, Grant dismissed whatever personal doubts he may have had and pitched in wholeheartedly. When Halleck instructed him to assist Lorenzo Thomas, the adjutant general, in enlisting freed slaves, Grant said frankly, "I never was an abolitionist, nor even what could be called antislavery. [However,] you may rely upon it I will give him all the aid in my power. I would do this whether arming the negro seemed to me a wise policy or not, because it is an order that I am bound to obey and I do not feel that in my position I have a right to question any policy of the government."[22]

Once in charge, Grant did what Taylor would have done, wasting no time or words. Grant wanted the entire Union Army to move in a coordinated fashion after the enemy, squeezing and chasing them relentlessly so that Lee and Joseph Johnston couldn't use their troops to help each other. He told Meade, "Lee's army will be your objective point."[23] Taking over Grant's former command was his friend William Sherman, whose foster father was the powerful Ohio politician Thomas Ewing, who had been a close friend of Clay's. Grant told Sherman "to move against [Joseph] Johnston's army in the south, to break it up and get into the interior of the enemy's country as far as you can, inflicting all the damage you can against their resources."[24] Sherman summarized the simple strategy: "He was to go for Lee and I was to go for Joe Johnston. That was the plan."[25]

The next year would be the busiest and bloodiest of the war. Grant and the Union Army would be tested as Lee's forces again brought the fight northward. Like other commanders before him, Grant faced organizational, structural, and personnel problems, including the fact that many units in the army were constrained to reporting directly to the secretary of war, not the commanding general. Lincoln assured Grant that, although he could not turn over control of these forces directly to Grant, "there is no one but myself that can interfere with your orders, and you can rest assured that I will not."[26]

Other than that, as Grant told his friend Jones, he knew he had "a pretty big job on my hands."[27]

II

From even before his first day in office, Lincoln worried about how the war might end, and if his army was victorious, how to mend the Union. Nearly a year before his second inaugural, on March 26, 1864, at a time when he expected to lose reelection, he met with a trio of Kentucky dignitaries—Albert Hodges, editor of the *Frank-fort Commonwealth*, Archibald Dixon, a former senator from Kentucky, and Kentucky's governor, Thomas Bramlette. They came to protest the enlistment of former slaves as soldiers. Lincoln gave them "a little speech," explaining why he felt obligated to change from his inaugural promise not to interfere with slavery to his decision to issue an emancipation proclamation. Acknowledging they had been persuaded by his remarks, Hodges asked Lincoln for a copy of what he had said. Lincoln's remarks were extemporaneous, but he promised to send a letter with his thoughts written down.

Nine days later, Lincoln sent the letter. He explained the series of events that had "driven [him] to the alternative of either surrendering the Union, and with it, the Constitution," or of arming Southern slaves.[28] He said, "I hoped for greater gain than loss; but of this, I was not entirely confident."[29] At the end of his missive, he wrote, "I add a word which was not in the verbal communication." He emphasized, "In telling this tale I attempt no compliment to my own sagacity. I claim not to have controlled events, but confess plainly events have controlled me." He added further that "after the end of three years struggle the nation's condition is not what either party or any man devised or expected. God alone can claim it."[30] His addendum reflects Lincoln at his best, manifesting both humility and piety in "telling this tale" of everything he had done thus far as president. Casting himself in the tale as an instrument of God could do him no harm in Kentucky.

Lincoln's two overriding concerns throughout 1864—ending the war and winning reelection—informed his judgment and leadership in virtually everything he did. It was no accident that Lincoln was the first incumbent president to be renominated by his party for president since Martin Van Buren in 1840. He had used his patronage to bolster party support, and he now decided to reorganize his Cabinet to solidify his support within the Republican Party.

Salmon Chase had been a thorn in Lincoln's side since joining the Cabinet. In 1863–1864, he was angling for the Republican nomination. Given that it was the custom for a sitting president not to openly campaign for reelection, Lincoln in those years avoided making public statements, openly soliciting support, or making campaign-related appearances. Instead, he had to work behind the scenes to stem the efforts of Radical Republicans to push him aside. Lincoln understood that the Radical Republicans did not just disapprove of his politics, but were also committed to the Jacksonian principle that he had championed as president, rotation in office. Neither Stuart nor Browning could be of any help since their connections were with the more conservative elements in Congress and the Republican Party. The most obvious choice for Radical Republicans was Chase, who gladly welcomed the attention and support. It was no secret that Chase resented Lincoln's partnership with Seward. Chase continued to believe he was superior to Lincoln both as a statesman and as an administrator, and he was not shy about expressing such sentiments. And Lincoln was aware of how, after almost each and every time he had a run-in with someone in the party—such as Frémont—Chase quickly found a way to befriend him.

Subtlety and self-awareness were not among Chase's strengths, however, whereas Lincoln always prided himself on his ability to read people. Under the tutelage of Stuart and with years of experience of outmaneuvering his opposition in elections and the state legislature, Lincoln had become adept at both recognizing and planning against subterfuge. The man who debated Douglas and outmaneuvered Chase and Seward to get the Republican Party's nomination in 1860 could do it again in 1864. Indeed, Lincoln had placed Chase in his Cabinet in part to keep an eye on him. Lincoln gave Chase ample room to make appointments from his cohort, because, as he said, he preferred to let "Chase have his own way in these sneaking tricks [rather] than getting into a snarl with him by refusing him what he asks."[31]

While Chase schemed with his friends in Congress and Ohio, Lincoln had his associates working on behalf of his renomination. Union Leagues were founded throughout the country to support the Union Army, and Lincoln succeeded in having them declare their support for his reelection. The first Union League, founded in Philadelphia, set an example for the other cities, which followed suit. In response, Chase's backers, particularly in Ohio, began pushing for public endorsements of their man, and circulated pamphlets urging Chase over Lincoln.

Public campaigning was a breach of etiquette not only for the president but also for a member of his Cabinet, as both Lincoln and Chase knew. Once newspapers caught wind of the pamphlets being circulated on Chase's behalf, including one signed by Senator Samuel Pomeroy of Kansas endorsing Chase, they reported it. Chase immediately wrote to Lincoln to assure him that he was only a reluctant candidate and that his friends had not consulted with him beforehand. When one Treasury Department official disputed Chase's statement, Chase offered his resignation, not for the first time, to Lincoln. He assured Lincoln, "I do not wish to administer the Treasury Department one day without your entire confidence."[32]

Lincoln said nothing for a week but then sent Chase a note saying he did not "perceive occasion for a change" at the Treasury Department.[33] He added that he had not read the circulars but only had heard of them. He told Chase that his friends "bring the documents to me, but I do not read them—they tell me what they think fit to tell me, but I do not inquire for more."[34] Lincoln did not need to make any further inquiries, since, as he had done before in outfoxing Chase in Chicago, his team was already laboring hard to secure his renomination at the national convention and support in the Northern and border states.

On February 22, 1864, the National Committee of the Republican Party met in Washington. Four-fifths of its members, most of whom had worked in the Lincoln administration, enthusiastically expressed support for his reelection. In closing his remarks thanking party leaders for their "renewed confidence" in him, the president said, "But I do not allow myself to suppose that either the [Republican National] Convention have concluded to decide that I am either the greatest or best man in America, but rather they have concluded that it is not best to swap horses while crossing the river, and further concluded that I am not so poor a horse that they might not make a botch of it in trying to swap."[35] Yet again it was characteristic humility and self-deprecation, reinforcing the image he relentlessly burnished of "old Abe Lincoln," the country lawyer, self-made man, as common as the rest of America.

On February 24, Lincoln's friends in Ohio rammed through a resolution at their party convention endorsing his reelection. On February 27, Lincoln's friend Frank Blair Jr., on leave from the army, launched an attack on the floor of the House against corruption in the Treasury Department and blamed Chase for it. On March 5, Chase withdrew his name for further consideration as an alternative nominee. In a transparent effort to make clear to voters what the party stood for (and to get around the resistance he faced from Radical Republican leaders), Lincoln worked with national Republican Party committee members to rename themselves the National Union Party for the 1864 election. They proclaimed themselves committed to prioritizing not party but the preservations of the Union and the Constitution. Unsure whether Chase was still trying behind the scenes to steal the nomination from Lincoln and weaken his support from within the party, Blair returned to the floor in late April again to denounce the Treasury Secretary's tolerance of corruption within his department and illicit efforts to "work there in the dark as he is now doing, and running the Pomeroy machine on the public money as vigorously as ever."[36]

While Lincoln had Blair keep Chase off balance, he secured the party's formal renomination for president. In late May, a convention of nearly two hundred disgruntled Republicans fizzled in its efforts to settle on an alternative, and on June 7, the party's convention in Baltimore unanimously renominated Lincoln. (Though he was now on the Supreme Court, David Davis managed Lincoln's reelection campaign but was so confident the convention would renominate that he didn't bother to come.) Two days later, a committee of delegates from the convention told Lincoln the news. "I will neither conceal my gratification, nor restrain the expression of my gratitude, that the Union people, through their convention [have] deemed me not unworthy to remain in my present position,"[37] Lincoln said. It was a typical display of humility, even though he had been planning for that result for some time.

When informed that the convention had endorsed a constitutional amendment banning slavery, Lincoln became more circumspect, noting that he could not endorse it "before reading and considering what is called the Platform."[38] He did not mention that, behind the scenes, he had been urging the convention to adopt that very amendment.

Securing the party's nomination gave Lincoln the upper hand in dealing with his Cabinet, particularly Chase. Less than a month after Lincoln was renominated, Chase failed to consult with him before nominating a friend of his, Maunsell Field, to replace John Cisco, who had resigned from his powerful post as the assistant treasurer of the United States in New York City. Lincoln was unhappy with Chase's failure to run appointments by him. When Chase asked to meet with him personally to discuss the matter, Lincoln declined. Instead, he wrote a candid letter to Chase acknowledging that the "difficulty does not, in the main part, lie within the range of a conversation between you and me. As the proverb goes, no man knows so well where the shoe pinches as he who wears it." This was not the congenial bumpkin Chase had long complained about and figured he could always outwit. It was a president who held all the cards, but Chase did not know it or refused to see it. Instead, Chase wrote back as if this time were no different than the others when he had gotten on the wrong side of Lincoln. He told Lincoln that Cisco, at his urging, agreed to withdraw his nomination, even though he reminded Lincoln, he only tried "to get the best men for the places" in his department.[39] The lack of congeniality in Lincoln's letter and the absence of any indication that Lincoln appreciated Chase's position prompted him to offer his resignation, for what turned out to be the last time. Lincoln's patience and support were at an end, and he responded, "Of all that I have said in commendation of your ability and fidelity, I have nothing to unsay; and yet you and I have reached a point of mutual embarrassment in our official relation which it seems cannot be overcome, or longer sustained, consistently with the public service."[40] Chase was stunned, but there was no turning back. He was out, and he had done it himself, his scheming used by Lincoln to justify his removal.

Chase's allies lobbied Lincoln to change his mind, but he refused and moved quickly to find a replacement he could work with. Without consulting anyone else (a striking departure for Lincoln), he nominated former Ohio governor David Tod, a Democrat who had supported his nomination in 1860. When Tod's nomination reached the Senate Finance Committee, its powerful chair, William Fessenden of Maine, was flabbergasted. He immediately came to see Lincoln. He told Lincoln that Tod knew nothing about finances and was opposed to the paper currency with which the administration had been conducting the war. He urged Lincoln to drop Tod, but Lincoln refused. Here again was Lincoln asserting the independence he thought to be embodied by Jackson. Fortuitously, Tod withdrew his nomination because of poor health.

The Tod debacle showed Lincoln's greater resolve not to bend to the will of either his Cabinet or the Senate. Particularly with his reelection at risk, he was determined to do what he had to do to get reelected. Yet being more independent did not mean Lincoln was less shrewd. The next morning, he nominated Fessenden to be his next Treasury Secretary. Fessenden was horrified. He let everyone know he had no desire to leave the Senate and immediately wrote a letter to Lincoln asking him to withdraw the nomination. Lincoln refused—he needed someone as soon as possible, and he knew that senators would likely be inclined to support a colleague's nomination. It was a clever move to coopt the Radical Republicans and appear to be appeasing the Senate at the same time.

Fessenden turned for advice to Stanton, telling Stanton that he feared that the job would kill him. Stanton, by this time fully in concert with Lincoln, responded, "Very well, you cannot die better than in trying to save your country."[41] When Fessenden asked for Lincoln's assurances that he would not interfere with Fessenden's administration of the department, Lincoln agreed to put down in writing that Fessenden was to have "complete control of the [Treasury] department."[42] In return, Fessenden agreed that in appointing subordinates he would "strive to give his willing consent to [Lincoln's] wishes in cases when [Lincoln] may let him know that [he had] such wishes."[43] One day later, on July 5, 1864, the Senate confirmed Fessenden as the new Treasury Secretary.

Lincoln was not done reconfiguring the Cabinet. While he made some concessions to conservatives in removing subordinates— like Hiram Barney, the collector of the port of New York City— Lincoln continued to feel unremitting pressure to appease Radical Republicans. Vetoing the Wade-Davis bill had alienated the powerful Radical Republican senator Benjamin Wade of Ohio. Wade agreed to back Lincoln's reelection but, as Senator Zachariah Chandler conveyed to Lincoln, only if Lincoln sacked his old friend Montgomery Blair. Lincoln had given Henry Davis control of the patronage in Maryland after he had passed him over for the Cabinet, but Davis blamed Blair for his failure and demanded his ouster to rid the administration of the Blair family influence—and to force Lincoln to prove to the world that he was nothing but a "mean and selfish dog who sacrificed his friend to his prospects."[44]

Lincoln's admiration for the Blair family was second to none. He had considered their support pivotal to his nomination, election, and administration thus far, and he resisted the pressure to fire Blair for as he long as he could. Sensing Lincoln's possible receptivity, Davis pushed harder. He found the fulcrum he needed when he suggested that if Lincoln got rid of Blair, Davis could get Frémont to drop his interest in the Radical Democratic Party's nomination for president, removing someone who could split votes in ways that might hurt Lincoln in the general election. Faced with a choice between reelection and his loyalty to a friend, adviser, and fellow partisan, Lincoln chose to protect his reelection. He could be ruthless when he had to be—after all, no president had been more ruthless than Jackson, about whose reelection he did not have to be reminded. He dismissed Blair in a letter that he left on Blair's desk, telling him that the dismissal was effective immediately.

On the day of Blair's dismissal, Welles and Edward Bates walked out of the White House with him, and Welles recorded the conversation for his daily diary of events. He recalled that, upon joining them, Blair said, "I suppose you are both aware that my head is decapacitated,—that I am no longer a member of the Cabinet."[45] Welles and Bates were surprised. Welles asked Blair to explain what happened and if he had had any warning he might be removed. According to Welles, Blair "said never until to-day; that he came in this morning from Silver Spring and found this letter from the President for him. He took the letter from his pocket and read the contents,—couched in friendly terms,—reminding him that he had frequently stated he was ready to leave the Cabinet when the President thought it best, etc., etc., and informing him the time had arrived."[46] Welles continued: "The remark that he was willing to leave I have heard both from him and Mr. Bates more than once. It seemed to me unnecessary, for when the President desires the retirement of one of his advisers, he would undoubtedly carry his wishes into effect. There is no Cabinet officer who would be willing to remain against the wishes or purposes of the President."[47]

"I asked Blair what led to this step," Welles later wrote, "for there must be a reason for it."[48] Blair responded that he was being sacrificed in retaliation for Frémont's resignation from the army and noted that Frémont had apparently told Lincoln "the Administration was a failure," except for both Bates and Welles.[49] "As Blair and myself walked away together toward the western gate," Welles added, "I told him the suggestion of pacifying the partisans of Fremont might have been brought into consideration, but it was not the moving cause; that the President would never have yielded to that, except under the pressing advisement, or deceptive appeals and representations of someone to whom he had given his confidence."[50] To remove all doubt what he meant, Blair told Welles that he had "no doubt Seward was accessory to this, instigated and stimulated by Weed."[51] Welles noted, "This was the view that presented itself to my mind, the moment he informed me he was to leave, but on reflection I am not certain that Chase has not been more influential than Seward in this matter."[52]

Welles later reflected, "In parting with Blair the President parts with a true friend, and he leaves no adviser so able, bold, sagacious.

Honest, truthful, and sincere, he has been wise, discriminating, and correct."[53] Welles did not add loyal, but, in spite of the fact that Blair never stopped grousing about his removal, he campaigned vigorously for Lincoln until the day of the election. The rest of the family remained loyal, too. Blair's wife consoled him that Lincoln had acted "from the best motives" and that "it is for the best all round."[54] Neither Frank Sr. nor Frank Jr. pressed the matter with Lincoln; instead, they campaigned hard for Lincoln's reelection. They were not just shrewd political operators, but they trusted Lincoln and considered his reelection indispensable for preservation of the Union. They also knew that if Lincoln and his party lost, they would have no clout with McClellan; their political careers would likely be at an end. But if the Union won the war and Lincoln were reelected, the door to the president's office would always be open to them, as it had been the past four years.

III

For much of 1864, nearly everyone, including Lincoln, expected McClellan to win the election. Everyone understood that Lincoln could reshuffle his Cabinet as much as he liked and orchestrate conventions, even his renomination, but none of that mattered if the Union failed to win the war. All eyes therefore were focused more on the new general in chief than Lincoln. If Lincoln won, it would be because of the difference Grant made in taking the fight to Lee.

It was not until late summer of 1864 that the tide began shifting decisively in favor of the Union. Throughout the year, everyone in the Union Army, from Grant on down, understood their instructions from Lincoln. Their tenacity and sacrifice—rebels would say their butchery and relentlessness—seemed limitless. The Confederate response was increasingly ferocious. As a result, the war turned, but at the cost of even more casualties than the army had faced before in a single year.

From 1861 through 1863, there had been less than eighteen major military engagements, but in 1864 there were nearly twice as many. In the first months after Grant's elevation to lieutenant general, Confederate forces had overwhelmed the Union garrison at Fort Pillow, Tennessee (where General Nathan Bedford Forrest's men slaughtered African American troops after they had surrendered), and had defeated Union forces in the Battle of the Wilderness (May 4–5, 1864), the Battle of Spotsylvania Courthouse (May 8–21), the Battle of Yellow Tavern (where confederate General J.E.B. Stuart was mortally wounded), the Battle of Cold Harbor (June 1–3, 1864), and the siege of Petersburg (June 15–18, 1864). Fueled by the flush of repeated victory, Lee ordered troops north to Washington, where the Army of the Potomac arrived just in time to rebuff the attack.

To avoid any chance of capture, or worse, by Lee's raging troops, Lincoln dashed into a carriage and headed straight to Fort Stevens, led by a cavalry escort shouting for soldiers and civilians to make way for the president. He arrived in time to see the fort's valiant rebuff of Lee's offensive on July 11–12, 1864. John Hay recorded that as Lincoln stood as high as he could to peer over the parapet at the attacking army, "a soldier roughly ordered him to get down or he would have his head blown off."[55] (Supreme Court Justice Oliver Wendell Holmes later claimed to have been that soldier.) With the fort secured, Lincoln ordered Generals Horatio Wright and Alexander McCook to pursue the fleeing Confederate troops, but they moved their forces too slowly. Once again, the enemy got away.

On August 23, 1864, eight days before the Democratic convention nominated McClellan as their presidential candidate, Lincoln drafted a private memorandum. "This morning, as for some days past," he wrote, "it seems exceedingly probable that this administration will not be re-elected. Then it will be my duty to so cooperate with the President elect, as to save the Union between the election and the inauguration; as he will have secured his election on such ground that he cannot possibly save it afterwards."[56] (The Democratic Party platform opposed continuing the war and restoring the Union, but Lincoln did not foresee that as soon as he became the party's nominee, McClellan would reject the party's platform.) Lincoln brought the document to a meeting of the Cabinet that afternoon, at which time he asked each member of the Cabinet to sign the back. It became known as the Blind Memorandum, because the Cabinet had signed it blind, without ever reading it. Lincoln placed the document in a safe so that it could be read by his successor once he was in office. It was an unprecedented move, but Lincoln recalled how Buchanan had declared in his last Annual Message that the federal government lacked the authority to prevent the Southern states from seceding, a declaration and stance that made Lincoln's presidency much harder than it would have been had Buchanan taken steps to protect the Union. Unlike Buchanan, he was determined to put the interests of the Union above his own.

Through it all, Grant's forces kept coming at the rebels. As Civil War historian James McPherson explained, Grant "did not think in terms of victory or defeat in single set-piece battles, which had been the previous pattern in this theater, but rather in terms of a particular stage in a long campaign."[57] His army followed Lee's men wherever they went. In the Battle of the Wilderness, May 5–7, 1864, in Virginia, Grant telegraphed Lincoln "there is no turning back."[58] Two days later, he added, "I intend to fight it out on this line if it takes all summer."[59] Though he walked the White House halls at night worrying aloud over the war's progress, Lincoln told others he was pleased. "The great thing about Grant," Lincoln said, "is his perfect coolness and persistency of purpose. [He] has the grit of a bull-dog! Once let him get his 'teeth' in, and nothing can shake him off.'"[60] Having praised Zachary Taylor in 1850 in similar terms, he now said, "It is the dogged pertinacity of Grant that wins."

Lincoln was equally pleased with Grant's order placing General Philip Sheridan, who had led the Army of the Potomac's cavalry, in charge the Army of the Shenandoah, pointedly admonishing Grant that Sheridan should "put himself South of the enemy and follow him to the death."[61] He added, "I repeat to you it will neither be done nor attempted unless you watch it every day, and hour, and force it."[62]

"Force it," they did. General Sherman's troops drove southward. On September 1, he notified Lincoln and Grant, "Atlanta is ours, and fairly won."[63] The day before, Democrats nominated George McClellan as their candidate for president. Earlier, on August 5, the Union fleet under the command of Admiral William Farragut captured one of the best-defended and most important ports in the South, Mobile, Alabama, which had rebuffed several earlier attacks. The Confederacy's navy never recovered. The Union was on a roll. Besides Sherman's march, Sheridan's men prevailed in the Third Battle of Winchester (September 19) and the Battle of Fisher's Hill (September 22). Then Union forces overwhelmed Fort Harrison outside of Richmond (September 29–30), and Sheridan's troops won a protracted contest for control of the Shenandoah Valley (October 19).

The string of Union victories in August and September transformed the election. With the removal of Montgomery Blair on September 24 in exchange for Frémont's agreeing to drop out of the race as a dangerous third-party candidate, Lincoln understood it was now a two-man race for the presidency. He did not have to be perfect, just a better alternative than the other man. McClellan was running on a platform that the war had failed. The cacophony of criticism (from him and many others, including Radical Republican leaders) leveled at Lincoln at every downturn of the war subsided with the unprecedented string of victories, as well as the awareness that if Lincoln lost, someone who would do far less for the Union's preservation would be president.

Buoyed by the news of Union victories and knowing his opponent's weaknesses, Lincoln fortified support among key constituencies, including free men of color in several states, Protestant religious groups, the growing German American population, and the army. Nineteen northern states passed laws allowing soldiers to vote away from home. Lincoln declared holding the election despite the war a "necessity," but Democrats were caught stuffing Democratic ballots into New York soldiers' absentee voting envelopes while War Secretary Stanton dismissed dozens of officers from the Union Army because they were Democrats, and commanders punished Democratic-leaning soldiers and granted furloughs for Republican soldiers to vote.[64] Radical Republican leaders and major newspapers increasingly recognized that, between the two alternatives, Lincoln was the only choice to be made by those who wanted to preserve the Union and the Constitution.

When the votes were counted on November 8, 1864, it was not close—Lincoln won in a landslide. As Civil War historian James McPherson notes, Lincoln "won 78 percent of the soldier votes in the states that tabulated them separately. The percentage was probably similar in states that lumped those votes" together with the civilian tallies.[65] Lincoln won 53 percent of the popular vote, but, as McPherson adds, "the most impressive thing about the 1864 election was that the men who would have to do the fighting and dying had voted overwhelmingly for their commander in chief to help him finish the job."[66] Lincoln won 212 electoral votes to McClellan's 21. It was a massive triumph by any measure, bigger than Jackson's reelection defeat of Clay in 1832.

IV

On hearing the news of Lincoln's reelection, Jefferson Davis proclaimed, "He does not attempt to deceive us. He affords us no excuse to deceive ourselves. He cannot voluntarily reaccept the Union; we cannot voluntarily yield it. Between him and us the issue is distinct, simple, and inflexible. It is an issue that can only be tried by war, and decided by victory."[67] Davis directed the Confederate armies to dig in their heels. (The nickname given to North Carolinians, "tar heels," described how their militias held their ground so fiercely, they must have had tar on their feet that prevented them from ever being budged.) Davis had not yet lost faith in his commander, Robert E. Lee, nor in his army. He intended to keep the war going until the South won, knowing that the more Union deaths, the more their zeal and energy could be broken. At some point, Northerners, in Davis's estimation, would tire of all the bloodshed, or their economy would collapse as the national government could not afford to keep the army funded and fully staffed for much longer.

One issue that had arisen before the election had yet to be settled. On October 12, 1864, Chief Justice Roger Taney died. Lincoln issued no public statement but did attend a simple funeral ceremony at Taney's home. Others expressed the relief that Lincoln likely felt. In a letter to Lincoln, Senator Charles Sumner wrote that "Providence has given us a victory in the death of Chief Justice Taney. It is a victory for Liberty and the Constitution."[68] Lincoln agreed, but he deliberately left the decision about who would replace Chief Justice Taney for after the election, the spoil of choice belonging to the victor. Given that Taney had died when Lincoln expected to win the election, he expected that selection to be his.

It is possible Lincoln may have also pushed the decision off until after the election to give him time to calmly think through who his choice should be. He had not rushed to fill the four other positions he had filled on the Court. This would be his fifth nomination— the same number Jackson had made, but Lincoln had achieved that number in nearly half the time it had taken Jackson, and Taney's appointment had not happened until near the end of his second term. Just as important, if not more so, such an appointment had the potential to transform the Court, both because it was Lincoln's fifth justice for the ten-member Court (with 5–5 splits reaffirming the lower courts' decisions) and because there had been only four other chief justices appointed in American history. Whoever led the Court would likely lead it for decades. Only Washington, Adams, and Jackson had appointed chief justices before. The fifth appointment would make this Lincoln's Court.

Unsurprisingly, there was a rush of people who wanted the position. Blair's family pushed for Montgomery, whose father pleaded with Lincoln "to remove the cloud which his ostracism from the Cabinet" had caused, but Lincoln had removed Blair not long before and those who had pushed for his ouster would likely not be pleased with a promotion.[69] Also, Lincoln was unsure whether Blair had the leadership and consensus-building skills that he believed the position required. Lincoln thought that the post should go to a Radical Republican, not only to appease that faction, but also to ensure that the person had strong, unshakable convictions about the war, the Union, and the constitutionality of Lincoln's actions and policies if they were to come further before the Court. That man was unlikely to be Montgomery Blair. Also jumping in was Orville Browning, who pushed for Edwin Stanton. Lincoln respected Stanton but decided it was more important for him to be by Lincoln's side for the remainder of the war and the reconstruction to follow.

In spite of many other candidates being pressed upon Lincoln, one name that kept crying for attention was that of Salmon Chase. After having pushed for himself as president for much of the year, Chase had grudgingly accepted Lincoln's candidacy. After Taney's death, Chase called upon Lincoln to lobby for his own appointment, but during the meeting Lincoln was, as Chase recorded, "not at all demonstrative, either in speech or manner."[70] Chase wrote Lincoln more than once to press his case, but the president gave no signal of his intentions. Once Chase realized that he could endear himself by campaigning for Lincoln, the ice thawed.

It is a credit to Lincoln that he was able to look beyond Chase's previous treachery and conclude that he had all the right qualities and convictions to fill the spot. As he explained to Ward Lamon shortly after making the nomination, Chase's "appointment will satisfy the Radicals and after that they will not dare kick up against [appointments] I may make."[71]

On December 6, 1864, Lincoln nominated Chase to be the nation's fifth chief justice; the Senate confirmed him that same day. Lincoln must have enjoyed having the power to replace Taney with his own former Treasury secretary, whose devotion to the Union and Lincoln's war policies was at least as strong as Taney's had been to Jackson's vision of a Union with a weaker federal government and stronger states.

V

When Congress reconvened in December 1864, Lincoln declared the "election has been of vast value to the national cause." Radical Republicans, emboldened, too, by Lincoln's and the party's successes at the polls, placed at the top of their agenda the drafting and approval of a new constitutional amendment abolishing slavery in the United States. Though he had not mentioned it to the committee of delegates from the convention informing him of his nomination, Lincoln had urged the National Union Convention to make ratification of the amendment a central component of its platform. Once again, and contrary to what he had said when he was in Congress and how Clay had argued about how presidents should defer to Congress in formulating national policy, Lincoln put all of his prestige, influence, and energy into pushing hard for the new amendment. Always keen on keeping track of his support in conventions or legislatures, Lincoln recognized that the time for historic change had finally come.

In his Annual Message in December 1864, Lincoln reminded Congress and the nation "the purpose of the people" to "maintain the integrity of the Union, was never more firm, nor more clearly unanimous, than now."[72] Accordingly, he urged Congress to support the proposed amendment abolishing slavery in the United States. He was aware that the House had fallen four votes short previously to approve the amendment, but he believed his election signaled the path forward. "Without questioning the wisdom or patriotism of those who stood in opposition," Lincoln pushed the House to approve the amendment, which the Senate had done earlier in the year.[73] "Of course," he acknowledged, "the abstract question is not changed; but an intervening election shows, almost certainly, that the next Congress will pass the measure if this does not."[74] Since approval was only a question of time, he asked, "may we not agree that the sooner the better?"[75] Echoing Jackson, he reminded the members of Congress that "some deference" should "be paid to the will of the majority, simply because it is the will of the majority."[76]

Lincoln worked closely with the sponsor of the bill, Ohio representative James Ashley, to identify any members who were wavering, and invited individual members of Congress to the White House so that he could lobby them in person, and he pressured Unionists from the border states to approve the new amendment. One of those invited to the White House was Representative James Rollins of Missouri, who had voted against the amendment the first time it had come before the House. Lincoln spoke to Rollins as a fellow Whig, who had, like him, revered Clay. Lincoln urged him as a follower of "that great statesman Henry Clay," to join in support of the amendment.[77] Once Rollins agreed, Lincoln urged him to rally other members to the cause. He described the amendment as "a king's cure for all the evils" that slavery had wrought upon the nation,[78] and assured him that its passage "will bring the war, I have no doubt, rapidly to a close."[79]

When rumors spread that Confederate peace commissioners were en route to Washington to negotiate the end of the war, Ashley considered delaying the vote, but Lincoln assured him that there were no peace commissioners in the city, and the vote went ahead as planned on January 31, 1865. More than two-thirds of the House voted in favor. Several Democrats joined in endorsing the proposed amendment, but one who did not was John Todd Stuart, reflecting the ideological divide that had arisen between him and Lincoln since Lincoln first campaigned for Stuart three decades earlier.

Because the amendment had previously been approved 38–6 in the Senate (exceeding the constitutionally mandated minimum of at least two-thirds), the resolution went from the House to the states for ratification. Even though the Constitution gave the president no role in authorizing a new amendment, Lincoln made a point of signing the resolution on February 1, 1865, as if it were a bill being made into law. When senators reminded him that his signature was unnecessary, he told them that he was confident that the new amendment would eliminate "the original disturbing cause" of the war and permanently settle any question about the validity of his Emancipation Proclamation.[80]

Yet Lincoln was not entirely truthful with Rollins. He knew that a peace commission was on its way—not to Washington but south of it, in Hampton Roads, Virginia. He later explained that he had kept the news to himself (and made a technically true but misleading statement to Ashley) because the "Democrats would have gone off on a tangent at the last moment had they smelt Peace."[81] Lincoln was more concerned with the need to get sufficient support in the House.

Leading the Confederate delegation was Lincoln's old friend Alexander Stephens of Georgia, who had reached out to Lincoln earlier to negotiate in 1863 and again in 1864. Coming with Stephens were former Supreme Court justice John Campbell of Alabama and Robert Hunter, a Virginia senator in the Confederacy. Lincoln had long resisted any such meetings because he had no interest other than having the rebels accept the conditions he had been suggesting since the war began—relinquishing their arms and pledging fealty to the federal Constitution.

There had been other efforts, too, to broker peace, though only a couple had Lincoln's blessing or approval. One involved a proposal brought to the White House's attention by Orville Browning. With Browning's support, a leading Illinois Peace Democrat (a faction within the party urging peace at any price), James Singleton of Illinois, received Lincoln's permission to go to Richmond to explore Confederate interest in ending the war. Singleton met with several leaders, including Davis and Robert E. Lee. When he returned to Washington, he told Lincoln that the Southerners were eager for peace but were unwilling to agree to any policy requiring them to give up their slaves unless they received in exchange "a fair compensation coupled with other liberal terms of reconstruction secured by Constitutional Amendments."[82] Lincoln was no longer interested in any scheme of compensated emancipation (in spite of his many years supporting such a plan, which Clay had long advocated), and the deal held no appeal for him or the Union.

Montgomery Blair's father, Frank Blair, went to Richmond with the president's approval. Whereas Singleton's efforts were focused on requiring the federal government to buy Confederate produce and products (a plan Lincoln never endorsed), Blair went with no instructions at all except perhaps for the long-standing confidence that Lincoln had in his fidelity to the Union. Blair had a lengthy meeting with Jefferson Davis, whom he had known for many years, as they had both been longtime faithful Jacksonian Democrats. Blair told Davis that slavery was no longer an "insurmountable obstruction to" peace, due to the recent enlistment of African Americans in the Union Army (effectively signaling to Davis that the Confederacy's objective of maintaining slavery was already a lost cause), and that reunion was inevitable.[83] Blair suggested that the only obstacle to peace came from France, which was scheming to take control of Mexico, and he proposed that Davis reach an armistice with the Union and send his armies to defeat the threat to the country from the south.

Blair relayed to Lincoln that this argument got Davis's attention. He told Lincoln that Davis did not trust Seward in any negotiations, but he did trust Blair and said he was willing to accept his assurance that Lincoln would "maintain his word inviolably."[84]

Davis gave Blair a letter, signed in Richmond on January 12, 1865, to take to Lincoln, which promised the appointment of a special commission that would enter into negotiations for peace. Lincoln rejected the offer and sent Blair back to deliver a letter to Davis, dated January 18, saying that he would be willing to meet with a Confederate commission that had serious interest in "securing peace to the people of our one common country."[85] Davis responded that he would send a commission to discuss "the issues involved in the existing war."[86] Lincoln found this unacceptable, because he did not wish to engage in negotiations with the commissioners as if the Confederacy was a separate nation. The war's premise was that it wasn't, and yet Lincoln was preparing to meet with this commission in Hampton Roads no doubt bent on parroting the Confederacy's rebellious views.

Before he agreed to attend the meeting himself, Lincoln had written down three nonnegotiable terms: "restoration of the National authority throughout all the United States," no "receding by" himself on "the Slavery question," and "no cessation of hostilities short of an end of war, and the disbanding of all forces hostile to the government."[87] Though wary, Lincoln brought Seward with him. For four hours, the five men discussed options. Stephens initially tried to steer the conversation to Blair's Mexican project, but Lincoln disavowed it. Campbell inquired about what terms of reconstruction would be offered if the Southern states returned to the Union. Lincoln insisted that he would not negotiate terms as long as the Southern states were in armed conflict against the United States. When Hunter pointed out how he had previously negotiated during wartime and Charles I had done the same, Lincoln responded, with a smile, "I do not profess to be posted in history. On all such matters I will turn you over to Seward. All I distinctly recollect about the case of Charles I, is, that he lost his head in the end."[88] Seward reminded the commissioners of Lincoln's pledge in his most recent message to Congress: "I shall not attempt to retract or modify the Emancipation Proclamation, nor shall I return to slavery any person who is free by the terms of that Proclamation, or by any of the acts of Congress."[89] Seward then told them of the recent approval in Congress, on January 31, of a Thirteenth Amendment abolishing slavery. The commissioners appeared too stunned to say much else. The meeting ended when they inquired about an exchange of prisoners, and Lincoln said he had put Grant in charge of that question. On leaving the boat where they had held their meeting, Stephens urged Lincoln to reconsider. He promised he would but pointedly added, "I do not think I will change my mind."[90] Nothing had ultimately been accomplished, except for, perhaps, the implicit agreement that the war would continue.

Not always reliable in his recollections, Stephens wrote later that during the discussions he had an exchange with Lincoln about reconstruction, in which Lincoln did not insist on the abolition of slavery as a condition for peace. He recalled Lincoln's telling him that he did not consider the Emancipation Proclamation to be anything other than "a war measure, and would have effect only from it being an exercise of the war power, as soon as the war ceased, it would be inoperative for the future. It would be held to apply to slaves as had come under its operation while it was in active exercise."[91] Stephens's recollection is not without confirmation from other sources, including Lincoln's telling Browning, just before Christmas in 1864, "that he had never entertained the purpose of making the abolition of slavery as a condition precedent to the termination of the war, and the restoration of the Union."[92]

It is hard to imagine that Lincoln would have had any such thoughts, especially given the fact that the House was on the verge of approving the Thirteenth Amendment. Yet according to Hunter as well as Stephens, Lincoln said during the meeting "that he would be willing to be taxed to remunerate the Southern people for their slaves."[93] As Stephens and Hunter recalled further, Seward interrupted Lincoln and said that "in his opinion the United States had done enough in expending so much money on the war for the abolition of slavery."[94] Lincoln, they claimed, believed that both sides were responsible for perpetuating slavery but that he "could give no assurance; enter into no stipulation" on paying slaveholders to release their slaves and then added that there were people "whose names would astonish you, who are willing to do this, if the war shall now cease without further expense, and with the abolition of slavery as stated."[95]

To remove any doubt that Lincoln was considering compensation (something in fact he had been pondering for years as a devotee of Clay), he drew up a proposal upon returning to Washington that asked for Congress to appropriate $400 million to be distributed to the Southern states in proportion to their slave population. If resistance to the Union ceased, half would be paid by April 1, and the remaining half by July 1, if the states ratified the Thirteenth Amendment.

Lincoln presented his proposal to his Cabinet on February 5. Everyone objected. Welles rejected it because he distrusted Southern leaders and because he thought the plan sent the wrong signal that the North was weak and desperate to end the war. Fessenden, as Treasury secretary, called the plan "unadvisable" because there would be no way to get the plan approved before Congress adjourned. Others felt only the use of force, not negotiation, could end the conflict. Whether it was the old Clay Whig in him or the absence of any support from within his administration for the idea, or both, Lincoln never made the proposal again.

VI

Almost everything about Lincoln's second inaugural differed from his first. When the inaugural parade began on the morning of March 4, 1865, he was not the outsider he'd been four years earlier. He was now the consummate insider and could be found early that day in the Capitol signing bills. As the time came for the ceremony to begin, it was raining, prompting the Committee on Arrangements to make the hasty decision to move the ceremonies inside the Senate chamber. At ten o'clock, the galleries were opened to the public, and at eleven forty-five the official procession began to file into the chamber. Lincoln was still signing bills.

At his first inaugural, Lincoln had had Hannibal Hamlin, a former Democrat from Maine, nearby as his vice president. This time, Hamlin was a lame duck. The convention had bypassed him and chose instead the pugnacious Andrew Johnson of Tennessee, the only Southern Democratic senator while Lincoln was president.

At noon, Hamlin began his farewell speech. Dignitaries continued to file in as he spoke. After Hamlin finished, Johnson rose to deliver his speech. Lincoln arrived not long after Johnson had begun. He saw and heard more than enough of the rambling remarks, coupled with Johnson's sweating and rocking back and forth, to know his new vice president was drunk. Lincoln directed Senator John Henderson of Missouri, seated nearby, "Do not let Johnson speak outside."[96]

By the time Johnson finished, the rain had stopped, and the procession happily moved back outside. When Lincoln finally rose and moved out from under the Capitol building into a narrow, open spot to deliver his address, the crowd erupted in applause. It was an immense gathering that watched the speech from every conceivable vantage point. Many people crowded directly in front of Lincoln and many others crammed close together watching from the portico over his left shoulder. Lincoln said the speech would be short, and it was—merely 701 words, the third-shortest Inaugural Address in American history. Speaking slowly, he was done in less than ten minutes.

Compared with Lincoln's other speeches, the Second Inaugural Address most closely resembles the Gettysburg Address. The two had in common his objective not to present any extended argument or complex plan for the future, but rather to set a mood. For the inaugural, as with the Gettysburg Address, Lincoln felt few would remember a longer oration—indeed, many would likely not listen to it at all. In Gettysburg, he hoped to cast a resolve to finish what the Southern states had started. Here he hoped to establish an atmosphere of reconciliation.

The day before his second inauguration, Lincoln signed the first in a series of laws that comprised the Reconstruction policies of the federal government. This first bill created the Freedmen's Bureau, designed to give help to millions of former slaves and poor whites in the South; it promised assistance in education, food, housing, and legal and medical services. It was an extension of Clay's conception of internal improvements.

A question that bothered some members of Congress throughout their deliberations on the Freedmen's Bureau was what constitutional basis Congress had to create it and to enact a civil rights act guaranteeing to the newly freed African Americans certain basic rights, such as to marry, to own property, and to negotiate contracts. Other amendments might be needed. One, urged by many Republicans, guaranteed freed slaves the right to vote. The new amendments under consideration were designed to guarantee newly freed slaves and their descendants the same rights as every other citizen and to empower Congress to enact legislation ensuring enforcement of those rights.

Lincoln mentioned none of that on March 4, 1865. He also left out many of the hallmarks of prior presidential inaugural addresses, the self-congratulation, the detailed plans for the future. He never mentioned himself. The term *war* appeared ten times and was referred to in nearly every line when not mentioned explicitly. The word *peace* appeared only once, in the last sentence. There were the contrasting images, alliteration, repetition of words, long sentences, and inversions of subject and verb that had become common to Lincoln, particularly in the Gettysburg Address. The Bible occupied a more prominent role in this speech than in any other that Lincoln gave. Here Lincoln declared slavery a sin, mentioned God fourteen times, quoted scripture four times, and invoked prayer four times.

Whereas at Gettysburg Lincoln had focused on the war's purpose, here he was focusing on its aftermath. Before any plan could be discussed, the country had to ready itself for reconciliation, but to do that the intensity of the conflict had to be replaced with a more collegial, more contemplative attitude, a solemn and reverential mood—indeed, the very one that had allowed the framers to put aside their differences to draft the Constitution that still governed the nation. Here, he hoped to recapture that mood when he pleaded with the American people, "Fondly do we hope—fervently do we pray—that this mighty scourge of war may speedily pass away. Yet, if God wills that it will continue, until all the wealth piled up by the bond-man's two hundred and fifty years of unrequited toil shall be sunk, and until every drop of blood drawn with the lash, shall be paid by another drawn with the sword, as was said three thousand years ago, so it still must be said 'the judgments of the Lord, are true and righteous altogether.'"[97] He encapsulated the atmosphere he hoped would prevail throughout the country in the very next sentence, the final unforgettable, lyrical

lines: "With malice toward none; with charity for all; with firmness in the right, as God gives us to see the right, let us strive on to
finish the work we are in; to bind up the nation's wounds; to take
care for him who shall have borne the battle, and for his widow,
and for his orphan—to do all which may achieve and cherish a
just, and a lasting peace, among ourselves, and with all nations."[98]

While Lincoln did not show anyone the address beforehand, he
was eager for feedback afterward. He read reviews of his speeches
and solicited reactions from people whose opinion he respected.
A descendent of John Adams, Charles Francis Adams Jr., wrote
his father, "That rail-splitter lawyer is one of the wonders of the
day. Once at Gettysburg and now again on a great occasion he has
shown a capacity for rising to the demands of the hour. [The] inaugural strikes me in its grand simplicity and directness as being
for all times the historical keynote of this war."[99] In contrast, the
strident abolitionist Charles Sumner dismissed the address as "an
augur [of] confusion & uncertainty in the future."[100]

Later in the day of his second inauguration, Lincoln spotted
Frederick Douglass as he entered the reception in the East Room
of the White House. "Here comes my friend Douglass," Lincoln
called out loudly enough for all to hear.[101] Taking Douglass by
the hand to the center of the room, Lincoln said, "I am glad to
see you. I saw you in the crowd today, listening to my inaugural
address; how did you like it?"[102] Lincoln knew Douglass had regarded his First Inaugural Address as weak and uninspiring. Douglass answered, "Mr. Lincoln, I must not detain you with my poor
opinion, when there are thousands waiting to shake hands with
you."[103]

"No, no," Lincoln responded, "you must stop a little, Douglass;
there is no man in the country whose opinion I value more than
yours. I want to know what did you think of it?"[104]

"Mr. Lincoln, that was a sacred effort," Douglass said.[105]

Lincoln's interest in hearing Douglass's opinion was likely not
merely his need for affirmation. After securing his freedom from
bondage, Douglass had become one of the nation's most revered
and impassioned orators and most uncompromising advocates for

complete abolition. He had long been one of Lincoln's most vocal critics. It was not unlike Lincoln to create a different picture for the attendees and newspapers, one showing he had Douglass in his corner.

Lincoln sought other opinions but did not hesitate to share his own. To Thurlow Weed, an ally who rarely hesitated to say what he thought, Lincoln said he expected his address "to wear as well as—perhaps better than—anything I have produced."[106] After a moment's pause, Lincoln added, "Lots of wisdom in that document, I suspect."[107]

Yet, absent in the speech was any sense of joy or gratification. Lincoln was not above gloating in private, but in public he hid that side of himself. He had spent a lifetime training himself not to take any public pleasure in anyone else's suffering or defeat. Of all the speeches that Lincoln admired from Clay and Webster, few evinced any joy. There could be satisfaction in saving the Union and in bringing the war to an end, but there was no pleasure in it. The hard work of reconciliation and reconstruction loomed ahead. But first, the war had to end, and for that to happen there had to be unconditional surrender.

VII

Three weeks after his second inauguration, Lincoln accepted an invitation from Grant to visit his headquarters in City Point, Virginia, eight miles from where Union lines had focused their attacks during the siege of Petersburg. Lincoln stayed for two weeks, from March 23 to April 8.

Ostensibly, Lincoln came for a long-needed break. More important, 1864 had ended with several significant Union victories. Grant's Army of the Potomac had the enemy on the run, and so did Sherman's, which had burned Atlanta and was marching to Savannah. The war appeared to be moving into its final stages. Lincoln wanted to be there when that happened. It was important to him personally, since his presidency had known nothing but war from the beginning and he was as eager as anyone for it to end. It was also important symbolically. No other office embodied American values more than the presidency. Washington was the "father of his country" based on his military and political leadership in helping to found the United States. He symbolized, too, the importance of courage and honesty in American life. Jackson symbolized the rise of the common man as the ultimate sovereign in America. He symbolized, too, directness, fearlessness, and determination in protecting American values and the sanctity of the Union. Building a presidency partly on Clay's achievements and vision, Lincoln symbolized the common decency and humility of the American people, the American way of life for which the Union stood, firmness in defending that unity, and the principle of grounding the Constitution in the values set forth in the Declaration of Independence. While Lincoln lacked the military leadership and experience of Washington, Jackson, and Taylor, he never failed to show solidarity with his men. (No president had devoted more time in office to visiting battlefields than he did.) They appreciated it, as reflected in their overwhelming votes in his favor in the recent presidential election. Every day at City Point, the president visited troops in camp and in the hospital, and the men cheered one day when he once grabbed an ax to help them cut timber.

There were other reasons for Lincoln's visit. Mary Todd agreed he needed to take a break from his routine, and the trip would allow him to see their son Robert, whom Grant had appointed to his staff. Lincoln came also to ensure that Grant, Sherman, and others in command kept pressing the Confederate troops wherever they went—and to ensure that he was a part of any peace negotiations. Shortly before the inauguration, Lee had written to Grant to propose a meeting to reach some accord to end the war, but Stanton, at Lincoln's urging, immediately telegraphed Grant, "You are not to decide, discuss, or confer upon any political question. Such questions the President holds in his own hands; and will submit them to no military conferences or conventions."[108] Whether in the field or the White House, Lincoln meant to enforce compliance within the chain of command throughout his presidency. Civilian control of the military meant the president, not the generals, made any policy decisions on war. Lincoln was determined to ensure that if the war ended, it did so in compliance with how he had defined the war's objective, including emancipation.

On March 28, Lincoln met with Grant, Sherman, and Admiral David Porter to discuss possible terms to end the war. He hoped, he told them, to be generous to the defeated rebels. "Let them once surrender and reach their homes," he said, and "they won't take up arms again. Let them all go, officers and all, I want submission, and no more bloodshed. [I] want no one punished, treat them liberally all around. We want those people to return to their allegiance to the Union and submit to the laws."[109] Lincoln still expected those laws to include the new Thirteenth Amendment.

Lincoln was with Grant when the Union Army scored a series of victories at the end of March and early April, hastening the war's end. Lincoln had arrived on his visit near the end of the last, futile efforts of Lee's men to break the Union's siege of Petersburg. He was there when Grant's counterattack in the Third Battle of Petersburg forced Lee's troops to retreat. He was there when Lee evacuated Petersburg and Richmond, and Lincoln again ordered Grant to pursue Lee's troops wherever they went.

At dusk on April 2, Jefferson Davis fled Richmond, defiantly vowing that the Confederacy would still prevail. With the Confederate capital abandoned, the flagship USS *Malvern* carried Lincoln and his son Tad to Richmond. En route, Lincoln told Admiral Porter, "Thank God I have lived to see this! It seems to me that I have been dreaming a horrid dream for four years, and now the nightmare is gone. I want to see Richmond."[110]

Into Richmond he went, against all advice that it was too dangerous. From an early age, Lincoln had read that physical courage was an integral attribute of presidential leadership—one of the many lessons of the biographies of Washington he had read as a child and of the many stories of Jackson and Taylor he knew. Unafraid to walk where the rebels once congregated and plotted the destruction of the Union (some of whom, Grant insisted, might still be lurking around), Lincoln was determined to set the right model of courage and leadership for his men, the nation, and his successors.

Richmond was still smoldering when Lincoln and Tad disembarked, within forty hours of Davis's departure. Almost immediately, Lincoln found himself surrounded by former slaves walking throughout the abandoned city. Admiral Porter said,

> *No electric wire could have carried the news of the President's arrival sooner than it was circulated in Richmond. As far as the eye could see the streets were alive with negroes and poor whites rushing in our direction, and the crowds increased so fast that I had to surround the President with sailors with fixed bayonets to keep them off. [They] all wanted to shake hands with Mr. Lincoln or his coat tail or even kneel down to kiss his boots!*[111]

They hailed "Father Abraham." When one former slave knelt down before Lincoln, he quickly asked him to rise: "Don't kneel before me. That is not right. You must kneel to God only and thank him for the liberty you will hereafter enjoy."[112] Lincoln came to see the Confederate White House, where Jefferson Davis had resided as recently as two days before. Tad watched as Lincoln sat in Davis's chair and asked for a drink of water.

Lincoln did not come to Richmond to talk about reconstruction, but he did. When he visited Davis's abandoned home, he met with a group of Union soldiers, too, one of whom asked what he thought should be done with the Confederates now that the war was ending. Rather than issue specific orders, Lincoln said, "If I were in your place, I'd let them up easy." Though he made a similar remark more than once in Washington circles, it lent little insight into what Lincoln planned for reconstruction. He might have been disposed to defer to Congress. He might not have thought of anything yet. He might have preferred to wait to allow developments to unfold before he made a commitment on anything specific.

As Lincoln enjoyed a moment of respite, the principal Confederate official left behind, John Campbell, Davis's assistant secretary of war, came to see him. Lincoln rarely underestimated people, but he might have done that, or been too eager, with Campbell, the former Supreme Court justice who would become, in the years after the war, one of the nation's most renowned appellate advocates. Campbell urged Lincoln to pursue a policy of "moderation" against the vanquished forces, sensing Lincoln's desperation for a workable and lasting peace. He got Lincoln to agree "not to exact oaths, interfere with churches, etc." and to allow "the Virginia Legislature to meet" in order "to repeal the ordinance of secession."[113] Lincoln failed to consult anyone beforehand, and the agreement was a mistake because it sent the wrong signal to the other secessionist states that Virginia had left and returned to the Union rather than as Lincoln and the Republican Party believed, that its government had been hijacked by rebels who were warring against the nation itself. (However, once the Confederate forces formally surrendered, the mistake would become moot.)

As he wrapped up his visit to Richmond, Lincoln refocused on the war, following the dispatches from the commanders in the field to ensure the final defeat of the rebels. On the passage back to Washington, Lincoln kept himself amused by regaling his fellow passengers with quotes from Shakespeare. A French journalist, who had been assigned to accompany the president on the journey, recounted that, on the trip back,

> Mr. Lincoln read aloud to us for several hours. Most of the passages he selected were from Shakespeare, especially Macbeth. The lines after the murder of Duncan, when the new king falls prey to moral torment, were dramatically dwelt. Now and then he paused to expatiate on how exact a picture here gives a murderer's mind when, the dark deed achieved, its perpetrator already envies the victim's calm peace. He read the scene over twice.[114]

Some listeners later wondered whether Lincoln had foreseen his own demise in the story.

Lincoln might have also read the monologue he liked best in

Hamlet, not the title character's famous "To be, or not to be" speech but instead the lament of Claudius, stepfather to young Hamlet and the murderer of Hamlet's father. It begins,

> *O, my offence is rank it smells to heaven;*
> *It hath the primal eldest curse upon't,*
> *A brother's murder. Pray can I not,*
> *Though inclination be as sharp as will.*

His conscience tears him apart, bemoaning,

> *What if this cursed hand*
> *Were thicker than itself with brother's blood,*
> *Is there not rain enough in the sweet heavens*
> *To wash it white as snow? Whereto serves mercy?*
> *But to confront the visage of offence?*
> *And what's in prayer but this two-fold force,*
> *To be forestalled ere we come to fall,*
> *Or pardon' being down? Then I'll look up;*
> *My fault is past. But, O, what form of prayer*
> *Can serve my term? "Forgive me my foul murder"?*
> *That cannot be; since I am still possess'd*
> *Of those effects for which I did the murder,*
> *. . .*
> *There is no shuffling; there the action lies*
> *In his true nature; and we ourselves compell'd,*
> *Aching with guilt, he worries still,*
> *Try what repentance can, what can it not?*
> *Yet what can it when one can not repent?*
> *Oh wretched state! Oh bosom black as death!*
> *Oh limed soul, that, struggling to be free,*
> *Art more engaged! Help, angels! Help assay!*

There can be little wonder why Lincoln was drawn to that passage filled with a brother's guilt over murdering his brother, for the Civil War was a battle of brother against brother. Claudius was distraught over killing his brother, while Lincoln felt the great weight of ordering the deaths of his brother citizens. He could only hope that in the end, as Claudius declares in the final line, "all may be well."[115] Lincoln could not help but see himself as different from Hamlet, who listens to Claudius confessing he's murdered Hamlet's father, yet Hamlet does nothing in the scene but walk away without avenging his father's death. In the end, Hamlet kills Claudius, and Lincoln, who hoped to avoid war, unleashed the Union's forces to put down the Southern rebellion, preserve the nation, and end slavery once and for all. Many of the same themes in Claudius's plea appear in both of Lincoln's inaugural addresses—mercy, prayer, freedom, angels, pardon, forgiveness, guilt, and sorrow. The war was not yet over, and Lincoln worried, like Claudius did, that the blood he was responsible for shedding could not be easily, or maybe ever, washed away.

Upon arriving back in Washington on April 9, Lincoln rushed to visit William Seward, who was in bed recuperating after a carriage accident. "I think we are near the end at last," Lincoln assured him.[116] Later that same evening, Lincoln received news from Grant that earlier that day he had met with Robert E. Lee, who formally surrendered his Army of Northern Virginia. Lee agreed to Grant's (that is, Lincoln's) terms of surrender, which included pardons for all officers and their men and allowed Confederate soldiers to return to their homes with their horses and side arms. Washington erupted in celebration.

VIII

The choice of Andrew Johnson as Lincoln's second vice president confounds people to this day. There was no obvious reason why Johnson was now the vice president. One possibility is that Whigs stuck with tradition. Whigs never attributed any importance to the vice presidency, and so perhaps neither did Lincoln, even though each of the times a vice president had ascended to the presidency was in a Whig administration. In neither case did these vice presidents—Tyler and Fillmore—advance the policies of the presidents they had served.

Lincoln said he had left the choice of vice president to the 1864 Republican convention, though he had taken the reigns of the party apparatus well before then. By the summer of 1864, the party was desperate to broaden its appeal to Democrats. Johnson left the Senate in 1862, but the freshly branded National Union Party lauded Johnson's fidelity to the Union, and Johnson held more appeal to the general electorate than Hamlin, because of Johnson's Southern connections. Party leaders figured those connections would help to ease reconstruction in the South.

Lincoln raised no question or objection to the choice of Johnson. The norm of the times treated the vice presidency as nothing more than a political expediency. Tyler and Fillmore each had been selected to give regional balance to the national ticket, while Hamlin brought both ideological balance as someone who had long been antislavery (in contrast with Lincoln's moderation) and balance in terms of experience, as Hamlin's public service spanned fifty years (in contrast with Lincoln's single House and four terms in the Illinois legislature).

But Lincoln did not treat the deaths of the Whig presidents as cautionary tales, because he did not expect to die in office. Harrison and Taylor died because of physical frailty and illness, while Lincoln was perfectly healthy and robust at fifty-six, much younger than Harrison, who passed away at sixty-nine, and Taylor, who died at sixty-five.

Of the fifteen presidents before Lincoln, few considered their vice presidents as political allies. Washington considered Adams a genuine partner, but in the presidential election of 1800, Adams's own vice president, Thomas Jefferson, ran against him. Jackson's first vice president, John Calhoun, was a competitor devoted to undermining him, whereas Jackson's second, Van Buren, was both a partner and an heir. Lincoln could not conceive of the vice president as a partner or an heir. For him, the vice presidency was a means to help keep the Union intact. Johnson's selection appeased factions Lincoln alone could not.

Johnson held less appeal to Lincoln than Hamlin did as a confidant, and Hamlin complained about not being consulted, listened to, or included in important meetings. Lincoln rarely confided in people. He trusted only a few—Browning as a sounding board, and Kentuckian James Speed, whom he brought into his administration as attorney general in December 1864, the brother of his close friend Joshua Speed. Lincoln developed affection and respect for Gideon Welles, his navy secretary, but he needed Welles in the Cabinet. He admired the Blairs, but then Montgomery had become a liability he could not ignore. William Seward had settled into a productive relationship with Lincoln after a rocky start, but he, like Welles, was where Lincoln needed him. Thurlow Weed and Horace Greeley inundated Lincoln with advice, but he steadfastly resisted relinquishing control of any kind over his administration to either of them. He listened patiently as many members of Congress lectured him, but he was wary of all and trusted only a few—Washburne and Stuart, among them. Radical Republicans, like Thaddeus Stevens of Pennsylvania, did not trust Lincoln, and so Lincoln did not trust them in return. The advantage of mentors such as Henry Clay, Jackson, and Taylor was that Lincoln could consult them as he pleased, and they never talked back. Mary Todd was a partner who had her own agenda. Lincoln frequently had to work around her, not with her, for the benefit of the nation.

Curiously, the lessons Lincoln took from Polk's passing were that he should avoid too extreme a workload but, like Polk, pay close attention to the day-to-day operations of his administration to ensure it functioned as he wished. But Polk had a weak constitution, and Lincoln did not. Nevertheless, Lincoln was often despondent and had dreams of dying. Orville Browning recalled that, when he once visited Lincoln in the White House, "After talking to me a while about his sources of domestic sadness, he sent one of the boys to get a volume of [Thomas] Hood's poems. It was brought to him and he read several of those sad pathetic pieces—I suppose because they were accurate pictures of his own experiences and feelings."[117] Yet, for a man who spoke often of death, as he did with Browning, Stuart, and Joshua Speed, Lincoln did not fear dying in office. When he suggested that fate controlled him more than he controlled it, it was not merely an expression of humility. It suggested that he left such great matters as life and death to a force beyond his control.

Johnson's coming from the South and the Democratic Party appealed to the party elders who wanted the Republican ticket to strip away some votes from McClellan with Democrats who still believed in the Union. There was no reason to think he could be a partner for Lincoln to handle the difficult path to reconstruction, and so unsurprisingly Lincoln never once consulted him. In fact, only near the end of his first term did Lincoln bring someone from the Southern end of the border states into his administration. Bates and Blair came from Missouri, but, after Bates departed, Lincoln brought into the Cabinet James Speed from the border state of Kentucky.

When all was said and done, Lincoln trusted no one's political judgment more than his own. He was educable but on his terms. As a result, no one in his administration, least of all his vice president, had any real insight into what he was planning for reconstruction.

IX

On Tuesday, April 11, 1865, Lincoln finished drafting his first major speech on reconstruction. He read some portions to his secretaries and the journalist Noah Brooks but to no one in the Cabinet. Whether he was feeling more confident in his own judgment, as had increasingly been the case with his public remarks, or less needful of input from others, no one knows for sure. But Lincoln had good reason to be more confident at this time than at any other time in his life. No one alive had done what he had done. No president, save possibly Washington, had accomplished more for the Union, and Lincoln was far from done.

The public rarely saw Lincoln's confidence and cockiness, obscured by his persistent proclamations of ordinariness, but it was perhaps more evident in the days after the second inauguration. Herndon said, "It was his intellectual arrogance and assumption of superiority that men like Chase and Seward never could forgive." The comment suggests that Chase and Seward could see Lincoln's arrogance and perhaps hear it in the way he talked to them and in his biting humor, which Lincoln often used to cut men down to size. Lincoln's remark, "Chase is about one and a half times bigger than any other man I know," was meant to cut Chase down to size. Seward, too, got his comeuppance more than once. Comparing his own penchant for telling anecdotes with that of Seward, Lincoln said, "Mr. Seward is limited to a couple of stories which from repeating he believes are true."

For all the humility Lincoln made a show of expressing, he never forgot—and did not let anyone else forget—that he was the president. He had outmaneuvered Chase and Seward at the convention and in the White House. They had their strengths and fancy educations (in his original Cabinet, Simon Cameron was the only member without any formal education), but he knew their weaknesses and had outplayed them in the only game that mattered: politics. If they had earned any glory for themselves, it was because of Lincoln, something he made sure none of them ever forgot.

Hundreds came to hear him on Tuesday evening, April 11, all crowding under his second-floor window at the White House, word having spread that Lincoln was going to read his first speech on reconstruction. Eventually he appeared, to great applause, and with no other fanfare, began to read his speech. Journalist Noah Brooks stood next to him, holding a light to illuminate the pages.

Lincoln acknowledged the important role that Congress would play in fashioning reconstruction. He told the crowd that he had "distinctly stated that this was not the only plan which might possibly be acceptable" and "that the Executive claimed no right to say when, or whether members should be admitted to seats in Congress from such States."[118] Lincoln addressed the question of whether Louisiana could "be brought into proper practical relation with the Union sooner by sustaining, or by discarding her new state government."[119] The answer, he said, was, "Concede that the new government of Louisiana is only to what it should be as the egg is to the fowl, we shall sooner have the fowl by hatching the egg than by smashing it."[120] If Louisiana were not to be readmitted, he said, "we also reject one vote in favor of the proposed amendment to the national constitution."[121] The new legislature, in other words, could still speak for Louisiana, since the state itself had never left the Union. Lincoln conceded he was not firmly committed to the current arrangement in Louisiana that he outlined. "As bad promises are better broken than kept, I shall read this as a bad promise, and break it, whenever I shall be convinced that keeping it is adverse to the public interest."[122] He added, "I have not yet been so convinced."[123]

Recognizing that Radical Republicans in Congress opposed the Louisiana constitution because it did not give African Americans the right to vote, he agreed "that it [should] now [be] conferred on the very intelligent [presumably meaning those who could read and write], and on those who serve our cause as soldiers."[124] Yet Lincoln was not dictating terms. In recognizing a right of suffrage for the newly freed slaves, he was still acting in conformity with his background as a Clay Whig, in deferring to Congress on the logistics of reconstruction.

Lincoln's April 11 speech marked the first time that a president acknowledged in public an African American right to vote. Though some of the crowd below grew bored and wandered away as Lincoln explained his thinking about reconstruction, many did not. One man in particular glared angrily at Lincoln from the shadows on the fringe of the crowd. "That means nigger citizenship," John Wilkes Booth told a friend.[125] "Now, by God, I'll put him through. That is the last speech he will ever make."[126]

This was not the first time Booth came to hear Lincoln speak.

Lincoln knew him by sight. He had been in the crowd at the inauguration. If Lincoln recognized Booth then, as he stared down at the president from a portico over Lincoln's left shoulder, Lincoln never mentioned it to anyone. One of the nation's preeminent actors, tall and handsome with a sleek moustache, Booth usually stood out. Lincoln had enjoyed seeing him perform Shakespeare. Yet even if Lincoln had tried on the evening of April 11 to make out particular people below his window, it was impossible, and people on the edge of the crowd were shrouded in shadows.

X

The first attempt to assassinate an American president was in 1835. On July 28, Andrew Jackson attended a funeral in the House chamber of the Capitol. Afterward he walked down the Capitol steps to be taken back to the White House, but as he finished descending, an unemployed house painter named Richard Lawrence suddenly broke loose from the crowd. He pressed a gun against Jackson's chest, and pulled the trigger. The gun misfired. Furious, Jackson began striking Lawrence with his cane. Lawrence broke free for a moment, drew a second pistol, and pulled the trigger again. This pistol, too, misfired. As he prepared to take another shot, Jackson's aides wrestled him to the ground. For the remainder of his presidency, Jackson worried about another attack. He was convinced that the Whigs had paid Lawrence, though there is no evidence to support the claim. In all likelihood, Lawrence was deranged.

After Lawrence's failed attack, every president was warned to take assassination attempts seriously, and most took precautions. Lincoln's head of security during the transition and in the administration, Allan Pinkerton, advised him to take a circuitous route from Springfield to Baltimore, to avoid any assassins lying in wait. Once in office, Lincoln frequently had bodyguards with him, including his loyal servant William Slade and old friend Ward Hill Lamon. In November 1864, the Washington police force created a special four-man detail to protect the president.

April 14, three days after Lincoln's first speech on Reconstruction, was Good Friday. Lincoln awoke feeling unusually refreshed. Though he had meetings scheduled all day, he was eager for a break. There was a play that evening, *Our American Cousin,* a popular comedy he wanted to see. Edwin Stanton pleaded with Lincoln not to go, sharing reports of assassins still plotting to kill him. Lincoln insisted that the play would be good for him because comedy always lightened his spirit. Unhappily, Stanton relented. The only person from his security detail available to go to the theater with Lincoln was John Parker, well known for his drinking habits. With Mary Todd, Parker, and their guests Major Henry Rathbone and his fiancée, Clara Harris, the daughter of Senator Ira Harris of New York, Lincoln left for the theater shortly before the scheduled curtain time.

Orville Browning was eager to see Lincoln, having not seen him since the formal surrender of the Army of Northern Virginia, when the two briefly conferred on reconstruction. Remembering the dark days when the war first started and he often visited alone with Lincoln, he hoped to have a celebratory moment with the president. He knew Lincoln would be busy, and he was—there was much work to be done on reconstruction, and the killing had not yet ended. Even after Grant's meeting with Lee at Appomattox, Sherman was still chasing General Johnston's army down south, and Nathan Bedford Forrest and his guerrilla units continued to terrorize Union forces and African Americans until they surrendered on May 9, 1865. For the moment, Browning was joyful, walking around his city. Most offices were still closed, the remnants of the partying the evening before still smoldering. In his diary for the evening of April 13 he had written, "Illumination of the city at night for General Lee's surrender."[127]

The next morning, some businesses and government offices were slowly beginning to reopen. Browning went to the War Department to "get passes for some refugee Germans to return to their families in Richmond."[128] From there, he walked to the Treasury Department, where he was following up on the "Singletons business," an arrangement that Browning and others had made with James Singleton, who had negotiated for peace earlier in the year, for the federal government to purchase cotton and tobacco from Virginia.[129] At three o'clock that afternoon, Browning and Nevada's first senator, William Morris Stewart, went to visit the president, but they were told that Lincoln "was done receiving for the day and we did not send in our cards."[130] Browning and Stewart returned to finish their business at the Capitol.

At seven that evening, Browning returned alone to the White House. He asked to see Lincoln and was led upstairs to Lincoln's office. Browning's diary recorded that he "went into [Lincoln's] room and sat there till 8 o'clock waiting for him, but he did not come. He was going to the theater."[131]

The first permanent memorial to Lincoln was one of the most difficult to arrange. Within days of his death, Mary Todd and their son Robert found themselves in heated dispute with John Todd Stuart and a self-appointed committee he led, the National Lincoln Monument Association, over where and how the fallen president should be buried. The ensuing "Battle of the Gravesite" was the first in an ongoing series of tussles over Lincoln's legacy.

On April 19, an elaborate ceremony was held in Washington to honor President Lincoln. Two days later, a funeral train began a twelve-day journey to return Lincoln's body to Springfield, following in reverse the route he had traveled from his home to his inauguration. Thousands lined the tracks to pay homage.

Initially, Mary Todd and Robert told Springfield leaders their preference was to bury Lincoln either in the empty crypt prepared for George Washington's body in the U.S. Capitol, or in Chicago, where Mary Todd hoped to settle. Eventually, Mary Todd relented and agreed with the rest of his family to bury Lincoln at the top of a hill in bucolic Oak Ridge Cemetery, next to Springfield. But Stuart's committee had other plans: they preferred for the murdered president to be buried at a site in the center of town, which they believed would be good for business in Springfield. Though Robert stayed with Stuart during the Springfield services, the skirmish continued, until Mary Todd made the ultimatum to bury Lincoln as she wished or she would withdraw her consent entirely for a burial in Springfield. Stuart's committee took a final vote, deciding by a narrow margin, 8–7, to acquiesce to her demands.

The principal themes of the eulogies were nearly the same everywhere except in the South. First, Lincoln had been the instrument of God's will. Among the longest orations was that of Bishop Matthew Simpson of the Methodist Episcopal Church of Philadelphia, who declared that

> *the great cause of this mourning is found in the man himself. Mr. Lincoln was no ordinary man; and I believe the conviction has been growing on the nation's mind, as it has certainly been on mine, especially in the last years of his administration, that by the hand of God he was especially singled out to guide our government in these troubled times. And it seems to me that the hand of God may be traced in many of the events connected with his history.*

In a ceremony in Washington, Dr. Phineas Gurley, the pastor of New York Avenue Presbyterian Church, which the president had attended, had sounded the same theme. "God raised him up for a great and glorious mission, furnished him for his work, and aided him in its accomplishment." Of Lincoln's many qualities, Simpson said the most impressive was his character. Lincoln's "moral power gave him pre-eminence. The convictions of men that Abraham Lincoln was an honest man, led them to yield to his guidance." A Springfield theology professor simply said, "Rest, Noble Martyr." One Springfield newspaper predicted, "Millions will drop a tear to his memory, and future generations will make pilgrimages to his tomb. Peace to his ashes."

The eulogies and Lincoln lore have great resonance because they fit the narrative of Lincoln's life as he had lived it. One essential element was his educability. Frederick Douglass often berated Lincoln for being too slow, cautious, incremental, and racist in his thinking, actions, and language. On April 14, 1876, eleven years after Lincoln's death, Douglass reiterated, "Truth compels me to admit, even here in the presence of the monument to his memory. [Lincoln] was not, in the fullest sense of the word, either our man or our model. In his interests, in his habits of thought, and in his prejudices, he [wa]s preeminently the white man's president, entirely devoted to the welfare of white men."[1]

Lincoln was all that Douglass said and more. In that same speech in 1876, Douglass expressed gratitude for Lincoln's "great works" and praised him as "a great and glorious friend and benefactor." Douglass, as clear-eyed as anyone assessing Lincoln in his own times, might have appreciated that Lincoln was educable, though not nearly as fast as Douglass had hoped from the man he called "the first martyr President of the United States." Lincoln never stopped studying and learning from people and events as much as he learned from books. In 1862, he met with a delegation of African American citizens from Washington, D.C. He told them, "You and we are different races," and suggested that "it was better for us both [to] be separated."[2] But later that same year, in 1862, Lincoln announced his intention to issue an Emancipation Proclamation. By the end of the war, he had moved beyond Clay's and his own past thinking, authorizing Douglass to put together an outfit of African American troops to fight for the Union, discarding the notion that slave-owners deserved compensation, and planning for an America of unprecedented equality. In 1864, Lincoln met in the White House with African American abolitionist Sojourner Truth, who had waited hours to see him. He shared with her a Bible that was given to him by African Americans in Baltimore. When she thanked him profusely for the Emancipation Proclamation, he assured her that Washington and other predecessors would have done the same "if the time had come." Lincoln was not above racist thinking and language, but he was also the first president to welcome African Americans into the White House—both literally and ideologically.

No one knows whether Lincoln's legacy would have been different had he not died as a martyr for his cause, even though he repeatedly expressed concern that he was headed to a "terrible end." Such premonitions did not lead him to take greater care to protect himself from the assassins he knew were hunting him.

Mary Todd had that and much more to regret as she settled in Chicago. Her debts hounded her, until she prevailed on Thaddeus Stevens to persuade his colleagues to enact legislation that covered much of the money she owed. When her son Tad died in 1871, the grief was too much for her. In 1875, Robert approved her commitment to an insane asylum. Six years later, she secured her release and went to Europe to escape the negative attention she was receiving in the United States. Eventually, she returned to the United States, where she died in 1882. She was buried with Lincoln, along with every other member of the family except Robert. When Robert died in 1926, his wife refused to allow her husband to be buried next to Lincoln. She did not wish Robert to be overshadowed in death by his father, as he had been in life. He was interred in Arlington National Cemetery, the last surviving member of the Cabinets of presidents James Garfield and Chester Arthur.

Slowly, other memorials to Lincoln began to appear outside Illinois, in most of the rest of the country, except, again, in the South. In 1869, Nebraska renamed its state capitol Lincoln in honor of the late president. Two years before that, Oliver Howard, a brigadier general known as the Christian General because of his determination to base his policies on his strong religious convictions, founded Howard University in Washington, D.C. (He later founded Abraham Lincoln Memorial University in Tennessee, the first such site in the South honoring the fallen president.)

As memorials and markers spread, however, a more extended battle was being waged over Lincoln's legacy. Andrew Johnson's legacy was not one of unity or racial progress, to say the least. Among the divisions that emerged was the question of whether and how to remember Lincoln. Republicans claimed Lincoln as their own. They defended his image the way he had shaped it in life. They burnished his memory as the first Republican president, the one who freed the slaves, whose rhetoric was unmatched, and who embodied calmness, steadiness, and humility during the most stressful years in American history. Lincoln had set the stage for the second founding, reconstructing the original Constitution to guarantee the freedom and equality of every American, regardless of race. Lincoln had done his part in both implementing the great promise of the Declaration of Independence that "all men are created equal" and crafting a new American rhetoric—plain, clear, and yet mellifluent and stirring. As Frederick Douglass observed,

In my interviews with him, I found him as I have already described him, a plain man. His manners were simple, unaffected, unstudied. His language, like himself, was plain strong and sinewy, just as it appears in his written productions. He spoke as he wrote, without ornament. Earnest always, but never extravagant. I never met a man who could state more clearly and forcibly, just what he wished to make apparent.[3]

Lincoln became mythic, nearly divine, in memorial after memorial paying homage to his martyrdom. Yet many Americans, particularly in the South, saw a different Lincoln, more devil than saint. They viewed him as a president elected by only a minority of the country who was a tyrant and waged war to force law-abiding Southerners to give up their way of life. The battle over Lincoln's legacy was essentially a war over a vision for America. It was a battle over which myth of Lincoln to advance and which story of the war to champion, more protracted than the war itself and ultimately more consequential for America's identity. For loyal Confederates, reconstruction and reunion required rebranding the purpose of the conflict. For the South, it became a noble contest to vindicate "states' rights" over federal supremacy, as Jefferson Davis proclaimed in his address to the Confederate Congress on April 29, 1861: "All we ask is to be let alone."[4] In the remainder of that address, which not only defined the terms of engagement at the start of the war but was drawn upon by sympathizers long after Lee's surrender, Davis denounced the "wrongs" and "evils" that the North had imposed on the Confederates. The wrongs and evils were the Union's efforts to contain slavery. Over the next few years, it was clear what Davis and other Confederate leaders wanted done if they were left alone—fortify and expand slavery to the fullest extent possible.

After Jefferson Davis died in 1881, the battle to rewrite the narrative on the reasons for the war did not stall but continued with greater fervor. Monuments sprouted up around the South, funded by the descendants of rebel soldiers who venerated their ancestors

and their "lost cause." They celebrated not Lincoln but instead retold the history of the war to recast it as having been waged for
reasons other than preserving slavery and to honor the valor of
Confederate war heroes and leaders. More than a century after
Davis died, Richmond, capital of the Confederacy, refused to allow
a mural of Lincoln to join the monuments of Confederate generals
lining its Monument Avenue. When a statue of Lincoln and his son
Tad was erected in a different part of town in 2003, more than a
century and a half since the end of the Civil War, over a hundred
Sons of Confederate Veterans protested. One complained that the
people erecting the statue "have no concept of history. . . . As a
southerner, I am offended. You wouldn't put a statute of Winston
Churchill in downtown Berlin, would you? What's next, a statue
of Sherman in Atlanta?"[5]

The debate over Civil War–era monuments still rages today.
The May 25, 2020, murder of George Floyd at the hands of a Minneapolis police officer sparked a renewed debate across the South
and the rest of the nation. Protests against police brutality directed
at African Americans spread like wildfire across the country, leading to the toppling of Confederate monuments, particularly in the
South, including those for Jefferson Davis and General Williams
Carter Wickham in Richmond (and prompting the governor to
take down a monument of Robert E. Lee); the House vote to take
down the seventeen monuments to Confederates in the Capitol;
the vote of both chambers in Congress to rename federal military
bases that had been named after Confederate military officers and
the removals of shrines to white supremacy and monuments or
celebrations of other Confederate figures in at least eleven states,
including Washington and Oregon.

In the midst of all this, Lincoln was not forgotten but venerated.
President Trump declared (falsely) that he had done as much for
African Americans as Lincoln had, if not more. Americans yearned
for a Lincoln, and President Trump was keen to align himself with
Lincoln's legend and to get on the bandwagon that Lincoln had put
in motion to secure equality throughout the land.

The finest Lincoln scholars—Sidney Blumenthal, Michael Burlingame, David Herbert Donald, Eric Foner, Doris Kearns Good-win, Allen Guelzo, Richard Hofstadter, Harold Holzer, James McPherson, Kate Masur, Allan Nevins, J. G. Randall, and Kenneth Winkle—to name but a few—have worked to restore Lincoln's humanity, to show that he was not a god or myth but a man.[6] His achievements are all the more impressive because he was not divine or superhuman but a mere mortal. He was not born to greatness but earned his way, his map drawn by the men, books, plays, and poetry that he took inspiration and instruction from.

When asked whether Lincoln was a weak man, Stephen Douglas said no, but quickly added that "he is preeminently a man of the atmosphere that surrounds him." Whether he intended it or not, Douglas captured an essential element of Lincoln's leadership—his ability to imbue and express, in all its complexity, the time in which he lived. Even if Lincoln were playing "chess" with other people's lives (as a Chicago lawyer friend suggested), his moves were not made in a series of sudden leaps ahead but rather incrementally, each step tracking the core values, sentiments, and ideals of the people and country he led. In being "a man of the atmosphere" around him, Lincoln had the unique capacity to absorb and adapt to his own ends the rhetoric, attitudes, and experiences of the leaders, visionaries, and poets of his era. As president, he was surrounded by Jackson men and pushed relentlessly to be firm and "manly" like Jackson. Having grown up among Jacksonian Democrats and counting many of them as close friends, Lincoln understood the allure of Jackson. It is no surprise that he wished to be a president like Jackson, who would be willing to die for his cause rather than to be a president, like Buchanan, who shrank from danger. Better to "be assassinated on this spot," as Lincoln said in front of Independence Hall in 1861, "than to surrender" the principle of liberty for all promised in the Declaration of Independence. His emulation extended to adopting Jackson's stories when it seemed appropriate. When approaching Richmond with his son Tad in April 1865, Lincoln told his shipmates of a Western stump speaker who had once sought [appointment to lead] a foreign embassy and was "only appeased by the gift of an old pair of breeches."

It was a story first told by Jackson. Lincoln had substituted himself for Jackson, his coda merely "But it is well to be humble."[7]

In the fight over Lincoln's legacy, Lincoln's mentors have largely been neglected. A rare exception can be found in the center of Philadelphia, once the nation's largest market for slave trade. A building dating back to 1862 houses the grandest Union League in the nation. On its second floor is a hall with portraits of every Republican president, beginning with the first, Abraham Lincoln. Yet not all the presidents in that great hall were Republicans. On the wall, in the lower right corner, sits a portrait of Andrew Jackson, painted during a visit to New Orleans in 1839. Above him is Zachary Taylor, the last Whig elected president. The largest painting of all in the Union League is not of Lincoln but is a nine-foot-tall portrait of his greatest mentor. Standing erect, Henry Clay is depicted as the "Father of the American System," with several emblems of his vision of industry and agriculture as indispensable to the nation's economic growth—a plow, an anvil, a shuttle, some cattle, a ship, and a globe with the American flag draped over it. Then in his sixties, Clay stands, looking as vibrant and imposing as ever. Above a bannister in another part of the Union League, there is a smaller portrait of Henry Charles Carey, who crafted the economic theory underlying Clay's American System and who had served as an adviser to Lincoln in his Treasury Department.

In the years following Lincoln's death, the legacies and reputations of his principal mentors have followed different paths. Of the three mentors who did not outlive him, history has been kindest to Clay. Clay is one of only five former senators commemorated by statues in the nation's capital. Historians acknowledge his strong influence on Lincoln and the role he played in congressional debates at critical moments of the antebellum period, none more so than in the Compromise of 1850. Yet, what continues to shine most from Clay's life is his oratory, still widely studied and emulated in the years after his death in 1852. No senator has been quoted as much by a president as Lincoln quoted Clay.

Andrew Jackson's reputation has waxed and waned in the years since his death in 1845. As the last president to serve for two terms before Lincoln's reelection in 1864, Jackson has received considerable attention from historians, political scientists, and presidential scholars. Among presidents, only George Washington, Lincoln, and Teddy and Franklin Roosevelt are the subjects of more biographical studies than Jackson. Jackson's record on forced removal of Native Americans is a permanent stain on his legacy. During his eight years in office, Jackson signed many laws, such as the 1830 Indian Removal Act, which authorized the government to negotiate with southern Native American tribes for relocation west. The vigorous enforcement of the law under both Jackson and Van Buren resulted in the forced expulsion of thousands of Native Americans from their homelands. The removals required forcibly moving about sixty thousand Native Americans westward from the southeast. The march became known as the Trail of Tears to signify the fact that thousands of Native Americans died during the march westward, including a fourth of the Cherokee population. Yet, Jackson still gets credit, as Lincoln gave him, for his strong stance against secession. Jackson's staunch partisanship—and the many years Lincoln had spent defending Jackson's nemesis Clay and combating Jacksonian Democrats—continue to distract people from considering how Jackson served as a mentor for Lincoln.

Historians largely treat Zachary Taylor as a footnote in American history. For them, his only importance was his death, which opened the way for Millard Fillmore to sign the Compromise of 1850 into law. Yet Lincoln did not overlook Taylor. Taylor was one of the two political leaders Lincoln eulogized, one of the three presidents Lincoln met while they were in office (the other two were Polk and Buchanan), one of the two most famous Kentuckians before his election as president, and a model to Lincoln and others for his toughness and ingenuity as a general and strong stand against threats of nullification and secession. Taylor was a cautionary tale, too, for Lincoln. In speaking about the presidency in Taylor's eulogy, Lincoln said, "No human being can fill that station and avoid censure." He was determined, too, not to repeat Polk's and Taylor's mistakes in failing to cultivate good, constructive relationships with members of Congress and his Cabinet, though he had difficulties in doing so with a number of Radical Republicans in Congress and Salmon Chase in the Cabinet.

John Todd Stuart and Orville Browning led productive lives for more than two decades after Lincoln's death. On the morning after the assassination, Browning was at the White House early consoling Lincoln's family and meeting with Andrew Johnson and shaken Cabinet members to discuss the delicate transition from Lincoln to Johnson as president. In subsequent and increasing visits with Johnson, the two men quickly realized they had important views on reconstruction in common. Browning had long favored policies that were sympathetic to the South, even though an enraged Southerner had killed Lincoln, who had supported harsh measures against the South for much of the war.

Unlike Lincoln, as his presidency went on, Johnson routinely sought Browning's advice, including on such matters as patronage and on whether he had the authority to dismiss Stanton as his secretary of war without Senate approval. The Cabinet split on whether Johnson had the authority on his own to dismiss Stanton or whether he needed Senate approval as required by the Tenure in Office Act. Browning suggested a middle course. Given that he believed the Tenure in Office Act did not clearly apply to Cabinet officers appointed before Johnson became president (because it was not modified to preclude him from doing so until after he became president), Browning thought Johnson should suspend Stanton and avoid a direct conflict with the statute or Congress. Johnson agreed, though the middle course was not enough to prevent Johnson from being impeached for his hostility to congressional Reconstruction policy.

When, in 1866, Johnson reshuffled Lincoln's Cabinet to rid himself of Radical Republicans (whom he believed were trying to impede his authority and force him to defer to congressional control over Reconstruction), he named Browning as his secretary of the interior. Later, when Henry Stanbery resigned as attorney general in order to represent Johnson in his impeachment trial (along with other eminent counsel, including former Supreme Court justice Benjamin Curtis), Browning became Johnson's acting attorney general. Johnson survived his trial, albeit barely, and the next president, Ulysses Grant, replaced Browning and the rest of Johnson's Cabinet. Having been alienated from the policies of the Radical Republicans, Browning, like Stuart before him, became a Democrat in his remaining years and returned to his law practice, serving as counsel to several railroads. Before his death in 1881, Browning communicated at length with Herndon as he was writing a life of Lincoln, but his pivotal role as a mentor to the aspiring Lincoln was mostly forgotten.

After losing his reelection bid in 1864, John Todd Stuart returned to Springfield, never again to return to Washington or to politics. He resumed his practice and prominence as one of Illinois's most successful trial lawyers. When he died in 1885, David Davis delivered his eulogy, speaking to the Illinois State Bar Association on November 23, 1885, of the man whom he knew "after half a century of unbroken friendship," said Davis. "The part which Stuart took in shaping Lincoln's destiny is not generally known outside of the circle of their immediate friends." He then recounted the two men's years together, living in the same boarding house, their engagement in Whig politics. David said,

> *Each estimated aright the abilities of the other. Both were honest men with deep convictions, and appreciated by their fellow members. The one was liberally educated and a lawyer; the other uneducated, and engaged in the humble occupation of a land surveyor. Stuart saw at once that there must be a change of occupation to give Lincoln a fair start in life, and that the study and practice of the law were necessary to stimulate his ambition and develop his faculties. [Every] lawyer, and indeed every thoughtful and intelligent person can readily see the influence which the choice of legal profession had on Lincoln's life.*

Davis added,

> *Stuart was as devoted to its fortunes equally with Lincoln. Their political friendship seemed to be as close and enduring as their*

personal friendship. [And] there was no sincerer mourner at his grave than Stuart. The beautiful monument erected in yonder cemetery to the memory of Lincoln, is a silent witness to the unceasing labors of Stuart, who cooperated with other distinguished citizens of Illinois in its construction. The men loved one another, and their political separation was a source of sorrow and grief to both.[8]

Davis took liberties with the truth, as such tributes often do, but the connection between Stuart and his greatest student could not be denied.

Indeed, Lincoln was that rare student who surpassed his teachers. He studied them closely not just to emulate them but to improve on what they did. He did not idolize his mentors but instead understood they were as human as he and thus prone to mistakes in judgment and action. Herndon recalled, "He read specifically for a special object and thought things useless unless they could be of utility, use, practice, etc."[9] He gradually abandoned the dense, systematic logic of Clay and the powerful imagery and declarations of Webster for plainer language, both easier to speak and easier to remember. He did not speak over the heads of the public, as so many presidents had done, or merely to the political elite, as so many members of Congress had done. Nor was he as conniving or duplicitous as some presidents had been in saying one thing and doing another. Jefferson had coined the great promise of the Declaration of Independence, but as president he declared in his first inaugural "We are all Republicans, we are all Federalists," just before his administration retaliated with fervor against the Federalists, who had attacked the Democratic-Republicans in the previous administration under President Adams. Jackson spoke with anger, harshness, and partisanship. Clay spoke powerfully (and memorably for those present) but often with partisan zeal, complicated analogies, and logical ferocity. Lincoln substituted for their excesses and mistakes simple, plain, poetic language, pitching what he had to say "low down, and the common people will understand you" as he once counseled Herndon. As Herndon told Jesse Weik, with whom he wrote Lincoln's biography, "Lincoln's ambition [was that] he wanted to be distinctly understood by the Common People."[10]

Lincoln had seen other presidents squander their public support, speak with the same kind of partisanship they had spoken with as candidates, and do little inspiring in either deeds or words. There were presidents who benefited from slogans that captured the essence of their visions—combatting the "corrupt bargain" for Jackson, achieving "manifest destiny" for Polk, Jefferson's timeless declaration that "all men are created equal," and Clay's "American System." But Lincoln went beyond slogans to craft a story of America that celebrated a renewed commitment guaranteeing equality and liberty to every American. That this story mirrored his own self-made journey reinforced his faith in its fundamental authenticity.

Actions could produce enduring results, as the Founders' generation did in winning the Revolutionary War. Actions were taken in response to the rebellion against the Union. Lincoln was cautious in taking the lead on issues he knew were dividing the nation—preserving the Union, whether to end slavery, and if so how to do it. But Lincoln saw a value to words that no other president, with the possible exceptions of Jefferson in the Declaration of Independence and Jackson in his proclamation against secession, had yet made use of. Words inspired action. Words inspired people to become their better selves. Words defined the war's purpose. Words defined the purpose of the Union. Words could entertain. Words could console. Words could wound. Words could divide. Words could unify. They could be used to free an enslaved people.

Memory was all-important to Lincoln. To him, what people remembered, even more than what happened, is what counted most. Lincoln lived a life—like the books, poems, and plays he loved—to be remembered. His actions and statements in public, from the hospitals and battlefields he visited, to the carefully constructed speeches he gave and Annual Messages he wrote to Congress, the many letters he wrote, and the steady stream of stories and jokes he told, were all done for a reason—to make people remember him, to write his story.

Lincoln saw a connection between Jackson and Clay that few others perceived. Jackson, as the champion of the "common man," and Clay, the champion of the "self-made man," were both championing something similar. Lincoln saw the connection between the two. He saw that the common man, with sufficient ambition and determination, could *become* a self-made man and that a self-made man was an ordinary man who realized his potential.

Some of Lincoln's closest associates saw the connection, including former Democrats, such as the Blair family, Gideon Welles, and Edwin Stanton. Poets and writers saw the connection, too. When Lincoln died, Herman Melville wrote the poem "The Martyr." Though he had been strongly committed to the Union in the 1850s, Melville met Lincoln briefly in 1861 and was unimpressed with his first few months in office. (Jackson had made an appearance as "The Hero" in Melville's *Moby-Dick*, published in 1851, and Melville wrote seventy-two poems during the Civil War.) But four years later, in 1865, Melville felt different:

He lieth in his blood——
    The father in his face;
They have killed him, the Forgiver——
    The Avenger takes his place,
The Avenger wisely stern,
    Who in righteousness shall do
    What the heavens call him to,
And the parricides remand;
    For they killed him in his kindness,
    In their madness and their blindness.
And his blood is on their hand.

There is sobbing of the strong,
    And a pall upon the land;
But the People in their weeping
    Bare the iron hand:
Beware the People weeping
    When they bare the iron hand.

For Melville, there was no conflict in celebrating Jackson's manliness and the "kingly commons," then also lauding another man, one who embodied different attributes and even proclaimed Jackson's nemesis as his teacher. Behind the Clay-like moderate tone and the jocularity was a man as firmly committed to the Union as Jackson. He gave his own "last full measure of devotion" to preserve it.

For much of his career, Walt Whitman had celebrated Jackson. In one famous poem, he paid homage to Jacksonian democracy and heroic manhood:

> *O the joy of a manly self-hood!*
> *To be servile to none, to defer to none, not to any tyrant known or unknown,*
> *To walk with erect carriage, a step springy and elastic,*
> *To look with calm gaze or with a flashing eye,*
> *To speak with a full and sonorous voice out of a broad chest,*
> *To confront with your personality all the other personalities of the earth.*

Jacksonianism aside, after Lincoln's death, Whitman wrote two poems to honor Lincoln, one perhaps the most famous poem to do so. It opened with the memorable line, "O Captain! my Captain! our fearful trip is done. . . ." Near the end, Whitman laments, "My Captain he does not answer . . . / But I with mournful tread, / Walk the deck my Captain lies, / Fallen cold and dead."

Melville and Whitman each saw a direct line connecting Jackson and Lincoln. Lincoln would have relished the irony that the line went straight through Henry Clay.

The poetry, like the sermons and eulogies, fed the narrative of Lincoln's story. They all celebrated the American ideals he exemplified and championed. They took what he gave them, the words, actions, attestations of humility and self-deprecation, homilies, the defense of the Union, and celebration of the common man to produce an enduring image of Lincoln as an American hero. Frederick Douglass had a nuanced view of Lincoln; in the same year, 1876, in which he stressed that Lincoln was a white man bent on serving other white people, Douglass reconsidered Lincoln's legacy, concluding, "Because of his commitment to liberty and equality, he is doubly dear to us, and his memory will be precious forever."

When Nathaniel Hawthorne met Lincoln in 1862, Lincoln struck him as a "country schoolmaster."[11] Hawthorne observed further,

> the president is teachable by events, and has now spent a year in a very arduous course of education; he has a flexible mind, much capable of expansion, and convertible towards far loftier studies and activities than those of his early life; and if he came to Washington a backwoods humorist, he has already transformed himself into [a] statesman. . . .

The educable country schoolmaster who became a statesman became in turn the teacher of presidents, a model and inspiration more than any other. No president is quoted more by other presidents than Abraham Lincoln. Every president after Lincoln in the nineteenth century had served the Union in some capacity under Lincoln (except for Grover Cleveland, who had arranged for a substitute to take his place in the Union Army). As a little boy, Theodore Roosevelt reputedly watched Lincoln's funeral procession pass by his grandparents' home, and later acknowledged Lincoln as "my great hero." And at his 1905 inauguration, he wore a ring containing a lock of Lincoln's hair, which had been given to him by Lincoln's secretary John Hay, who served as Roosevelt's secretary of state. Before Roosevelt placed Lincoln's image on the penny in 1909 to honor his fellow Republican, no American coin had featured an image of a president.

During his 1912 campaign for president, Woodrow Wilson traveled to Springfield to emphasize Lincoln's presidency as his inspiration. In 1929, Franklin Roosevelt told a journalist that "it was time for us Democrats to claim Lincoln as one of our own." As president, he spoke of Lincoln more than any other president, quoted him in support of his New Deal, and on July 3, 1938, delivered his own brief address upon the seventy-fifth anniversary of Gettysburg, on which occasion he met the oldest living veteran of the Civil War. Harry Truman studied Lincoln's firing of General George McClellan when he was considering whether to relieve General Douglas McArthur from his command of U.S. forces in Korea because of insubordination. Dwight Eisenhower kept a set of Lincoln's collected works in the Oval Office and even painted a portrait of Lincoln that he hung in the Cabinet Room of the White House.

In daring to broaden protections for African Americans' civil and voting rights in 1964 and 1965, Lyndon Johnson understood that he was extending Lincoln's hard-fought vision of equality and opportunity for all Americans. Richard Nixon had a picture of Lincoln hung over his bed when he was a boy and later visited the Lincoln Memorial for inspiration as he wrestled with how to end the Vietnam conflict. In speaking to a junior high school class visiting the Federal Executive Office Building (next to the White House) in 1987, Ronald Reagan spoke of how as a young boy he knew "Americans who could remember Abraham Lincoln" and of Lincoln's rise to the presidency as the quintessential American success story.

Bill Clinton mused to one historian that he hoped to write a biography of Lincoln, while George W. Bush read fourteen biographies of Lincoln in the aftermath of the terrorist attacks against the United States on 9/11 and met with a group of Lincoln scholars to better understand Lincoln "as a war-time president." Bush's Justice Department used Lincoln's refusal to have war declared against the seceding states as a model for not requesting a declaration of war against the terrorists who attacked the United States, since in both cases the United States was combatting rebels and terrorists, not formally recognized foreign states.

When Barack Obama was president, he placed a portrait of Lincoln so that when he looked up from his desk in the Oval Office, Lincoln's eyes met his, and he acknowledged Lincoln, above all others, as his inspiration, model, and teacher. Perhaps with Lincoln's team of rivals in mind, Obama appointed Hillary Clinton, his chief opponent for the Democratic nomination, as secretary of state, the position Clay held under John Quincy Adams.

President Donald Trump elevated, as Lincoln did, a portrait of

Andrew Jackson as a symbol of the toughness a president requires, and he has repeatedly likened his presidency to that of Lincoln's. On May 3, 2020, in the midst of the nation's struggling with the deaths and economic destruction wrought by a pandemic, Trump convened a virtual town hall at the Lincoln Memorial in the hopes of showing solidarity with America's greatest president. Faced with the fallout, protests, and violence spurred by George Floyd's murder at the hands of a Minneapolis police officer, President Trump continued comparing himself to Lincoln, complaining that he was being "treated worse" than Lincoln ever was. Lincoln never lived to see the Union made whole, but making it whole was his last wish, "to cherish," as he said in his second inaugural, "a just and lasting peace among ourselves and with all nations."

All presidents look to Lincoln as their metric. They claim Lincoln's project as their own, hope to be associated with his achievements, and aspire to connect their stories with his. He has become a mentor to them all.

ACKNOWLEDGMENTS

Abraham Lincoln and the Civil War have been with me since the beginning. I spent my first eighteen years living in Mobile, Alabama, where I read or heard about them often. My father and mother stressed the importance of education above all, and they instilled within me a love of learning. My father, born and raised in Alabama, shared with me and my brothers, Doug and Jim, his many books on the life of Lincoln and the battles of the Civil War. He loved taking us to the battlefields. I will never forget marveling at how small the battlefield was at Gettysburg. At school, I frequently heard about the "War Between the States," the "Lost Cause," and states' rights as the main objective of the war. The textbooks I read taught me much about Lincoln's rise to power and the war but little about Reconstruction.

In college, my eyes widened as I learned more about Lincoln, the war, and its aftermath. C. Vann Woodward and Skip Gates taught me about the frustrations of Reconstruction, Edmund Morgan about the founding, and Rollin Osterweis about the oratory of both Clay and Lincoln. Robin Winks and I talked at length about our shared love of detective fiction, and his belief that historians are really detectives solving past mysteries has had a profound influence on my reading and writing as a legal academic for the past thirty years.

Many people have helped me in trying to find a solution to the intriguing mystery about how Lincoln became Lincoln. The University of North Carolina Law School has supported me throughout this project. The law library at the UNC Law School, led by Anne Klinefelter, has been a great help throughout the writing of and research for this book. Research librarians Melissa Hyland and Nick

Sexton have been invaluable resources. For several years, Nick patiently fielded my questions about Lincoln documentation, which he thoroughly addressed at every step along the way to completion of this book. I am grateful for enormously helpful assistance from UNC law students Anna Conaway, Rob Harrington, Tanner Caplan, Joseph Wakeford, and the indefatigable Hailey Klabo. I am especially grateful to Alex Grosskurth of UNC Law School and Michael Christ of the University of Chicago Law School for their meticulous review of the manuscript.

Several libraries have been hospitable homes when I have visited them for research. My son Noah and I visited the Lincoln Library in Springfield, Illinois, and resident historians Ian Hunt, Christian McWhirter, Christian Schnell, and Samuel Wheeler could not have been more helpful. Noah and I toured not just the library but the town of Springfield. We visited Lincoln's grave and traced the Blairs and the *Dred Scott* case in St. Louis. Characteristically, Noah asked terrific questions everywhere we went, and patiently scoured the secondary literature for this project. He is our resident Lincoln scholar.

I spent days wading through the papers of the Blair family and Albert Beveridge at the Library of Congress. And the Yale library, which I loved as a student, welcomed me back with its friendly assistance on several lines of inquiries. I had fruitful conversations with many historians on this project. For their helpful feedback, I thank Mary Sarah Bilder, David Blight, Douglas Brinkley, Thavolia Glymph, Harold Holzer, and Robert Strauss. I cannot thank UNC historians Mike Morgan, Harry Watson, and Molly Worthen enough for their patience and insights in fielding my many questions about studying and writing about Lincoln. I am grateful, too, to John Meko, executive director of the Foundations of the Union League, and his wonderful team, for welcoming me into the Union League and sharing its rich archives, history, and remarkable artifacts and paintings with me. I could not cite all the archives and works I consulted throughout the writing of this book, but I am grateful to those who have collected and edited the corpus of Lincoln and of the papers of each of the people who were in his ambit and are mentioned herein.

And there are some people I must thank because I could not have completed this book without them. Bob Strauss introduced me to my agent, Jane Dystel. Jane's support, advice, patience, and confidence in this project have been invaluable and heartening. I am also grateful to her colleague Miriam Goderich and Geoff Shandler for their guidance and counsel. My colleague John Orth, my friend Jeff Rosen, and my wife, Deborah, carefully read through every word of the manuscript, for which I am eternally grateful. Our entire family—Deborah and our sons, Ben, Daniel, and Noah—stood by me and the idea of this book throughout its completion; they were patient, thoughtful sounding boards every day of this project. Peter Hubbard, Molly Gendell, and the wonderful team at Mariner Books have all worked tirelessly to make this a better work, though I alone am responsible for any errors.

I had hoped I could share the finished product with my mother, whose love, unyielding support, and patience have brought me to this point in my life. She died weeks before I finished the book but not before telling me (as she did every time I spoke with her) how much she adored and respected my wife, Deborah, and our three sons. (We had that and many other things in common.) Truly, these two women have made me the man I am today. I had hoped to see my mother's eyes light up when I gave her a signed copy of this book. She was the archivist and memory of our family's history, and I would have loved for her to see how I used what she taught me. Instead, I have dedicated this book to her, my very first mentor, whose lessons on the importance of family, stories, and memory are imprinted on our hearts and souls forever.

NOTES

INTRODUCTION: THE SEARCH FOR LINCOLN'S TEACHERS

1. September 30, 1859, address before the Wisconsin State Agricultural Society, Milwaukee Wisconsin, Reprinted from the Proceedings of the Society, 1859, Lincoln Fellowship of Wisconsin Madison (1943).

CHAPTER ONE: FINDING HIS MENTORS (1809-1834)

1. Abraham Lincoln, *Autobiography*, December 20, 1859, in *Collected Works of Abraham Lincoln*, 8 vols., ed. Roy Basler et al. (New Brunswick, NJ: Rutgers University Press, 1953–1955).
2. Nathaniel Grigsby, interview with Herndon, September 12, 1865, in William Henry Herndon and Jesse William Weik, *Herndon's Informants: Letters, Interviews, and Statements About Abraham Lincoln*, ed. Douglas L. Wilson and Rodney O. Davis (Champaign: University of Illinois Press, 1998), 113.
3. Dennis F. Hanks, interview with Herndon, June 13, 1865, in *Herndon's Informants*, 37.
4. Id.
5. David Herbert Donald, *Lincoln* (New York: Simon & Schuster, 1995), 30.
6. Id.
7. Id. (different page).
8. Michael Burlingame, *Abraham Lincoln: A Life*, vol. 1 (Baltimore, MD: Johns Hopkins University Press, 2008), 25.
9. Louis A. Warren, *Lincoln's Youth: Indiana Years, 1816–1830* (Indianapolis: Indiana Historical Society, 1959), 69.
10. Kenneth J. Winkle, *Abraham and Mary Lincoln* (Carbondale: Southern Illinois University Press, 2011), 14.
11. Id.
12. Id.
13. Sarah Bush Johnson, interview with Herndon, September 8, 1865, in *Herndon's Informants*.
14. Carl Sandburg, *Abraham Lincoln: The Prairie Years and the War Years* (one-volume edition) (New York: Harcourt, Brace, 1954), 13.
15. Burlingame, *Abraham Lincoln: A Life*, 1:34.
16. Donald, *Lincoln*.
17. Sandburg, *The Prairie Years*, 71.
18. Written to Jesse W. Fell on December 20, 1859, as an autobiographical sketch.
19. Lincoln, *Autobiography*, June 1860.

20. Sarah Bush Johnson, interview with Herndon, September 8, 1865, in *Herndon's Informants.*

21. Dennis Hanks to Herndon, June 13, 1865, in *Herndon's Informants.*

22. Id.

23. Matilda Johnston Moore to Herndon, September 8, 1865, in *Herndon's Informants,* 109.

24. Id.

25. Dennis Hanks to Herndon, September 8, 1865, in *Herndon's Informants,* 106.

26. Sarah Bush Lincoln to Herndon, September 8, 1865, in *Herndon's Informants,* 107.

27. Burlingame, *Abraham Lincoln: A Life,* 1:39.

28. John Langdon Kaine, "Lincoln as a Boy Knew Him," *Century Magazine* 85 (February 1913): 557; and Reply to loyal colored people of Baltimore upon presentation of a Bible, September 7, 1864, Lincoln, *Collected Works,* 7:542.

29. William E. Barton, *The Soul of Abraham Lincoln* (George H. Doran Co., 1920), 47.

30. Walter Barlow Stevens, *A Reporter's Lincoln,* ed. Michael Burlingame (Lincoln: University of Nebraska Press, 1998), 61.

31. Owen T. Reeves, *Abraham Lincoln by Some Men Who Knew Him* (Pantagraph Printing & Stationery Co., 1910), 21.

32. Mason Locke Weems, *A History of the Life and Death, Virtues and Exploits of General George Washington* (1809), 8.

33. Id. at 41, 129, 176, 179, 181, 186, 191.

34. Abraham Lincoln, Address to the New Jersey State Senate, Trenton, New Jersey, February 21, 1861.

35. William H. Herndon, *Herndon's Lincoln* (Herndon's Lincoln Pub. Co., 1888), 437.

36. Id.

37. Douglas L. Wilson, "Lincoln's Rhetoric," *Journal of the Abraham Lincoln Association* 34, no. 1 (Winter 2013): 1–17.

38. Grimshaw's *History of the United States* (1820).

39. Abraham Lincoln, Speech on the Kansas-Nebraska Act, October 16, 1856.

40. Abraham Lincoln, Peoria Speech, October 16, 1854.

41. Dennis Hanks to Herndon, June 13, 1865, in *Herndon's Informants,* 37.

42. Richard Carwardine, *Lincoln's Sense of Humor* (Carbondale: Southern Illinois University Press, 2017), 9.

43. John L. Scripps to Herndon, June 24, 1865, in *Herndon's Informants,* 57.

44. Joseph C. Richardson to Herndon, September 14, 1865, in *Herndon's Informants,* 120.

45. Doris Kearns Goodwin, *A Team of Rivals: The Political Genius of Abraham Lincoln* (New York: Simon & Schuster, 2005), 51.

46. Sidney Blumenthal, *A Self-Made Man: The Political Life of Abraham Lincoln,* vol. 1 (New York: Simon & Schuster, 2016), 36, originally Beveridge, *Abraham Lincoln,* 1:86; and Whitney, *Life of Lincoln,* 1:48.

47. Whitney, *Life of Lincoln,* 1:48.

48. Originally in *Herndon's Informants,* 58, 114–15.

49. Dennis Hanks, interview with Herndon, June 13, 1865, in *Herndon's Informants,* 41.

50. Id.

51. Id.
52. Blumenthal, "Self-Made Man at 37" (originally in *Herndon's Informants*, 127, 132).
53. Blumenthal, "Self-Made Man at 46" (originally in *Herndon's Informants*, at 355, 374, 457.
54. Id.
55. Herndon, *Herndon's Lincoln*, 2:57.
56. Herndon interview, September 8, 1865, in *Herndon's Informants*, 103, 105.
57. Harry L. Watson, *Andrew Jackson v. Henry Clay: Democracy and Development in Antebellum America* (Boston: Bedford/St. Martin's, 1998), 23–55.
58. Henry Clay to B. B. Minor, May 3, 1851.
59. U.S. Senate, Art & History, "Blount Expulsion," https://www.senate.gov/artandhistory/history/common/expulsion_cases/Blount_expulsion.htm.
60. Henry Clay, Letter to Dr. R. Pindell, October 15, 1828, *The Private Correspondence of Henry Clay*, ed. Calvin Colton (1855), 207.
61. Aaron Burr to Henry Clay, November 27, 1806, *The Papers of Henry Clay: The Rising Statesman, 1797–1814* (2015), 1:256.
62. Aaron Burr to Henry Clay, December 1, 1806, *Papers of Henry Clay*, 1:256–57.
63. Defense of Aaron Burr, December 2, 1806; Defense of Aaron Burr, December 3, 1806, *Papers of Henry Clay*, 1:257–59.
64. Henry Clay to Col. Thomas Hart, February 1, 1807, *Papers of Henry Clay*, 1:273.
65. Dr. Anthony Hunn's Reply to "Regulus," June 7, 1808, *Papers of Henry Clay*, 1:338.
66. Andrew Jackson, *The Papers of Andrew Jackson: 1821–1824*, ed. Harold D. Moser et al. (1980), xiii–xiv.
67. John H. Eaton, *The Life of Andrew Jackson* (1817).
68. Henry Clay, "On American Industry," Speech before the House of Representatives, March 30 and 31, 1824, reprinted in *The Speeches of Henry Clay: Delivered in the Congress of the United States*, 268.
69. Id. at 283.
70. Donald, *Lincoln*, 110.
71. Richard R. Stenberg, "Jackson, Buchanan, and the 'Corrupt Bargain' Calumny," *Pennsylvania Magazine of History and Biography* 58, no. 1 (1934): 61–85, JSTOR, https://www.jstor.org/stable/20086857.
72. For a broader discussion of Jackson's influence on modern campaigning, see Lynn Hudson Parsons, *The Birth of Modern Politics: Andrew Jackson, John Quincy Adams, and the Election of 1828* (Oxford University Press, 2009).
73. Andrew Jackson, Veto Message Regarding Funding of Infrastructure Development, May 27, 1830, Miller Center, University of Virginia, https://millercenter.org/the-presidency/presidential-speeches/may-27-1830-veto-message-regarding-funding-infrastructure.
74. Id.
75. Id.
76. George Denison Prentice, *Biography of Henry Clay*, vol. 9 (1831).
77. Dennis Hanks, interview with Herndon, June 13, 1865, in *Herndon's Informants*, 41.
78. Robert L. Wilson to Herndon, February 10, 1866, in *Herndon's Informants*, 201.

79. Mentor Graham to Herndon, May 29, 1865, in *Herndon's Informants,* 8–9.
80. Royal Clary, interview with Herndon, [likely October 1866], *Herndon's Informants,* 370.
81. John Todd Stuart, interview with James Q. Howard, [May 1860], copy in John G. Nicolay's hand, John Hay Papers, RPB.
82. Graham to Herndon (interview), Petersburg, Illinois, May 29, 1865, in *Herndon's Informants,* 10.
83. Id.
84. Kunigunde Duncan and D. F. Nickols, *Mentor Graham: The Man Who Taught Lincoln* (Chicago: University of Chicago Press, 1944), 132.
85. J. Rowan Herndon to Herndon, May 28, 1865, in *Herndon's Informants,* 9.
86. Hardin Bale to Herndon, 1866, in *Herndon's Informants,* 528.
87. Caleb Carman to Herndon, October 12, 1866, in *Herndon's Informants,* 374.
88. Lincoln, *Collected Works,* vol. 8, January 25, 1865.
89. N. W. Branson to William Henry Herndon, August 3, 1865, in *Herndon's Informants,* 90.
90. Kenneth J. Winkle, *The Young Eagle: The Rise of Abraham Lincoln* (Lanham, MD: Taylor Trade Publishing/Rowman & Littlefield, 2001), 70.
91. Id.
92. T. G. Onstot, *Pioneers of Menard and Mason County* (1902), 70.
93. Abner Y. Ellis to Herndon, Letter 173.
94. Abner Y. Ellis to William Herndon, December 6, 1866, in *Herndon's Informants,* 502.
95. Lincoln, *Autobiography,* December 20, 1859.
96. Id., June 1860.
97. Id., December 20, 1859.
98. Edward J. Kempf, *Abraham Lincoln's Philosophy of Common Sense: An Analytical Biography of a Great Mind* (New York: New York Academy of Sciences, 1965), 1:171.
99. John Todd Stuart, interview with Herndon, [1865–1866], in *Herndon's Informants,* 481.
100. John Todd Stuart, interview with John G. Nicolay, June 23, 1875, in Michael Burlingame, ed., *An Oral History of Abraham Lincoln: John G. Nicolay's Interviews and Essays* (Carbondale: Southern Illinois University Press, 2006), 8–9.
101. Id. at 9.

CHAPTER TWO: FINDING THE PATH TO CONGRESS (1834–1844)

1. Henry Clay, "The American System," Speech made in U.S. Senate, February 2, 3, and 6, 1832.
2. Abraham Lincoln, Address to the People of Sangamon County, Mar. 9, 1832, http://history.furman.edu/benson/fywbio/LincolnSangamon_1832.htm.
3. Id.
4. Id.
5. George D. Prentice, *Biography of Henry Clay* (1831), 25.
6. Id. at 25–26.
7. Abraham Lincoln, First Political Announcement, New Salem, Illinois, March 9, 1832.

8. Id.

9. Abraham Lincoln, *Collected Works of Abraham Lincoln*, 8 vols., ed. Roy Basler et al. (New Brunswick, NJ: Rutgers University Press, 1953–1955), 1:5.

10. Id. at 5–7.

11. Id. at 8.

12. Id.

13. Michael Burlingame, *Abraham Lincoln: A Life*, vol. 1 (Baltimore, MD: Johns Hopkins University Press, 2008), 73; and Abner Ellis to Herndon, January 1866, in William Henry Herndon and Jesse William Weik, *Herndon's Informants: Letters, Interviews, and Statements About Abraham Lincoln*, ed. Douglas L. Wilson and Rodney O. Davis (Champaign: University of Illinois Press, 1998), 171.

14. S. T. Logan interview with John G. Nicolay, July 6, 1875, in Michael Burlingame, ed., *An Oral History of Abraham Lincoln: John G. Nicolay's Interviews and Essays* (Carbondale: Southern Illinois University Press, 2006), 35.

15. President Jackson's Proclamation Regarding Nullification, December 10, 1832.

16. Sydney Blumenthal, *A Self-Made Man: The Political Life of Abraham Lincoln* (New York: Simon & Schuster, 2016), 1:61.

17. John Todd Stuart, interview with John G. Nicolay, Springfield, Illinois, June 23, 1875, in Burlingame, ed., *Oral History of Abraham Lincoln*, 11.

18. Id. at 10.

19. Lincoln, *Autobiography*, June 1860, in Lincoln, *Collected Works*.

20. John Todd Stuart, interview with John G. Nicolay, Springfield, Illinois, June 23, 1875, in Burlingame, ed., *Oral History of Abraham Lincoln*, 10.

21. William H. Herndon and Jesse William Weik, *Herndon's Lincoln: The True Story of a Great Life* (Springfield, IL: Herndon's Lincoln Publishing Co., 1888), 1:181.

22. Lincoln, *Autobiography*, June 1860.

23. Id.

24. Ron J. Keller, *Lincoln in the Illinois Legislature* (Carbondale: Southern Illinois University Press, 2019), 19.

25. Id.

26. Id.

27. John G. Nocolay, conversation with Hon. J. T. Stuart, June 23, 1875, in Burlingame, ed., *Oral History of Abraham Lincoln*, 11.

28. John Todd Stuart, interview with John G. Nicolay, Springfield, Illinois, June 23, 1875, in Burlingame, ed., *Oral History of Abraham Lincoln*, 11.

29. Id.

30. John G. Nicolay and John Hay, *Abraham Lincoln: A History* (1914), 1:103.

31. Herndon and Weik, *Herndon's Lincoln*, 2:375.

32. The original source is Caroline Owsley Brown writing in the *Journal of the Illinois State Historical Society* 15, no. 1 (1922): 490, JSTOR, https://www.jstor.org/stable/pdf/40186857.pdf.

33. This is from the Scripps autobiography that Lincoln prepared and was published first in the *Chicago Press and Tribune* in 1860 and then later issued by Horace Greeley as *Tribune Tracts*, no. 6.

34. Lincoln to Isham Reavis, November 5, 1855, in Lincoln, *Collected Works*, 2:328.

35. Conversation with Hon. J. K. Dubois in Burlingame, ed., *Oral History of Abraham Lincoln*, 30.

36. J. Rowan Herndon to Herndon, May 28, 1865, in *Herndon's Informants*, 7–8.

37. Blumenthal, *A Self-Made Man*, 1:91.

38. Lincoln gave this speech on June 20, 1848, to the U.S. House of Representatives.

39. Blumenthal, *A Self-Made Man*, 1:73.

40. Keller, *Lincoln in the Illinois Legislature*, 33.

41. Id. at 34.

42. Id. at 45.

43. Id.

44. Stephen A. Douglas, Letter to the Editor of the *Illinois Patriot*, March 8, 1837.

45. Robert L. Wilson to Herndon, February 10, 1866, in *Herndon's Informants*, 204.

46. Burlingame, *Abraham Lincoln: A Life*, 1:120, fn. 209.

47. *Lincoln: A Corporate Lawyer*, 397.

48. Abraham Lincoln to William A. Minshall, December 7, 1837, in Lincoln, *Collected Works*, 1:107.

49. Kenneth J. Winkle, *The Young Eagle: The Rise of Abraham Lincoln* (Lanham, MD: Taylor Trade Publishing/Rowman & Littlefield, 2001), 164.

50. Lincoln speech in Chicago on October 27, 1854, as reported on October 30 in the *Chicago Daily Journal*.

51. Id.

52. Abraham Lincoln and Dan Stone, "Protest in Illinois Legislature on Slavery, March 3, 1837," in Lincoln, *Collected Works*, 1:74–75.

53. Address by Abraham Lincoln before the Young Men's Lyceum of Springfield, Illinois, as it appeared in the *Sangamo Journal*, February 3, 1838, in Lincoln, *Collected Works*, 1:108–15.

54. Id.

55. Id.

56. Id.

57. Id.

58. Id.

59. Id.

60. Id.

61. Id.

62. Id.

63. Id.

64. Id.

65. Id.

66. Id.

67. Burlingame, *Abraham Lincoln: A Life*, 1:151.

68. Abraham Lincoln, Speech on National Bank, December 20, 1839, in *The Papers and Writings of Abraham Lincoln*, 1:70.

69. Id. at 71.

70. Id. at 72.

71. Id. at 73.

72. Id.

73. George W. Smith, *When Lincoln Came to Egypt* (Carbondale: Southern Illinois University Press, 2016), 51.

74. Id.
75. Hezekiah Morse Wead, Diary, July 15, 1847, in *Herndon's Informants*.
76. Brian R. Dirck, *Lincoln the Lawyer* (Champaign: University of Illinois Press, 2007), 25.
77. Burlingame, *Abraham Lincoln: A Life*, 1:184.
78. *Sangamo Journal*, April 13, 1843.
79. Id.
80. "Conversation with Hon. Stephen T. Logan," in Burlingame, ed., *Oral History of Abraham Lincoln*, 38.
81. John G. Nicolay, conversation with Hon. Stephen T. Logan, Springfield, Illinois, July 6, 1875, in Burlingame, ed., *Oral History of Abraham Lincoln*, 37.
82. Id.
83. Id.
84. Id.
85. Usher F. Linder, *Reminiscences of the Early Bench and Bar of Illinois* (Chicago: Chicago Legal News Company, 1879), 155.
86. Reminiscences of R. R. Hitt, in Otis B. Goodall, "Hon. Robert Roberts Hitt," *Phonographic Magazine* 7 (June 1, 1893): 206–7.
87. *Illinois State Journal* (Springfield), July 19, 1880.
88. Burlingame, *Abraham Lincoln: A Life*, 1:186.
89. Id.
90. McClernand was an Illinois Democratic legislative leader.
91. Howard Gillman et al., *American Constitutionalism*, vol. 1: *Structures of Government* (New York: Oxford University Press, 2013), supplementary material, *Field v. People of the State of Illinois, ex rel. McClernand*, 3 Ill. 79 (1839).
92. Protest dated February 26, 1841, in Lincoln, *Collected Works*, 1:245–49.
93. Id. at 247.
94. Id. at 245–47.
95. Burlingame, *Abraham Lincoln: A Life*, 1:164.
96. Id.
97. Ivor D. Spencer, *The Victor and the Spoils: A Life of William L. Marcy* (Providence, RI: Brown University Press, 1959), 58–60.
98. Blumenthal, *A Self-Made Man*, 1:265.
99. *Lost Townships* (The Rebecca Letter), August 27, 1842, in *The Papers and Writings of Abraham Lincoln*, 1:163.
100. James Shields to Lincoln, September 17, 1842, in *The Papers and Writings of Abraham Lincoln*, 1:168.
101. Walter Barlow Stevens, *A Reporter's Lincoln*, ed. Michael Burlingame (Lincoln: University of Nebraska Press, 1998), 16–18.
102. U.S. Constitution, Art. I, § 6, cl. 2.
103. Lincoln to John Todd Stuart, January 23, 1841, in Lincoln, *Collected Works*, 1:229.
104. Joshua F. Speed to Herndon, 1865–66, in *Herndon's Informants*, 475.
105. Joshua F. Speed to Herndon, February 7, 1866, in *Herndon's Informants*, 197.
106. Lincoln to Joshua F. Speed, July 4, 1842, in Lincoln, *Collected Works*, 1:289.
107. Herndon and Weik, *Herndon's Lincoln*, 1:513.
108. Conversation with Hon. O. H. Browning at Leland Hotel, Springfield, Illinois,

June 17, 1875, in *Oral History of Abraham Lincoln*, 1–3; Herndon and Weik, *Herndon's Lincoln*, 1:229; and John Todd Stuart, interview with Herndon, in *Herndon's Informants*, 64.

109. For an in-depth historical analysis of this theory, see Wayne Calhoun Temple, *Abraham Lincoln: From Skeptic to Prophet* (Mahomet, IL: Mayhaven Publishing, 1995).

110. Henry Clay Whitney, *Life on the Sixth Circuit with Lincoln: With Sketches of Generals Grant, Sherman and McClellan, Judge Davis, Leonard Swett, and Other Contemporaries* (1892), 460.

111. Edward Sylvester Ellis, *The History of Our Country from the Discovery of America to the Present Time* (1900), 782.

112. Daniel Webster, Andrew Jackson, in Andrew Sloan Draper, *Draper's Self Culture: Ideals of American History* (1918), 135.

113. Alexis de Tocqueville, *Democracy in America* (G. Adlard, 1839), 1:412.

114. Id. at 262.

115. Robert V. Remini, "Texas Must be Ours," *American Heritage* (February–March 1986): 37.

116. Id. at 38.

117. Henry Clay to the editors of the *Washington Daily National Intelligencer*, April 17, 1844, in *The Papers of Henry Clay: The Rising Statesman, 1797–1814* (2015), 10:42.

118. Id. at 43–44.

119. Id. at 43.

120. Id.

121. Id. at 44.

122. Id. at 48.

123. *Washington Globe*, April 27, 1844.

124. Andrew Jackson to Francis Preston Blair, May 7, 1844, Manuscript/Mixed Material, Library of Congress, https://www.loc.gov/item/maj017662/.

125. Andrew Jackson to Francis Preston Blair, March 10, 1845, Manuscript/Mixed Material, Library of Congress, https://www.loc.gov/item/maj017996/.

126. See Eugene Irving McCormac, *James K. Polk: A Political Biography* (1922), 590 n. 64.

127. Lincoln to Williamson Durley, October 3, 1845, in Lincoln, *Collected Works*, 1:347.

CHAPTER THREE: CLAY MAN IN THE HOUSE (1844-1850)

1. Robert Merry, *A Country of Vast Designs* (New York: Simon & Schuster, 2009), 131.

2. James J. Polk, Inaugural Address, March 4, 1845, via Avalon Project at Yale Law School.

3. Id.

4. *Connecticut Herald* 28, no. 41 (August 30, 1831).

5. James J. Polk, Inaugural Address.

6. Id.

7. Id.

8. Id.

9. Id.

10. Id.

11. Id.

12. Ron J. Keller, *Lincoln in the Illinois Legislature* (Carbondale: Southern Illinois University Press, 2019), 108–9.

13. Id. at 109, quoting Douglas L. Wilson, *Honor's Voice: The Transformation of Abraham Lincoln* (New York: Vintage, 1998), 210.

14. Joseph Gillespie to Herndon, January 31, 1866, in William Henry Herndon and Jesse William Weik, *Herndon's Informants: Letters, Interviews, and Statements About Abraham Lincoln,* ed. Douglas L. Wilson and Rodney O. Davis (Champaign: University of Illinois Press, 1998), 181.

15. Ron Keller, *Lincoln in the Illinois Legislature,* 106, quoting Ida M. Tarbell, *The Life of Abraham Lincoln* (1900), 167.

16. Id., quoting *Alton Telegraph,* April 11, 1840.

17. Id., quoting *Illinois State Register,* October 16, 1840.

18. Id. at 108, quoting Ralph Gary, *Following in Lincoln's Footsteps: A Complete Annotated Reference to Hundreds of Historical Sites Visited by Abraham Lincoln* (New York: Carroll & Graf Publishers, 2001), 13.

19. Lincoln to John Hardin, January 19, 1846, Springfield, Illinois.

20. Lincoln to John Hardin, February 7, 1846, Springfield, Illinois.

21. Id.

22. Abraham Lincoln, Handbill Replying to Charges of Infidelity, in Lincoln, *Collected Works of Abraham Lincoln,* 8 vols., ed. Roy Basler et al. (New Brunswick, NJ: Rutgers University Press, 1953–1955), 1:383.

23. Sydney Blumenthal, *A Self-Made Man: The Political Life of Abraham Lincoln* (New York: Simon & Schuster, 2016) 1:326–27; and Ida M. Tarbell, *Abraham Lincoln and His Ancestors* (1924), 270–71. I found a longer version of Lincoln's reply that comes from the first Sandburg volume: Stephen Mansfield, *Lincoln's Battle with God: A President's Struggle with Faith and What It Meant for America* (Nashville, TN: Thomas Nelson, 2012).

24. Published on July 7, 1847, in the *New York Tribune;* also in Blumenthal, *A Self-Made Man,* 1:336.

25. Blumenthal, *A Self-Made Man,* 1:342, citing the website for Ashland, Henry Clay's estate.

26. Id., citing Robert V. Remini, *Henry Clay: Statesmen of the Union* (New York: W. W. Norton, 1991), 692–94.

27. Id. at 343.

28. Market speech, November 13, 1847.

29. Id.

30. Id.

31. Id.

32. Id.

33. Id.

34. Id.

35. Blumenthal, *A Self-Made Man,* 1:334.

36. Id.

37. Charles Dickens, *American Notes* (London: Hazell, Watson and Viney, 1932), 97.

38. Michael Burlingame, *Abraham Lincoln: A Life*, vol. 1 (Baltimore, MD: Johns Hopkins University Press, 2008), 258, quoting Alexander MacKay, *The Western World, or, Travels in the United States in 1846–47*, 3 vols. (London: Richard Bentley, 1850), 3:177.

39. Chris DeRose, *Congressman Lincoln: The Making of America's Greatest President* (New York: Simon & Schuster, 2013), 76.

40. Abraham Lincoln to Mary Todd Lincoln, April 16, 1848, in Lincoln, *Collected Works*, 1:465.

41. Id.

42. Interview with Orlando Ficklin, *The Classmate: A Paper for Young People* (Cincinnati), February 6, 1926.

43. Abraham Lincoln, Speech at Peoria, Illinois, October 16, 1854, in Lincoln, *Collected Works*, 2:252.

44. Speech of the Hon. Alexander H. Stephens, February 12, 1878, in Richard Malcolm Johnston and William Hand Browne, *Life of Alexander H. Stephens* (1883), 624.

45. Abraham Lincoln to William H. Herndon, February 2, 1848, in Lincoln, *Collected Works*, 1:448.

46. *Congressional Globe,* 30th Congress, 1st Session, Appendix, 163 (February 2, 1848).

47. Abraham Lincoln to William Herndon, January 8, 1848, in Lincoln, *Collected Works*, 1:430.

48. Abraham Lincoln, Remarks in the United States House of Representatives Concerning Postal Contracts, January 5, 1848, in Lincoln, *Collected Works*, 1:426, from *Congressional Globe,* 30th Congress, 1st Session, January 5, 1848.

49. Samuel C. Busey, *Personal Reminiscences and Recollections of Forty-Six Years in the Medical Society of the District of Columbia* (Washington, D.C., 1895), 25.

50. *Congressional Globe,* 30th Congress, 1st Session, 64 (1847).

51. *Congressional Globe,* 30th Congress, 1st Session, 95 (1848).

52. Abraham Lincoln, Speech in United States House of Representatives: The War with Mexico, January 12, 1848, in Lincoln, *Collected Works*, 1:432.

53. Henry Clay, *The Works of Henry Clay*, ed. Calvin Colton (1904), 67.

54. Id. at 68.

55. Abraham Lincoln, Speech in United States House of Representatives: The War with Mexico, January 12, 1848, in Lincoln, *Collected Works*, 1:433–38.

56. Id. at 432.

57. Id. at 433.

58. Id.

59. Id. at 440.

60. Id.

61. Id.

62. Abraham Lincoln to William H. Herndon, January 8, 1848, in Lincoln, *Collected Works*, 1:431.

63. Id. at 437.

64. Id. at 438.

65. Abraham Lincoln, Speech to the United States House of Representatives: The War with Mexico, January 12, 1848, in Lincoln, *Collected Works*, 1:438–39.

66. Burlingame, *Abraham Lincoln: A Life*, 1:267.
67. Osborn H. Oldroyd, ed., *The Lincoln Memorial: Album-Immortelles* (1882), 241.
68. Id.
69. Kenneth J. Winkle, *Lincoln's Citadel* (New York: W. W. Norton, 2013), 252.
70. Id. at 35.
71. Id. at 48.
72. Id. at 47.
73. Id. at 59.
74. Id. at 42.
75. Speech by James Singleton in Jacksonville in 1858, quoted in the Lincoln Illinois correspondence, June 4, 1860, *Missouri Republican* (St. Louis), June 7, 1860, and in the Jacksonville correspondence, n.d., *Missouri Republican* (St. Louis), n.d., copied in the *Illinois State Register* (Springfield), September 24, 1858.
76. Caleb B. Smith to Allen Hamilton, February 15, 1848, Hamilton Papers; Thomas M. Brewer to William Schouler, March 28, 1848, Schouler Papers, Massachusetts Historical Society; and Mangum to William Graham, January 23, 1848, *The Papers of Willie Person Mangum*, ed. Henry Thomas Shanks (1956), 5:92–96.
77. Burlingame, *Abraham Lincoln: A Life*, 1:275.
78. Abraham Lincoln, *Life and Works of Abraham Lincoln*, Marion Mills Miller, ed. (1907), 3:156.
79. Abraham Lincoln, Speech in United States House of Representatives on the Presidential Question, July 27, 1848, in Lincoln, *Collected Works*, 1:504.
80. Id. at 505.
81. Richard Carwardine, *Lincoln's Sense of Humor* (Carbondale: Southern Illinois University Press, 2017), 24.
82. Id.
83. Lincoln, *Collected Works*, 1:502.
84. Id. at 509–10.
85. Id. at 514.
86. Id.
87. Abraham Lincoln to William H. Herndon, June 22, 1848, in Lincoln, *Collected Works*, 1:491.
88. Id. at 492.
89. Francis B. Carpenter, "A Day with Governor Seward at Auburn," July 1870, Seward Papers, University of Rochester.
90. Frederick W. Seward, *Seward at Washington as Senator and Secretary of State: A Memoir of His Life, with Selections from His Letters* (1891), 1:80.
91. *A Sketch of the Life and Character of Gen. Taylor* (1847), 11–12.
92. Id.
93. Id. at 34–35.
94. Abraham Lincoln to William H. Herndon, January 8, 1848, in Lincoln, *Collected Works*, 1:430–31.
95. Abraham Lincoln to Davis, February 12, 1849, in Roy P. Basler, ed., *Collected Works of Abraham Lincoln: Supplement 1832–1864* (Westport, CT: Greenwood Press, 1974), 14.
96. Abraham Lincoln to Mary Todd Lincoln, April 16, 1848, in Lincoln, *Collected Works*, 1:465–66.

97. Mary Todd Lincoln to Abraham Lincoln, May 1848.

98. Abraham Lincoln to William B. Warren and others, April 7, 1849, in Lincoln, *Collected Works*, 2:41.

99. Burlingame, *Abraham Lincoln: A Life*, 1:297, quoting Abraham Lincoln to William B. Warren and others, April 7, 1849, in Lincoln, *Collected Works*, 2:41.

100. Abraham Lincoln to Josiah M. Lucas, April 25, 1849, in Lincoln, *Collected Works*, 2:43.

101. Id.

102. Burlingame, *Abraham Lincoln: A Life*, 1:300.

103. Abraham Lincoln to Josiah M. Lucas, April 25, 1849, in Lincoln, *Collected Works*, 2:43.

104. Abraham Lincoln to Elisha Embree, May 25, 1849, in Lincoln, *Collected Works*, 2:51.

105. Thomas F. Schwartz, "An Egregious Political Blunder: Justin Butterfield, Lincoln, and Illinois Whiggery," *Papers of the Abraham Lincoln Association* 8 (1986), 15, JSTOR, https://www.jstor.org/stable/20148848?seq=1#metadata_info_tab_contents.

106. Abraham Lincoln to David Davis, July 6, 1849, in Lincoln, *Collected Works, First Supplement*, 16.

107. Kenneth J. Winkle, *The Young Eagle: The Rise of Abraham Lincoln* (Lanham, MD: Taylor Trade Publishing/Rowman & Littlefield, 2001), 248.

CHAPTER FOUR: LEARNING FROM FAILURE (1849–1856)

1. William Herndon, *Herndon on Lincoln: Letters*, ed. Douglas L. Wilson and Rodney O. Davis (Galesburg, IL: Knox College Lincoln Studies Center, 2016), 102.

2. David H. Donald, *We Are Lincoln Men* (New York: Simon & Schuster, 2003), 96.

3. Id. at 28.

4. Id.

5. Leonard Swett to Herndon, January 17, 1866, in William Henry Herndon and Jesse William Weik, *Herndon's Informants: Letters, Interviews, and Statements About Abraham Lincoln*, ed. Douglas L. Wilson and Rodney O. Davis (Champaign: University of Illinois Press, 1998), 168.

6. Donald, *We Are Lincoln Men*, 76.

7. John T. Stuart to Herndon, late June 1865, in *Herndon's Informants*, 63.

8. David Davis to Herndon, September 19–20, 1866, in *Herndon's Informants*, 346, 348.

9. Elizabeth Todd Edwards to Herndon, 1865–1866, in *Herndon's Informants*, 443.

10. Kenneth J. Winkle, *The Young Eagle: The Rise of Abraham Lincoln* (Lanham, MD: Taylor Trade Publishing/Rowman & Littlefield, 2001), 229.

11. Gustave Koerner, *Memoirs of Gustave Koerner*, ed. Thomas J. McCormack (Cedar Rapids, IA: Torch Press, 1909), 2:112, accessed via HathiTrust.

12. Alexander McClure, *Abraham Lincoln and Men of War-Times*, 4th ed. (Times Pub. Co., 1892), 74.

13. Id. at 77.

14. Letter by John W. Bunn, *Abraham Lincoln by Some Men Who Knew Him* (Bloomington, IL: Pantagraph Printing and Stationery Co., 1910), 150–51.

15. Frank Van der Linden, *Lincoln: The Road to War* (Golden, CO: Fulcrum Publishing, 1998), 109.

16. Donald, *We Are Lincoln Men,* 139.

17. Abraham Lincoln, "Fragment: Notes for a Law Lecture," July 1, 1850, in *Collected Works of Abraham Lincoln,* 8 vols., ed. Roy Basler et al. (New Brunswick, NJ: Rutgers University Press, 1953–1955), 2:81.

18. Abraham Lincoln, "Fragment on Stephen A. Douglas," December 1856?, in Lincoln, *Collected Works,* 2:382–83.

19. Id. at 7.

20. Id.

21. Abraham Lincoln, "Communication to the People of Sangamo County," March 9, 1832, in Lincoln, *Collected Works,* 1:8–9.

22. Abraham Lincoln, "Letter to George B. McClellan," October 13, 1862, in Lincoln, *Collected Works,* 5:461.

23. Abraham Lincoln, "Fragment: Notes for a Law Lecture," July 1, 1850, in Lincoln, *Collected Works,* 2:81.

24. Abraham Lincoln, "Letter to Isham Reavis," November 5, 1855, in Lincoln, *Collected Works,* 2:327.

25. Abraham Lincoln, "Letter to William Grigsby," August 3, 1858, in Lincoln, *Collected Works,* 2:535.

26. Abraham Lincoln, "Letter to James Thornton," December 2, 1858, in Lincoln, *Collected Works,* 3:344.

27. Abraham Lincoln, "Letter to Isham Reavis," November 5, 1855, in Lincoln, *Collected Works,* 2:327.

28. John M. Hay, *Addresses of John Hay* (Washington, D.C: Divine Press, 1906), 335, per Google Scholar.

29. Abraham Lincoln, "Letter to James H. Hackett," August 17, 1863, in Lincoln, *Collected Works,* 6:392.

30. William Shakespeare, *Julius Caesar,* Act III, Scene II.

31. Herndon, *Herndon's Lincoln,* 332.

32. Id. at 317–18.

33. David Herbert Donald, *Lincoln* (New York: Simon & Schuster, 1995), 127, quoting Herndon to Weik, November 19, 1885, and January 8, 1886; and "Lincoln's Domestic Life," undated Herndon monograph, copy, Herndon-Weik Collection.

34. Brian R. Dirck, *Lincoln the Lawyer* (Champaign: University of Illinois Press, 2007), 39.

35. Abraham Lincoln, "Letter to William H. Herndon," July 10, 1848, in Lincoln, *Collected Works,* 1:497–98.

36. Donald, *We Are Lincoln Men,* 73.

37. Id.

38. William H. Herndon, interview with David Davis, September 20, 1866.

39. Donald, *We Are Lincoln Men,* 73.

40. Id. at 73–74.

41. Id. at 74.

42. Henry Clay Whitney, *Life on the Circuit with Lincoln* (Boston: Estes and Lauriat, 1892), 255.

43. Michael Burlingame, *Abraham Lincoln: A Life*, vol. 1 (Baltimore, MD: Johns Hopkins University Press, 2008), 1:467.

44. Id.

45. Donald, *We Are Lincoln Men*, 75.

46. Thurlow Weed, *Life of Thurlow Weed* (autobiography) (Boston: Houghton Mifflin, 1884), 610–11.

47. Burlingame, *Abraham Lincoln: A Life*, 1:231.

48. Id. at 468.

49. Donald, *We Are Lincoln Men*, 75, quoting Herndon to Weik, February 9, 1886, Herndon-Weik Collection.

50. Id.

51. Carl Sandburg, *Abraham Lincoln: The Prairie Years and the War Years* (one-volume edition) (New York: Harcourt, Brace, 1954), 125.

52. Sydney Blumenthal, *A Self-Made Man: The Political Life of Abraham Lincoln* (New York: Simon & Schuster, 2016), 2:460.

53. Id.

54. Id.

55. Id.

56. Abraham Lincoln, "Fragment: Notes for a Law Lecture," July 1, 1850, in Lincoln, *Collected Works*, 2:81–82.

57. Abraham Lincoln, "Temperance Address," February 22, 1842, in Lincoln, *Collected Works*, 1:273.

58. Abraham Lincoln, "Fragment: Notes for a Law Lecture," July 1, 1850, in Lincoln, *Collected Works*, 2:81.

59. Henry B. Rankin, "Lincoln's Cooper Institute Speech: Fifty-Six Years Ago," *Illinois State Register* (Springfield), February 11, 1917, 8, The Builder, http://www.tbm100.org/Lib/Ran17.pdf.

60. Blumenthal, *A Self-Made Man*, 2:467.

61. Henry Clay, "Letter to James Harlan," March 16, 1850, in *The Works of Henry Clay: Comprising His Life, Correspondences, and Speeches*, ed. Calvin Colton (New York: G. P. Putnam's Sons, 1904), 603–4, via HeinOnline.

62. Taylor to John Allison, September 4, 1848, in Holman Hamilton, *Zachary Taylor*, vol. 2, *Soldier in the White House* (Indianapolis: Bobbs-Merrill, 1951), 121–24.

63. Zachary Taylor, Inaugural Address, March 5, 1849, via Avalon Project at Yale Law School.

64. Id.

65. Frank Freidel, *Presidents of the United States of America* (Washington, D.C.: White House Historical Association, 1996), 30.

66. Elbert B. Smith, *The Presidencies of Zachary Taylor and Millard Fillmore* (Lawrence: University Press of Kansas, 1988), 60.

67. Id.

68. Abraham Lincoln, "On the Life and Services of the Late President of the United States," July 25, 1850, in Lincoln, *Collected Works*, 2:83.

69. Id.

70. Id.

71. Id.

72. Id.

73. Id.
74. Id.
75. Id.
76. Id.
77. Id.
78. Id.
79. Id.
80. Id.
81. Id.
82. Id.
83. Id.
84. Id.
85. Id.
86. Id.
87. Id.
88. Id.
89. Id.
90. Henry Clay, Speech, January 29, 1850, via HathiTrust.
91. Id.
92. Id.
93. Id.
94. Id.
95. Henry Clay, *Speech of the Hon. Henry Clay, of Kentucky: On Taking Up His Compromise Resolutions on the Subject of Slavery, Delivered in Senate, Feb. 5th & 6th, 1850; As Reported by the National Intelligencer* (New York: Stringer & Townsend, 1850), 31–32.
96. Id.
97. Id.
98. Speech quoted from Daniel Webster, *"The Completest Man": Documents from the Papers of Daniel Webster,* ed. Kenneth E. Shewmaker (Lebanon, NH: Dartmouth College Press, 1990), 121–30, https://www.dartmouth.edu/~dwebster/speeches/seventh-march.html.
99. Id.
100. William H. Seward, speech, "On the Admission of California, U.S. Senate, March 11, 1850, https://archive.org/stream/williamhspeech00sewarich/williamhspeech00sewarich_djvu.txt.
101. Id.
102. Id.
103. John C. Calhoun, Speech to the United States Senate Against the Compromise of 1850, March 4, 1850, in John C. Calhoun Papers (Library of Congress).
104. Id.
105. Id.
106. Id.
107. Id.
108. Id.
109. Id.
110. Id.

111. Eulogies Delivered in the Senate and House of Representatives of the United States on the Life and Character of Hon. John C. Calhoun, of South Carolina, Hon. Henry Clay, of Kentucky, and Hon. Daniel Webster, of Massachusetts (Washington, D.C.: Foster & Cochran, 1856), 15.

112. Id.

113. Blumenthal, *A Self-Made Man*, 2:71.

114. Id. at 542.

115. Speech of Henry Clay, "A General Review of the Debate on the Compromise Bills," July 22, 1850, in *The Works of Henry Clay*, 9:542–43.

116. Id.

117. Id. at 560.

118. Id.

119. Id. at 555.

120. Id. at 540.

121. Id. at 557.

122. Id. at 561.

123. Id. at 563.

124. *The Annual Register; or, A View of the History and Politics of the Year 1850* (1851), 347.

125. Daniel Webster, "Speech at Syracuse," May 1851, *Mr. Webster's Speeches at Buffalo, Syracuse, and Albany* (New York: Mirror Office, 1851), 37.

126. Id.; "Speech at Buffalo," May 1851, 8.

127. Id.

128. *Southern Historical Society Papers* (Virginia Historical Society, 1888), 16:329.

129. Daniel Webster, *The Writings and Speeches of Daniel Webster*, ed. Edward Everett (1903), 13:439.

130. John T. Stuart, interview with William Henry Herndon, late June 1865, in *Herndon's Informants*, 64.

131. Id.

132. Abraham Lincoln, "Honors to Henry Clay," July 6, 1852, in Lincoln, *Collected Works*, 2:122–23.

133. Id. at 122.

134. Id.

135. Id.

136. Id. at 123.

137. Id.

138. Id.

139. Id. at 124.

140. Id. at 125.

141. Id.

142. Id.

143. Id. at 126.

144. Id.

145. Id.

146. Id. at 128.

147. Id. at 130.

148. Id.

149. Id.

150. Id.
151. Id. at 131.
152. Id.
153. Id.
154. Id.
155. Id. at 132.
156. Id.
157. Id.
158. Abraham Lincoln, Speech at Peoria, Illinois, October 16, 1854, in Lincoln, *Collected Works*, 2:248.
159. Id. at 249.
160. Abraham Lincoln to Henry L. Pierce and others, April 6, 1859, in Lincoln, *Collected Works*.
161. Abraham Lincoln, Speech at Peoria, in Lincoln, *Collected Works*, 2:248.
162. Id. at 251.
163. Id.
164. Id. at 255.
165. Id.
166. Id.
167. Id. at 256.
168. Id.
169. Id. at 265–66.
170. Id. at 266.
171. Id.
172. Id. at 255.
173. Id.
174. Id. at 266.
175. Id. at 267.
176. Id. at 274.
177. Id.
178. Id. at 272.
179. Id.
180. Id.
181. Id. at 271.
182. Id. at 259.
183. Id. at 268.
184. Id. at 261.
185. Id. at 262.
186. Id. at 261–62.
187. Id. at 282.
188. Id. at 248–83.

CHAPTER FIVE: BECOMING PRESIDENT (1856–1860)

1. Abraham Lincoln, "Fragment on Stephen A. Douglas," December 1856, in *Collected Works of Abraham Lincoln*, 8 vols., ed. Roy Basler et al. (New Brunswick, NJ: Rutgers University Press, 1953–1955), 2:383.

2. Lincoln's eulogy of Clay, in Lincoln, *Collected Works*, vol. 2 (Michigan archives).

3. James Oakes, *The Radical and the Republican: Frederick Douglass, Abraham Lincoln, and the Triumph of Antislavery Politics* (New York: W. W. Norton, 2007), 83, citing William Henry Herndon and Jesse William Weik, *Herndon's Informants: Letters, Interviews, and Statements About Abraham Lincoln*, ed. Douglas L. Wilson and Rodney O. Davis (Champaign: University of Illinois Press, 1998), 161–62.

4. Letter of John Whitfield Bunn from Springfield, Illinois, November 8, 1910, in Owen Thornton Reeves, *Abraham Lincoln, by Some Men Who Knew Him* (Bloomington, IL: Pantagraph Printing & Stationery, 1910), 150.

5. David Herbert Donald, *Lincoln* (New York: Simon & Schuster, 1995), 180, and Michael Burlingame, *Abraham Lincoln: A Life*, vol. 1 (Baltimore, MD: Johns Hopkins University Press, 2008), 514, citing Lincoln to Ichabod Codding, Springfield, Illinois, November 27, 1854.

6. Burlingame, *Abraham Lincoln: A Life*, 1:363.

7. Id. at 523, citing Lincoln to William H. Henderson, Springfield, Illinois, February 21, 1855.

8. Burlingame, *Abraham Lincoln: A Life*, 1:524, citing Davis to Julius Rockwell, Bloomington, Indiana, March 4, 1855.

9. Burlingame, *Abraham Lincoln: A Life*, 1:531.

10. Lincoln to Speed, August 24, 1855.

11. Id.

12. Id.

13. Id.

14. Citing Lincoln, *Collected Works*.

15. Id.

16. Id.

17. Browning to Trumbull, May 18, 1856, Trumbull Papers.

18. Burlingame, *Abraham Lincoln: A Life*, 1:540.

19. Id.

20. Maurice G. Baxter, *Orville H. Browning: Lincoln's Colleague and Critic* (Bloomington: Indiana University Press, 1957), 87.

21. Browning to Mrs. Browning, July 24, 1844.

22. Burlingame, *Abraham Lincoln: A Life*, 1:420.

23. Daniel Webster, Second Reply to Hayne, January 26–27, 1830, U.S. Senate, https://www.senate.gov/artandhistory/history/resources/pdf/WebsterReply.pdf, p. 77.

24. Franklin Pierce, speech to the Senate and House of Representatives, January 24, 1856.

25. Burlingame, *Abraham Lincoln: A Life*, citing Lincoln to Trumbull, Springfield, Illinois, June 7, 1856.

26. Burlingame, *Abraham Lincoln: A Life*, 1:546.

27. Id.

28. Id. at 547; and Donald, *Lincoln*, 193.

29. Donald, *Lincoln*, 193.

30. Speech at a Republican Banquet, Chicago, Illinois, December 10, 1856, in Lincoln, *Collected Works*, 2:385.

31. 60 U.S. 393, 407 (1857).

32. Id. at 450.

33. Speech at Chicago, Illinois, October 27, 1854, in Lincoln, *Collected Works*, 2:283.

34. Speech at Galena, Illinois, July 23, 1856, in Lincoln, *Collected Works*, 2:355.

35. Douglas speech on Kansas, Utah, and the *Dred Scott* decision, delivered at the State House in Springfield, Illinois, June 12, 1857.

36. Id.

37. Id.

38. Speech at Springfield, Illinois, June 26, 1857, in Lincoln, *Collected Works*, 2:401.

39. January 1857 speech, in Lincoln, *Collected Works*, 2:388.

40. June 26, 1857, speech, in Lincoln, *Collected Works*, 2:401.

41. Id. at 405.

42. Id. at 404.

43. Id. at 405.

44. Id. at 406.

45. Donald, *Lincoln*, 202.

46. Abraham Lincoln to B. Clarke Lundy, August 5, 1857, in Lincoln, *Collected Works*, 2:413.

47. Speech at Springfield, Illinois, June 26, 1857, in Lincoln, *Collected Works*, 2:400.

48. Robert W. Johannsen, *The Frontier, The Union, and Stephen A. Douglas* (Champaign: University of Illinois Press, 1989), 236; Stephen A. Douglas, Speech of Senator Douglas, of Illinois, on the President's Message, Delivered in the Senate of the United States, December 9, 1857.

49. Abraham Lincoln to Lyman Trumbull, June 23, 1858, in Lincoln, *Collected Works*, 2:472.

50. William H. Herndon, *Herndon's Lincoln* (Herndon's Lincoln Pub. Co., 1889), 396.

51. Leonard Swett to William H. Herndon, January 17, 1866, in *Herndon's Informants*, 163.

52. Herndon, *Herndon's Lincoln*, 398.

53. *Speeches of Haynes and Webster in the United States Senate* (1853), 37.

54. Abraham Lincoln, "A House Divided," Speech at Springfield, Illinois, in Lincoln, *Collected Works*, 2:461.

55. Id.

56. Id.

57. Donald, *Lincoln*, 206.

58. Lincoln, *Collected Works*, 2:465–66.

59. Id. at 467.

60. *Congressional Globe*, July 9, 1861, p. 30.

61. Abraham Lincoln, *Selections from the Writings of Abraham Lincoln*, ed. J. G. de Roulhac Hamilton (New York: Scott, Foresman & Co., 1922), 169.

62. Abraham Lincoln, "Speech at Springfield, Illinois," July 17, 1858, in Lincoln, *Collected Works*, 2:506.

63. Herndon, *Herndon's Lincoln*, 336–37.

64. Don F. Fehrenbacher and Virginia Fehrenbacher, *Recollected Words of Abraham Lincoln* (Redwood City CA: Stanford University Press, 1996), 371.

65. Joseph Gillespie to William H. Herndon, December 8, 1866, in *Herndon's Informants*, 507.

66. Chapman Coleman, ed., *The Life of John J. Crittenden* (1873), 2:152.
67. Allen Johnson, *Stephen A. Douglas: A Study in American Politics* (1908), 352.
68. Id. at 299.
69. Abraham Lincoln, Second Debate, in Freeport, Illinois, August 27, 1858.
70. Stephen Douglas, Second Debate, in Freeport, Illinois, August 27, 1858.
71. Id.
72. Id.
73. Abraham Lincoln to Henry Asbury, July 31, 1858, in Lincoln, *Collected Works,* 2:530.
74. Enoch Walter Skies and William Morse Keener, *The Growth of the Nation, 1837–1860* (1905), 13:444.
75. Josiah Gilbert Holland, *Life of Abraham Lincoln* (1866), 190.
76. Id.
77. Mr. Lincoln's Reply, in Lincoln, *Collected Works,* 3:28.
78. Id.
79. Id.
80. John G. Nicolay and John Hay, eds., *Abraham Lincoln: Complete Works* (1894), 1:447.
81. Id. at 448.
82. Abraham Lincoln, Sixth Debate, in Quincy, Illinois, October 13, 1858.
83. Id.
84. Stephen Douglas, Sixth Debate, in Quincy, Illinois, October 13, 1858.
85. Abraham Lincoln, Seventh Debate, in Alton, Illinois," October 15, 1858.
86. Id.
87. *Political Debates Between Hon. Abraham Lincoln and Hon. Stephen A. Douglas* (1860), 232.
88. Id. at 234.
89. Stephen A. Douglas, Seventh Debate, in Alton, Illinois, October 15, 1858.
90. Id.
91. Id.
92. Donald, *Lincoln,* 228.
93. Abraham Lincoln to Anson G. Henry, November 19, 1858, in Lincoln, *Collected Works,* 3:339.
94. Abraham Lincoln to Henry Asbury, November 19, 1858, in Lincoln, *Collected Works,* 3:339.
95. Abraham Lincoln to George Robertson, August 15, 1855, in Lincoln, *Collected Works,* 2:318.
96. James F. Rhodes, *History of the United States* (MacMillan, 1920), 2:328.
97. Abraham Lincoln, Speech at Columbus, Ohio, September 16, 1859, in Lincoln, *Collected Works,* 3:425.
98. Abraham Lincoln, Address at Cooper Institute, New York City, February 27, 1860, in Lincoln, *Collected Works,* 3:522.
99. Harold Holzer, *Lincoln at Cooper Union: The Speech That Made Abraham Lincoln President* (New York: Simon & Schuster, 2006), 128.
100. Lincoln, Address at Cooper Institute, in Lincoln, *Collected Works,* 3:549.
101. Id. at 550.
102. Holzer, *Lincoln at Cooper Union,* 121.

103. Id. at 122.

104. Id. at 122–23.

105. Id. at 124.

106. Gregory A. Borchard, *Abraham Lincoln and Horace Greeley* (Carbondale: Southern Illinois University Press, 2011), 59.

107. Orville Hickman Browning, *The Diary of Orville Hickman Browning: 1850–1864*, ed. Theodore Calvin Pease (Champaign: University of Illinois, 1925), 1:406.

108. Michael S. Green, *Lincoln and the Election of 1860* (Carbondale: Southern Illinois University Press, 2011), 55.

109. Abraham Lincoln, Telegraph to a Member of the Illinois Delegation, May 17, 1860, in *The Papers and Writings of Abraham Lincoln*, 5:687.

110. Horace Greeley, *Proceedings of the Republican National Convention* (1860), 108.

111. Doris Kearns Goodwin, *A Team of Rivals: The Political Genius of Abraham Lincoln* (New York: Simon & Schuster, 2005), 253.

112. Donald, *Lincoln*, 251.

113. Green, *Lincoln and the Election of 1860*, 63.

114. John B. Alley, *Reminiscences of Abraham Lincoln by Distinguished Men of His Time*, ed. Allen T. Rice (North American Pub. Co., 1886), 575.

CHAPTER SIX: "HE WAS ENTIRELY IGNORANT NOT ONLY OF THE DUTIES, BUT OF THE MANNER OF DOING BUSINESS" (1860–1861)

1. Robert L. Wilson to William H. Herndon, February 10, 1866, in William Henry Herndon and Jesse William Weik, *Herndon's Informants: Letters, Interviews, and Statements About Abraham Lincoln*, ed. Douglas L. Wilson and Rodney O. Davis (Champaign: University of Illinois Press, 1998), 207.

2. James K. Polk, *The Diary of James K. Polk During His Presidency: 1845–1849* (A.C. McClurg & Co., 1910), 261.

3. Orville Hickman Browning, diary entry for July 3, 1861, in *The Diary of Orville Hickman Browning: 1850–1864*, ed. Theodore Calvin Pease (Champaign: University of Illinois, 1925).

4. Joseph Holt and Winfield Scott to Lincoln, March 5, 1861.

5. *Diary of Orville Hickman Browning*, 1:xvi.

6. Harold Holzer, *Lincoln President-Elect: Abraham Lincoln and the Great Secession Winter 1860–1861* (New York: Simon & Schuster, 2008), 59.

7. Id. at 78.

8. Henry Villard, *Memoirs of Henry Villard* (Boston: Houghton, Mifflin, 1904), 1:93.

9. Holzer, *Lincoln President-Elect*, 89.

10. Id. at 90.

11. Henry Villard, *Sixteenth President-in-Waiting: Abraham Lincoln and the Springfield Dispatches of Henry Villard, 1860–1861*, ed. Michael Burlingame (Carbondale: Southern Illinois University Press, 2018), 134.

12. Id. at 135.

13. Id. at 136.

14. Id.

15. Holzer, *Lincoln President-Elect*, 189.

16. Abraham Lincoln, "Letter to Daniel Ullman," February 1, 1861, in Abraham

Lincoln, *Collected Works of Abraham Lincoln*, 8 vols., ed. Roy Basler et al. (New Brunswick, NJ: Rutgers University Press, 1953–1955), 4:184.

17. Holzer, *Lincoln President-Elect,* 189.

18. Ted Widmer, *Lincoln on the Verge: Thirteen Days to Washington* (New York: Simon & Schuster, 2020), 277 (quoting both the newspaper and Fillmore).

19. Lincoln, *Collected Works,* 4:214.

20. Id.

21. Abraham Lincoln, Speech in Independence Hall, Philadelphia, February 22, 1861, in Lincoln, *Collected Works,* 4:2401–41.

22. Quoted in David M. Potter, *The Impending Crisis, 1848–1861* (New York: Harper, 1976), 432.

23. Holzer, *Lincoln President-Elect,* 60.

24. Id.

25. John B. Alley, *Reminiscences of Abraham Lincoln by Distinguished Men of His Time,* ed. Allen T. Rice (North American Pub. Co., 1886), 603.

26. Id.

27. Holzer, *Lincoln President-Elect,* 312.

28. Id.

29. Id.

30. Id.

31. Id.

32. Id.

33. Id. at 296.

34. Seward to Lincoln, February 1861.

35. Diary entry for February 9, 1861, in *Diary of Orville Hickman Browning.*

36. Id.

37. Browning to Lincoln, February 17, 1861.

38. Id.

39. Maurice G. Baxter, *Orville H. Browning: Lincoln's Colleague and Critic* (Bloomington: Indiana University Press, 1957), 110.

40. Id. at 109–10.

41. President Andrew Jackson's Proclamation Regarding Nullification, December 10, 1832, via Avalon Project at Yale Law School.

42. Abraham Lincoln, First Inaugural Address, March 4, 1861, in Lincoln, *Collected Works,* 4:265.

43. Jackson's Proclamation Regarding Nullification, December 10, 1832, via Avalon Project at Yale Law School.

44. Lincoln, First Inaugural Address, in Lincoln, *Collected Works,* 4:265.

45. Jackson's Proclamation Regarding Nullification.

46. Id.

47. Lincoln, First Inaugural Address, in Lincoln, *Collected Works,* 4:268.

48. Id. at 267.

49. Id. at 268.

50. Jackson's Proclamation Regarding Nullification.

51. Lincoln, *Collected Works,* 4:265, 270.

52. Jackson's Proclamation Regarding Nullification.

53. Id.

54. Lincoln, First Inaugural Address, in Lincoln, *Collected Works*, 4:265.

55. Id.

56. Jackson's Proclamation Regarding Nullification.

57. Lincoln, *Collected Works*, 4:271.

58. Id.

59. Henry Clay, Speech of Mr. Clay, of Kentucky, On the Measures of Compromise: Delivered in the Senate of the United States, July 22, 1850 (Washington, D.C.: J. T. Towers, 1850), 25.

60. Id.

61. Lincoln, Inaugural Address, in Lincoln, *Collected Works*.

62. Id. at 270.

63. Id. at 271.

64. Id.

65. Henry Clay, Speech, January 29, 1850, via HathiTrust, 24.

66. Lincoln, First Inaugural Address, in Lincoln, *Collected Works*, 4:271.

67. Richard Carwardine, *Lincoln's Sense of Humor* (Carbondale: Southern Illinois University Press, 2017), 33.

68. Joshua F. Speed to Herndon, February 7, 1866, in *Herndon's Informants*, 197.

69. Abraham Lincoln, First Debate with Stephen Douglas, Ottawa, Illinois, August 21, 1858.

70. Abraham Lincoln, Annual Address to Congress, December 1, 1862, in Lincoln, *Collected Works*, 5:535.

71. Abraham Lincoln to William H. Seward, December 8, 1860, in Lincoln, *Collected Works*, 4:148.

72. Abraham Lincoln to Thurlow Weed, March 15, 1865, in Lincoln, *Collected Works*, 8:356.

73. Holzer, *Lincoln President-Elect*, 103.

74. Walter Stahr, *Seward: Lincoln's Indispensable Man* (New York: Simon & Schuster, 2012), 244.

75. Michael Burlingame, *Abraham Lincoln: A Life*, vol. 1 (Baltimore, MD: Johns Hopkins University Press, 2008), 740.

76. Abraham Lincoln to Simon Cameron, January 3, 1861, in Lincoln, *Collected Works*, 4:169.

77. Noah Brooks, *Washington in Lincoln's Time* (New York: The Century Co., 1895), 49; and *Century Illustrated Monthly Magazine*, November 1894–April 1895, p. 147.

78. Holzer, *Lincoln President-Elect*, 104.

79. Id.

80. The other three were Polk, Taylor, and Van Buren.

81. William O. Stoddard, *Abraham Lincoln: The True Story of a Great Life* (Fords, Howard & Hulbert, 1885), 245.

82. John G. Nicolay and John Hay, *Abraham Lincoln: A History* (1890), 380–81.

83. Noah Brooks to George Witherle, December 23, 1863, in *Lincoln Observed: Civil War Dispatches of Noah Brooks*, ed. Michael Burlingame (Baltimore, MD: Johns Hopkins University Press, 1998), 97–98.

84. Gideon Welles, *Diary of Gideon Welles: Secretary of the Navy Under Lincoln and Johnson* (New York: Houghton Mifflin Co., 1911), 13.

85. Id.

86. Francis P. Blair to Montgomery Blair, March 12, 1861, Lincoln Papers, Library of Congress.

87. Allan Nevins, *The War for the Union: The Improvised War, 1861–1862* (New York: Charles Scribner's Sons, 1959), 48.

88. Welles, *Diary of Gideon Welles*, 13–14.

89. Id. at 14.

90. Francis P. Blair to Montgomery Blair, March 12, 1861.

91. Abraham Lincoln, Letter from the President to the Secretary of State, March 15, 1861, in *Lincoln: Speeches and Writings, 1859–1865* (New York: Library of America, 1989), 225.

92. Montgomery Blair to Lincoln, March 15, 1861.

93. Charles Francis Adams, Sr., March 29, 1861, diary entry, in Charles Francis Adams, Sr.: *The Civil War Diaries (Unverified Transcriptions)* (Boston: Massachusetts Historical Society, 2015), http://www.masshist.org/publications/cfa-civil-war/view?id=DCA61d0889.

94. *Diary of Gideon Welles*, 6, via Archive.org.

95. Id. at 9; and John G. Nicolay and John Hay, *Abraham Lincoln: A History* (1890), 390.

96. Letter from Francis Blair to A. Lincoln, March 18, 1861, quoted in Allan Nevins, *The War for the Union* (New York: Scribner, 1959), 1:48.

97. Stephen A. Hurlbut to Abraham Lincoln, May 27, 1861, in *Abraham Lincoln Papers: Series 1. General Correspondence, 1833–1916*, Library of Congress, https://www.loc.gov/item/mal2813300/.

98. John G. Nicolay and John Hay, *Abraham Lincoln: A History* (1890), 394.

99. Id. at 395.

100. Id. at 345.

101. Id. at 394.

102. William H. Seward to Abraham Lincoln, April 1, 1961, in *Abraham Lincoln Papers: Series 1. General Correspondence, 1833–1916*, Library of Congress, https://www.loc.gov/item/mal2813300/.

103. John G. Nicolay and John Hay, *Abraham Lincoln: A History* (1890), 443.

104. *Diary of Gideon Welles*, 21, 25.

105. Id. at 24.

106. Virginia Woodbury Fox, Diary, April 18, 1861, available in microfilm format in the Levi Woodbury Family papers, Manuscript Division, Library of Congress.

107. *Abraham Lincoln, His Speeches and Writings*, quoting on-camera tour of Lincoln's presidential office, with Harold Holzer, C-SPAN (2007); and Mark E. Neely Jr., "Wilderness and the Cult of Manliness: Hooker, Lincoln, and Defeat," in Gabor S. Boritt, ed., *Lincoln's Generals* (New York: Oxford University Press, 1994), 51–77.

108. Abraham Lincoln, Reply to Baltimore Committee, April 22, 1861, in Lincoln, *Collected Works*, 4:342.

109. Id.

110. Abraham Lincoln, Proclamation Calling Militia and Convening Congress, April 15, 1861.

111. John Savage, *The Life and Public Services of Andrew Johnson, Seventeenth President of the United States* (1866), 163.

112. Paul Angle, ed., *The Lincoln Reader* (New Brunswick, NJ: Rutgers University Press, 1947), 357.

113. Abraham Lincoln, Reply to Baltimore Committee, April 22, 1861, in Lincoln, *Collected Works*, 4:341.

114. Id. at 342.

115. For a discussion of the myth of this quotation, see Stephen M. Engel, *American Politicians Confront the Court: Opposition Politics and Changing Responses to Judicial Power* (New York: Cambridge University Press, 2011), 134 n. 9.

116. Abraham Lincoln, Message to Congress in Special Session, July 4, 1861, in Lincoln, *Collected Works*, 4:430.

117. Abraham Lincoln, Speech at Havana, Illinois, August 14, 1858, in Lincoln, *Collected Works*, 2:542.

118. *General Orders, 1861, 1862 & 1863, Adapted for the Use of the Army and Navy*, ed. Thomas M. O'Brien (1864), 1:62.

119. Baxter, *Orville H. Browning*, 123.

120. Orville H. Browning to Abraham Lincoln, March 26, 1861, in *Abraham Lincoln Papers: Series 1. General Correspondence, 1833–1916*, Library of Congress, https://www.loc.gov/item/mal2813300/.

121. Henry Wilson to William Henry Herndon, Natick, Massachusetts, May 30, 1867, in *Herndon's Informants*, 562.

122. Diary entry for July 3, 1861, in *Diary of Orville Hickman Browning*, 1:476.

123. Ari Hoogenboom, "Gustavus Fox and the Relief of Fort Sumter," *Civil War History* 9, no. 4 (December 1963): 383–98, at 396.

124. Abraham Lincoln, Message to Congress, July 4, 1961, in *Abraham Lincoln Papers: Series 1. General Correspondence, 1833–1916*, Library of Congress, https://www.loc.gov/item/mal2813300/.

125. Michael Burlingame, ed., *With Lincoln in the White House: Letters, Memoranda, and Other Writings of John Nicolay, 1860–1865*, Memorandum, July 13, 1861, 48.

CHAPTER SEVEN: COMMANDER IN CHIEF (1861–1864)

1. *The American Quarterly Register and Magazine*, vol. 1, p. 533, via Google Books.

2. Lucien Bonaparte Chase, *History of the Polk Administration* (1850), 435, via Google Books.

3. Neely, "War and Partisanship: What Lincoln Learned from James K. Polk," *Journal of the Illinois State Historical Society* 74, no. 3 (1981): 213.

4. Edgar Curtis Taylor, "Lincoln the Internationalist," *Abraham Lincoln Quarterly* 4, no. 2 (June 1946): 73, https://quod.lib.umich.edu/a/alajournals/0599998.0004.002/21.

5. Abraham Lincoln, First Inaugural Address, March 4, 1861, in *Collected Works of Abraham Lincoln*, 8 vols., ed. Roy Basler et al. (New Brunswick, NJ: Rutgers University Press, 1953–1955), 4:268.

6. Abraham Lincoln, Message to Congress, July 4, 1961, in *Abraham Lincoln Papers: Series 1. General Correspondence, 1833–1916*, Library of Congress, https://www.loc.gov/item/mal2813300/.

7. Citing speech to Wisconsin State Agricultural Society, Milwaukee, September 30, 1859; and Lincoln, *Collected Works*, 3:479.

8. Id.
9. Michael Burlingame, *Abraham Lincoln: A Life,* vol. 1 (Baltimore, MD: Johns Hopkins University Press, 2008), 63.
10. William H. Herndon, *Herndon's Lincoln* (Herndon's Lincoln Pub. Co., 1889), 337.
11. James M. McPherson, *Tried by War: Abraham Lincoln as Commander in Chief* (New York: Penguin, 2008), introduction.
12. Michael Burlingame, ed., *Lincoln's Journalist: John Hay's Anonymous Writings for the Press, 1860–1864* (Carbondale: Southern Illinois University Press, 1999), 366 n. 1.
13. Abraham Lincoln to Winfield Scott, April 1, 1861, in Lincoln, *Collected Works,* 4:316.
14. Carl Sandburg, *Abraham Lincoln: The Prairie Years and the War Years* (one-volume edition) (New York: Harcourt, Brace, 1954), 258.
15. Id.
16. Burlingame, *Abraham Lincoln: A Life,* 2:199.
17. David Herbert Donald, *Lincoln* (New York: Simon & Schuster, 1995), 319.
18. David Donald, "Getting Right with Lincoln," *The Atlantic* (1956), https://www
    .theatlantic.com/past/docs/issues/95nov/lincoln/lincrite.htm.
19. Abraham Lincoln to Carl Schurz, November 10, 1862, in Lincoln, *Collected Works,* 5:494.
20. Robert Remini, *Daniel Webster: The Man and His Time* (New York: W. W. Norton, 1997), 520–21.
21. Burlingame, *Abraham Lincoln: A Life,* 2:224–25.
22. Id. at 360.
23. McPherson, *Tried by War,* 66. (It appears there are variations of this quote, but this is the only book where I could find it.)
24. Lincoln, *Collected Works,* 5:111.
25. Burlingame, *Abraham Lincoln: A Life,* 2:297.
26. McPherson, *Tried by War,* ch. 3.
27. Id.
28. Id.
29. George B. McClellan, *McClellan's Own Story: The War for Union, the Soldiers Who Fought It, the Civilians Who Directed It and His Relations to It and to Them* (New York: Charles L. Webster & Co., 1887), 546.
30. Lincoln, *Collected Works,* 5:486.
31. Ethan Rafuse, *McClellan's War: The Failure of Moderation in the Struggle for the Union* (Bloomington: Indiana University Press, 2011), 376.
32. Burlingame, *Abraham Lincoln: A Life,* 2:430.
33. McPherson, *Tried by War,* 145.
34. Id.
35. Donald, *Lincoln,* 402.
36. Orville Hickman Browning, *The Diary of Orville Hickman Browning: 1850–1864,* ed. Theodore Calvin Pease (Champaign: University of Illinois, 1925), 1:600–601.
37. Id. at 600.
38. Burlingame, *Abraham Lincoln: A Life,* 2:453.
39. Sandburg, *The Prairie Years* (one-volume edition), 333.
40. Doris Kearns Goodwin, *A Team of Rivals: The Political Genius of Abraham Lincoln*

(New York: Simon & Schuster, 2005), 490. It's possible the longer quote is elsewhere and I just couldn't pin it down.

41. Donald, *Lincoln,* 403.
42. Id.
43. Id. at 404.
44. Id.
45. Id.
46. Id.
47. Id.
48. Id.
49. Id.
50. Id.
51. Id.
52. Id. at 405.
53. Id.
54. Id.
55. Id.
56. Id. at 406.
57. Burlingame, *Abraham Lincoln: A Life,* 2:174.
58. *Diary of Orville Hickman Browning,* 1:478.
59. Orville Browning to Abraham Lincoln, September 17, 1861, reproduced in Burrus M. Carnahan, *Act of Justice: Lincoln's Emancipation Proclamation and the Law of War* (Lexington: University of Kentucky Press, 2011), 146.
60. Lincoln, *Collected Works,* 4:531.
61. Id.
62. Id. at 532.
63. Id.
64. Id.
65. Id. at 5:48–49.
66. Id. at 7:281.
67. McPherson, *Tried by War,* 86.
68. Abraham Lincoln, Message to Congress, March 6, 1862, in Lincoln, *Collected Works,* 5:144.
69. Abraham Lincoln, To the Senate and House of Representatives, July 17, 1862, in Lincoln, *Collected Works,* 5:331.
70. Id. at n. 3.
71. William Whiting, *The War Powers of the President, Military Arrests, and Reconstruction of the Union* (1864), 58.
72. *National Quarterly Review* 13 (1867): 387.
73. Francis Bicknell Carpenter, *Six Months at the White House with Abraham Lincoln* (1866), 22.
74. Illinois State Historical Society, *Journal of the Illinois State Historical Society* (1955): 448.
75. Id.
76. William Henry Herndon and Jesse William Weik, *Herndon's Informants: Letters, Interviews, and Statements About Abraham Lincoln,* ed. Douglas L. Wilson and Rodney O. Davis (Champaign: University of Illinois Press, 1998), 197.

77. Abraham Lincoln, Emancipation Proclamation, January 1, 1863, in Lincoln, *Collected Works*, 6:29.

78. Abraham Lincoln, Annual Message to Congress, December 1, 1862, in Lincoln, *Collected Works*, 5:537.

79. Id.

80. General Order No. 11 (1862).

81. Id.

82. Ron Chernow, *Grant* (New York: Penguin, 2017), 85 n. 20.

83. Albert Deane Richardson, *A Personal History of U.S. Grant* (1868), 277.

84. Francis Bicknell Carpenter, *Six Months at the White House with Abraham Lincoln* (1866), 269.

85. Frederick William Seward, *Seward at Washington as Senator and Secretary of State* (1891), 151.

86. Carpenter, *Six Months*, 269.

87. Id. at 87.

88. Id. at 270.

89. H. W. Halleck to Ulysses S. Grant, January 4, 1963, in United States War Department, *The War of the Rebellion* (1887), 1:17, 2:530.

90. Ulysses S. Grant, *The Papers of Ulysses S. Grant: December 9, 1862–March 31, 1863*, vol. 7, ed. John Y. Simon (Carbondale: Southern Illinois University Press, 1979), 54.

91. *Washington Correspondence*, January 8, 1863; "The Last of General Grant's Order," *Washington Correspondence*, January 23, 1863; *Washington Correspondence*, January 7, 1863; *New York Tribune*, January 8, 1863.

92. H. W. Halleck to Ulysses S. Grant, Washington, January 21, 1863, United States War Department, in *The War of the Rebellion*, 1:9, 24.

93. Elihu B. Washburne to Ulysses S. Grant, January 6, 1863, in *Papers of Ulysses S. Grant*, 7:55–56.

94. Id.

95. Jonathan D. Sarna, *When General Grant Expelled the Jews* (New York: Nextbook/Schocken, 2012), 25.

96. Don Seitz, *Artemus Ward: A Biography and Bibliography* (New York: Harper & Bros., 1919), 113–14.

97. Herndon, *Herndon's Lincoln*, 208.

98. Id.

99. Ted Widmer, *Martin Van Buren* (New York: Times Books, 2003), 147.

100. Tara McLellan McAndrew, "Flashback Springfield: Lincoln, Van Buren Had Unlikely Meeting in Rochester," *State Journal Register*, October 31, 2015, https://www.sj-r.com/article/20151031/NEWS/151039892.

101. Herndon, *Herndon's Lincoln*, 503.

102. Id. at 504.

103. Id.

104. Id.

105. Edward Bates, *The Diary of Edward Bates: 1859–1866*, ed. Howard K. Beale (CreateSpace Independent Publishing Platform, 2013), 244.

106. John T. Stuart to Abraham Lincoln, January 24, 1862, Lincoln MSS.

107. *Diary of Orville Hickman Browning* 1:621.
108. *Prize Cases,* 67 U.S. 635, 667 (1863).
109. Id. at 669.
110. Mark E. Neely Jr. *Lincoln and the Triumph of the Nation: Constitutional Conflict in the American Civil War* (Chapel Hill: University of North Carolina Press, 2011), 206.
111. Eliakim Littell, *Littell's Living Age* (1916), 289, 629.
112. T. Harry WIlliams, *Lincoln and His Generals* (New York: Vintage, 2011), 269.
113. *Papers in Illinois History and Transactions for the Illinois State Historical Society for the Year 1906* (1906), 143.
114. Id. at 142.
115. Abraham Lincoln to James M. Cutts, Jr., October 26, 1863, in *Lincoln: Speeches and Writings 1859–1865* (New York: Library of America, 1989), 530.
116. Abraham Lincoln, Address Delivered at the Dedication of the Cemetery at Gettysburg, November 19, 1863, in Lincoln, *Collected Works,* 7:17.
117. Id.
118. Id. at 20–21.
119. Daniel Webster, *The Great Speeches and Orations of Daniel Webster,* ed. Edwin P. Whipple (1879), 257.
120. Lincoln, *Collected Works,* 7:264.
121. Id. at 265.
122. Id.
123. Abraham Lincoln, Address Delivered at the Dedication of the Cemetery at Gettysburg, in Lincoln, *Collected Works,* 7:19.
124. Id.
125. *The Living Age* 85 (1865): 283.
126. Ralph Waldo Emerson, *Emerson in His Journals,* ed. Joel Porte (Cambridge, MA: Harvard University Press, 1982), 421.
127. Herndon, *Herndon's Lincoln,* 571.
128. *Lincoln and the Civil War in the Diaries and Letters of John Hay,* ed. Tyler Dennett (1939), 121.
129. Edward Everett to Abraham Lincoln, November 20, 1863, *Abraham Lincoln Papers: Series 1, General Correspondence, 1833 to 1916,* Manuscript/Mixed Material, Library of Congress, https://www.loc.gov/item/mal2813300/.
130. Id.
131. Abraham Lincoln, Annual Message to Congress, December 8, 1863, in Lincoln, *Collected Works,* 7:49.
132. Id. at 50.
133. Id.
134. Id. at 49.
135. Abraham Lincoln, Proclamation of Amnesty and Reconstruction, December 8, 1863, in Lincoln, *Collected Works,* 7:53–56.
136. Id. at 54.
137. Abraham Lincoln, Proclamation about Amnesty, March 26, 1864, in Lincoln, *Collected Works,* 7:269.
138. Donald, *Lincoln,* 510.

CHAPTER EIGHT: FINAL ACT (1864-1865)

1. Elizabeth Keckley, *Behind the Scenes; Or, Thirty Years a Slave, and Four Years in the White House* (1868), 59.
2. Gettysburg Address.
3. Orville Hickman Browning, *The Diary of Orville Hickman Browning: 1850–1864,* ed. Theodore Calvin Pease (Champaign: University of Illinois, 1925), 1:600.
4. David Herbert Donald, *Lincoln Reconsidered: Essays on the Civil War Era* (New York: Vintage, 2001), 131.
5. Michael Burlingame, *Abraham Lincoln: A Life,* 2 vols. (Baltimore, MD: Johns Hopkins University Press, 2008), 2:379.
6. Carl Sandburg, *Abraham Lincoln: The Prairie Years and the War Years* (New York: Harcourt, Brace, 1954), 2:537.
7. Ron Chernow, *Grant* (New York: Penguin, 2017), 329.
8. David Herbert Donald, *Lincoln* (New York: Simon & Schuster, 1995), 491.
9. Jean Edward Smith, *Grant* (New York: Simon & Schuster, 2001), 286.
10. Donald, *Lincoln,* 491.
11. Smith, *Grant,* 290.
12. Id. at 290–91.
13. Chernow, *Grant,* 42.
14. Id. at 41.
15. Smith, *Grant,* 259.
16. Abraham Lincoln, *Collected Works of Abraham Lincoln,* 8 vols., ed. Roy Basler et al. (New Brunswick, NJ: Rutgers University Press, 1953–1955), 7:88.
17. Smith, *Grant,* 259.
18. G.W.S., "British Topics: Home and Foreign Affairs," *New-York Tribune (New York Herald-Tribune),* July 6, 1877, 1, col. 5.
19. Smith, *Grant,* 40.
20. Id. at 68.
21. Chernow, *Grant,* 42.
22. Smith, *Grant,* 259–60.
23. Id. at 298.
24. Id.
25. Id. at 296.
26. Id.
27. Chernow, *Grant,* 329.
28. Abraham Lincoln to Albert G. Hodges, April 4, 1864, in Lincoln, *Collected Works,* 7:282.
29. Id.
30. Id.
31. Donald, *Lincoln,* 480.
32. Id. at 482.
33. Id.
34. Id.
35. Abraham Lincoln, *Life and Works of Abraham Lincoln,* ed. Marion Mills Miller (1907), 5:197.
36. Donald, *Lincoln,* 496.

37. Id. at 506.

38. Lincoln, *Collected Works*, 7:380.

39. Id. at 414.

40. Abraham Lincoln to Salmon Chase, June 30, 1864, in Lincoln, *Collected Works*, 7:419.

41. Donald, *Lincoln*, 509.

42. Id.

43. Id.

44. Id. at 533.

45. Gideon Welles, diary entry for September 23, in *Diary of Gideon Welles: Secretary of the Navy Under Lincoln and Johnson* (New York: Houghton Mifflin Co., 1911), 156.

46. Id.

47. Id.

48. Id.

49. Id.

50. Id. at 156–57.

51. Id. at 157.

52. Id.

53. Id.

54. Doris Kearns Goodwin, *A Team of Rivals: The Political Genius of Abraham Lincoln* (New York: Simon & Schuster, 2005), 660.

55. John Hay, *Inside Lincoln's White House: The Complete Civil War Diary of John Hay*, July 11, 1864, p. 221. In *Battle Cry of Freedom: The Civil War Era* (New York: Oxford University Press, 1988), James M. McPherson says that Holmes shouted "Get down, you damn fool, before you get shot!" (757).

56. Lincoln, *Collected Works*, 7:514.

57. James M. McPherson, *Tried by War: Abraham Lincoln as Commander in Chief* (New York: Penguin, 2008), 218.

58. Burlingame, *Abraham Lincoln: A Life*, 2:649.

59. Id.

60. Donald, *Lincoln*, 501.

61. Abraham Lincoln, *The Papers and Writings of Abraham Lincoln*, vol. 7, ed. Arthur Brooks Lapsley (Project Gutenberg, 2009), https://www.gutenberg.org/files/2659/2659-h/2659-h.htm#link2H_4_0138.

62. Id.

63. Donald, *Lincoln*, 530.

64. Lincoln's policy of allowing soldiers to vote in the presidential election became an issue during the impeachment of President Donald Trump in 2019. Trump's defenders likened his solicitation of foreign assistance to defame a likely political rival (former vice president Joseph Biden) in the 2020 election to Lincoln's policy of allowing Union soldiers to vote, that both presidents were simply making policy decisions that inured to their personal benefits. The analogy is false, however. Lincoln's policy was stated publicly and purported to allow all soldiers, not just Republicans, the opportunity to vote, and it was consistent with the polices of nineteen states, which were constitutionally empowered to regulate the manner and timing of elections. President Trump's action in soliciting foreign interference in the election was not national policy enacted beforehand

by Congress, and he opposed every effort of Congress to get information about his actions. True, both presidents benefited personally from their actions, but only Lincoln's was cast as an actual openly stated position of the federal government backed by the states in the exercise of their lawful authority under the Constitution. Trump's attempt to condition U.S. aid to Ukraine on Ukraine's president doing him a "favor" was not the official policy of the land and no other constitutional authority recognized this as anything more than a purely private and personal benefit for the president, precisely the kind of misconduct that the Constitution created the impeachment process to address. To be sure, federal officials other than Lincoln abused their powers in making it difficult for Democratic soldiers to vote, but Lincoln's position still resulted in votes being cast against him, whereas President Trump's so-called policy would never have become public but for a whistleblower whom he denounced. In short, Lincoln's policy was imperfectly executed but Trump's position was illegitimate in every way.

65. McPherson, *Tried by War*, 250.

66. Id.

67. Id. at 151.

68. Timothy S. Huebner "'The Unjust Judge': Roger B. Taney, the Slave Power, and the Meaning of Emancipation," *Journal of Supreme Court History* 40 (2015): 249.

69. Donald, *Lincoln*, 536.

70. Salmon Chase to Kate Chase Sprague, September 17, 1864, in Salmon Portland Chase, *The Salmon P. Chase Papers: Correspondence, April 1863–1864,*ed. John Niven (Kent, OH: Kent State University Press, 1993), 432.

71. Donald, *Lincoln*, 552.

72. Abraham Lincoln, Annual Message to Congress, December 6, 1864, in Lincoln, *Collected Works*, 8:149.

73. Id.

74. Id.

75. Id.

76. Id.

77. Isaac N. Arnold, *The Life of Abraham Lincoln* (1887), 358.

78. Abraham Lincoln, *Response to a Serenade*, February 1, 1865, in Lincoln, *Collected Works*, 8:224.

79. Id. at 359.

80. Id.

81. Donald, *Lincoln*, 555.

82. Washington correspondence, February 1, 1865; *New York Tribune*, February 2, 1865; and Jewett to the editor of the *New York Tribune*, February 4, 1865; *New York Tribune*, February 6, 1865.

83. Chester G. Hearn, *Lincoln, the Cabinet, and the Generals* (Baton Rouge: Louisiana State University Press, 2010), 278.

84. Conversation with Francis Preston Blair, January 12, 1865, in Jefferson Davis, *The Papers of Jefferson Davis: July 1846–December 1848*, ed. Lynda Lasswell Crist (Baton Rouge: Louisiana State University Press, 1971), 318.

85. Jefferson Davis to Hon. R. M. T. Hunter, January 28, 1865, *Official Records of the Union and Confederate Navies in the War of the Rebellion* (1922), 191.

86. Id.

87. Abraham Lincoln to William H. Seward, Washington, February 1, 1865, in Lincoln, *Collected Works*, 8:250.
88. *The Century* 38 (May–October 1889): 850.
89. Abraham Lincoln, Annual Message to Congress, December 6, 1864, in Lincoln, *Collected Works*, 8:152.
90. *The Century* 38 (May–October 1889): 851.
91. Id. at 849.
92. *Diary of Orville Hickman Browning*, 1:699.
93. *The Century* 38 (May–October 1889): 849.
94. J. William Jones, *Southern Historical Society Papers* (1877), 3:174.
95. *Southern Historical Society Papers*, ed. R. A. Brock (1899), 27:375.
96. Donald, *Lincoln*, 565.
97. Abraham Lincoln, Second Inaugural Address, March 4, 1865, in Lincoln, *Collected Works*, 8:333.
98. Id.
99. Louis P. Masur, *Lincoln's Last Speech* (New York: Oxford University Press, 2015), 152.
100. Id. at 153.
101. Frederick Douglass, *The Life and Times of Frederick Douglass: From 1817–1882*, ed. John Lobb (1882), 321.
102. Id.
103. Id.
104. Id.
105. Id.
106. Abraham Lincoln to Thurlow Weed, March 15, 1865, in Lincoln, *Collected Works*, 8:356.
107. Francis Bicknell Carpenter, *The Inner Life of Abraham Lincoln: Six Months at the White House* (1872), 234.
108. Abraham Lincoln to Ulysses S. Grant, March 3, 1865, in Lincoln, *Collected Works*, 8:330–31.
109. David Dixon Porter, *Incidents and Anecdotes of the Civil War* (1886), 314.
110. Clifton Melvin Nichols, *Life of Abraham Lincoln: Being a Biography of His Life from His Birth to His Death* (1896), 235.
111. Jeff Rosenheim, *Photography and the American Civil War* (New York: Metropolitan Museum of Art, 2013), 224.
112. Porter, *Incidents and Anecdotes of the Civil War*, 295.
113. Donald, *Lincoln*, 577–79.
114. Id. at 580.
115. William Shakespeare, *The Tragedy of Hamlet, Prince of Denmark*, Act III, Scene III.
116. Donald, *Lincoln*, 581.
117. Conversation with Orville H. Browning, June 17, 1875, in Michael Burlingame, ed., *An Oral History of Abraham Lincoln: John G. Nicolay's Interviews and Essays* (Carbondale: Southern Illinois University Press, 2006), 4.
118. Abraham Lincoln, Last Public Address, April 11, 1865, in Lincoln, *Collected Works*, 8:401.
119. Id. at 404.
120. Id.

121. Id.
122. Id. at 402.
123. Id.
124. Id.
125. John Wilkes Booth, "Right or Wrong," in *God Judge Me: The Writings of John Wilkes Booth,* ed. John Rhodehamel and Louise Taper (Champaign: University of Illinois Press, 1997), 15.
126. Id.
127. *Diary of Orville Hickman Browning,* 2:18.
128. Id.
129. Id.
130. Id.
131. Id.

EPILOGUE

1. DeNeen L. Brown, "Frederick Douglass Delivered a Reality Check at Emancipation Memorial Unveiling," *Washington Post,* June 27, 2020 (quoting Douglass's April 14, 1876, speech).
2. Abraham Lincoln, Address on Colonization to a Deputation of Negroes, in *Collected Works of Abraham Lincoln,* 8 vols., ed. Roy Basler et al. (New Brunswick, NJ: Rutgers University Press, 1953–1955), 5:371, 372.
3. Douglas L. Wilson, "Lincoln's Rhetoric," *Journal of the Abraham Lincoln Association* 34, no. 1 (Winter 2013): 8.
4. Jefferson Davis, Messages to the Provision Congress, Second Session (Called) (Met at Montgomery, Ala., April 29, 1861), in James D. Richardson, ed., *A Compilation of Messages and Papers of the Confederacy, Including the Diplomatic Correspondence, 1861–1865* (Nashville, TN: United States Publishing Co., 1905), 82.
5. "Lincoln Statue Is Unveiled, and Protestors Come Out," *New York Times,* April 6, 2003.
6. See, for example: Sidney Blumenthal, *A Self-Made Man: The Political Life of Abraham Lincoln* (New York: Simon & Schuster, 2016); Michael Burlingame, *Abraham Lincoln: A Life* (Baltimore, MD: Johns Hopkins University Press, 2008); David Herbert Donald, *Lincoln* (New York: Simon & Schuster, 1995); Eric Foner, *The Fiery Trial: Abraham Lincoln and American Slavery* (New York: W.W. Norton & Company, 2010); Doris Kearns Goodwin, *A Team of Rivals: The Political Genius of Abraham Lincoln* (New York: Simon & Schuster, 2005); Richard Hofstadter, *The American Political Tradition* (New York: A.A. Knopf, 1948); Harold Holzer, *Lincoln President-Elect: Abraham Lincoln and the Great Secession Winter, 1860–1861* (New York: Simon & Schuster, 2008); Louis P. Masur, *Lincoln's Last Speech* (Oxford: Oxford University Press, 2015); James McPherson, *Tried by War: Abraham Lincoln as Commander in Chief* (New York: Penguin, 2008); Allan Nevins, *The War for the Union: The Improvised War, 1861–1862* (New York: Scribner, 1959); Allen Guelzo, *Lincoln's Emancipation Proclamation: The End of Slavery in America* (New York: Simon & Schuster, 2004); J. G. Randall, *Lincoln, the President* (multivolume) (New York: Dodd, Mead, 1945); and Kenneth J. Winkle, *The Young Eagle:*

The Rise of Abraham Lincoln (Lanham, MD: Taylor Trade Publishing/Rowman & Littlefield, 2001).

7. David Porter, *Incidents and Anecdotes of the Civil War* (D. Appleton & Co., 1885), 294–95.

8. David Davis, Memorial Address: The Life and Services of John Todd Stuart (Read Before the Illinois State Bar Association, at Its Annual Meeting Held at Springfield, January 12th and 13th, 1886), in *Proceedings of the Illinois State Bar Association at Its First Annual Meeting* (Springfield, Illinois, 1878), 54.

9. Hofstadter, *The American Political Tradition*, 124 n. 1 (citation omitted in original).

10. William H. Herndon to Jesse W. Weik, January 9, 1886, Herndon-Weik Collection, Library of Congress.

11. Nathaniel Hawthorne, "Chiefly About War Matters," printed anonymously and with omissions as "A Peaceable Man," *The Atlantic* (July 1862).

INDEX

75,000 volunteers, 297–98

abolitionism. *See also* slavery
  Bleeding Kansas, 201, 212–17, 224–25,
    231, 236, 246, 261
  election of 1846, 111
  election of 1848, 135–36
  Giddings and Wilmot, 120–21, 130–31
  Lincoln-Douglas debates, 240–42
  Wilmot Proviso, 116, 121, 131, 136,
    137, 166, 167, 179, 198–99, 207,
    243, 306
Abraham Lincoln Memorial University,
  412
Adams, Charles Francis, Jr., 392
Adams, John, 33, 218, 392
  education of, 263
  election of 1800, 32, 33, 400
Adams, John Quincy, 147
  death of, 131–32
  education of, 263
  election of 1824, 33–34
  election of 1824 and "corrupt bargain,"
    34, 90, 101, 421
  election of 1828, 25, 34–35
  later congressional career, 97, 129,
    305–6
  legal experience of, 55
  military experience of, 305–6
  presidency of, 55, 215, 253, 273, 285,
    381, 420, 425
  secretary of state, 30, 89
Adams-Onis Treaty, 30, 89
Address at Independence Hall (1861),
  269–70
Address to Congress. *See* State of the
  Union Address
Aesop's Fables, 16–17, 202–3, 229

African Americans. *See* Emancipation
  Proclamation; fugitive slaves;
  slavery
African American soldiers, 335, 355, 377,
  386, 406, 411
Allen, John, 28
Allison, John S., 139–40, 164, 216
Alvarado, Luis de Moscoso, 88
Alvarez de Piñeda, Alonso, 88
American Colonization Society, 30, 116,
  130, 187, 238
American Revolution, 19, 26, 293, 421
American System, 31–32, 36, 38, 39, 47,
  50, 72, 80, 95, 140, 156, 218, 306,
  416, 421
Anderson, Robert, 264, 273, 292, 297
Anti-Nebraska Movement, 206, 207–9,
  248
antiphony, 251–52
anti-Semitism, 332–33, 336, 338
Arabian Tales, The, 12
Archer, William, 216
Aristotle, 70
Arizona Territory, 215
Arkansas secession, 297–98
Arlington National Cemetery, 412
Armstrong, Jack, 40, 44
Army of Northern Virginia, 344, 399,
  406
Army of the Potomac, 310, 316–19,
  344–45, 377, 378–79, 393–94
Arthur, Chester, 412
Ashley, James, 384
assassination of Lincoln, 405–7, 409–11

Back-to-Africa movement, 116, 130, 187,
  195–96
Baker, Edward, 74, 83, 108, 110, 141

Bank of the United States, 36–37, 51, 61, 97, 125, 135, 218, 237

Banks, Nathanial, 310

Bank War, 36–37, 51, 61, 81–82, 97, 125, 237

Barnburners, 136, 145

Barney, Hiram, 374

Bates, Edward, 113, 202
  attorney general, 287, 341, 374–75, 402
  Blair's dismissal, 374–75
  election of 1860, 247, 255–56, 258–59, 292
  post-election, 271–72, 273

Bates, Hervey, 274

Bates House, 274

Battle of Antietam, 318, 330, 345

Battle of Buena Vista, 106, 112, 114–15

Battle of Bull Run, 310, 323, 362

Battle of Chancellorsville, 345, 354

Battle of Chattanooga, 353

Battle of Chickasaw Bayou, 333

Battle of Cold Harbor, 377

Battle of Fisher's Hill, 379

Battle of Fort Sumter, 296–98, 303–4

Battle of Fredericksburg, 318–19, 345

Battle of Gettysburg, 344–45, 354

Battle of Mine Run Creek, 353

Battle of Monterrey, 105

Battle of New Orleans, 29, 299, 300, 355

Battle of Palo Alto, 105

Battle of Resaca de la Palma, 105

Battle of Spotsylvania Courthouse, 377

Battle of the Monongahela, 18

Battle of the Wilderness, 377, 378

Battle of Vicksburg, 333, 354

Battle of Winchester, 379

Battle of Yellow Tavern, 377

Battle of York, 305

Battle of Yorktown, 119

Baxter, Maurice, 210–11

Beecher, Henry Ward, 156

Bell, John, 260

Benton, Thomas Hart, 29–30, 132, 147, 166, 178, 216

Bible, 15–16, 17, 23, 71, 229, 391

Biddle, Nicholas, 36, 38, 97

biographies, 17–20

Birney, James, 91

birth of Lincoln, 10

Bissell, William, 217

Black Code, 9

Black Hawk War, 5, 6–7, 43–45, 59, 63, 170, 293, 305

black suffrage, 209, 390–91, 395, 404

Blair, Francis Preston, 90, 219
  Civil War, 290–94, 318, 361, 386–87
  election of 1860, 255–56, 258
  election of 1864, 376
  opposition to slavery, 219, 248, 290–91
  Supreme Court and, 381–82

Blair, Francis Preston, Jr., 288, 371, 376

Blair, Montgomery, 401
  Civil War, 290–94, 295, 329
  dismissal of, 374–76, 379
  Dred Scott case, 219–20, 288
  postmaster general, 288, 290–94, 374–76
  Supreme Court and, 381–82

Bleeding Kansas, 201, 212–17, 224–25, 231, 236, 246, 261

Bloomington Convention (1856), 208–12

Blount, William, 27

Blumenthal, Sidney, 82, 117, 414–15

Boone, Daniel, 119

Booth, John Wilkes, 404–5

Boston Slave Riots, 181

Botts, John, 123

Bowdoin College, 263

Braddock, Edward, 18

Bragg, Braxton, 353

Bramlette, Thomas, 368

Brayman, Mason, 252

Breckinridge, John, 260

Breese, Sidney, 112

Bright, John, 290

Brooks, Noah, 288, 291, 402–3

Brooks, Preston, 213

Brown, John, 214

Browning, Orville
  ambition of Lincoln, 48, 153
  background of, 45
  Civil War, 264, 317, 318, 319–20, 324, 325–27, 330–31, 385, 388, 406–7
  election of 1858, 226

election of 1860, 256, 257, 258
election of 1864, 360–61
First Inaugural Address of Lincoln, 276–77, 282
formation of Republican Party, 202, 204, 209–11
later life and death of, 418–19
legal career of, 54, 75, 108, 157, 353–54
"Long Nine" and, 62–63
Mary Todd and, 84, 85, 151
presidency of Lincoln, 273–74, 315, 317, 318, 319–20, 322, 324, 325–27, 330–31, 340–42, 353–54, 361, 369, 382, 385, 388, 401–2, 406–7
relationship with Lincoln, 7, 45, 48, 151, 158, 264, 303–4, 330, 353–54, 360, 361, 369, 401–2, 406–7
Senate appointment of, 303–4
Springfield Debates, 74, 230
Supreme Court appointments, 340–42, 343, 382
Brown's Indian Queen Hotel, 120
Buchanan, James
education of, 263
election of 1832, 37
election of 1856, 201–2, 214–17, 221
presidency of, 219, 224, 253, 277–78, 289, 291, 293, 306, 312, 314, 338, 378, 415
secretary of state, 101
Bunn, John, 150, 203
Bunyan, John, 23
Burlingame, Michael, 16, 72, 76, 77, 129, 310–11, 414–15
burning of Francis McIntosh, 68
Burns, Robert, 22, 41–42, 154, 332
Burr, Aaron, 27–29, 337
Bush, George W., 425
Butler, Andrew Pickens, 213
Butler, Benjamin, 306
Butterfield, Justin, 142, 143

Cabeza de Vaca, Álvar Núñez, 88
Cabinet. See also specific members of Cabinet
assembling, 6, 271–72, 273–74, 284–89, 290
crisis of 1862, 319–22

first meetings, 290–92
presidential relations, 315–16
principle of rotation, 311–15
reconfiguring of, 372–76
Cadwallader, George, 299
Calhoun, John (surveyor), 6, 74
Calhoun, John C., 63, 132, 147, 278
death of, 176–77
election of 1828, 35
secretary of war, 39, 92
Senate career of, 52, 167, 175, 176–77, 348–49
Texas annexation, 92, 99, 100
vice presidency of, 33, 35–36, 52, 98, 99, 100, 275, 276, 400
California, 99, 165, 168, 171, 176–77
Cameron, Simon
death of Douglas, 303
secretary of war, 159, 272, 286–88, 295, 309, 313–14, 403
Campbell, Alexander, 187
Campbell, John, 338, 340–41, 385, 397
caning of Charles Sumner, 213
Carey, Henry Charles, 156, 416
Carlin, Thomas, 78
Cartwright, Peter, 110–11
Cass, Lewis, 135–36, 137, 139, 140, 144, 214
Catron, John, 219
Centre College, 44, 63
chain of command, 308–9, 395
Chambers, John, 313
Chandler, Zachariah, 374
Charleston Bay, 264, 273, 293, 295
Chase, Salmon P.
election of 1856, 215
election of 1860, 121, 248, 254, 255, 258–59
election of 1864, 368–73
formation of Republican Party, 202
post-election, 271–72, 286–87
Supreme Court appointment, 382–83
treasury secretary, 286–87, 289, 293, 312, 313, 314, 319, 321–22, 370, 372–73, 403, 418
Chenery House, 276
Chernow, Ron, 365
Chicago Tribune, 236, 253–54

"Chronicles of Reuben" (Lincoln), 22

Churchill, Winston, 414

Cicero, 70

Cisco, John, 372

Civil War. *See also specific battles and figures*

    Confederate surrender, 394–95, 399, 406

    Confiscation Acts, 324–29

    early war, 264, 273, 277, 290–98

    election of 1864, 359–62, 367–73, 376–77, 379–80

    Emancipation Proclamation, 329–32, 334, 335–36, 357, 388, 411

    Gettysburg Address (1863), 345–53, 390, 391

    Hampton Roads Conference, 385–87, 389

    Peace Conference of 1861, 270–71

    Proclamation of Amnesty and Reconstruction, 355–57

    Proclamation of April 15, 297–98

    suspension of habeas corpus, 298–302

Civil War–era monuments, 413–14

Civil War Military Draft Act, 344

Clausewitz, Carl von, 308

Clay, Cassius, 248

Clay, Henry

    "American System" of, 31–32, 36, 38, 39, 47, 50, 72, 80, 95, 140, 156, 218, 306, 416, 421

    background of, 26–27

    Bank War, 36–37, 51, 61, 125, 237

    Browning and, 210–11

    Buchanan and, 201–2

    Burr and, 27–29

    Compromise of 1850, 173–80, 186, 198–99, 208, 249, 267, 280–82, 328

    death of, 182–83

    early political career of, 27–29, 30–31

    election of 1824, 32–34, 53

    election of 1824 and "corrupt bargain," 34, 90, 101, 421

    election of 1828, 34–35, 53

    election of 1832, 4–5, 6, 9–10, 35–39, 48–49, 52, 53–54, 206, 247, 359, 380

    election of 1840, 88, 90–91

    election of 1844, 88–92, 93–94, 110, 117, 144, 210, 281

    election of 1848, 132–40

    Fillmore and, 171, 173, 174–75, 177, 178–80

    as "the Great Compromiser," 31, 93–94, 151

    Jackson's death and, 86, 87

    legal career of, 26–27, 55

    Lincoln-Douglas debates and, 233–35, 238–43

    Lincoln's eulogy for, 168, 182–88, 193

    Lincoln's possible meeting with, 113–17

    Market Street Speech (1847), 114–17, 118, 126–27

    Mary Todd and, 85, 114

    as a mentor, 5, 38–39, 41, 47–48, 49–50, 67–68, 74, 88, 108, 113–14, 116–18, 148, 151, 152–53, 182–88, 194–95, 224, 247, 250–51, 274, 289, 335–36, 360, 384, 416–17, 420

    Mexican War, 113–18, 125–27, 169

    Missouri Compromise, 30–31, 47, 195, 219, 220, 249

    oratory of, 31, 71, 108, 114–18, 147, 160, 175, 177, 227, 272, 346–47, 349, 350–51

    political vision of, 32–33, 36–37, 62, 87, 163, 357, 422

    Polk and, 144–45

    secretary of state, 273, 285

    as "self-made man," 5, 47–48, 55, 422

    Taylor and, 132–44, 152–53, 164, 166, 168, 169

    Texas annexation and, 88–90

    Van Buren and, 66, 67

    Whig Party and, 25, 183, 185, 206, 210–11

Clay, Henry, Jr., 113, 114, 125, 169

Clay, James, 271

Cleveland, Grover, 424

Clifford, Nathan, 221

Clinton, Bill, 425

Clinton, Hillary, 425

Cobb, Howell, 131–32

College of William & Mary, 263

Columbian Class Book, 12

Columbus Speech (1859), 246–47

"common man," 47, 66, 263, 394, 422, 423

compensation, 324, 331, 385–86, 388, 411

Compromise of 1850, 173–82, 189, 190,
198–99, 208, 267, 280–82, 328

Confederate monuments, 413–14

Confederate States of America, 289, 295,
297–98, 299

Confiscation Acts, 324–29

Congressional Globe, 123

Congressional Taylor Club (Young
Indians), 134–35

Constitution, U.S., 4, 20, 21, 87, 92,
249–50

Constitutional Convention, U.S., 27, 134,
242

Constitutional Unionist Party, 260

Cooper, James Fenimore, 17

Cooper Union Speech (1860), 247–52, 255

Cornwallis, Charles, Lord, 119

"corrupt bargain," 34, 90, 101, 421

Corwin, Thomas, 288

court packing, 78–80

COVID-19 pandemic, 1, 426

Cowan, Edward, 360

Crawford, Elizabeth, 25

Crawford, George, 167

Crawford, William, 33–34

Crisis of 1819, 37

Crittenden, John, 202, 272, 276, 288,
323–24
election of 1848, 115, 132–33, 137–38,
140, 233
election of 1860, 244, 262

Crittenden-Johnson Resolution, 323–24,
327

Cumberland Road, 36

Curtin, Andrew, 347–48

Curtis, Benjamin, 221, 338, 418

Daniel, Peter, 338, 339–40

Davis, David, 157, 205
death of Stuart, 419–20
election of 1856, 216
election of 1860, 14, 255–59

election of 1864, 371
relationship with Lincoln, 75, 143–44,
149–50, 419–20
Supreme Court appointment, 340–42

Davis, Henry Winter, 356–57, 374

Davis, Jefferson, 147
Civil War, 289, 307–9, 311, 353, 380–81,
385, 386, 395, 396–97
death of, 413–14
death of Taylor, 170–71
election of 1860, 306
Mexican War, 167, 170, 307–8
secretary of war, 191–92
Senate career of, 95, 99, 132, 167,
170–71, 175, 189–90, 246

Dayton, William, 202, 216

Declaration of Independence, 5, 21, 119,
223, 269–70, 335, 348, 420, 421

Democracy in America (Tocqueville), 87

Democratic Convention (1860), 259–60

Democratic Party, establishment of,
34–35

Dick, John, 300

Dickens, Charles, 17, 119

Dickey, Theophilus Lyle, 201

Dickinson College, 263

"Dilworth's Spelling-Book," 11–12

Dix, John, 306

Dixon, Archibald, 368

Donald, David Herbert, 11, 14, 31, 42,
229, 244, 312, 415

Douglas, Stephen, 162, 415
court-packing plan, 78–80
death of, 303–4
debates with Lincoln, 74, 107, 147, 200,
230–31. *See also* Great Debates
of 1858
election of 1838, 64–67, 109
election of 1856, 7, 202, 214–15
election of 1858, 206, 227
election of 1860, 202, 254, 260, 261–62,
302
last months of, 297–98, 302–3
"Long Nine" and, 62–63
nickname of, 64–65
rivalry with Lincoln, 73, 152, 157,
196–97, 222–23, 230, 415

Douglas, Stephen (*cont.*)
  Senate career of, 112, 132, 179–80,
    189–94, 196–97, 225–26, 227
  slavery question, 2–3, 179–80, 189–94,
    196–97, 200, 221–23, 225–26, 230
Douglass, Frederick, 232, 236, 241,
    392–93
  legacy of Lincoln, 410–11, 412–13,
    423–24
Dred Scott v. Sandford, 219–23, 225, 229,
    237, 299, 323, 328–29
Dresser, Charles, 85–86
Drummer, Henry, 54
Dubois, Jesse, 257

Eaton, John, 30, 34, 36, 38
education, 11–15, 41, 50, 55–56
Edwards, Benjamin, 75
Edwards, Cyrus, 141–42
Edwards, Elizabeth, 150
Edwards, Ninian W., 133, 141
Eighth Judicial Circuit of Illinois, 75
Eisenhower, Dwight, 425
election of 1824, 30, 32–34
election of 1828, 25, 34–35, 96–97
election of 1832, 4–5, 9–10, 34–39, 53–54
election of 1844, 88–92, 93–94
election of 1848, 95, 132–40, 233
election of 1852, 189–90
election of 1856, 7, 214–18
election of 1860, 14, 247–48, 252–60
  Democratic National Convention,
    259–60
  electoral votes, 261–62
  Lincoln's campaign organization,
    253–54
  Lincoln's compelling vision, 253
  Lincoln's lack of experience, 261, 262
  party unity, 254
  Republican National Convention,
    254–59
election of 1864, 359–62, 367–73, 376–77,
    379–80
election of 2020, 1, 461–62n
Electoral College
  1824, 33–34
  1828, 35

  1860, 261–62
  Polk on, 96
"Elegy in a Country Churchyard"
    (Gray), 21–22
Elliot, Jonathan, 249
Emancipation Proclamation, 329–32,
    334, 335–36, 357, 388, 411
Emerson, John, 219
Emerson, Ralph (lawyer), 161
Emerson, Ralph Waldo, 156, 350
Enrollment Act of 1863, 344
Era of Good Feelings, 32
Erie Railroad, 181
Euclid, 3, 155–56, 270
Everett, Edward, 345–46, 347, 350, 352
Ewing, James, 17
Ewing, Thomas, 141, 142, 143, 367

Farragut, William, 379
Federalist Party, 32, 218, 265
Fell, Jesse, 14
Fessenden, William, 320, 373–74, 389
Ficklin, Orlando, 120–21
Field, Alexander, 78–80
Field, David Dudley, 113, 343
Field, Maunsell, 372
Field, Stephen, 343
Field v. People of the State of Illinois,
    78–80
Fifth Amendment, 191, 220
Fifteenth Amendment, 404
Fillmore, Millard
  Compromise of 1850, 173–74, 175, 178,
    180–81
  death of Taylor, 170–72, 178
  election of 1848, 135, 138, 139
  election of 1856, 215, 217–18
  Lincoln and, 268–69
  presidency of, 2, 171–75, 178, 265,
    288–89, 312, 400
First Inaugural Address (1861), 19, 272–74,
    277–82, 303, 322–23, 389, 392
First Judicial Circuit of Illinois, 75, 157
Florida, 7, 20, 27, 30, 35, 43
Floyd, George, 414, 426
Ford, Thomas, 60
Ford's Theater, 406–7

Forrest, Nathan Bedford, 333, 377, 406
Fort Harrison, 379
Fort Henry, 299
Fort Moultrie, 264, 273, 297
Fort Pickens, 294, 295–96
Fort Pillow, 377
Fort Snelling, 219
Fort Stevens, 377
Fort Sumter, 264, 273, 277, 290–98
Fox, Gustavus, 293–94, 295–96, 304
Fox, Virginia Woodbury, 296
Frankfort Commonwealth, 368
Freedmen's Bureau, 390–91
Free Soil Party, 136, 145, 193, 208, 224
Frelinghuysen, Theodore, 182
Frémont, Jessie Benton, 216
Frémont, John
    background of, 215–16
    Civil War, 324–27, 330–31, 375
    election of 1856, 215–16, 217–18, 221,
        254, 270
    election of 1864, 374, 379
Frémont Emancipation, 324–27, 330–31
French and Indian War, 293
Fugitive Slave Act, 179, 180–81, 188, 190,
    207–8, 265
fugitive slaves, 111, 157, 166, 176

"gag rule," 97
Gaines, John, 142
Garfield, James, 412
Garrison, William Lloyd, 265
General Order No. 1, 317
General Orders No. 11, 332–36
Gettysburg Address (1863), 345–53, 390,
    391
Giddings, Joshua, 120–21, 124, 130–31,
    132, 236, 241, 243, 247
Gillespie, Joseph, 107, 232
Graham, Mentor, 40, 41
Grant, Ulysses S., 376–77, 378–79
    Battle of Chattanooga, 353
    General Orders No. 11, 332–36
    Hampton Roads Conference, 386–88
    Lincoln's visit to City Point, 393–95
    Mexican War, 332, 362–63, 365
    presidency of, 419

promotion to general-in-chief, 362–67,
    377
surrender of Lee, 399, 406
Gray, Thomas, 21–22
Great Debates of 1858, 230–47
    first debate, 233–34
    second debate, 234–37
    fourth debate, 237–38
    fifth debate, 238
    sixth debate, 238–39
    seventh debate, 240–44
Great Reaper Trial, 2, 161–62
Great Southern Mail, 122–23
Greeley, Horace, 113, 255, 273, 287, 290,
    401
Green, Bowling, 42–43, 48, 54, 57, 74
Green, Duff, 120, 132–33
Greene, William, 42
Grier, Robert, 219
Grigsby, Aaron, 22
Grigsby, Billy, 22
Grigsby, Charles, 22
Grigsby, Nathaniel, 22, 24–25
Grigsby, Reuben, 22
Grigsby, Sarah Lincoln, 11, 12, 22
Grigsby, William, 154
Grimshaw, William, 20–21
Grundy, Felix, 96
Gurley, John, 334
Gurley, Phineas, 410

habeas corpus, 5, 298–302
Habeas Corpus Suspension Act of 1863,
    302
Hackett, James, 154
Hall, Dominick, 300
Halleck, Henry, 309–10, 332–35, 362–63,
    364, 366
Hamilton, Alexander, 27–28, 337
Hamlet (Shakespeare), 154, 347, 398–99
Hamlin, Hannibal, 132, 136, 259, 389–90,
    400–401
Hammett, William, 90
Hampton Roads Conference, 385–87,
    389
Hanks, Dennis, 11–16, 21, 24, 25, 38, 41
Hanks, John, 12, 14

Hardin, John J., 81, 82, 83, 108–10, 112, 125, 169, 226
Harper's Ferry, Virginia, 214
Harper's Weekly, 256
Harris, Clara, 406
Harris, Ira, 322
Harrison, William Henry
  election of 1840, 71–73, 78, 88, 90–91, 132, 262, 285
  Inaugural Address, 100, 114*n*
  presidency of, 94, 98, 107, 144, 164, 254, 313, 400
Harvard College, 124, 263
Hawthorne, Nathaniel, 17, 424
Hay, John, 154, 271, 307, 308, 322, 351–52, 377, 424
Hayne, Robert, 228, 272, 278, 348, 349
Henry, Anson G., 143
Herndon, John Rowland, 41
Herndon, William, 19, 122, 140
  biography of Lincoln, 58, 107, 149, 150, 151, 155, 205, 260, 337, 340–41, 403, 420–21
  law partnership with Lincoln, 2, 86, 148, 155, 156–60
  political career of Lincoln, 205, 208–9, 255
Hicks, Thomas, 273–74
Hill, Samuel, 56
History of the Life and Death, A (Weems), 17–19
History of the United States (Grimshaw), 20–21
Hodges, Albert, 368
Holmes, Oliver Wendell, 377
Holzer, Harold, 251, 274, 415
Hood, Thomas, 401–2
Hooker, Joseph, 345
House Committee on Post Offices and Roads, 123
House-Divided Speech (1858), 227–30, 250
House of Representatives, U.S., 2, 27, 33, 81, 111–13, 118, 140–41
  Clay in, 30, 33
  election of 1842, 81, 82, 83
  election of 1844, 83

  election of 1846, 95, 108–11
  Thirtieth Congress, 119–32
House Ways and Means Committee, 97, 173
Howard, Oliver, 412
Howard University, 412
Hubbard, Gurdon, 60–61
humility, 19, 49–50
Hunter, Robert, 385, 387–88
Hurlbut, Stephen, 293–94

Illinois and Michigan Canal, 60–61
Illinois Central Railroad, 158, 252
Illinois drought, 65
Illinois House of Representatives, 47, 59–61, 107, 205, 206
  court-packing plan, 78–80
  election of 1832, 47, 48–52
  election of 1834, 56–58
  election of 1836, 61
  election of 1838, 64–68
  election of 1854, 205
  Lincoln's departure, 81
  "Long Nine," 62–63
Illinois Peace Democrat, 385
Illinois Republican Party, 7, 204, 206, 207, 209–11, 226–28, 246, 256
Illinois Senate election of 1855, 203–4, 212
Illinois Senate election of 1858, 224, 226–28, 244, 245, 247
Illinois's Seventh District, 111–13, 118, 140–41
  election of 1842, 81, 82, 83
  election of 1844, 83
  election of 1846, 95, 108–11
  Thirtieth Congress, 119–32
Illinois State Journal, 200
Illinois Supreme Court, 59, 77, 78, 158
Illinois Whig Party, 47, 48, 60–61, 71–72
Inaugural Addresses. *See* First Inaugural Address; Second Inaugural Address
Independent Spy Corps, 43
Indiana, 287
Indian Removal Act, of 1830, 417
Ivanhoe (Cooper), 17

Jackson, Andrew
  assassination attempt on, 405
  background of, 26–27
  Bank War, 36–37, 51, 61, 97, 125, 237
  Black Hawk War, 5, 43, 104
  championing of "common man," 47,
      66, 394, 422
  death of, 86–87
  declaration of martial law, 5, 299–301
  early political career of, 27
  education of, 26, 55, 263
  election of 1824, 32–34
  election of 1828, 25, 34–35, 96–97
  election of 1832, 4–5, 6, 9–10, 34–39,
      52, 247, 276, 359, 380
  Lincoln's postmaster appointment, 56
  as a mentor, 4–5, 47–48, 61, 148, 247,
      264–65, 274, 289, 292, 360, 416–17,
      420
  nickname of "Old Hickory," 29, 189,
      263
  nullification and, 35, 52–53, 100, 212,
      265, 274–76, 277–80, 293
  political vision of, 32–33, 47–48, 61,
      86–87, 421, 422
  Polk and, 90, 96–102
  presidency of, 4, 5, 61, 65–66, 83,
      88, 96–97, 98, 105, 215, 218–19,
      263–65, 299–301, 311–15, 400, 417
  principle of rotation, 83, 311–15
  Revolutionary War, 26, 299–300, 301
  Seminole Wars, 30, 43, 309
  trial and fine of, 300
  War of 1812, 29–30, 104
Jackson, Robert, 26
Jackson, Thomas Jonathan "Stonewall,"
    354
Jacksonians (Jacksonian Democrats), 6,
    42, 61, 80, 87, 89, 93, 94–95, 288
Jay Treaty, 306
Jefferson, Thomas, 18–19, 55, 202
  Declaration of Independence, 5, 194,
      420
  education of, 263
  election of 1800, 32, 33, 400
  as a mentor, 5, 186, 194–95, 234
  presidency of, 27, 28–29, 32, 285, 311

John, Vanderlyn, 119
John Brown's raid on Harpers Ferry, 214
Johnson, Andrew, 132
  impeachment of, 314–15, 418–19
  legacy of, 412–13
  presidency of, 78, 314–15, 418–19
  vice presidency of, 389–90, 399–402
  War Aims Resolution, 323–24, 327
Johnson, John, 15–16
Johnson, Lyndon, 425
Johnson, Matilda, 15
Johnson, Reverdy, 167, 168
Johnston, Joseph, 367, 406
Joint Committee on the Conduct of the
    War, 317, 323
Jonas, Abraham, 75
Jones, J. Russell, 363
Jones, William, 23–25
Judd, Nathan, 157
Judd, Norman, 206, 226, 254–55, 258, 259
Julius Caesar (Shakespeare), 155

Kansas Constitution, 224–25
Kansas-Nebraska Act, 2–3, 190–97. See
    also Bleeding Kansas
  aftermath of, 203, 205–8, 212, 216, 231,
      246, 286, 290–91
  Peoria Speech (1854), 194–200
Kaskel, Cesar, 334
Keller, Ron, 107
Kelso, Jack, 41
Kentucky, 326–27
Kentucky General Assembly, 27, 48
Kentucky Preceptor, 12
King, Preston, 319
Kirkham, Samuel, 41
Knapp, Nathan, 259–60
Know Nothing Party, 204, 207, 215
Knox, William, 154, 172
Koerner, Gustave, 150, 258, 259

Lamon, Ward Hill, 157, 255, 293, 382, 406
Land Office, 141–44
Last Public Address (1865), 403–5
Lawrence, Kansas, sacking of, 201,
    213–14
Lawrence, Richard, 405

Lecompton Constitution, 217, 224–26, 239
Lee, Robert E., 354–55, 367, 377, 381, 385, 414
  Battle of Antietam, 318, 345
  Battle of Fredericksburg, 318–19, 345
  Battle of Gettysburg, 344–45, 354, 362
  Battle of the Wilderness, 377, 378
  Black Hawk War, 170
  capture of Brown, 214
  Mexican War, 144
  surrender of, 394–95, 399, 406
legacy of Lincoln, 412–26
Liberian colonies, 195–96
Lincoln, Abraham (paternal grandfather), 10
Lincoln, Mary Todd
  assassination of husband, 406, 409–10
  background of, 84–85
  Civil War, 394
  Clay and, 85, 114
  death of son William, 330
  Herndon and, 156
  later life and death, 411–12
  marriage and home life, 7, 83–86, 119–20, 141
  political ambitions for husband, 3, 401
Lincoln, Mordecai, 10
Lincoln, Nancy Hanks, 11, 15
Lincoln, Robert Todd, 84, 394, 409, 411–12
Lincoln, Sarah Bush, 11–15, 161, 272
Lincoln, Thomas (father), 10–13, 14–15, 21, 23, 39, 162, 272
Lincoln, Thomas "Tad" (son), 395–96, 411–12, 414, 415–16
Lincoln, William Wallace, 330
Lincoln-Douglas debates, 74, 107, 147, 200, 230–31. *See also* Great Debates of 1858
Lincoln Memorial, 7, 425, 426
Linder, Usher, 117, 211
Logan, Stephen, 51–52, 58, 74, 157
  Illinois House, 140, 205
  law partnership with Lincoln, 75–78, 86, 156–60
logrolling, 60, 112, 217

"Long Nine," 62–63
Longstreet, James, 353
Louisiana Purchase, 89, 186, 190
Louisville Gazette, 25
Louisville Journal, 38, 41
Lovejoy, Elijah, 67–68, 251
Lovejoy, Owen, 251
Lowell, James Russell, 260
Lucas, Joshua M., 143
Lyceum Address (1837), 67–71, 129

McArthur, Douglas, 425
Macbeth (Shakespeare), 22, 154–55, 397
McClellan, George, 153, 269, 310–11, 314, 425
  Civil War, 316–20, 328, 366, 402
  election of 1864, 359–60, 362, 376–78, 379–80
McClernand, John, 78, 306
McClure, Alexander, 117, 150
McCook, Alexander, 377
McCormick, Cyrus, 2, 161–62
McCormick, Richard, 255
McCulloch v. Maryland, 218, 237
McDowell, Irvin, 310
MacKay, Alexander, 119
McLean, John, 148, 215, 220–21, 338–39
McPherson, James, 328, 378, 380, 415
Madison, James, 33, 55, 263, 285, 305
Maine, 30–31, 186
Malvern, USS, 395
Mangum, Willie, 134
"manifest destiny," 99, 421
Manny, John, 161–62
Mansfield, Joseph, 310
Marcy, William Learned, 80, 105, 285
Marshall, John, 27, 29, 120, 218, 278–79, 300–301
martial law, 299–301, 324–25
"Martyr, The" (Melville), 422–23
Maryland, 297, 298–99
Mason, James, 176–77, 315
Mattison, Joel, 205
May, Henry, 301–2
Maysville Road veto, 36
Meade, George, 345, 362, 366–67
Medill, Joseph, 236, 254, 255, 256, 342

Meigs, Montgomery, 295

Melville, Herman, 422–23

mentors of Lincoln, 1, 3, 4–7. *See also* specific mentors

Meredith, William, 167

Merryman, John, 299

Mexican War, 103–6
aftermath of, 112, 113, 131, 167
Clay's Market Street Speech (1847), 114–17, 118, 126–27
Lincoln's opposition to, 2, 110, 122, 125–28, 305–6

Mexico. *See also* Mexican War
Texas annexation, 88–90, 99–104

Michigan Territory, 135, 137, 140, 142

Mill, John Stuart, 156

Miller, Samuel Freeman, 339–40

Minnesota Territory, 219

Mississippi River, 9–10

Missouri, 9, 30–31, 212–13, 219–20, 220, 287, 324–25

Missouri Compromise, 30–31, 47, 186, 190–200, 207, 219, 220, 221, 249

Monroe, James, 55, 285
education of, 263
election of 1816, 33, 285
presidency of, 30, 35, 43, 221, 309

Mormonism, 82, 108

Morrison, J.L.D., 141

Murray, Lindley, 20

myth of Lincoln, 7, 18, 19, 413, 415

National Committee of the Republican Party, 370–71

National Intelligencer, 89–90

National Lincoln Monument Association, 409

"native born," 148

Nebraska. *See also* Kansas-Nebraska Act
Anti-Nebraska Movement, 206, 207–9, 248
naming of state capitol, 412

New Deal, 424–25

New Mexico, 99, 165–66, 168, 171, 265

New Salem, Illinois, 10, 39–43

New York Herald, 265–68

New York Historical Society, 87

New York Telescope, 25

New York Times, 252

New York Tribune, 113, 252, 255, 287

Nicolay, John, 271, 290, 304, 309

Nixon, Richard, 425

North Carolina secession, 297–98

Northwest Ordinance, 194–95, 198, 219, 249

Northwest Territory, 36

nullification, 35, 52–53, 100, 180–81, 212, 265, 274–80

Oak Ridge Cemetery, 409–10

Obama, Barack, 359, 425

Offutt, Denton, 39

On War (Clausewitz), 308

Ordinance of Nullification, 52–53, 212

Oregon Territory, 99, 100–102, 142–43

Oregon Treaty, 99, 102

Our American Cousin (play), 406

Pacific Railroad Acts, 306

Palmer, John, 206, 209, 216, 227, 255, 256, 257

Panic of 1819, 37

Panic of 1837, 65, 67

Paredes y Arrillaga, Mariano, 103

Parker, John, 406

Parker, Theodore, 349

Pascal, Blaise, 347

patronage, 143, 192, 312, 368, 418. *See also* spoils system

Peace Conference of 1861, 270–71

Peck, Ebenezer, 74

"peculiar," 149–50

Peoria Speech (1854), 194–200, 204

Philadelphia Speech (1861), 269–70

Phillips, Wendell, 229

Pierce, Benjamin "Bennie," 191

Pierce, Franklin, 4
education of, 263
election of 1852, 189–90
Kansas-Nebraska Act, 2–3, 191–93, 203
presidency of, 191–93, 213, 216–17, 253, 277–78, 288, 308, 315, 338

Pilgrim's Progress, The (Bunyan), 23, 154

Pinkerton, Allan, 405–6

poetry, 21–22, 41–42, 422–24
police brutality, 414
"political education," 6, 269
Polk, James, 4
　background of, 96–97
　death of, 144–45, 401
　education of, 263
　election of 1844, 88–92, 93–94, 98,
　　110, 255
　governor of Tennessee, 90, 97–98
　Jackson and, 90, 96–102
　Mexican War, 2, 103–6, 125–27, 305–6,
　　309
　nickname of "Young Hickory," 87, 96
　presidency of, 87, 94, 96–106, 112,
　　125–26, 135, 144, 262, 282, 401,
　　417–18, 421
　Texas question, 99–104
Pomeroy, Samuel, 370, 371
Poore, Ben Perley, 136
Pope, John, 362
popular vote, 33, 34, 35, 91, 96, 140, 217,
　244, 261, 380
Porter, David, 296, 395, 396
postmaster general, 123, 215, 288, 291
Powhatan, 295–96
Prentice, George, 38–39, 41, 71, 234, 300
president-elect, 263–66, 268–72
Princeton University, 263
principle of rotation, 311–15
Prize Cases, 342–43
Proclamation of Amnesty and
　Reconstruction, 355–57
Proclamation of April 15, 297–98
Purple, Norman, 159

Radical Republicans, 78, 223, 291, 313,
　323, 343, 356, 357, 369, 373, 374, 380,
　382, 383, 401, 404, 418–19
Ramsay, David, 18–19
Rathbone, Henry, 406
Rawlins, John, 333
Raymond, Henry, 252
reading, 3–4, 12–14, 15–23, 41–43, 154–56
Reagan, Ronald, 425
Reavis, Isham, 153–54
reconstruction, 385–88, 390–91, 402–5

Reeves, Owen, 17
Remini, Robert, 89
Republican National Convention (1860),
　254–59
Republican National Convention (1864),
　370–72, 400
Revolutionary War, 19, 26, 293, 421
Richardson, Joseph, 22
Richardson, William, 342
Richmond, 297, 379, 386, 395–97
Richmond Dispatch, 268
Rivers and Harbors Bill, 112–13, 124
Robinson Crusoe (Defoe), 12
Rollins, James, 384–85
Roosevelt, Franklin, 417, 424–25
Roosevelt, Theodore, 417, 424
Rule of Three, 14
Rutgers College, 182

Sandburg, Carl, 14
Sangamo Journal, 51, 61, 64, 66, 70, 76,
　81–82
Santa Anna, Antonio López de, 103, 105,
　106
Scott, Dred, 219–20. See also Dred Scott
　v. Sandford
Scott, John, 211–12
Scott, William, 22
Scott, Winfield
　Civil War, 264, 294, 306, 308–10, 354
　election of 1852, 189–90, 254
　election of 1856, 252
　Mexican War, 103–4, 105–6, 144, 293
Scripps, John Locke, 22, 58–59
secession, 1, 5, 6, 122, 175–76, 181–82,
　297–98, 307
　Compromise of 1850, 175–82
　Cooper Union Speech (1860), 251–52
　First Inaugural Address (1861), 276–82
Second Inaugural Address (1865), 389–93
"self-made man," 5, 6, 47–48, 55, 152, 162,
　202, 263, 361, 422
Seminole Wars, 7, 30, 43, 104, 309, 345
Senate Committee on Territories, 190
Senate election of 1855, 203–4, 212
Senate election of 1858, 224, 226–28, 244,
　245, 247

Senate Finance Committee, 373
Seneca, 70
Seward, Frederick, 319
Seward, William, 401, 403
    Cabinet crisis of 1862, 319–21, 322
    carriage accident, 399
    Civil War, 291, 293–97, 316, 329–30,
        364, 386–88, 399
    election of 1838, 80
    election of 1848, 273
    election of 1856, 215
    election of 1860, 248, 252, 254, 255,
        256, 258–59, 262, 271–72, 369
    Emancipation Proclamation, 329–30,
        331
    governor of New York, 113
    New York Senator, 138
    president-elect's transition, 273, 274,
        276, 282
    secretary of state, 273, 285–87, 291,
        293–97, 312, 313, 314, 319–21, 322,
        329–30, 331, 369, 375, 386–88
    slavery question, 173, 176, 202, 243,
        251
    Taylor and, 171, 273
Shakespeare, William, 22, 41, 71, 154–55,
    277, 332, 352–53, 397–99, 405
Sheridan, Philip, 378–79
Sherman, William, 367, 379, 393–94, 395,
    406, 414
Shields, James, 81–83, 205
siege of Petersburg, 377, 393–94, 395
Simpson, Matthew, 410
Singleton, James, 242–43, 385, 386, 407
Slade, William, 351, 406
slavery
    Compromise of 1850, 173–82, 189, 190,
        198, 208, 267
    Cooper Union Speech (1860), 247–52
    Dred Scott case, 219–23, 225, 229, 237,
        299, 323, 328–29
    election of 1860. See election of 1860
    Emancipation Proclamation, 329–32,
        334, 335–36, 357, 388, 411
    House-Divided Speech (1858), 227–30
    Kansas-Nebraska Act. See Kansas-
        Nebraska Act

Lincoln-Douglas debates, 234–42
Lincoln's eulogy of Clay, 186–88
Lincoln's letters to Speed, 206–7, 284,
    330
Missouri Compromise, 30–31, 47, 186,
    190–200, 207, 219, 220, 221, 249
Northwest Ordinance, 194–95, 198,
    219, 249
Peoria Speech (1854), 194–200
Second Inaugural Address (1865),
    389–93
Thirteenth Amendment, 360, 361–62,
    383–88, 395
Slidell, John, 102–3, 315
Smith, Caleb, 134, 257–58, 287, 294, 341
Smith, Jean Edward, 365
Smith, Joseph, 108
Sons of Confederate Veterans, 414
South Carolina
    Battle of Fort Sumter, 296–98, 303–4
    Ordinance of Nullification, 52–53, 212
    secession threat, 264, 265, 274, 277,
        290
Spanish Florida, 27, 30, 35
Specie Circular, 65
Spectator, The, 20
Speed, James, 401, 402
Speed, Joshua, 84, 330, 401, 402
    Lincoln's letters on slavery, 206–7,
        284, 330
spoils system, 80, 138, 143, 311–12
Sprigg, Ann, 120, 128
Springfield, Illinois, 2, 40, 43, 62, 63–64
Springfield Debates (1839), 74
Springfield Speech (1857), 222–23
Springfield Washington Temperance
    Society, 163
Springfield Young Men's Lyceum Speech
    (1837), 67–71, 129
Stanbery, Henry, 418
Stanton, Edwin, 422
    assassination of Lincoln, 406
    Civil War, 317–18, 322, 336, 382,
        394–95
    McCormick Reaper Trial, 2, 161–62
    secretary of war, 78, 313–15, 317–18,
        322, 373–74, 382, 418

State of the Union Address
  1861, 307
  1862, 331–32
  1863, 355–56
  1864, 383–84
Stephens, Alexander, 121–22, 129–30,
    134, 385, 387–88
Stevens, Thaddeus, 401, 411–12
Stewart, William Morris, 407
Stoddard, William, 290
Stuart, J.E.B., 377
Stuart, John Todd
  assassination of Lincoln, 409
  background of, 44, 63
  Black Hawk War, 6–7, 44–45, 59, 63
  debates with Douglas, 230
  election of 1834, 57–61, 255
  election of 1838, 64–67, 109
  Illinois House, 53
  Illinois's 8th District, 353–54, 369, 384,
    401
  Illinois Senator, 111–12
  later life and death, 418, 419–20
  law partnership with Lincoln, 63–64,
    75–76, 77, 156–60
  Lincoln wrestling match, 40, 315
  Mary Todd and, 84, 85
  mentorship and friendship with
    Lincoln, 6–7, 48, 51, 53, 54, 81,
    111–12, 142, 149, 208, 341, 361,
    384, 402
  nickname of, 64–65
  presidency of Lincoln, 341, 342, 354,
    356, 369, 384
  slavery question, 154, 208, 384
Sub-Treasury Speech (1839), 71–74, 78
suffrage. See black suffrage; women's
    suffrage
Sullivan, John Louis, 99
Sumner, Charles, 213, 381, 392
Supreme Court, 218–23
  Dred Scott case, 219–23, 225, 229, 237,
    299, 323, 328–29
  Lincoln's appointments to, 338–43,
    381–83
suspension of habeas corpus, 5,
    298–302

Swayne, Noah, 339, 341
Swett, Leonard, 75, 149, 157, 202, 203,
    227, 232, 255, 257, 259, 341, 354

Taney, Roger, 132, 147
  death of, 381, 382–83
  Dred Scott case, 219–20, 221, 223, 299
  education of, 263
  Jackson and Bank War, 36–37
  Lewis v. Lewis, 148
  Merryman decision, 298–99
  Prize Cases, 343
"tar heels," 380–81
Tariff of 1824, 31, 32, 37–38, 52
tariffs, 52, 88, 98–99, 101, 110, 135, 211,
    275
Taylor, Sarah Knox, 170
Taylor, Zachary
  background of, 104, 133–34
  Black Hawk War, 6–7, 43, 44, 104, 359
  death of, 170–72, 178
  election of 1848, 2, 6, 95, 115, 129,
    132–40, 144, 242, 254, 262, 269,
    273
  election of 1850, 95
  Grant and, 365–67, 378
  Inaugural Address of, 164
  Land Office and, 2, 141–44
  as a mentor, 5–6, 360, 416–18
  Mexican War, 5–6, 103–6, 168–70,
    306, 365
  presidency of, 140–44, 145, 164–70,
    252, 265, 268–69, 282–83, 417–18
  as "self-made man," 6
  Seminole Wars, 43, 104, 309
  War of 1812, 104, 133–34
Tennessee, 27, 297–98
Tennessee Supreme Court, 27
ten percent plan, 355–57
Tenure in Office Act, 314–15, 418
Texas annexation, 88–90, 92, 99–104
Thirteenth Amendment, 360, 361–62,
    383–88, 395
Thomas, Lorenzo, 366
Thornton, Seth, 104–5, 154
Tocqueville, Alexis de, 87
Tod, David, 373

Todd, John Stuart, 157
Todd, Polly, 160
Todd, Robert Smith, 85, 114, 160
Todd Heirs v. Wickliffe, 160
Toombs, Robert, 122
Topeka Constitution, 212–13
Trail of Tears, 417
Transylvania University, 85, 340
treaty of 1818, 99
Treaty of Ghent, 300
Treaty of Guadalupe Hidalgo, 106
Trent Affair, 315–16
Truman, Harry, 425
Trumbull, John, 119
Trumbull, Lyman, 205, 206, 209, 215,
   226, 303
Trump, Donald, 414, 425–26, 461–62n
Truth, Sojourner, 411
Turney, James, 40
Turnham, David, 25
Twelfth Amendment, 33–34
Twenty-Second Amendment, 92
Tyler, John, 88, 92, 263, 311–12, 400

Ullman, Daniel, 268
Unionist Party, 260, 302, 354, 384
Union League, 370, 416, 428
United States Telegraph, 120
University of North Carolina, 263

Van Buren, Martin, 4, 55, 286
   ambassador to Britain, 275–76
   death of, 336–37
   election of 1828, 34–35
   election of 1832, 34–35, 36, 52,
      275–76
   election of 1840, 72, 78, 89–90, 368
   election of 1848, 135–36, 140
   Lincoln's meeting with, 337
   military experience of, 305
   presidency of, 65–66, 97, 99, 417
   secretary of state, 36, 275
   vice presidency of, 276, 400
Vanderlyn, John, 119
Van Dorn, Earl, 333
Vázquez de Coronado, Francisco, 88
Villard, Henry, 265–68, 287

Vincennes University, 24
Virginia Court of Chancery, 27
Virginia secession, 297–98
voting age, 61
voting rights, 80. *See also* black suffrage;
   women's suffrage

Wade, Benjamin, 320, 356–57, 374
Wade-Davis Bill, 356–57, 374
War Aims Resolution, 323–24, 327
War of 1812, 29–30, 104, 300, 305
Washburne, Elihu, 333, 335, 363, 401
Washington, George, 263, 352
   biographies, 17–19, 417
   French and Indian War, 293
   Northwest Ordinance, 249
   Revolutionary War, 19, 105, 119, 293
   Supreme Court appointments, 338
Washington Globe, 89–90
Washington Intelligencer, 25
Watts, Isaac, 172
Webster, Daniel, 136, 288
   Clay and, 52, 71, 124
   Compromise of 1850, 173–74, 177–78,
      180–82, 235
   death of, 188
   oratory of, 71, 87, 147, 175–76, 212, 228,
      272, 278, 346, 348–49, 350–51
   secretary of state, 313
   Winthrop and, 124
Webster, Edward, 125
Webster's Speller, 13
Weed, Thurlow, 113, 273, 285, 375, 393,
   401
   election of 1848, 139, 173
   election of 1860, 256, 262
Weems, Mason "Parson Weems," 17–19
Weik, Jesse, 420–21
Welles, Gideon, 422
   background of, 286
   Blair's dismissal, 374–76
   Civil War, 295–96, 298, 313, 389
   election of 1860, 264–65
   secretary of the Navy, 285, 286, 287,
      291, 292, 293, 295–96, 313, 401
Wentworth, John, 226–27
Western Register, 25

West Point, 288, 307, 310, 332, 345, 362

Whig Party, 2, 7, 25, 271. *See also* Illinois
    Whig Party
  Clay and, 25, 183, 185, 206
  election of 1848, 132–33, 137–39, 144
  Jackson and, 86–87
  Taylor and, 164–65, 166–67

Whitman, Walt, 423

Whitney, Henry Clay, 24, 86, 159

Wickham, Williams Carter, 414

Wickliffe, Robert, 160

Widmer, John, 154

William, Herndon, 231

Wilmot, David, 116, 121, 130–31, 136

Wilmot Proviso, 116, 121, 131, 136, 137,
    166, 167, 179, 198–99, 207, 243, 306

Wilson, Robert, 108, 262

Wilson, Robert L., 62–63

Wilson, Woodrow, 424

Winkle, Kenneth, 130, 145, 415

Winthrop, Robert, 124, 131

women's suffrage, 61

Woodbury, Levi, 296

Worcester v. Georgia, 300–301

Wright, Horatio, 377

Wythe, George, 27, 42

Yates, Richard, 303